The Real Worlds of Welfare Capitalism

The Real Worlds of Welfare Capitalism traces how individuals fare over time in each of the three types of welfare state. Through a unique analysis of panel data from Germany, the Netherlands and the US, tracking individuals' socio-economic fate over fully ten years, Goodin, Headey, Muffels and Dirven explore issues of economic growth and efficiency, of poverty and inequality, of social integration, stability and autonomy. It is common to talk of the inevitability of trade-offs between these goals, but in this book the authors contend that the social democratic welfare regime, represented here by the Netherlands, equals or exceeds the performance of the corporatist German regime and the liberal US regime across all these social and economic objectives. They thus argue that, whatever one's priorities, the social democratic welfare regime is the best choice for realizing them.

ROBERT E. GOODIN is Professor of Philosophy at the Research School of Social Sciences, Australian National University. He is the editor of *The Journal of Political Philosophy*, and of the Cambridge University Press series *Theories of Institutional Design*. His books include *Political Theory and Public Policy* (1982), *Not Only the Poor* (with Julian Le Grand, *et al.*, 1987), *Reasons for Welfare* (1988) and *Social Welfare and Individual Responsibility* (with David Schmitz, 1998).

BRUCE HEADEY is Associate Professor of Political Science and Public Policy at the University of Melbourne. He is the author of various articles and books on housing, well-being and income dynamics. His publications include *Housing Policy in the Developed Economy* (1978) and *Understanding Happiness: A Theory of Subjective Well-Being* (with Alex Wearing, 1992).

RUUD MUFFELS is Research Professor of Labour Market and Social Security at Tilburg University, and Research Director of the Tilburg Institute of Social Security Research. His work on the labour market, poverty and welfare states includes *Welfare Economic Effects of Social Security* (1993), and several articles and book chapters.

HENK-JAN DIRVEN is project manager at the Central Bureau of Statistics of the Netherlands. He has published journal articles on income poverty and relative deprivation.

The Real Worlds of Welfare Capitalism

Robert E. Goodin, Bruce Headey, Ruud Muffels and
Henk-Jan Dirven

CAMBRIDGE
UNIVERSITY PRESS

PUBLISHED BY
THE PRESS SYNDICATE OF THE UNIVERSITY OF CAMBRIDGE
The Pitt Building, Trumpington Street, Cambridge CB2 1RP,
United Kingdom

CAMBRIDGE UNIVERSITY PRESS
The Edinburgh Building, Cambridge, CB2 2RU, UK
http://www.cup.cam.ac.uk
40 West 20th Street, NY 10011-4211, USA http://www.cup.org
10 Stamford Road, Oakleigh, Melbourne 3166, Australia

© Robert E. Goodin, Bruce Headey, Ruud Muffels and Henk-Jan Dirven 1999

First published 1999

Printed in the United Kingdom at the University Press, Cambridge

Typeset in Plantin 10/12pt [VN]

A catalogue record for this book is available from the British Library

Library of Congress Cataloguing in Publication data

The Real Worlds of Welfare Capitalism/Robert E. Goodin ... [et al.].
    p. cm.
    Includes bibliographical references and index.
    ISBN 0 521 59386 7 (hardbound)
    1. Welfare state.   2. Welfare state – Case studies.   3. United
States – Social policy.   4. Netherlands – Social policy.   5. Germany –
Social policy.   I. Goodin, Robert E.
JC479.R4   1999
361.6'5 – dc21   98-49778   CIP

ISBN 0 521 59386 7 hardback
ISBN 0 521 59639 4 paperback

Contents

vi   Contents

Preface

This book represents an unusual collaboration between a philosopher, a political scientist, an economist and a sociologist. The preoccupation we share is with the central question, 'What are the best institutional arrangements for promoting each of a variety of social, political and moral values which the welfare state has historically been supposed to serve?'

Investigating that in the way we have done was made possible, however, only by the painstaking work of many others who have, over the past decade and more, conducted on-going socio-economic household panel studies in the three countries we study. We should like to take this opportunity to pay tribute to their incalculable contribution to the social sciences generally. Our small study, purely parasitic upon their vast labours, merely serves as a sample of the treasure trove that waits to be discovered within those larger data sets.

Others before us – in a distinguished line running from Richard Titmuss to Gøsta Esping-Andersen – have theoretically and empirically elaborated the view that there are three distinct worlds of welfare capitalism. It is our aim to use the evidence from those panel studies to help us discover what life is 'really like' in each of those three worlds. The panel data are by their nature limited to a few hundred pre-coded items bearing primarily on people's socio-economic circumstances. Clearly, there are myriad aspects to life that cannot be captured by such cold statistics. While our analysis necessarily lacks the full ethnographic richness that the phrase 'real life' might imply, we hope it nonetheless captures an important part of what welfare states are supposed to be about. Whatever else, welfare regimes are supposed to serve some clear socio-economic goals, and their success in so doing can indeed be measured through panel data in some interesting and surprising ways.

Acknowledgments

Our first and largest debt is to those who have conducted the panel studies upon which we draw. For willingness to share their data with us, and the scholarly community more generally, we are most grateful to:

- the Panel Study of Income Dynamics, conducted by the Survey Research Center at the University of Michigan under the direction of James N. Morgan;
- the German Socio-Economic Panel, jointly by the Wissenschaftszentrum, Berlin under the direction of President Wolfgang Zapf and the Deutsches Institut für Wirtschaftsforschung, with Gert G. Wagner heading its panel group;
- the Dutch Socio-Economic Panel Survey, conducted by the Centraal Bureau voor de Statistiek (CBS).

We should particularly like to thank Brian Galligan and David van Iterson, the Dutch Consul in Melbourne, for helpful interventions at a crucial stage in facilitating our collaboration. We should also record our gratitude for subventions from our home institutions in helping to finance the project: the Philosophy Program, Research School of Social Sciences, Australian National University and the Collaborative Research Scheme of ANU's Institute of Advanced Study; the Centre for Public Policy of the University of Melbourne; and the Work and Organization Research Centre (WORC) of the University of Tilburg.

While new technology makes trans-oceanic collaboration more feasible than ever before, at crucial stages it remains essential actually to meet. The four of us met in Melbourne and Canberra in February 1996 to plan the project; the first three authors met again in Canberra in May 1997 to advance it; and the Australian and Dutch sub-teams met together more often still, in pursuit of it. We are all grateful for the hospitality, from time to time, of each others' home institutions. Bruce Headey also gratefully acknowledges the hospitality of Erasmus University Rotterdam, the WORC at the University of Tilburg, the Wissenschaftzentrum, Berlin, and the Deutsches Institut für Wirtschaftsforschung, Berlin, where much of the initial work was done; and Bob Goodin gratefully acknowledges the hospitality of the Kennedy School of Government at Harvard University, where the final write-up was completed.

We must also record our great debts to Peter Krause, who was the source of continuous advice and assistance with the US–German matching file. We are also grateful to Barbara Butrica for advice on and research assistance supplementing the US data file and to Didier Fourage for contributing to the Dutch longitudinal data file. Our thanks too to those who have helped us with computing, prominently among them Ewa Karafilowska and Craig Lonsdale.

Finally, we are most grateful for those who have taken the time to discuss these issues with us. Important early input came from Tony Atkinson, Diane Gibson, Desmond King, Julian Le Grand, David Miller, Deborah Mitchell, Stein Ringen, Diane Sainsbury and David Soskice. As the project began to take shape, we also benefited from extensive commentaries by Frank Castles, Claus Offe and Göran Therborn. From well before the conception of the present project, Bruce Headey has been profiting from the advice of the Director of the German Socio-Economic Panel, Gert G. Wagner. All of those people have been continuing sources of advice throughout the project, and we are immensely grateful to them for it. Many others also commented most helpfully, intensively or (often even more helpfully) in passing. Among them are: Jim Alt, Brian Barry, Michael Bittman, Bruce Bradbury, Richard V. Burkhauser, Johan De Deken, Tony Eardley, Jon Elster, Gøsta Esping-Andersen, Peter Hall, Karl Hinrichs, Sandy Jencks, Olli Kangas, Stefan Leibfried, Bernard Manin, Jenny Mansbridge, Bernd Marin, Ted Marmor, Jane Millar, Ulrich Mückenberger, Dick Neustadt, Joakim Palme, Paul Pierson, Martin Rein, Peter Saunders, Anneloes Smitsman, Frank Vandenbroucke, Robert van der Veen, Wim van Oorschot, Philippe Van Parijs, Michael Shalev, Shirley Williams, Eric Olin Wright and anonymous readers for Cambridge University Press.

An interim version of our preliminary results comparing the first five years of panel data was presented at the Second German Socio-Economic Panel Conference at Potsdam in July 1996 and published under the title 'Welfare over time: three worlds of welfare capitalism in panel perspective, 1985–89' in the *Journal of Public Policy*, 17 (September/December 1997): 329–59. We are grateful for the comments both of that conference audience and of Richard Rose and his *JPP* referees. Other sections of the book have been tried out on colleagues at our home institutions and on various other conference audiences, among them: the Workshop on Political Theory and Social Policy (Paris, May 1998); the Third German Socio-Economic Panel Conference (Berlin, July 1998); Research

Committee 19 of the International Sociological Association (Montreal, July 1998); and lectures at the A. E. Havens Center for the Study of Social Structure and Social Change, Department of Sociology, University of Wisconsin, Madison (September 1998). We are grateful to all those audiences for invaluable feedback that shaped the final book.

Finally, the standard disclaimer: we alone are responsible for what is written here, which does not necessarily reflect the views of either our advisors or our employers.

1 Introduction

1.1 Dry statistics / real lives

To get a good sense of how real lives are really lived, of what it is really like to be poor or old or disabled, we read novels or biographies, social histories or social commentaries. We read Charles Dickens' *Hard Times* (1854) or George Orwell's *Down and Out in Paris and London* (1933) or John Steinbeck's *The Grapes of Wrath* (1963); we read Jane Addams' *Twenty Years at Hull House* (1919) or Michael Harrington's *The Other America* (1962) or *The Autobiography of Malcolm X* (1965). Any of these offer far more evocative accounts than we social scientists can ever hope to muster out of the dry statistics which are our stock in trade.[1]

Inept though we may be at evoking the real lives of social unfortunates, social scientists are nevertheless relatively good at counting how common each of those patterns of social misfortune actually is in any given society. That is a crucial step in transforming 'personal troubles' into 'public issues' (Mills 1959, ch. 1; Gibson 1998, ch. 1). Ever since the days of Charles Booth's magisterial sixteen-volume study of *Life and Labour of the People in London* (1892–1903) and Seebohm Rowntree's study of York (1901; 1941), social reformers have been keenly aware that it is as essential to enumerate instances of social distress as it is to describe them evocatively. Social statisticians both inside and outside government have, by now, gone a long way toward helping us understand not only what sorts of problems people have but also how many people have them.

While providing us with many good head counts, however, social statisticians still provide us with far too little by way of connected stories. In purely mathematical terms, 'transition matrices' may succeed in rendering their models dynamic, but such devices hardly constitute a continuous narrative thread. Much of the appeal of 'qualitative' methods in the social sciences derives from their promise to recapture the sequencing and patterning that constitutes the real lives of real people (King, Keohane and Verba 1994).

---

[1] Though more 'qualitative' work – such as Edin's (1991) on 'how AFDC recipients make ends meet in Chicago' – comes much closer.

1

Sequences and longer-term patterns clearly matter enormously to people's welfare. It makes an enormous difference whether people are poor for just one year or several, whether their deprivations are singular or multiple, whether ruptures in their family lives or employment histories are isolated instances or recurring patterns.[2] If bad things keep happening to the same people over and over again, then that is more problematic for those people.[3] If the bad things happen to different people over time, then that is less problematic for any given individual but obviously involves more people.[4] The sociology and politics and perhaps the morality of social policy as well varies, depending upon which of those ways social risks are distributed among people over time. Important though those factors undeniably are, however, they are captured only very imperfectly in conventional social surveys.

Conventional compilations of social statistics have traditionally amounted simply to a succession of cross-sectional 'snapshots' of the population, frozen at some particular moment in time. By taking repeated cross-sectional snapshots at regular intervals we can build up what social statisticians proudly call a 'time series'. But that inevitably remains a series of disconnected snapshots. What exactly has happened in between successive snapshots – how one cross-section has transformed itself into the next – inevitably remains a mystery. Successive snapshots record the fact of change without revealing the mechanism. Furthermore, those snapshots are of cross-sections representing group profiles rather than

---

[2] The best brief discussion of this issue is perhaps Ruggles (1990, ch. 5), though of course all the wider literature on income dynamics makes this same point at more length (see, e.g., Levy 1977; Lilliard 1977; Duncan et al. 1984; Atkinson, Bourguignon and Morrisson 1992, ch. 1; Bane and Ellwood 1994; Leisering and Leibfried 1998).

[3] In the purple prose of Milton Friedman (1962, pp. 171–2): 'A major problem in interpreting evidence on the distribution of income is the need to distinguish two basically different kinds of inequality: temporary, short-run differences in income, and differences in long-run income status. Consider two societies that have the same distribution of annual income. In one there is great mobility and change so that the position of particular families in the income hierarchy varies widely from year to year. In the other, there is great rigidity so that each family stays in the same position year after year. Clearly, in any meaningful sense, the second would be the more unequal society. The one kind of inequality is a sign of dynamic change, social mobility, equality of opportunity; the other of a status society. The confusion behind these two kinds of inequality is particularly important, precisely because competitive free-enterprise capitalism tends to substitute the one for the other. Non-capitalist societies tend to have wider inequality than capitalist, even as measured by annual income; in addition, inequality in them tends to be permanent, whereas capitalism undermines status and introduces social mobility.'

[4] As pointed out by Rowntree's (1901, p. 172) analysis of poverty as a lifecourse phenomenon: 'The proportion of the community who at one period or another of their lives suffer from poverty to the point of physical privation is ... much greater, and the injurious effects of such a condition are much more widespread, than would appear from a consideration of the number who can be shown to be below the poverty line at any given moment.' See similarly Duncan et al. 1984.

individual faces. In the sorts of 'time series' which social statisticians conventionally compile, there is no way of tracking what happens to particular individuals over time. All we can say is how many people – but not which people – fell into each category at successive moments in time. That sort of information is obviously very useful, and for certain sorts of purposes a series of disjointed cross-sectional time slices may be all that we really need. But for lots of other purposes it will inevitably be woefully inadequate (Ruggles 1990, ch. 5).

Great strides were made in the 1980s through the heroic efforts of the Luxembourg Income Study (LIS) toward compiling individual unit-record data on a genuinely cross-nationally comparable basis.[5] Thanks to LIS, our statistical snapshots now have recognizably individual faces: we can now link up an individual's response to one question to the same individual's response to other questions within a single survey. But snapshots they remain. It is still impossible, even in the LIS data, to track individuals through time since each successive five-yearly wave of LIS surveys is based on a different, unconnected sample of individuals.[6]

With long-term panel studies now coming on stream, we can at long last do better than that. In these 'panel studies', the same individuals are re-interviewed, time and again, over a protracted period. The interviews are conducted according to a strictly predetermined questionnaire. The responses are pre-coded, computerized and calculated in the ordinary way. The results are therefore highly quantitative and, in that sense, still dryly statistical – certainly compared to the more richly textured accounts

---

[5] Smeeding, O'Higgins and Rainwater (1990); Mitchell (1991); Smeeding *et al.* (1993); Atkinson, Rainwater and Smeeding (1995); Gottschalk and Smeeding (1997). Further information on LIS can be obtained from CEPS/INSTEAD, B.P. 48, L-4501 Differdange, Luxembourg; http://www.ceps.lu.

[6] Anyway they are reported on that basis. Occasionally, as in the case of the Netherlands, a country's LIS data was generated through a panel study; but when depositing those data with LIS, they recoded individual identifiers in such a way as to preclude linkage across the two surveys.

As an adjunct to the LIS project, there is now a central collection of panel studies, PACO (the Panel Comparability project); further information on this project, too, can be obtained from CEPS/INSTEAD, B.P. 48, L-4501 Differdange, Luxembourg; http://www.ceps.lu. The surveys held in the PACO archive at the time of writing are: Belgium, 1992; France (Lorraine), 1985–90; Germany 1984–92; Hungary, 1992–94; Luxembourg 1985–92; Poland, 1987–90; Spain (Galicia), 1992–93; Sweden, 1984, 1986, 1988, 1991; US, 1968–88; UK, 1991–94. So far, only seven of those countries' data have been rendered comparable and incorporated in the PACO database (the three as yet non-comparable panels being those from Belgium, Spain and Sweden). Eventually a more systematic study might be conducted on the basis of those resources. For the time being, however, none of the other panels represented in that collection have been systematically surveyed for fully a decade, as have the panels in our study. Note that the Dutch Socio-Economic Panel Survey which we will be analysing is not included in the PACO project.

that might emerge through qualitative investigations. Nevertheless, those panel-study statistics reveal far more about the ebb and flow of real life events in real people's lives than could ever be done through any set of successive aggregate snapshots, and they do so in a much more systematic way than could ever be accomplished through purely qualitative methods alone.

That is the basis upon which this book purports to reveal more than has hitherto been known about the 'real worlds' of welfare capitalism. For the first time, we can look at those questions through panel data tracking real people's lives across a whole decade in at least one representative of each of the three basic types of welfare regime. We can, in this way, tell more about the real lives of real people than could have been told by previous cross-sectional time-series studies, however sophisticated.

These new developments do not render the older-style compilations of cross-sectional time-series data irrelevant. There are many respects in which cross-sections might be more useful than panels. Certainly cross-sections at a single point in time are more readily interpretable than panel data spanning several years, in which natural ageing and lifecourse effects at the individual level must somehow be disentangled from genuine changes at the systemic level. While there will thus remain an important role for both types of data, panel data nonetheless provide an important new perspective – and one which, in all its complexities, better reflects lives as they are really lived.

1.2   Welfare states / welfare regimes

The 'welfare state' is not one thing. Many subtly different particular programmes and policies, and different combinations of them, are pursued under its banner. Many subtly different objectives, goals and values are served, intentionally or otherwise, by all those various programmes and policies.

Within that diversity, however, are a few clear clusters. There seem to be broadly three distinctive styles of welfare state. These represent prototypes as much as ideal types. They represent intellectual constructions on the basis of which particular welfare regimes have been self-consciously modelled, as much as they do intellectual abstractions from the messy reality that has emerged haphazardly around us.

Different welfare regimes represent different 'worlds of welfare capitalism'.[7] They represent, almost literally, whole different 'worlds' – each

---

[7] The phrase is Esping-Andersen's (1990) but the basic idea had been expressed by many before: see particularly Titmuss (1958; 1974) and Mishra (1984), the first of which in particular is fully acknowledged by Esping-Andersen (1994, p. 715). Note also Myrdall

world being internally tightly integrated, and each being sharply differentiated from one another. Welfare regimes bunch particular values together with particular programmes and policies. Different sorts of welfare regime pursue different policies, and they do so for different sorts of reasons. Each fixates narrowly on its own reasons, not denigrating the values that drive other welfare regimes so much as de-emphasizing them or perhaps just taking them for granted.

Welfare regimes also bundle together programmes and policies which transcend the 'welfare state', narrowly conceived. They are indeed worlds of 'welfare *capitalism*'. Welfare regimes represent different ways of organizing not only the transfer sector, represented by social welfare policy, but also the productive sector of the capitalist economy. (Non-capitalist states perform transfer functions too, but such states lie outside the discussion of this book;[8] so too do the 'Confucian' welfare states of the Asian tigers.[9]) All of the various sorts of welfare state we shall be discussing here are set in the context of a capitalist economy: and in a capitalist market economy, what the market can be made to do the state does not need to do.

Thus, while the 'welfare state' is often associated narrowly with public transfers, in cash or in kind, welfare states of that narrower sort are all embedded in larger socio-economic orders which promote people's welfare – their well-being, more broadly construed – by various other means as well. The term 'welfare regime' refers to that larger constellation of socio-economic institutions, policies and programmes all oriented toward promoting people's welfare quite generally. It certainly includes the transfer-oriented 'welfare state' sector, narrowly conceived. But it also includes the tax as much as the transfer sector of the public economy.[10] And it also includes, alongside both, the productive sector of the economy.[11]

(1944, p. 152): 'Social reform policies may be conceived of as passing through three stages: a paternalistic conservative era, when curing the worst ills is enough; a liberal era, when safeguarding against inequalities through pooling the risks is enough; and a social democratic era, when preventing the ills is attempted. The first was the period of curative social policy through private charity and public poor relief; the second was the period of social insurance broad in scope but yet merely symptomatic; and the third may be called the period of protecting and cooperative social policy.'

[8] For discussions on the former approach of the command economies of communist states see Pryor (1968) and Deacon (1983).

[9] These are well surveyed by Jones (1990; 1993), who also characterizes them as 'oikonomic welfare states', falling within Titmuss' (1974) 'institutional redistributive' class but placing particular emphasis upon education and family as keys to stable social progress.   [10] Titmuss (1958).

[11] It also includes institutional arrangements facilitating private home ownership, the rates of which vary considerably cross-nationally and with real consequences for the welfare of people, particularly in their later years (Castles 1996a).

Particular sorts of tax-transfer arrangements thus tend to be associated with particular sorts of strategies within the productive sphere. These clusters, which we map in chapter 3 below, represent intellectually and pragmatically unified packages of programmes and policies, values and institutions. It is between these whole packages – these welfare regimes as a whole – that social engineers are obliged to choose.[12] It is the performance of these welfare regimes, taken as a whole, that we ought to try to compare.

Inevitably there are limits in the extent to which we can do that in data available to us. (Education, health, and labour-market policies all lie largely outside the remit of the socio-economic panels upon which we will be relying for our data.) But at least at the level of broad conceptualization, if alas not at the level of operationalization, we ought to take that broader perspective on welfare regimes as a whole.

1.3   Our aims and methods: ethics, institutions and panels

Our aims in this book are ambitious. We will strive to produce an overall assessment of alternative welfare regimes, looking across all the various values that they have traditionally been supposed to serve and across all the various institutional shells that they have traditionally been supposed to inhabit.

Our *object* of assessment is institutions. Our concern is to find out which type of welfare regime best serves the values that welfare states have traditionally been supposed to serve. The *criterion* for assessment is moral, embodied in social and political values. We are concerned to discover how the values traditionally associated with welfare states are best served. The *mechanism* of assessment is by means of empirical socio-economics. We draw upon socio-economic panel studies across three countries (the United States, Germany and the Netherlands) for evidence as to how well each of those countries – and each of the styles of welfare regime that they in turn represent – promote those central social goals.

Those vaunting ambitions must be moderated in the light of the limits of the evidence which is empirically available to us through those panel studies. Not all welfare-state values are readily couched in terms of socio-economic outcomes tracked in panel studies, and the measures which those studies report often represent only imperfect or indirect indicators of what it is that concerns us. The particular countries scrutinized may or may not be perfectly representative of the others in that

---

[12] Although, as will be evident from the discussion in chapter 3 below, there is also considerable scope for choosing between various 'options' within each basic package.

cluster, or hence of that style of welfare regime more generally. The particular decade under scrutiny may or may not be peculiar in ways that might confound our findings.

Despite these risks and shortcomings (about which we will say a little more at the end of this chapter, and indeed throughout the book), these panel studies represent not only the best but, ultimately, the only real way of answering the sorts of evaluative questions that we generally want to pose of our social institutions. They and they alone afford us genuine, quantitatively grounded insights into what life is *really like* for individuals and families under alternative social arrangements.

Limited though these first fruits of panel techniques are in time and place, they allow us to say – in ways that we never could with older cross-sectional snapshot techniques – what really happens to real people over time. Only by knowing what happens to particular people, individually, can we *really* know what has happened to them in aggregate. And only by knowing what happens to the same people over time can we evaluate what the *actual* consequences of welfare regimes are for real people. Unfortunate though it may be that anyone ever falls into poverty, brief spells of poverty are much less worrying (both to them and to us) than persistent poverty plaguing the same persons year in and year out.

The central finding of the American Panel Study of Income Dynamics – which recurs cross-nationally, and will recur yet again in our analysis of Germany and the Netherlands below – is that people's economic fortunes are vastly more volatile than most of us would ever have expected. The stability of the overall cross-sectional aggregates trick us into supposing that there is an underclass of citizens, economically deprived and socially excluded, which is stable over time. Probing beneath those cross-sectional aggregates through panel data, we now know that this is largely untrue. Many more people than we ever imagined are poor in one or two years out of ten; far fewer than we would ever have dared to hope are poor for eight or more.[13]

These differences really do matter. In the first instance, and most importantly, they obviously matter to the people themselves. If poverty

---

[13] Duncan *et al.* (1984); see similarly Levy (1977); Ruggles (1990, ch. 5); Bane and Ellwood (1994, esp. chs. 2–3). Previous international and cross-national findings are contained in: Duncan *et al.* (1993, 1995) (eight countries); Muffels and Dirven (1993) (US and the Netherlands); Headey and Krause (1994) (Germany and Australia); Headey, Krause and Habich (1994) (Germany); Muffels and Dirven (1995) (Germany and the Netherlands); Dirven (1995) (Germany and the Netherlands); Dirven and Berghman (1995) (the Netherlands); Dirven and Fouarge (1995) (Belgium and the Netherlands); Fouarge and Dirven (1995) (Belgium, Germany and the Netherlands); Schluter (1996a, b); Burkhauser and Poupore (1997) (US and Germany). A preliminary report on the first five years of our own three-country study is contained in Headey, Goodin, Muffels and Dirven (1997).

were in effect a life sentence, that would be much worse than if poverty were a state from which many (if not all) of the poor might hope soon to escape. The good news from panel studies, and obtainable only through such studies, is that most poverty spells are of this more transient, short-lived character.[14]

These new perspectives on the nature of poverty have implications for welfare philosophy and policy as well. If poverty spells strike broadly but usually just briefly, then social welfare policies to alleviate poverty look much less like unidirectional transfers between ossified classes and much more like 'insurance' policies which any of us, rich or poor, might some-day need.[15] Even those who are presently not in need, looking at the evidence of income volatility contained in the panel data, might come to regard welfare policies as a good insurance investment.

It is of course a sheer fallacy to say that, just because most do escape poverty in relatively short order, all can.[16] This amounts to a fallacy of false universalization.[17] True, most people's poverty spells are brief. But there is no reason to suppose that what is true of most people is (or can be) true of all of them. To assume otherwise ignores the variety of causes of poverty spells, the variety of escape routes from poverty, and the differen-tial impact they have on different people's lives.[18] The panel evidence indicates that there is indeed a group – smaller than traditionally sup-posed, but nonetheless a very important presence in real human terms – who are persistently poor and genuinely need public assistance on a

[14] That is demonstrated on a broadly cross-national basis, albeit on the basis of less long-term panel data, in Duncan *et al.* (1993).

[15] Note in this connection the striking survey finding that, in the Netherlands *circa* 1995, fully 79 per cent of those under sixty-five said that they had received or fully expected to receive at some future time unemployment, disability, sickness or social assistance benefits; and that proportion rises to a staggering 92 per cent if we include those with some other household member or close acquaintance who is presently receiving such benefits (van Oorschot 1997, p. 14).

[16] The American welfare reform of 1996 – eventually enacted as the 'Personal Responsibility and Work Opportunity Reconciliation Act of 1996', Public Law 104–193 [H.R. 3734] August 22, 1996, 110 Stat. 2105 – was largely predicated on precisely that fallacy, based in no small part on the panel data we shall here be re-analysing. Mary Jo Bane, who has done so much to analyse welfare spells using these data, served as Assistant Secretary for Children and Families in the US Department of Health and Human Services under Clinton. Of course a key part in her strategy, and indeed the President's, was to target education and training on those at risk of long-term welfare dependency (Bane and Ellwood 1994: 36–7). How well the 1996 reforms succeed in that is a much contested question which must, at the time of writing, remain an open one (Moynihan 1995; Friedlander and Burtless 1995).

[17] Akin to the more standard 'fallacy of composition'.

[18] For just one example, within the white community the dominant path out of poverty among women thrown into poverty by divorce is through remarriage to a more affluent man. Given the realities of mating practices within impoverished black ghettos, that is an option simply unavailable to large proportion of single black mothers.

protracted basis. It is an open question what form that differential public assistance ought to take – whether cash benefits, or in-kind assistance and services, or education and training, or some combination of all of these.

1.4   Our focus: three countries, ten years

Panel studies, by their nature, are difficult and expensive to run. You must keep track of particular individuals as they change names and addresses over the years. Furthermore, you must accumulate the evidence of several years before any important long-term patterns start to emerge with any clarity. Because of these difficulties and the attendant expenses, social scientists have been slow to mount on-going panel studies. Only a very few have been conducted with any regularity, over any substantial period.[19] Furthermore, not all of them contain strictly comparable questions, further complicating both cross-time and cross-national comparisons.

Consider, for example, the case of Sweden. Obviously, we would very much like to have been able to include that classic exemplar of social democracy in our study. But, alas, the Swedish panel study is virtually useless, given the way in which it has been conducted to date. Whereas the panels we will be using here were all surveyed at least once a year, the Swedish panel was surveyed only sporadically – only every other year (in 1984, 1986 and 1988) or worse (not again then until 1991). In the first two waves (1984 and 1986), the Swedish study administered long questionnaires comparable to those used in the other three panel studies we examine. In the latter two waves (1988 and 1991), it administered only a very short battery of largely non-comparable questions.[20] Consequently the Swedish panel data are just not sufficiently continuous or comparable to serve our purposes, however desirable it might otherwise have been to include that country in our study.[21] So too for the other Scandinavian panels, such as the Swedish Level of Living Survey (SLLS), which characteristically contain good income information drawn from tax records but often have such grossly inadequate information about house-

[19] The European Community Household Panel, begun in 1994, has a high degree of cross-national comparability but has not been running long enough for meaningful results to have emerged, and so too with most of the panels contained in the PACO project, discussed in footnote 6.

[20] These problems will obviously remain even after the HUS (Household Market and Non-Market Activities) Panel is updated to include 1993 and 1996. For details, see http://silver.hgus.gu.se/econ/econometrics/hus.husin.htm.

[21] Tellingly, these Swedish studies are among those which the Luxembourg PACO team has not been able to render comparable for incorporation into their database. Duncan *et al.* (1995) report results based instead upon the Swedish Household Income Survey (HINK), which show very similar poverty rates to those of the Netherlands.

hold structure that 'we do not know the number of children in the household, nor do we know the number of other adults' (Aaberge *et al.* 1996: 7).[22] And so too, in less dramatic fashion, for the great many other panel studies underway across the world: either they have not been running long enough, or they have not been running regularly enough, or they have not been using sufficiently comparable questions from year to year to provide the sort of data needed for the present study.

US panel researchers waited until the first ten years' worth of panel data were in before offering the results of that project to a wider public in their *Years of Poverty, Years of Plenty* (Duncan *et al.* 1984). That timing was not accidental. Ten years is about what it takes for any really conclusive long-term results to emerge from a panel study. The virtue of panels is that they allow us to track individuals through time. The disadvantage is that this necessarily takes quite some time.

If, however, ten years' worth of panel data are required for conclusive long-term results to emerge, then that drastically limits the scope of any comparative cross-national study relying upon panel data. There are only three major countries for which regular, comparable collections of socio-economic panel data have been collected over ten years or more.[23] The US Panel Study of Income Dynamics, pioneered by James N. Morgan at the University of Michigan's Institute for Social Research, has been tracking its panel since 1968. The German Socio-Economic Panel, run by the Deutsches Institut für Wirtschaftsforschung, Berlin, has been tracking its panel since 1984. The Dutch Socio-Economic Panel Survey, run by the Centraal Bureau voor de Statistiek, has been tracking its panel since 1984. These are the panel data we will be using.[24]

Our choice of countries to study was opportunistic and data-driven. We focus on the countries we do – the United States, Germany and the Netherlands – simply because those are the only countries for which ten-year socio-economic panel data are available. It is sheer good fortune that each of those countries can credibly be taken to represent one of each of the 'three worlds of welfare capitalism'.[25]

---

[22] Thus precluding construction of 'equivalence scales', upon which all serious work in this area is based: see section 6.3.2 below.

[23] Strictly speaking there are two other socio-economic panels which meet our ten-year test, but one is sub-national in scope (Lorraine) and the other is of an economically peculiar micro-state (Luxembourg).

[24] Our efforts at working across these data sets were greatly facilitated by the 1995/6 release of an official Equivalent File, organized through the University of Syracuse, combining the results of the German and American studies.

[25] We will be speaking here primarily of the tax-transfer aspects of countries' welfare regimes. Rankings based on countries' labour market policies would look different (Esping-Andersen 1996c; 1999). Basing the categorization on the extent of capital-labour intermediation in economic policy-making would make rankings more different again,

The United States is conventionally regarded as the archetypical example of a 'liberal welfare regime' and Germany is equally conventionally regarded as the archetypical example of a 'corporatist welfare regime'.[26] Of course even those archetypes turn out not to be completely pure cases. Over four-fifths of the money the US government spends on social protection goes not on means-tested benefits of the sort most strongly associated with the liberal welfare regime but rather on social insurance schemes of a more corporatist sort; and forgetting that fact leads in domestic American politics to many misguided attacks on 'America's misunderstood welfare state' (Marmor, Mashaw and Harvey 1990). For the purposes of international comparisons of welfare regime types, however, what is crucial is that the US relies much more heavily than most (three times the OECD average) on classically liberal means-tested benefits (Esping-Andersen 1990, p. 70). It is purely in this comparative sense that we say the US and Germany are archetypical liberal and corporatist welfare regimes respectively.

The Netherlands may be a still less archetypical representative of the 'social democratic welfare regime' type. Nonetheless, the Netherlands does sit squarely within that camp defined in terms of the vigorous public pursuit of income redistribution and, through that, social equality. The original foundations of the Dutch welfare state may have been essentially corporatist, and its path to its present form very different from the 'labour mobilization' path of the Scandinavian social democracies;[27] it may lack the heavy commitment to active labour market policies and high levels of public employment and public consumption that characterize the Swedish welfare state today;[28] its health system is income-tested; and it may not be nearly so 'women-friendly' as the Swedish model.[29] In the words of the title of one classic article on the subject, the Dutch model was – certainly in the period under study, at least – one of 'a passive social democratic welfare state in a Christian democratic ruled society' (van

with the Scandinavian countries (and sometimes the Netherlands) appearing very much at the top and Germany only in the middle of the list (Schmitter 1981; Lehmbruch 1984).

[26] Esping-Andersen (1987b, p. 7; 1990, p. 27).

[27] But perhaps none the less solidaristic for that: see Baldwin's (1990, ch. 1) forceful critique of the fallacy of thinking that the 'laborist approach' exhausts all socially based explanations of solidaristic social policy. Cf. Esping-Andersen and van Kersbergen (1992).

[28] Mahon (1991); Therborn (1992); cf. Kloosterman (1994). Note that the Netherlands today spends well above the OECD average on active labour market policies; note furthermore that Sweden began spending substantially larger proportions than the Netherlands on such programmes only in recent years (OECD 1996c, Table 2.9, p. 30).

[29] In the sense employed by Hernes (1987). For evidence see: Bussemaker and van Kersbergen (1994); Knijn (1994); Esping-Andersen (1996b); Lewis and Astrom (1992); Jenson and Mahon (1993); Sainsbury (1996). For more general discussions, see Orloff (1996) and Sainsbury (1996).

Kersbergen and Becker 1988). Still, at least in respect of the tax-transfer side of social policy, the Netherlands clearly qualifies as social democratic, and it has done so for the duration of the period under study.[30] And, as we shall go on to argue in section 1.5 below, in certain crucial respects it is actually a better representative of the social democratic welfare regime than is Sweden itself.

There are of course many other ways of categorizing welfare regimes other than these three, and there were many people who had the basic idea before Esping-Andersen popularized it.[31] Esping-Andersen has many critics, some of whom think that they said the same thing first, others of whom think that they have refuted Esping-Andersen decisively.[32] The point remains that, however compelling those refutations, they have not succeeded in laying to rest Esping-Andersen's 1990 book. Not only does it remain the firm focus of most on-going discussions in these areas, it has by now become a well-established landmark in relation to which any subsequent work – theirs as much as ours – must situate itself.

In certain quarters, the whole idea of a typology of welfare regime types is an anathema. Those deeply immersed in the particular facts of particular countries' national experiences see each country's welfare institutions as *sui generis* – a case unto itself. That is standardly said even of those countries which, among those prepared to countenance typologies at all, are regarded as archetypical instances of a certain class. American exceptionalism, as regards its welfare state as well as much else, is a familiar refrain (Skocpol 1995; Lipset 1996). Germans say much the same of their peculiar history. And those who want to make history the litmus test would similarly say the Dutch welfare state was built on far too many corporatist foundations to count as social democratic in the way the

---

[30] The key tables in Esping-Andersen's (1990, pp. 52, 74) own original presentation so classify it; and all the standard international comparisons of cross-sectional data on income distribution confirm that the Netherlands is in broadly the same league as Sweden (Atkinson, Rainwater and Smeeding 1995; Sweden, Ministry of Finance 1996). In a subsequent paper discussing the Netherlands alongside Germany, France, Italy and Belgium as instances of a 'conservative Continental welfare state', Esping-Andersen's (1996b, c) data once again show that the Netherlands is very much an outlier among that group, with much higher 'social minimum' payments and higher 'replacement rates' than those countries whose benefit systems are more occupationally based. Esping-Andersen (1996c, p. 84) admits as much in his first footnote to that article, where in effect he apologizes for the inclusion of the Netherlands among 'conservative Continental welfare states', saying, 'The Netherlands is a partial exception in that important elements of her income maintenance system are closer to the Nordic universalistic model.'

[31] Most especially Wilensky and Lebeaux (1958) and Titmuss (1958; 1974). See also: Furniss and Tilton (1977); Marshall (1977); Korpi (1983); Therborn (1986).

[32] Among them: Ringen (1991); Castles and Mitchell (1992; 1997); Lewis (1992); Castles (1993; 1996a, b); Sainsbury (1996). Esping-Andersen (1994; 1999, ch. 4) has himself subsequently conceded that at least some of those counterclaims might have merit.

Scandinavian countries do.[33] (Of course, those steeped in Swedish history say that there, too, the story is much more complicated than any simple, stylized social democratic account would make it appear.[34])

Those inclined to this line of thought might say that welfare typologies can, at best, identify ideal types which are inevitably intermingled in any particular country's welfare institutions. Thus, no single country – still less, they would say, pointing to the peculiarities of the national histories of the countries under examination, the particular countries we have 'chosen' – can truly be taken as representative of a regime type as a whole (Bolderson and Mabbett 1995).[35]

We respect the position of such sceptics. Certainly we share their strong sense that there are indeed many respects in which 'history matters'. Toward that end, we provide (in chapter 4) a brief historical and institutional sketch of welfare institutions in each of the countries under study to complement our more abstract, stylized account of welfare regimes (in chapter 3). Nonetheless, we cannot help thinking that it is useful to try to put particular countries' welfare arrangements in some more general perspective – just as it is to look at general typologies of welfare regimes through the experiences of particular countries.[36] On that latter proposition if not the former one, we should surely have the sceptics on our side.

Those conciliatory gestures notwithstanding, many will no doubt resist either the 'three worlds' hypothesis in general or our categorizations of those three particular countries within that scheme. We invite them to approach this book as a report on the real effects of social welfare arrangements in three important – and, we hope to show, importantly different – countries. That is a much more modest understanding of the task we have set for ourselves, and it is not the way we ourselves prefer to regard it. Nonetheless, that would be a perfectly interesting and worthwhile project in its own right, as must be agreed even by those who do not suppose that any more general conclusions follow from it.

In the process of showing the ways in which these countries differ, we will of course be providing further evidence bearing on our classifications

---

[33] Van Kersbergen (1995); Hemerijck and van Kersbergen (1997). Cf. Korpi (1997, pp. 46–8) who, analysing the same history, focuses upon the universal, flat-rate old age pension and concludes that by virtue of that 1956 enactment the Netherlands 'move[d] over to a basic security [i.e., social democratic] model'.

[34] Therborn (1989); Tilton (1990).

[35] Economists would therefore advise us to construct mathematical models in which these institutional differences figure as variables, which may be present to a greater or lesser degree in any case. But such mathematical models would of course be even more of an anathema to those sceptical of even the more informal modelling involved in regime typologies.

[36] A point which Esping-Andersen (1987b, p. 7) is of course happy to concede.

of countries and on the 'three worlds' hypothesis more generally. Those who remain unconvinced by chapter 4's institutional and programme-specific arguments that the Dutch tax and transfer mechanisms really do approximate to a social democratic welfare regime should simply wait to see whether (come chapter 14's application of the panel results to that model) the Netherlands turns out to look like one.

1.5   The best worlds of welfare capitalism

The logic of the comparative research design ideally requires that the countries be maximally different on the dimensions under study and maximally similar on all other dimensions (Mill 1843; Przeworksi and Teune 1970). As we hope to show over the course of this study, these three countries are indeed strikingly different, both in their welfare regimes and in the effects that those regimes have on people's lives, particularly among people of prime working age.[37]

In most other obvious respects, these three countries are pretty similar to one another. They represent the largest and economically most successful example of each regime type. In that sense, they might be said to constitute not just 'representative cases' but, indeed, the 'best cases' of each regime.

Certainly that is true of the United States. Judged in terms of population or GDP, the US is indisputably the largest liberal regime; and judged in terms of economic growth rates it is a highly successful one. Among Esping-Andersen's other (1990) liberal welfare regimes – Australia, Canada, Japan and Switzerland – only Japan's per capita GNP grew at a higher average annual rate over the period under study (World Bank 1996, pp. 18–19).[38]

Germany, likewise, is indisputably the largest and it was among the economically most successful corporatist regimes over this period. Among Esping-Andersen's (1990) other conservative-corporatist welfare regimes – France, Italy, Austria and Belgium – only the latter (smaller) two did economically better, and then not by much, over this period (World Bank 1996, pp. 18–19).

The Netherlands is by far the largest country in Esping-Andersen's (1990, p. 74) social democratic regime cluster. It is twice the size of Sweden and three times the size of Denmark in terms of population and

---

[37] The regimes and their effects are rather less distinctive in their treatment of the elderly, whose experiences we report separately.

[38] Of course, the Japanese welfare state is very different from those of Western welfare generally – more Confucian than liberal some would say (Jones 1993; Goodman and Peng 1997) – and in any case Japanese economic growth rates have plummeted in the period since 1994.

GDP. It is also economically the most successful member of that regime cluster. The more standard social democratic exemplars such as Sweden and Denmark have seen their economies unravel, with potentially serious consequences for their social welfare arrangements as well.[39] The Dutch economy, in contrast, has been performing remarkably well.[40] Domestic Dutch discourse may suggest otherwise, but seen from abroad the Netherlands seems to be 'a country that has exceptionally high job growth, radiantly healthy public finances, a relatively low rate of unemployment and an attractive climate for investment – and moreover . . . a country that sees the opportunity to combine all this with a high level of social protection'.[41] As *The Economist* once editorialized: 'If somewhere must be found to sit out the recession, Holland must be the nicest, comfiest place to choose' (quoted in van Kersbergen and Becker 1988, p. 477).

As we have frankly admitted in section 1.4, our real reason for choosing the Netherlands as our social democratic exemplar was that the Netherlands is the only even remotely social democratic welfare regime on which we have long-run, continuous panel data. But, as it happens, the choice thus forced upon us might not be a bad one. The Netherlands might be taken to represent not some deviant version of a social democratic welfare regime but, rather, a paradigmatic case of a social democratic-style welfare regime that looks likely to be economically sustainable in the long run (Hemerijck and van Kersbergen 1997; Visser and Hemerijck 1997).

If we want to assess regime performance there is much to be said for taking 'best cases' or best practice. Best cases tell you how to achieve good outcomes and avoid unnecessarily damaging trade-offs between 'hard' economic goals and 'soft' social welfare goals. They are what you need, in order to answer the question, 'What is the best we can do?' That is the right question to ask, for the development of future policy.

Previous assessments of welfare regimes and the 'big trade-off' have usually averaged the performance of regime types. This has the advantage

---

[39] For a striking contrast, compare Marquis Childs' 1936 celebration of Sweden as 'the Middle Way' with his 1980 reconsideration. For economic analyses see: Moene and Wallerstein (1993); Lindbeck (1995; 1997); Lindbeck *et al.* (1994). On social policy retrenchment see: Ploug and Qvist (1994); Clasen and Gould (1995); Stephens (1996); Andersen (1997). For a comparison with previous, more successful periods see Erikson and Åberg (1987).

[40] Its growth in real GNP per capita over the period 1985–94 averaged 1.9 per cent per year, compared to zero in Sweden, – 0.3 per cent in Finland, 1.3 per cent in Denmark and 1.4 per cent in Norway (World Bank 1996, pp. 18–19).

[41] In the words of A. P. W. Melkert, Minister for Social Affairs and Employment, in the introduction to a report which was addressed much more to the very different domestic perceptions of 'a highly developed welfare state where the associated costs, legislation and institutional structure create a contented society, but also create such an obstacle to economic dynamics that it is difficult to talk in terms of a bright future' (Netherlands Ministry 1996a, p. 4).

of using all available cases. But poor performers are arguably irrelevant. There are many ways of failing to achieve the social optimum. The interesting question is, 'Is there some way of having the best of all possible worlds, without any trade-offs?' Our answer, to foreshadow what follows, will be, 'Yes!'

1.6   Is it a fair test?

This book is clearly no more than a first cut at the cross-national analysis of these socio-economic panel data, and these three data sets are themselves only a precursor of many others still to come. A different decade or different countries might make a difference, maybe a big one, to our overall conclusions.

Still, while ours is only a first cut it is nonetheless a perfectly reasonable one. These three countries are all very much in the OECD mainstream, with successful market economies. They all have 'big governments', which take between 30 and 60 per cent of GDP in taxes and spend half of that on health, education and welfare (Rose 1984). They are, in those terms, all 'big social policy' states.

The years under study – the mid-1980s to the mid-1990s[42] – were not particularly peculiar, in global economic terms. The first half of the period corresponded to a worldwide economic boom, the second contained an economic slump in all three countries (OECD 1996f, annex table 1, p. A4). Economic growth, expressed as change in real (inflation-adjusted) GDP, was around 26 per cent in all of these three countries.[43]

All the countries under study were affected, at different times and some more than others, by broadly the same global economic, social and demographic trends. All three countries have around two people in the working-aged population for every person who is too old or too young to be expected to engage in paid labour.[44] Over four-fifths of men in all these countries were in the paid labour force. And while female labour force participation rates did differ across the three countries, they rose over this period in Germany and especially in the Netherlands and by the end of

---

[42] More precisely: 1985–94 for Germany and the Netherlands (though the 1994 income data in the Netherlands is adduced from the 1995 survey); for the US, 1983–92, representing the latest results available at the time of writing.

[43] Owing to differential population growth rates, growth in GDP per capita – which as we argue in section 7.2 is actually a better measure of people's well-being – varied between 17 per cent in Germany and the US and 19 per cent in the Netherlands. For details see appendix table A1, Eff 1B and sources cited therein.

[44] 'Dependency ratios' measuring the ratio of non-working-age population to the working-age population (16–64) were in the mid-40 per cent range for both Germany and the Netherlands throughout this period, and only just over 50 per cent in the US (ILO 1984–96, table 1 and UN 1984–95, table 7).

the period they were beginning to approach US levels (where about two-thirds of women were in the paid labour force throughout the period).[45]

Politically, of course, the period was one of great rupture, with the collapse of communism and the reunification of Germany. In terms of social welfare policy, however, that had little immediate impact.[46] At least in their formal institutional structures, East German social welfare arrangements were very like those of West Germany, sharing as they did common pre-war roots.[47] The welfare costs to the Federal Republic were certainly higher after unification than before, but their form was not materially different – certainly not, anyway, as regards members of the original West German panel to whom we confine our attention for the purposes of this study.[48]

The comparability of the items upon which we focus in these panel studies is underwritten by the imprimatur of an official Equivalent File merging the results of the German and American panel studies.[49] Of course we have had to supplement that official US–German file with the corresponding Dutch data; and we also had occasion to supplement it with other variables from the larger underlying files which were omitted from the official Equivalent File. But the great advantage of having that official Equivalent File as the starting point for our work is that, at least as regards those key variables which it does contain, we can compare across the data sets in the confidence that the variables we are using are ones that the data managers themselves regarded as being well matched for precisely these purposes.

In all these ways, ours seems to be a perfectly fair 'first cut' – but definitely only a first cut – at the analysis of alternative welfare regimes as viewed through the lens of panel data.

---

[45] Male labour force participation rates were in the mid-80 per cent range for all countries at the beginning of the period and stayed there in Germany and the US, rising in the Netherlands into the mid-90s (although most of that increase came in the form of part-time labour). Female labour force participation rates were in the mid-60 per cent range in the US throughout the period, whereas in Germany they moved from the mid-50s to around 60 per cent by the end, and in the Netherlands they rose from the middle 40 per cent range to the middle 50 per cent range (OECD 1996a, table II; ILO 1984–96, table 1; OECD 1984–95, Statistical Appendix).

[46] At least in the period upon which we focus, ending in 1994; cf. Hauser (1995).

[47] US SSA (1983, pp. 94–5).

[48] A panel of former East Germans was added to the panel in 1990, but they are clearly identified as such in the panel, and they can easily be discarded for the purposes of our study.

[49] Syracuse University Center for Aging and Demography and German Institute for Economic Research (1998). For a brief description see Wagner, Burkhauser and Behringer (1993).

Part I

Setting the scene

2 Reasons for welfare

There are many reasons for states to concern themselves with the welfare – the well-being – of their citizens. In terms of pragmatic politics, governments wanting to stay in office must satisfy the desires of their electors. Providing people with 'bread and circuses' is a time-honoured formula for securing social peace. Economically, improving human capital is a good productive investment, and giving poor people more purchasing power stimulates the demand side of the economy. Sociologically and psychologically, attending to social welfare is a sign that 'we care', unifying the nation and stirring people to greater sacrifices when required.

None of those, however, represent the sorts of 'reasons for welfare' with which we will be concerned in this chapter. The reasons which concern us here pertain not to causes and pragmatic motives but, rather, to more high-minded moral reasons. What we will be looking for here are good reasons, from a moral point of view, for attending to the welfare of our fellow citizens. Empirical matters – the 'hows' and 'whys' – will be addressed in later chapters. Our stance in the present chapter is insistently normative rather than empirical, evaluative rather than explanatory.

It would nonetheless be wrong to draw an overly sharp distinction between the two sets of concerns. Moral norms matter, socially and politically (and hence ultimately morally as well), only insofar as people can actually be motivated to act upon them (Goodin 1993). Morals, to be of any consequence, have to be internalized and acted upon by real actors in the real world. In the end, then, an analysis can really succeed in being normative in the ethical sense only if it succeeds in becoming normative in the sociological sense as well.

Neither do we mean to prise these moral propositions radically apart from the larger constructs of social ideology within which they are politically lodged. But while those larger ideological constructs may form the 'natural home' for each of these values, it is also the case that each of these values also has (as we hope the balance of this chapter will show) an appeal that transcends its traditional ideological home. Different ideologies often interpret the values differently, and states in the service of different ideologies characteristically pursue them through different strategies.

Still, each of these values seems to represent things which, in one way or another and to some extent or another, all of us would like to see served by our various social welfare arrangements. Different ideologies may interpret those values differently, operationalize them differently, weight them differently. But in one way or another, everyone would apparently like ideally to see all of them being served.

In so far as these values thus form the core of a loose social consensus across various ideologies, they can be taken to represent 'external standards of assessment' by which the performance of various alternative welfare regimes can be assessed. We will use them in just this way when it comes to assessing specific sorts of welfare regimes in chapters 7–12 below, before then going on also to assess each welfare regime in terms of the more 'internal' standard of whether it achieves what it tries to achieve in the way it tries hardest to achieve it (in chapters 13–15).

In our discussion of 'external standards of assessment', we focus upon six moral values which welfare states have traditionally been supposed to serve:

- promoting economic efficiency;
- reducing poverty;
- promoting social equality;
- promoting social integration and avoiding social exclusion;
- promoting social stability; and
- promoting autonomy.

There are many different ways of phrasing those points, and various different ways of splitting them up into distinct values, but there is broad consensus upon some such list as this, across a broad range of commentators.[1]

---

[1] Compare our list with that provided by the Commission on Social Justice (1994, p. 8):
- Prevent poverty where possible and relieve it where necessary.
- Protect people against risks arising in the labour market and from family change.
- Redistribute resources from richer to poorer members of society.
- Redistribute resources of time and money over people's life-cycles.
- Encourage personal independence.
- Promote social cohesion.

Our 'promoting economic efficiency' and 'reducing poverty' correspond to the first of those, our 'promoting equality' to the third and fourth together, our 'promoting social integration' to the last, our 'promoting social security' to the second, and our 'promoting autonomy' to the fifth.

There is also a broad consensus across all welfare regimes on this list of desiderata. These are the terms in which capitalist welfare regimes of all stripes legitimize themselves to their publics (Habermas 1975; Offe 1984). Different welfare regimes accord them different emphases, to be sure; we detail those differences in chapter 3. But similarities ought to be emphasized too. Low poverty rates, social stability, social integration and – most especially – high economic growth rates are all goals that are internalized by all welfare regimes of every sort. So too are freedom and equality, differently though different regimes would understand those terms.

These external moral standards are listed in no particular order, whether of 'moral importance' or anything else. In listing and discussing efficiency first, we do not mean to imply by that alone that economic efficiency is morally more (or less) important than reducing poverty or inequality; and in discussing poverty second, we do not mean to imply that reducing poverty is necessarily more (or less) important than reducing inequality. Nor do we mean to imply that promoting economic efficiency or reducing poverty is a prerequisite, logically or sociologically, for promoting equality. Nor do we even mean to imply that there is some sort of developmental sequence, in which one focus of attention characteristically gives way to the other with the maturation of social policy or political or economic systems.

These values may well sometimes come into conflict. Where they do, one will simply have to decide which of these moral criteria matters most. Having offered no ranking of their comparative moral importance, we offer no basis for choosing between them in cases of conflict.

All we will be able to do is to make weak rankings among welfare regimes. If one regime meets all the criteria that another meets, and more, then the former regime is morally to be preferred to the latter. Such weak rankings take us a long way, as we hope to show in our concluding chapter. Indeed, it will be our contention there that those weak rankings can take us all the way to a determinate choice, uniquely favouring one particular welfare regime over all others.

It is thus important to eschew any temptation to rush to judgment. It is altogether too easy to plump for one sort of welfare regime because it is the one supposedly most concerned with the value which is of most concern to you, without stopping to examine whether that welfare regime actually does what it is supposed to do, much less whether some other welfare regime altogether might champion that value less loudly while actually serving it more effectively.

2.1   Promoting economic efficiency

Efficiency is a constraint incumbent upon all purposive social action, be it in the realm of welfare policy or any other. It is better to do things efficiently than inefficiently, simply because by doing things efficiently we can achieve more of whatever it is that we want (Barr 1985). But that constraint has standardly been thought to apply with particular force to the design of welfare policy (Okun 1975).

When economists critique the welfare state in terms of its economic inefficiency, however, they mean more than merely that there is some alternative administrative arrangement which would yield 'more bang for the buck'. The inefficiencies introduced into the economy by welfare policies are said to hinder economic growth and through that people's 'well-being', broadly construed. That is what makes 'equity versus efficiency' the 'big trade-off', in the terms of the title of Arthur Okun's (1975) classic text on the topic.

For economists and politicians critiquing welfare regimes in terms of it, 'efficiency' serves as shorthand for a set of alternative ways of conceiving of social welfare and of alternative ways of promoting it. Welfare policy, as standardly understood, is supposed to remedy the failures of the market. It aims to provide an income flow to people who have, for whatever reason, failed to secure an adequate income flow from ordinary market dealings – people who are out of work or could never find any, or people whose productive contributions are valued so little by the market that they would not be able to live adequately on the basis of their market incomes alone.

Where welfare policy-makers would remedy the failure of the market to provide those people with a living wage, others of a more economistic bent would pause to query why their wages are so low and what might be the broader welfare implications of artificially increasing them. After all, markets promote welfare, just as do welfare states.[2] When social policy-makers intervene into the operations of markets through welfare policies, what they risk upsetting are instruments and institutions which are also working to promote welfare. They risk undermining the sorts of incentives by which markets evoke hard work in the service of others' interests,

---

[2] In support of that view, welfare economists can offer one of the most impressive accomplishments of modern social science, General Equilibrium Analysis, and the two Fundamental Theorems of Welfare Economics derived from it (Arrow and Hahn 1971). Of course, the proofs of those Fundamental Theorems presuppose certain ideal conditions which are nowhere realized in the real world; and the very 'market failures' which welfare policy-makers strive to remedy when aiding poor people go to the heart of crucial mathematical assumptions required for General Equilibrium Analysis – and the economic market – to work its welfare magic.

or private savings which form the basis of national investment, or whatever.[3]

The fundamental notion of efficiency underlying all economists' discussions of the issues is of course that of 'Pareto efficiency': when no one can be made better off without anyone being made worse off. If that is their basic definition of efficiency, economists nonetheless talk of various specific mechanisms by which such efficiency might be promoted or compromised. They talk of 'productive' efficiency, in the 'bang for the buck' sense: given factor inputs of this level, there is no way to rearrange the productive process in such a way as to get more outputs from them.[4] They talk of 'allocative' efficiency: there is no way to rearrange our resources across the whole range of things we do that would lead to a set of outcomes which is Pareto superior to the one we currently achieve. They talk of 'x-efficiency': there is no way to better motivate people to invest more of the intangible resources of mental energy and enthusiasm into the process (Leibenstein 1966).

Across all of these more specific senses, the fundamental moral value underlying notions of efficiency is simply the value of 'waste not, want not'. Inefficiency, in Paretian terms, is a matter of waste pure and simple. The existence of Pareto inefficiency is *ipso facto* evidence that we could have done more, of whatever it is we wanted to do, with the same resources.

The virtue of the value of efficiency, among morally agnostic economists, is that it is in this way utterly non-committal as regards the deeper values it is to serve. Whatever we want to do, we could do more of it if we did it efficiently than if we did it inefficiently. That is true if we are trying to promote people's welfare: it is better to do it efficiently than inefficiently, because we can do more of it if we do it efficiently. That is also true if we are trying to kill people: if that is our goal, we can do more of that, too, by doing it efficiently rather than inefficiently (hence the injunction of McNamara's Pentagon cost-benefit analysts that we should try to get the 'most bang for the buck' (Hitch and McKean 1960)).

The value of efficiency is, thus, morally agnostic in a major way. Economists regard that as a benefit of the notion. But that moral agnosticism is also a burden from larger evaluative perspectives. First of all, we must recognize that efficiency is not an ultimate value but merely an

---

[3] At the same time, certain sorts of interventions – education and training schemes, for example – also promote efficiency through the development of human capital, and so on (Van Parijs 1991).

[4] What we shall be discussing in chapter 7 below as 'target efficiency' is a sub-species of that: it is a matter of whether, for welfare budgets of a fixed size, we could help more genuinely deserving people.

instrumental one. It is not good in itself.[5] Rather, it is good only in so far as we would be able to achieve more of the other goods that we are pursuing, if we pursued them efficiently rather than inefficiently (Goodin 1988, ch. 8; Le Grand 1990; Barry 1990, p. xl). A second proposition, which follows from the first, is that we must recognize that the value of efficiency is morally speaking parasitic upon the value of the goals which are being pursued efficiently. It may well be true that it is always better to do X efficiently than inefficiently; but it is not necessarily true that it is always better to do Y efficiently than X inefficiently. It all depends upon the relative moral values of X and Y respectively.

2.2   Reducing poverty

The poor will always be with us: the Bible tells us so. But since time immemorial societies have nonetheless tried to reduce poverty's ineradicable presence, moderating its extent and mitigating its effects as much as humanly possible. Famine relief and food rationing in times of war or drought or pestilence or other natural disasters was the most traditional form. In one way, the modern welfare state is the latest in a long line of such public interventions aimed at reducing poverty and its effects on people (Himmelfarb 1984).

Poverty might be defined simply as having resources inadequate to meet one's needs.[6] That definition, like all good definitions, does not so much solve problems as shift them. What it does usefully do, though, is to shift the focus to what genuinely are the two central issues – 'what are needs?' and 'what is adequate?' Those two issues lie substantively at the heart of disputes over different conceptions of poverty and different approaches to ameliorating it.[7]

There is, first, the classically 'minimalist' position. This clings to a notion of 'needs' as 'basic requirements for physical functioning'; and it deems those needs to have been met 'adequately' whenever physical

---

[5] One of the things economic efficiency is instrumental for (and which the term often serves as code for) is of course material well-being, which is arguably of more than merely instrumental value.

[6] According to this definition, you are not poor if you have resources which would be sufficient to meet your needs, whether or not you actually spend them on things required to meet your needs. We agree with Ringen (1988) that it is wrong to call the starving miser 'poor', just because money which was present in abundance was not spent on needed foodstuffs.

[7] While discussions ordinarily focus on economic resources and poverty defined in terms of them, we can also discuss in like fashion poverty defined in terms of social and cultural resources as well (as the European Council does). On the concept of needs see: Braybrooke (1987); Doyal and Gough (1991); and, more generally, Goodin (1988, ch. 2) and sources cited therein.

existence is sustained. This is the 'food, clothing and shelter' school of needs analysis. Operationalized through nutritionist notions such as 'minimum caloric intake', this approach forms the core of classically 'absolute'-style standards of poverty.[8]

But even in terms of the narrowly restricted set of 'food, clothing and shelter' as the only strictly needed goods, how much is 'adequate' along each of those dimensions surely depends on what you want to do with them. And even if your aspirations are fixed as low as possible, at just 'staying alive', that still leaves the standard arguably indeterminate. Is the 'nutritional minimum', thus understood, one which will allow one sufficient energy just to eat? Or to collect one's food as well? Or to work in the fields to cultivate it? Or, if one is an urban dweller without access to arable land, to work in the factories to earn money to buy it? In such ways, even a tight initial focus just on what is needed for physical functioning inevitably leads us to think about what is needed for 'social functioning' more broadly (Dasgupta 1993, chs. 14–16).

As we broaden our horizons in these ways, we have increasingly to take notice of 'relative' as well as absolute necessities. Your need for 1,500 calories a day may be as absolute as you like, defined purely in terms of nutritional requirements for physical functioning. But suppose rice is the only available foodstuff from which you could derive those calories, and that we are in the midst of a famine so there is not enough rice to go around to all who need it. Then you are in competition with others for the rice you need, instrumentally, to get your 1,500 calories. How much money you need to bid successfully for 1,500 calories' worth of rice depends, crucially, upon how much money others against whom you are bidding have available. Your need for calories, and hence rice, may be absolute: how much you need has nothing to do with how much anyone else has. But your need for money with which to buy the rice, derived from that, is very much relative: how much money you need depends crucially upon how much others have (Sen 1981; 1983; Drèze and Sen 1989). Many of the 'needs' served by welfare states are relative in structurally just the same way (Hirsch 1976; Goodin 1990a).

In moving from an initial concern with relieving absolute poverty with respect to basic necessities (food, clothing and shelter), the concern of poverty researchers has thus expanded. It has come to embrace not just

[8] Ruggles (1990) suggests the original US poverty line was built on some such premises. See similarly Leibfried's (1992) discussion of 'nutritional minima' in interwar Germany. Early poverty researchers (Rowntree and Booth in England, and so on) almost certainly operated with some such standard at the back of their minds – not necessarily because that was where their analysis of poverty would have stopped, but just because when such palpable poverty of that sort existed its eradication must surely be a first priority, however anxious one might later be to go on to eradicate other forms as well.

basic necessities but also a broader range of more 'instrumental' goods necessary to secure those more basic ones. And in the process it has come to embrace a broader standard of adequacy, couched in terms of 'social functioning' rather than just 'physical functioning'.

The limiting case is perhaps best represented by Peter Townsend's monumental study of *Poverty in the United Kingdom* (1979). His concern there is with the extent to which people have the basic material resources which would allow them to participate effectively in the ordinary life of their community: television, holidays at the coast, a Sunday roast, and so on.[9] The extent to which people did not have resources is taken, by Townsend, as a measure not just of social deprivation or hardship but, literally, of poverty.

Most would demur at going quite as far as Townsend (1954; 1962; 1979) toward a notion of completely 'relative poverty'. Nevertheless, more moderate measures of relative deprivation are by now very much the most widely accepted standards of poverty. Some of the relativizations of notions of social need (as for money with which to buy rice) are justified as having an absolutely objective basis (Sen 1983). Others are rooted in people's subjective senses of status and justice, which are powerfully shaped by expectations and aspiration levels determined by those around them (Stouffer 1949; Runciman 1966). People feel themselves to be poor, and think others to be poor, in ways that matter both sociologically and ultimately morally, if they have substantially less than what is commonplace among others in their society (Kapteyn, Kooreman and Willemse 1988; van Praag 1993).

2.3   Promoting social equality

Concern with promoting 'social equality' has proceeded through many phases over the centuries (Marshall 1949). Initially, it was almost exclusively a concern with status concepts. Everyone was supposed to be 'equal under the law', or later 'equally entitled to vote'. Those battles won, concern with equality came to focus on an equality of material condition and with the state's role in underwriting it. That is where the real story of the welfare state, as an aid to equality, begins.

Again, how best to understand the sort of 'equality' the welfare state is supposed to be serving is much debated. The mathematical analogy suffices to make the formal meaning of equality clear enough. But its referent – 'equality of what?' (Sen 1980; Cohen 1989) – remains much disputed.

---

[9] An odd standard to apply to vegetarians or pensioners who prefer radio, as Piachaud (1981) pointed out.

One version would cash out the notion of equality simply in terms of 'equal concern and respect' (Dworkin 1978). This, the most conservative interpretation of the egalitarian ideal sometimes amounts to little more than the 'equal status' concerns that animated demands for the Magna Carta and the Bill of Rights. While this has long ceased to be the cutting edge of egalitarian concern, sadly enough it has never completely lost its salience. That is the form of equality still being fought for by various civil rights movements in the American South and indeed throughout the world (Rose 1976).

Moving beyond mere equal status, some egalitarians argue for 'equal opportunity' while others argue for 'equal outcomes'. In the realm of welfare policy, that typically translates into an argument for 'equal resources' as against 'equal welfare' (Dworkin 1981). We tend to regard the former item in each of these pairs as the less demanding one, and all the more attractive for that reason.

Those seemingly more modest demands turn out to be radically underspecified, however. We have no good way of knowing whether opportunities ever were equal, except by checking to see to what extent the outcomes ensuing from them have, over the long haul, been equal (Nell 1980). Similarly, given the different things people want to do with their resources and the different amounts of resources it takes to achieve each of them, we have no way of calibrating resource equality except by reference to the welfare effects produced by alternative portfolios of resource holdings (Roemer 1985).

The upshot is that the less demanding forms of the egalitarian ideal (equal opportunities, equal resources) are radically unspecified, in ways causing them ultimately to collapse into the other more demanding forms. We are thus left with the more demanding forms of social equality (equal outcomes, equal welfare) as the socially preferred ones, insofar as social equality is thought to matter at all.

There is yet another side to social equality. Walzer (1983) calls it 'complex equality', Tobin (1970) 'specific egalitarianism', Elster (1990; 1992; 1995) 'local justice'. The basic idea running across all these discussions is that we do, and think we ought to, distribute different sorts of goods according to different rules. We think certain sorts of things, like food, housing and health care, ought to be distributed more equally than money income; and we institute non-tradeable systems of food stamps, public housing and subsidized medical care toward that end.

The very fact that we address inequalities in those realms through in-kind services, which we are not prepared to allow people to cash out for money, is evidence of a sort for thinking that there is something special about those goods. It is evidence, anyway, that we think for some reason that the distribution of those specific things should be relatively more equal, rather than just that the standards of living which people enjoy across all goods they consume should be more equal.

What it is that is special about those goods is something of a mystery which has so far eluded any general theory. Elster has now largely abandoned his quest for a theory of local justice, accepting defeat. Walzer rather tends to regard it as a curious anthropological fact where any particular society will draw the lines. It may well have something to do with 'needs' as discussed above: lots of the goods provided in strictly egalitarian fashion seem to speak to what we might more naturally regard as people's needs, rather than their mere preferences.

Crucially they also have to do with 'status rights', of the sort with which this discussion of equality began. One specific egalitarian policy is the requirement that everyone do jury duty and military service, rather than buying in replacements. Another, presumably, would be the ban on selling your vote or other civic entitlements. The thought, perhaps, is that however poor or rich, everyone should be equally citizens.

Much of the modern case for welfare rights has been couched precisely in these terms of the 'rights of social citizenship' (Marshall 1949; King and Waldron 1988). In so far as decent levels of welfare provision – unemployment benefit, old age pension and the like – are seen as part and parcel of the rights of citizenship in a modern society (and citizenship is a quintessentially single-status concept: it is built into the notion of citizenship that all citizens are equally citizens), it then follows that the distribution of those rights of citizenship and the welfare benefits conferring them should be equal.

A final feature of social citizenship, of particular concern to egalitarians because it is of particular concern to citizens themselves, is the 'right to work' (Elster 1988). Work is indeed 'special' in several respects. People not only derive income from it, they also derive social status, self-respect, satisfaction and self-realization from it – at least if the work is of the right sort (Elster 1988; Arneson 1990). Many social theorists want people to work for many different reasons. But the distinctively egalitarian concern with work is that its unique benefits should be shared equally between everyone in the community, which is what leads egalitarians to promote 'full employment' policies as a crucial component of the egalitarian social programme (Therborn 1986).

2.4   Promoting social integration, avoiding social exclusion

In stark contrast to the rugged individualism of market society, notions of community, fraternity and solidarity mark at one and the same time both a descriptive reality and a social ideal. Descriptively, all of us are much more rooted in on-going social relations of a more intimate sort than some forms of individualism and market liberalism seem to suggest. Morally, most of us deem this to be something of a mixed blessing, perhaps, but on balance definitely a good thing.[10]

Where society is regarded as essentially a 'family', welfare policies follow logically from that conception. The family takes care of its members; and in a familist world, whom you are prepared to take care of effectively defines the boundaries of your kin. As Walzer (1983, p. 31) writes in a famous passage:

The idea of distributive justice presupposes a bounded world within which distributions take place: a group of people committed to dividing, exchanging and sharing social goods, first of all among themselves. That world ... is the political community, whose members distribute power to one another and avoid, if they possibly can, sharing it with anyone else.

Mutual aid is both the cause of and consequence of (both constitutive of and correlative with) tightly integrated communities. It constitutes a virtuous circle, whereby social ties are reaffirmed, reinforced and renewed. The sort of trust which this mutual aid builds has been dubbed 'social capital' (Putnam 1993). But whereas other forms of capital might diminish with use, social capital of this sort instead expands with use. The more often people have occasion to trust one another, and find one another trustworthy, the more trusting they become (Cornford 1972).

Much of this social capital and community spirit must perforce be developed in face-to-face interactions. But there are certain things that the state can do to facilitate such interactions, or anyway not get in the way of them. A primary task in developing caring communities thus understood is to protect and nurture the 'intermediary institutions' of society. Primary among them is, of course, the 'family'. But also among them are churches, civic groups, trade unions and trade associations, sports clubs and voluntary associations which together constitute what has today come to be called 'civil society' (Habermas 1962/1989; Berger and Neuhaus 1977; Cornuelle 1965; Green 1993).

Although ordinarily content to leave social welfare primarily to the workings of these intermediary institutions, communitarians are sometimes prepared to countenance collective provision of a social safety net for anyone who slips through those other more natural nets of society. What is crucial for communitarians is that the state's safety net should

---

[10] Hence the 'communitarian' challenge to liberalism (Sandel 1982; MacIntyre 1988; Taylor 1989; Benhabib 1992; cf. Gutmann 1985 and Goodin 1998a). Hence too the so-called 'new communitarianism' of Etzioni (1993).

complement and strengthen what is provided by broader social institutions, rather than in any way competing or undermining them (Tocqueville 1835; Himmelfarb 1994). But that said, a collectively organized social safety net to supplement society's other structures might well be justified in these terms as further expression of the full integration of all members into society (Young and Halsey 1995).

The most recent expression of this integrationist thought is through the European Union's language of 'social exclusion'. Rather than just worrying about poverty as such, what policy-makers there now worry about are the deeper sources of poverty, which they conceive to be the exclusion of people from central elements of the life of their society right across the board. Cumulative disadvantages combine to exclude people from ever wider sectors of social life. Low levels of education, poor health and housing, low job skills, insecure and intermittent labour force attachment, low income and so on all feed on one another, leading to the increasing marginalization of already marginal members of society.[11] And that social exclusion is all the more problematic when the marginalized groups are culturally distinct, whether by reason of race or ethnicity or of national origins.

2.5   Promoting social stability

Those concerned that people be integrated into communities are, quite naturally, concerned with the security and stability of those on-going social institutions. But quite apart from those larger concerns with social integration and the stability of overarching social structures, we also more simply want some stability in our own personal lives.

Much of what is called 'social security' policy aims precisely at these concerns, stabilizing people's incomes when their ordinary earnings are interrupted. In case of sickness or industrial injury, social insurance benefits typically replace lost earnings at a rate very close to the person's previous wage rate for a fairly long period of time. Only after a year or so, in most places, are people moved across to 'disability' benefits; and those, too, are explicitly earnings-related albeit typically with replacement rates of a rather lower level. The old age pension, too, is almost everywhere set up on an earnings-related basis to support people in retirement at a level proportionately close to what they enjoyed while in work. And so on down all the major headings of 'social insurance', across most countries (US SSA 1993).

The ethical case to be made for this practice is quite unlike that

[11] See, e.g., Silver (1994; 1995); Rogers (1995); Room (1995); Dryzek (1996); Jordan (1996); Atkinson (1998c). Cf. Goodin (1996).

underlying many of the more familiar arguments for welfare-state transfers. At least on the face of it, earnings-related benefits are more pro-rich
than pro-poor. Earnings-related benefits pay more to those who have
historically earned more, and who presumably will have more accumulated capital in consequence.[12] Earnings-related benefits are, if not strictly
inegalitarian, a dramatically less efficient way of achieving overall social
equality than flat-rate or progressive welfare payments would be.

Despite all that, we nonetheless pay a good many of our social benefits
in this earnings-related form. One reason, of course, derives from the
social integrationist concerns just discussed. Earnings-related benefits
essentially preserve people's position in the social structure. Insofar as
social status is a function of income, social programmes which ensure
high replacement rates when ordinary income streams are interrupted in
effect guarantee that those interruptions to ordinary earnings will not
upset the existing status hierarchy in society.

This is the sense in which such earnings-related benefits, and corporatist states organized around them, are said to be fundamentally 'conservative' institutions (Esping-Andersen 1990). They conserve – protect and
restore – the existing pecking order of society. For those who regard that
pecking order as being itself arbitrary and unjustified, that constitutes a
criticism of such arrangements. But for those who value tradition, stability and order, either as ends in themselves or as necessary preconditions of
any other major achievements in social life, that is seen as a major service
(Oakeshott 1962; Hayek 1973–79).

Quite independent of those larger conservative claims, however, there
is another reason for being concerned with security and stability in our
individual lives. We are intentional agents, who want to 'make something'
of our lives. We commit ourselves in consequence to certain plans and
projects, people and principles (Sen 1977; Williams 1973). Our on-going
commitment to those people, plans, projects and principles constitute, in
some deep sense, our 'identity' and 'sense of self'. Inevitably, some of
those commitments will have to be revised from time to time. But we do
not want to, or to ask others to, give up such commitments lightly. We do
not want them to be buffeted unduly in respect of those most fundamental commitments. That is at least part of what we are trying to do, through
the stability-inducing aspects of earnings-related social welfare policies:
to prevent people from having to revise more than strictly necessary the
basic plans and projects that constitute their lives (Goodin 1990b).

[12] To some extent of course this is just to say that they 'pay back' more to those people, for
earnings-related benefits are characteristically financed by workplace contributions
compulsorily extracted in part from those individuals themselves during their working
lives (and from their employers, characteristically in equal proportions).

2.6   Promoting autonomy

Finally, social welfare policy is designed to serve goals of promoting personal autonomy. Under circumstances of grinding poverty, people have very little freedom for manoeuvre. They must secure the preconditions for their continued survival, and they must do whatever it takes to accomplish that.

In conditions of great inequality, where grinding poverty on one side is matched by considerable affluence on the other, that natural necessity gives rise to relations of subservience and hence social unfreedom. Those in need will be utterly at the mercy of those upon whom they depend to meet their needs. They will have to bow and scrape (Pettit 1997). They are prey to exploitation and manipulation of the cruellest sort (Goodin 1988, chs 5–7).

Therein lies the classic case for the welfare state. To avoid unwarranted manipulation and exploitation of the most vulnerable members of society, welfare assistance should be run by state agencies rather than private charities; and payments should be made as entitlements on the basis of well-specified 'welfare rights' rather than at the discretion of social-service caseworkers (Goodin 1985, ch. 7; 1988, chs. 5–8). In the limiting case, this logic leads to an argument for 'basic income', paid to all, absolutely without any conditions whatsoever (Van Parijs 1990; 1991; 1992; 1995; van der Veen and Van Parijs 1987; van der Veen 1998a).

Even in much less dramatically unconditional assistance regimes, however, social assistance is often said to serve a vital function in underwriting the autonomy and independence of those in receipt of it. Few welfare programmes could be hedged with more qualifications and conditions than was the now defunct US programme of Aid to Families with Dependent Children (AFDC). But hedged with conditions though it may have been, AFDC nonetheless made – quite unintentionally, of course – a massive contribution to the independence and autonomy of the young (and sometimes not so young) women receiving it, in terms of getting them out from under the yoke of fathers and boyfriends and allowing them to establish an independent household (Orloff 1993; Young 1995).[13]

Feminist critics of the 'male breadwinner model' not only want the welfare state to help young women escape domination in their father's home but also insist that welfare states should be arranged in such a way as to make women economically independent within marriage. The control over the family's economic resources within marriage is often highly

---

[13] For a particularly sensitive feminist treatment of the notion of 'independence', see James (1992).

unequal (Young 1952; Piachaud 1982; Pahl 1983; 1989). Some sorts of welfare states exacerbate those inequalities, by enforcing the dependency of non-waged (usually female) members of the household upon the (usually male) breadwinner's attachment to the labour market. The dependency of women upon men's wages and welfare entitlements is mitigated by other sorts of welfare states which actively encourage female labour force participation, or at least give all members of the household entitlements to welfare benefits in their own right rather than by virtue of the labour force participation of their household's (typically male) head (Sainsbury 1994; 1996; Orloff 1996; MacDonald 1998).

Receiving unconditional state support – without doing anything to qualify for it, and without any conditions on what one should do with it – clearly enhances the freedom and independence of people in receipt of it. In terms of the classical distinction, it increases people's 'positive freedom', freedom *to do* various things and to live in certain ways (Berlin 1958). Equally clearly, refusing to let the people paying the tax bill to put any strings on the assistance financed by their taxes constitutes a restriction on those people's freedom of action. Precisely because the welfare state is financed by a regime of compulsory taxation, it is said to restrict taxpayers' 'negative freedom' – freedom *from* state interference. The high-tax, high-transfer is sometimes dubbed a 'servile' state, in consequence (Hayek 1960; 1973–79). Some go so far as to equate the hours you spend generating income that goes toward paying your tax bill to 'forced labour' (Nozick 1974, p. 169).

How you draw the balance sheet on the welfare state, in terms of its impact on values of freedom and autonomy, is of course a matter of judgment. Clearly, there are entries on each side to be weighed in the balance. But while much must be left to judgment in these realms, the one thing that ought to be firmly insisted upon is that it is fundamentally the same kind of freedom at work on both sides of the ledger. If what the welfare state takes away from people, in taxing them, is properly described in terms of 'freedom' at all, then what it gives to people, in paying them welfare benefits, must be describable in the self-same terms of 'freedom' (Jones 1982; Goodin 1988, ch. 11). The only issue is how to weight the competing freedoms involved.

A larger issue concerns the extent to which those who rely upon the state for subsistence can truly be said to be 'autonomous'. Of course, as already noted, some forms of state support impinge on people's autonomy more than others; and a system of unconditional assistance, minimally subject to the discretionary judgments of programme administrators, is the form most consistent with autonomy on the part of recipients. But critics have long claimed that recipients' autonomy is compromised by the sheer fact of their 'welfare dependency', relying year in and year out upon the state for their support (Tocqueville 1835; Mead 1986; 1992; Himmelfarb 1994; Bane and Ellwood 1994, chs. 3–4; cf. Fraser and Gordon 1994; Gibson 1998, ch. 10).

When critics of 'welfare dependency' argue that people should instead be 'self-reliant' or 'self-sufficient', however, it is not the 'self' alone upon which they would have people rely. Rather than eliminating dependency altogether, these critics of welfare dependency just propose shifting its locus: from the state to the market or, even more often, the family (Goodin 1988, ch. 12; 1998b). Which is the preferable form of dependency is, again, an open question. All we would care to emphasize at this point, again, is that the choice before us in this realm is between competing dependencies. Autarky is simply not an option.

2.7   A matter of priorities

In the following chapter, and indeed throughout the rest of this book, we will be associating each of the values just canvassed primarily with one or another of the welfare regimes we will be discussing. But it is important to remember that those differences are largely just differences of emphasis.

All the welfare regimes we will be discussing attach positive value to all the sorts of considerations we have been discussing in this chapter. None can afford to ignore altogether considerations of economic efficiency. None thinks poverty is a good thing. None thinks social disintegration is preferable to social integration, or that social instability is something to be desired. Each of the welfare regimes we will be discussing strives to promote freedom and equality, at least on its own understanding of those terms.

Where the regimes differ from one another is in how much weight they attach to each of those goals. Liberal welfare regimes attach relatively more importance to economic efficiency than do other welfare regimes. Social democratic welfare regimes value economic efficiency too: they just attach relatively more importance to equality than do other welfare regimes. Corporatists value economic efficiency, too; they just attach relatively more importance to social integration and social stability than do other welfare regimes. Those differing emphases are what is distinctive about each welfare regime, and inevitably much of our discussion will be couched in terms of them. But all these discussions of differences between welfare regimes must be set firmly against the backdrop of commonality. In many respects, what all these welfare regimes share is at least as important as their differences.

3 Alternative institutional designs

In this chapter, we present stylized models of different types of welfare regimes. These models represent alternative 'institutional designs' (Goodin 1996). 'Design', here, does not necessarily imply a designer, some Rousseau-style Lawgiver from whose brow institutional structures sprang fully formed. The institutions of welfare states, and of the larger socio-economic orders in which they are set, emerged over many years, the product of many hands and much political horse-trading.

In the course of all this wrangling over the design and redesign of our inherited institutions, though, patterns nonetheless emerge and clusters form. To some extent this has to do with intentions, ideas and values. According to received wisdom, there are only so many ways of pursuing any given social objective; and unless they can think up some altogether new way of doing things, people (particularly people closely engaged in the day-to-day fray of political life) tend to fall into whichever of the old intellectual ruts suits their principles and purposes. Furthermore, to some extent these ruts are real. That is to say, there is, to some extent, an internal 'regime logic' that dictates what institutional options can fit together coherently and work together well.

These institutional designs, by their very nature, blend many different elements. Moral values and social goals are the guiding lights; but they must be given more operational form than ordinarily is the case in more abstract philosophical argumentation. Institutional forms and social practices are the practical embodiments; but their salient features must be isolated more clearly than in more descriptive institutional analysis. Thus, in building bridges between social values and political forms, institutional design is also bridging between levels of abstraction, making the former less abstract and the latter more so.

The particular institutional designs here in view represent alternative ways of constituting welfare regimes. Each model to be discussed will be characterized by:

- a distinctive set of fundamental *values*;
- a distinctive analysis of what *produces social welfare* and, connected to that, a distinctive analysis of why some people *fail to benefit* from that process; and
- deriving from that analysis, a distinctive *policy response* to such people's failures to benefit from the productive process, together with a distinctive way of construing the *social goal* which that response is aimed at achieving and a distinctive set of *threats* to be avoided in the process.

These correspond loosely to the 'politics', 'economics' and 'social policy' underlying each type of welfare regime.

There are, of course, a great many different ways of categorizing welfare regimes. Not only does every commentator strive for some 'novel twist'; all of us are also inclined to make our own country's history a central axis in whatever typology we construct. It is in the nature of typologies, however, that they abstract from every particular country's history and therefore are not literally true to any of them. And most of the 'novel twists' seem almost to amount to changes of nomenclature alone, with most of the distinctions they mean to identify apparently collapsing into broadly the same basic dimensions.

The nomenclature we prefer, and which has become virtually standard across these discussions in recent years, distinguishes between 'liberal', 'social democratic' and 'corporatist' welfare regimes. We shall say more about the substantive implications of each of those categories shortly. First, however, we simply want to point out the parallels between this and other sorts of typology. What Esping-Anderson (1990) calls a 'liberal welfare regime' is essentially the same as, for example, Titmuss' (1974) 'residual welfare model of social policy' or Furniss and Tilton's (1977) 'positive state'; and Esping-Andersen's 'social democratic welfare regime' is essentially identical to Titmuss' 'institutional redistributive model' or Furniss and Tilton's 'social welfare state'. Esping-Andersen's 'corporatist welfare regime' is broadly the same, in its policy instruments if not necessarily its underlying logic, as Titmuss' 'industrial achievement-performance model' and Furniss and Tilton's' 'social security state'.

Those writing from a more continental European tradition tend to put corporatism nearer centre stage, distinguishing between 'Bismarck' and 'Beveridge' styles of welfare states (Liebfried 1993; Hills, Ditch and Glennerster 1994). 'Bismarck' clearly represents the corporatist pole. Beveridge, as a historical figure, actually occupies an ambiguous position in all these categorizations.[1] But in terms of the contrast that those employing this language mean to draw, 'Beveridge'-style welfare regimes – by virtue of their emphasis upon universal flat-rate entitlements – clearly represent the social-democratic pole.

Still others distinguish states and styles of social policy according to the role they assign to the state (active or passive) and according to the relative responsibilities they assign to the state versus the individual (Schmidtz and Goodin 1998). In this sort of typology, the 'liberal welfare regime' is one which assigns individuals primary responsibility for their own welfare and consigns the state to an essentially passive role. The 'corporatist welfare regime' envisages a more active state but still assigns primary responsibility for welfare to individuals – organized, it would emphasize, into various social units (families, guilds, corporations and so on). The 'social democratic welfare regime' assigns the state both a more active role and the preponderance of responsibility for promoting the welfare of its citizens.

What matter, of course, are the distinctions themselves rather than the terminology with which we choose to talk about them. As this brief discussion has shown, the basic distinctions are essentially the same in whatever language we choose to demarcate them. In what follows, there-fore, we shall revert to the 'liberal'/'social democratic'/'corporatist' which has by now become standard.

These three types of welfare regime are familiar, in both theory and practice. The classically *liberal welfare regime* is rooted in capitalist econ-omic premises and confines the state to a merely residual social welfare role. The classically *social democratic welfare regime* is rooted in socialist economic premises and assigns the welfare state a powerfully redistribu-tive role. The classically *corporatist welfare regime* is rooted in communitar-ian 'social market' economics and sees the welfare regime as primarily a facilitator of group-based mutual aid and risk pooling.[2]

The balance of this chapter is devoted to elaborating each of these theoretical models of welfare regime, in turn. The aim in this chapter is to

---

[1] William Beveridge himself was a member of the Liberal Party. His early work was on labour-market-oriented solutions to poverty, by promoting state-run employment ex-changes (Beveridge 1907): that looks like a social democratic concern. His famous 1942 report on *Social Insurance and Allied Services* provides essentially an insurance-based remedy for poverty, which therefore looks corporatist in its basic orientation. Of the other two reports Beveridge issued around the same time, which were to be taken together as his 'blueprint' for postwar Britain, one (the report promoting *Voluntary Action* (Beveridge 1948)) reinforces those corporatist emphases while another (the report on *Full Employ-ment in a Free Society* (Beveridge 1945)) reinforces his earlier social democratic concerns.

[2] We say 'classically' in each case, because there are of course many variants of each extant in the actual social politics of particular places.

lay out these theories as theories. The next chapter is devoted to showing how each of these first three theoretical constructs is given concrete form in one particular country's welfare arrangements. These are to be taken merely as examples. We hope that they are good examples, but obviously none are perfect examples of the theoretical constructs developed below; equally obviously, there are many other ways that each theoretical model might play itself out institutionally. In the end, it is only the practices of particular states that we can examine. But the interest in examining any particular country's performance lies not in praising or blaming particular places and practices, but rather in assessing the more abstract theoretical logic underlying each type of strategy for promoting social welfare.

3.1   The liberal welfare regime

The liberal welfare regime is characterized by (1) liberal politics, (2) capitalist economics and (3) residualist social policies. Historically, this model arose in the course of the 'great transformation' associated with the industrial revolution, and it found its fullest flowering in England with the New Poor Law of 1832 (Polanyi 1944; Blaug 1963). It remains a dominant model, particularly in the United States, the World Bank and those within their respective spheres of influence. We will discuss the particular form this model takes in the United States in the next chapter. Here, however, we concentrate on developing the underlying logic of the model in more abstract, stylized form.

The *fundamental value* underlying liberalism as an ideology has been variously characterized. The most favoured recent formulation is couched in terms of the state's being 'neutral' among all competing conceptions of the good life which citizens may harbour (Dworkin 1978; Waldron 1987). But that is only part of the larger liberal story. Certainly it is true to the tradition to say that the liberal state is, fundamentally, not a crusading state. Earlier liberals, however, provide a rather better account of why exactly a liberal state ought not to ram basic values down people's throats. Today's talk of 'epistemological abstinence' (Raz 1990) seems a thin reed upon which to found a political ideology. Far better to talk in more old-fashioned terms, like John Stuart Mill (1859), of freedom and autonomy. Etymology and argumentation converge on the obvious conclusion that liberty is what liberalism is centrally about.

Of course there are in turn many different ways of understanding 'liberty'. The notion clearly admits of a more activist, enabling interpretation, such as that given it by British 'New Liberals' and American progressives at the turn of the nineteenth century (Freeden 1978), and by egalitarians campaigning under the banner of 'liberalism' in the United

States today (Dworkin 1978).[3] Traditionally, however, liberals have understood 'liberty' in much more 'negative' terms, as freedom 'from' interference by other human agents in one's own pursuits (Berlin 1958). The fundamental liberal value of liberty, thus understood, gives rise to a characteristically liberal *economic theory*. Liberalism, as ordinarily understood, is committed to endorsing 'capitalist acts between consenting adults' (Nozick 1974, ch. 7). Valuing liberty as liberalism does, paradigmatically liberal economic relations must necessarily be relations of free exchange.

Precisely because no one can be forced into relations of free exchange, such exchanges must necessarily be mutually beneficial. Indeed, such arrangements are arguably maximally productive of 'social welfare', in the sense of getting everyone as far along towards their conception of the good life as we can without detracting from anyone else's.[4] Liberals value high disposable incomes and low tax rates, not as a matter of sheer acquisitiveness, but rather as a fundamental contribution to people's autonomy to make and spend their money as they please.[5]

Just as there are many different ways of fleshing out liberal notions of liberty, so too are there many different ways of fleshing out a liberal economy. Many commentators, while clinging firmly to core liberal values, nonetheless recommend strong state intervention to overcome the imperfections of free markets in one way or another. But recourse to the coercive apparatus of the state is, for liberals, at best an unfortunate necessity to remedy an imperfect situation. The liberal economic ideal would clearly be to leave as much as possible to the free play of market forces (which are themselves, ideally, just the products of free exchange). The corresponding liberal political ideal would be to relegate the state, insofar as possible, to a 'nightwatchman' role of simply safeguarding the conditions of free exchange and fair competition.[6]

A corollary to the liberal analysis of what promotes social welfare is its analysis of the reasons for some people *failing to benefit* from those

[3] 'Welfare rights' movements are a particularly interesting manifestation of this left-liberalism. See, e.g., Marshall (1949); Handler (1979).
[4] Arrow and Hahn (1971) provide the formal proof of the truth of Adam Smith's (1776) early insight. 'Arguably', because the proof of the proposition presupposes various conditions which almost never obtain in practice.
[5] Hence Nozick's (1974, p. 169) denigration of taxation as 'forced labor' and the emphasis by liberal regimes on low taxes and correspondingly low levels of public spending.
[6] Thus, instead of redistributing income and wealth, liberals would characteristically prefer to let the rich get richer and let their wealth 'trickle down' to the poorer members of the community. That strategy of 'supply-side economics' was self-consciously adopted by the Reagan Administration (Gilder 1981; Murray 1982; cf. Goodin 1988, ch. 9); but the notion of a 'chain connection' between the prosperity of the rich and the poor also figures in Rawls's (1971: 80–3) 'liberal theory of justice' (Barry 1973, pp. 110–12; Shue 1974).

processes. In an idealized model of free exchange, every productive resource (be it labour or capital) migrates to its most socially valued use; and, in that idealized world, every productive resource is rewarded according to what it deserves in terms of its marginal contribution to social welfare. If the market fails to reward certain people very much, then in this sort of world that can mean only one thing: those people do not make very much of a contribution that other people value very much. They do not have anything that very many other people want very badly.

Of course, the world that this idealized economic model describes is not necessarily our own. The idealizations required to make the liberal's economic model mathematically tractable – the idealizations which are required to make the proofs go through – abstract away from the real world in many important respects. That fact provides liberal economic theory with a second sort of analysis of why some people may fail to benefit from processes of free exchange. They may have things that others want, and indeed they may be making contributions that others genuinely value, but because of market imperfections these resources fail to find their most productive employment or to realize their full reward.

Those two very different analyses of why some people fail to benefit from the ordinary operation of free markets lead liberals to two different sorts of *policy response*. In so far as certain people are poor because of market imperfections, liberals are inclined to attack that problem at its root, correcting the market failures themselves. The liberal has no hesitation in recommending an energetic state response to problems such as these. Those, after all, are precisely what the liberal's nightwatchman state is supposed to be watching out for – barriers and blockages to free exchange. The precise policy response will depend upon the particulars of the market imperfections in view. But, broadly speaking, we are here in the realm of regulatory policy and macro-economic management.

There will inevitably remain some people who fail to benefit from the operations of free markets because of ineradicable imperfections in those markets, try as we might through regulatory policy and macro-economic management to eradicate them. But assuming our efforts in those realms meet with broad and substantial success, most of those remaining poor are poor because they have no real social contribution that they are willing or able to make.

The first task of liberal social welfare policy, as such, is to separate out those who are genuinely *unable* to make any productive contribution from those who are merely *unwilling* to do so. Liberals respect people's free choices. If people genuinely had the option of entering into market exchanges that would have improved their material standard of living, but opted not to do so, then liberals infer from that fact that they think themselves better off as they are – poor, but happy, living in the crumbling mansion or surfing the day away. Liberals have no grounds for denigrating those people's choices. But they do have good grounds, in terms of respecting people's choices, for not meddling with the consequences of those choices.

Those who are genuinely unable to make any productive contribution represent a different case altogether. They genuinely constitute the social residual – those left out of and left behind through the operations of free markets. Liberalism as such has little to say about the proper treatment of such social unfortunates. But as a matter of sheer humanity, if not of liberal socio-economic theory, we might say that people who are in distress through no fault of their own are in some larger sense 'deserving of our sympathy'. As a matter of social charity – as a largesse, rather than an entitlement in any sense – a liberal state ordinarily organizes a social welfare policy to relieve the worst of the distress of those who are genuinely unable to benefit from the ordinary operations of the market economy (Waldron 1986).

In a liberal welfare regime, these benefits will typically be tightly targeted in several respects.[7] First, they will be targeted on those genuinely in need of them. Income support and social services will be given only to those in demonstrable need of the service (medical care only to the sick, public housing only to those inadequately housed, and so on). Second, benefits will be targeted on those who cannot meet those needs through ordinary free exchange. Assistance will be given only to those with insufficient resources (taking account of their income and assets, and in some cases those of family and friends) to meet those needs themselves.[8] Third, benefits will be targeted on those lacking resources for legitimate reasons. Toward that end, liberals have sometimes imposed a 'character test' directly, as when Guardians charged with administering the Poor Law were enjoined to assess the deservingness of claimants. The

[7] On the practice and problems of targeting more generally, see Townsend (1975, esp. chs. 7, 9); Goodin (1985); Atkinson (1995a, ch. 12). There is, we should say, a deviant liberal position here. As becomes clear in their confrontations with communitarians or nationalists, liberals are fundamentally universalists (Sandel 1984; Tamir 1993). Left-liberals of the sort who favour a more positive conception of freedom and a more interventionist state (in the welfare sector and various others) in general tend to appeal to such notions of liberal universality to argue for universal rather than selective welfare-state benefits (Titmuss 1967). Paradigmatic here is Beveridge's (1942) original plan for a low but universal flat-rate old age pension for Britain.

[8] A tax claw-back – paying the same benefit to everyone, but then including that benefit in taxable income – constitutes in its own way a form of income-testing of the benefit (US DHEW 1969, pp. 53–4; Saunders 1991). The difference, of course, is that well-off people would receive none of an income-tested benefit whereas they would be allowed to keep whatever portion of the universal benefit that is not clawed back by the highest marginal rate of taxation.

'available for work' test imposed on unemployment benefits is the principal residue of that practice today (King 1995). Rather than imposing any direct character tests, today we more often allocate benefits through 'categorical' programmes whose categorical qualifications are designed to pick out certain classes of people (the very old, the very young, the sick and disabled) who are deemed to be legitimately exempt from participation in ordinary labour markets (Titmuss 1958; Gal 1997).[9]

The primary policy task in liberal welfare policy lies in separating out those unwilling to work from those genuinely unable to do so. One strategy – favoured in the 1832 revisions in the English Poor Law (Blaug 1963), and arguably still practised in many places today – is to make the condition of welfare beneficiaries so wretched that only those genuinely in need of them would be remotely tempted to apply for such benefits. But that assumes of course that the able-bodied poor can always find work if they want it, which may not of course be true. So liberal welfare regimes have from the turn of the twentieth century onwards operated schemes of 'labour exchanges' to facilitate matching up workers and jobs, and they have made payment of any state unemployment benefits conditional upon proof on the part of the poor that they have been 'actively seeking work' (Beveridge 1907; King 1995). The current preoccupations of those advocating a 'punitive welfare state', offering 'workfare' as a solution to problems of 'welfare dependency' (Murray 1984; Mead 1986; 1992), should be seen as only the latest in a long line of liberal policies. There is a long-standing concern among liberals with problems of separating out the 'able-bodied poor' who are merely unwilling to work from those who are genuinely unable to work and therefore deserving of public sympathy and support.

(There is, of course, an important deviant strand of that liberal tradition, which, as we have said, culminates in just the opposite analysis of people's plight and leads to just the opposite policy prescriptions. Those liberals who see freedom in essentially positive terms and poverty as the product of deep flaws in the market economy recommend an activist state, energetically intervening in the economy and positively promoting people's freedom. Thus, things like the 'welfare rights' movement clearly grew out of recognizably liberal stock. Undeniably important though it is to acknowledge the diversity within each of these traditions, none more so than liberalism, it is also important to recognize clearly where the main

[9] Targeting on categorical groups can be a good surrogate for targeting on low income, so long as low household equivalent income is tightly correlated with the category in question. Thus, for example, South Africa's policy of making large cash transfers to the elderly seems an effective anti-poverty strategy, in part because the elderly themselves would otherwise be poor, and in part because they tend to live in households composed of extended families with many children who would otherwise be poor (Case and Deaton 1998).

line of that tradition's analysis lies. In the context of liberalism, it is clearly left-liberalism that is the off-shoot and what we have been calling 'classic liberalism' that constitutes the main strand.)

The classic *goal* of liberal social welfare policy follows straightforwardly from that characterization of its essential components. Being essentially a charitable response to human distress, liberal social welfare policy aims merely to alleviate undeserved distress. The liberal call is merely upon ordinary human sympathy. Sympathy does not require us to make people positively happy; it merely requires us to help people cease being miserable.

The way that goal is operationalized in liberal welfare regimes is as the 'alleviation of poverty', at least for the 'deserving poor'. We set a certain level, below which we think that no one in our society should have to live. Inevitably somewhat arbitrary, this 'poverty line' varies over time and across cultures, with different things being considered socially demeaning at different times and places (Townsend 1979). Wherever we draw the line, however, the point of the line is to serve as a social minimum. The policy tied to the operation of such a line is, accordingly, a minimalist one. The liberal welfare policy's goal is not to make anyone particularly well off. It is merely to get everyone over the line.

The primary *threat* which liberal policies for alleviating poverty are designed to protect against is the threat of 'dependency'. The fear is that people will see public assistance as a first rather than last recourse, that they will come to depend upon public hand-outs rather than their own efforts for securing a living. This is the threat against which the 1832 revisions in the English Poor Law were aimed (Polanyi 1944; Blaug 1963), and it is the threat which still looms largest among contemporary critics of social welfare arrangements (Murray 1984; Mead 1986; 1992). The New Poor Law protected against that threat through a principle of 'lesser eligibility' – making poor relief so undesirable (so 'less eligible') an option that only those who had no other recourse would come to rely on it. Contemporary critics supplement that strategy with administrative arrangements of various sorts, screening applicants and forcing recipients into the workforce. But in one form or another these same preoccupations have persisted among liberal theorists of welfare across the centuries.

3.2   The social democratic welfare regime

The social democratic welfare regime is characterized by (1) class politics, (2) socialist economics and (3) redistributive social policies. Historically, this model arose in direct reaction to the social consequences of free market economics and liberal politics. To this day, it remains a dominant model in Scandinavia and elsewhere (Castles 1978; Rothstein 1996). We discuss in the next chapter the particular form that certain key elements of this model take in the Netherlands. Here, however, we concentrate on developing the underlying logic of the model in a more abstract, stylized form.

The *fundamental value* underlying the social democratic welfare regime is social equality. Again, equality assumes various forms (Rae 1981), with seemingly endless disputes among philosophers as to which matters most (Sen 1980). Classic social democrats themselves, however, are relatively clear on what is fundamentally of value and how they propose to achieve it. Their aim is to transform political equality, via the 'democratic class struggle', into economic and thence social equality (Korpi 1983; 1989; Esping-Andersen 1985a, b; 1987a; 1990, ch. 5; Esping-Andersen and van Kersbergen 1992; cf. Baldwin 1990). But both political and even economic equality, important though they may be, are important to social democrats principally as the means to the further end of a society without class or caste distinctions. And a minimal precondition of that is, of course, the elimination of poverty.

As with liberalism, so too with social democracy: that classical version has subsequently spun off several variants, many substantially softer than the original. Many self-styled social democrats would now soft-pedal the 'labour-versus-capital' class struggle emphasis in that formulation (and in the ones that follow). 'Soft social democrats', like deviant 'left-liberals' discussed in section 3.1, are left emphasizing 'social equality' as an end, while embracing little of this larger apparatus of more classical social democratic analysis to sustain that claim. Furthermore, like left-liberals, soft social democrats are accordingly particularly at pains to pare down the scope of their egalitarian claims (often to little more than 'equality of opportunity').[10]

In these discussions, the social democratic ideal is often expressed in terms of 'social citizenship' (Marshall 1949) – of everyone's having the wherewithal to 'participate fully' in the life of the community (Townsend 1979). That does not necessarily entail a strict equality of income or wealth; it involves something much more like 'equal concern and respect' (Dworkin 1978), or the 'equal worth' of all citizens (Commission on Social Justice 1993, pp. 7–8, 17–91; 1994, p. 18). 'Equal opportunities' may be a token of that; and 'equal access to opportunities' or 'equal resources' may in turn be a means of achieving that (Dworkin 1981). So too might neutralizing the power of private capital and equalizing power

---

[10] See, for example, the UK Labour Party's Commission on Social Justice (1993, p. iii): 'We do not claim that all inequalities are unjust. In fact, few people believe that arithmetic equality is either feasible or desirable. But structural inequalities of power and position such as discrimination or abuse of power in the labour market are unjust.'

in wage bargaining, to take another more classic social democratic preoccupation. But all those are merely means. The end in view is this fundamental social equality of a more abstract sort.

Allied with this social vision is a characteristically socialist *economic theory*, explaining why that ideal is not and cannot be achieved under conditions of unfettered capitalist competition and what economic reforms must be instituted if that ideal is to be attained. Unfettered capitalism, this theory says, systematically exploits labour. It allows owners to take systematic advantage of rules of property and the structure of competition to pay workers less than they should (and, under alternative property rules and competitive regimes, would) receive.[11] A few gain from productive relations so organized, but many lose.

This social democratic analysis of the dynamics of the capitalist economy leads, straightforwardly, to a social democratic analysis of why some people *fail to benefit* from productive relations, so organized. They are disadvantaged, at root, by the 'relations of production'. They are at a competitive disadvantage in market relations either (or both) because of certain features of the allocation of power over productive assets or/and because of certain features of the structure of competition.

The *policy response* that follows from this analysis spreads across several dimensions. One set of responses has to do with weakening the power of private capital, ranging from regulations restricting what can be done with it to programmes of nationalization taking private capital into social ownership. Another set of responses has to do with strengthening the power of labour to organize, strike and bargain collectively, most dramatically through systems of compulsory arbitration and consolidated nationwide wage-bargaining.[12] Full employment policies, obviously, could be seen as part and parcel of that: eliminating the 'reserve army of the unemployed' and its drag on labour's bargaining power. Yet another set of responses focuses on protecting individual workers: legislatively regulating working hours, conditions and wages; providing education, training and labour exchanges to assist those not in work; and public employment for those for whom no work is to be found in the private sector. All of those 'active labour market' policy responses fall essentially within the realm of economic policy.[13]

---

[11] To older work along these lines by economic theorists (Sraffa 1926; Robinson 1933) have recently been added works drawing on economics (Roemer 1982; Bowles and Gintis 1990), philosophy (Cohen 1983) and political science (Elster 1978).

[12] As, at one point anyway, was seen in Sweden (Olson 1982) and Australia (Hancock 1979; Castles 1985). For a more formal account of the underlying logic, see Moene and Wallerstein (1995).

[13] For summaries of social democratic thought on those issues, see: Rothstein (1996, ch. 6); Esping-Andersen (1990, ch. 7); and Moene and Wallerstein (1993; 1995). On the liberal corporatist logic of such policies, see King (1995) and Janoski (1994). For an evaluation of those policies see Calmfors and Skedinger (1995).

It should also be emphasized that social democrats are, first and fore-most, democrats.[14] As such, they would be unwilling to implement those reforms, or any others, without the full support of a democratic majority. Many such fundamental reforms to the structure of the capitalist economic system fail to command the support of democratic majorities, for perfectly understandable reasons to do with the structure of democratic competition.[15]

Thus, many of the broader economic aspects of the social democrats' preferred welfare regime prove politically infeasible. Classic social democrats then find themselves left relying largely upon what are, from their own perspective, very much second-best ameliorist responses, trying to use the shallow instruments of social policy to fix deep problems in the fundamental structure of capitalist economies. The basic aim of these narrowly welfare-state interventions may, for classic social democrats, remain the same as for those other broader interventions they would have wished to be able to make in labour or capital markets – to strengthen the social claims of labour. But even classic social democrats committed to the class struggle see these narrower welfare-state interventions as the best means practically available for achieving that end.

Those whom we have called 'soft social democrats' – committed more to social equality than the class struggle – would probably have preferred the latter sort of emphasis all along. What the hard-nosed 'classic social democrats' see as second-best fall-backs they would regard as first-best. The two groups might largely converge on the same policy proposals, since the hard-nosed economic reforms that 'classic social democrats' would prefer are politically impossible in most places and at most times. But the differences between the two do lead to a moderately sharp bifurcation between two styles of social democratic social welfare policy, one (associated with 'classic social democrats') emphasizing labour market interventions and the other (associated with 'soft social democrats') emphasizing transfer payments and the welfare sector.[16]

[14] That, after all, is what makes them social 'democrats' and what distinguishes them from other brands of less (or differently) democratic state socialists, whose fundamental economic theories they broadly share.

[15] The key to the Przeworski and Sprague (1986) argument is that the working class has never had an electoral majority in its own right, and the need to construct cross-class coalitions has necessarily compromised the capacity of 'working-class parties' to implement a full socialist agenda. In the economic realm, similar cross-pressures – there, of capital accumulation to satisfy the needs of producers and of public spending to satisfy the needs of consumers of state services – are similarly said to lead to a 'fiscal crisis' of the welfare state (O'Connor 1973; Gough 1979; Offe 1984; cf. Klein 1993).

[16] In the cases standardly discussed, Sweden typifies the former, the Netherlands the latter (Therborn 1989). Australia historically enjoyed a high degree of income equality through full employment policies and the efforts of an Arbitration Commission committed to policing a flat wage structure; because it also paid only very low social welfare benefits,

The best way social democrats have devised for pursuing their redistributive goal through the welfare state, as such, is by means of 'decommodification' (Esping-Anderson 1987a; 1990, ch. 2). That ominously technical term has a clear and precise meaning, and a political logic to go with it. The social democratic approach to the welfare state is to concede the world of commodities – that which is bought and sold – to the realm of capitalist economic relations. What social democratic welfare states do is simply to try to take certain goods and services out of that realm. Health care, education, housing and income security – formerly all things purchased as commodities in exchange for cash in the market economy – are, in social democratic welfare states, allocated instead as state benefits and services. No longer bought and sold, their distribution is no longer dictated by the underlying distribution of income and wealth within the community. That opens the way, in turn, for those things to be distributed more equally across the community than is income or wealth itself.

Ideally, both the allocation of goods and services and the way of paying for them would be more egalitarian than they would have been in a market economy. Social democrats would also favour a regime of progressive taxation. Of course notionally progressive taxes are rarely very progressive, if progressive at all, in their actual implementation. But if they were, progressive taxation would redouble the redistributive effect of welfare-state programmes by causing people in higher income brackets to pay a larger proportion of their income in tax, with those taxes being used to finance benefits and services used disproportionately by people in lower income brackets.

Redistributing resources in these ways will, social democrats hope, have the further effect of strengthening the hand – both economically and politically – of the characteristically poorer working classes. By increasing their resources, a redistributive welfare state shifts the terms of trade – both economically and politically – more to their advantage. In this way, social democrats hope, their social welfare policies might create the conditions for their own further success (Korpi 1983; 1989; Esping-Anderson 1985a, b; 1990).

That grander strategic aim is not to be discounted, nor can we ignore the larger intellectual structure underlying the classic social democratic case for the welfare state. There is much more to that labourist way of looking at the world than finds any expression in the social democratic analysis of the purposes and prospects of a welfare state, as such. Still, that narrower focus is the one we must fix upon for the purposes of the

Castles and Mitchell (1990) dub it a 'fourth world of welfare capitalism', but really it just represents a limiting case of the labour-market-oriented version of the social democratic form.

present book. Recognizing it is a partial perspective on classic social democrats' wider social teachings, we can nonetheless isolate one characteristic goal which social democrats (hard as well as soft) ascribe to the welfare state as they conceive it.

That goal is one of redistribution. For social democrats, the point and purpose of the welfare state, narrowly conceived, is to transfer resources – goods and services, and income and wealth more generally – from the richer to the poorer members of society. That constitutes a relatively direct contribution to the social democrats' fundamental goal of deeper social equality, in so far as the particular goods and services in question are particularly crucial for creating a sense of 'equal worth' and for contributing to full participation in the life of the community. Sometimes they seem to be: overcoming homelessness and destitution, while hardly a sufficient condition for full participation, is certainly a necessary one (Waldron 1991; Jencks 1994). And so too is overcoming poverty, in general. At other times, the contribution seems to be of a more indirect sort, with redistributive policies enhancing economic equality and personal autonomy, which hopefully in turn will eventually lead to greater social equality.

At yet other times, state benefits themselves seem to be literally constitutive of the deeper social equality that social democrats seek. That is particularly the case with what might be seen as the 'rights of citizenship'. Just as citizenship in the political sense is literally constituted by being eligible to vote in elections in the polity, so too is citizenship in the social sense sometimes seen to be literally constituted by being in receipt of certain state benefits (Marshall 1949; King and Waldron 1988). Old age pensions, child benefits and family allowances have all been made universal entitlements, paid irrespective of means-testing, in a range of welfare states for just those reasons (Beveridge 1942; Titmuss 1967).

Universal flat-rate benefits may not look very redistributive (Baldwin 1988). Certainly they are less redistributive than would have been the same amount of money spent through a system of benefits targeted more tightly on the poor. But increasing the number of people who benefit from public programmes increases their political constituency and hence the budget available for distribution (Korpi and Palme 1998). In any case, universal flat-rate benefits may be redistributive after a fashion (Tawney 1931; cf. Le Grand 1982). First of all, it is a mathematical truism that adding the same absolute sum to everyone's income will necessarily reduce the proportional differences between their incomes; and this mathematical truism might have real social significance, particularly if the sums involved are relatively large. Furthermore, in so far as the taxes used to finance the benefits are even weakly progressive, universal benefits will involve taking disproportionately from the rich and giving equally to rich and poor alike. Here again, it is a mathematical truism that such a scheme simply must be redistributive; and that truism may take on real social significance, once again, depending on the size of the sums involved and the progressivity of the tax structure.

Of course, both those mathematical truisms remain true only so long as universal benefits really do go to everyone universally. Empirical evidence suggests that often they do not, and that there is differential take-up not only of state-provided services but also of state income support (Le Grand 1982; Goodin, Le Grand *et al.* 1987). In so far as those higher up the income distribution take up these state subsidies more frequently than those lower down the income distribution, their redistributive effects are compromised. Then it is simply an open empirical question just how redistributive, if at all, universal flat-rate benefits might be. Those empirical questions are best left for later chapters.

The *threat* to social democratic welfare policies is, quite simply, one of greed. Just as early socialists such as Tawney (1921) railed against the 'acquisitive society', so too are generous social democratic welfare regimes at risk of being undermined by greedy individuals 'playing the system', pretending to be in need or unable to work when actually they are not (Goodin, Le Grand *et al.* 1987). Whereas liberal welfare regimes establish elaborate mechanisms to protect against those risks, social democratic welfare regimes rather trust to the character of their people not to do so; and there is good reason to suppose that trusting to people's better motives in turn actually helps to reinforce and evoke those better sides of people's characters (Goodin 1982, ch. 5).

3.3   The corporatist welfare regime

The corporatist welfare regime is characterized by (1) group politics, (2) communitarian economics and (3) mutualist social policies. This model is essentially a residue of pre-industrial feudal forms, particularly as they have been codified in the social teachings of the Roman Catholic church.[17] It remains a dominant model particularly in Germany and Austria and across the Catholic world. We will discuss the particular form this model takes in Germany in the next chapter. Here, once again, it is merely our task to set out the underlying logic of the model in a more abstract, stylized form.

The *fundamental value* underlying corporatism is 'social cohesion'.

---

[17] For surveys, see McQustra (1990) and Dierickx (1994). These and analogous Protestant doctrines are applied to the welfare state in particular by van Kersbergen (1995, chs. 8–10).

However, this value is to be understood as social integration of the very special sort best captured in notions of 'my station and its duties' (Bradley 1876), rather than of any of the more diffuse sorts of social cohesion that might be characterized variously as 'fraternity' or 'brotherhood' or even 'solidarity' (Hobsbawm 1975). The value in view is not simply 'belonging', not simply attachment to some group or another. Solidarity might be with some class, caste or ethnic group, and it alone; fraternity might imply universal brotherhood – solidarity with all humanity. Corporatists would eschew both of those visions.

Corporatists cherish, above all else, attachment to one's community. But theirs is a very specific idea about how communities themselves are constituted. Communities, in the corporatist vision, are composed of groups nested within groups – each of which, under the principle of 'subsidiarity', is 'sovereign in its own realm'.[18] The fundamental value for the corporatist is for an individual to be integrated into a group, which alongside other groups is integrated in turn into a larger community. Cohesion with other members of one's group, and of one's group with other groups in the society, is the corporatist's fundamental value.[19]

The primary social group, for corporatists as well as many others, is of course the family. The corporatist vision is, traditionally, one of a highly patriarchal family, with the male head of household as the breadwinner connecting the household to the wider society through his labour force attachments, and the female homemaker being connected to that wider society primarily through the her husband's work (Pateman 1988a; Davidoff 1995; Sainsbury 1996; Esping-Andersen 1996c).

Here, as before, there are many who share this ideology in diluted form. There is, for example, a quasi-corporatist fixation on 'family policy' across most developed countries; and a 'family allowance' or 'child benefit' is typically one of the earliest and is by now one of the most common forms of universal social entitlements across all countries.[20] And much in 'new communitarianism', as a political movement, seems to amount to a 'soft corporatism' embracing the social policy if not necessarily all the Catholic social teachings underlying it (Etzioni 1993; Etzioni et al. 1991/ 2). Interesting though this 'soft corporatism' may be where it is found, it is the classic, undiluted form which constitutes the clearest version of the model. It is that upon which we will be focusing here.

As regards its underlying *economic theory*, corporatism operates on

---

[18] Therborn (1989); McQustra (1990); van Kersbergen (1994, chs. 8–10).
[19] For a particularly rich, desecularized statement of this model, as applied to the welfare state, see Unger (1975, pp. 174–90).
[20] See, e.g., Land (1975) on the British case.

socialist-cum-communitarian premises. Much is made in papal encyclicals of the 'dignity' of labour as deserving of respect – and, these teachings go on to emphasize, 'mutual recognition'. What produces wealth, according to this philosophy, is social cooperation and collaboration. In the classically corporatist account, capitalist economics are right to emphasize the economic advantages of a 'division of labour' and of specialization within spheres; but they are wrong to suppose that competition is the best way to evoke the gains that can be realized through such specialization. Instead, the corporatist recommends cooperation between all the main groups within society – capital and labour, and all others besides – for the greater good. That is the force of the term 'social' in the standard description of corporatist economy as a 'social market economy'.[21]

The practical implementation of this theory will no doubt involve a fair bit of horse-trading and interplay of sectional interests, as the leaders of the 'peak associations' representing all these groups get together to haggle over details of proposed solutions to various social and economic problems. But in practice just as in theory, the solution which these negotiators will be seeking is one which is mutually agreed. In corporatist-style interest group intermediation, negotiations are conducted under a decision rule of (rough) unanimity rather than of merely majority rule. No one (or virtually no one) will be left out; broadly speaking, all major groups in society have to agree (Schmitter and Lehmbruch 1975; Lehmbruch 1984). Wage bargaining, most conspicuously, is done this way in a corporatist community.[22] But all other major decisions – economic and otherwise – are ideally supposed to be handled the same way.

This corporatist analysis of the sources of economic productivity leads, in turn, to a distinctively corporatist account of why certain people *fail to benefit*. Basically, no whole sector of society will be left behind in the process of corporatist economic growth, because every group with distinctive interests in society has a veto at the bargaining table.[23] It is

---

[21] Daly and Cobb (1989) provide a strong contemporary statement of this general theory, with a particular green tinge.

[22] In this sense, Sweden is nearer the corporatist than the social democratic pole (Olson 1982; Lehmburch 1984, p. 66), and there is much in the early history of the Swedish welfare state to confirm that general suspicion (Therborn 1989; Tilton 1990). Ironically, this is minimally true of industrial relations in Germany – our archetypical corporatist state for the purposes of analysing welfare regimes – although even there echoes of it are found in the sort of 'co-determination' practised at the level of firms.

[23] Insofar as some sectors (e.g., agriculture) have to shrink for others to grow, that sector will demand – and since it has a veto over the overall policy, will be granted – a subsidy as compensation for those losses. Occasionally this might show up in social welfare policy, but more often such subsidies will come through industrial or regional policies of one sort or another.

individuals, much more often than groups, who corporatists imagine will most often be left behind.

They will be left behind for one of two reasons. Either they are particularly unlucky members of some group or another; and while the group as a whole is prospering, they individually are suffering. Alternatively, people might be left out of the benefits of corporatist economic growth because they are not properly integrated into any of the central groups of the society at all. Those are 'the excluded' – people who have yet to be properly 'inserted' into the natural economic life of the community (Evans *et al.* 1995; Silver 1994; 1995; Atkinson 1998c).

From that diagnosis follows the characteristically corporatist *policy response*, which is simply to try to ensure (1) that people are properly integrated into groups and (2) that groups in turn take care of their own. This might be dubbed a 'mutualist' approach to the welfare regime. Just as corporatists rely on mutual aid across groups to promote growth in the larger economy, so too do they rely on 'mutual aid' within groups to take care of those who fall upon hard times.

This amounts, in the first instance, to a particular way of assigning responsibility for aiding those in need. Under the corporatist principle of 'subsidiarity' (Føllesdal 1998), that responsibility falls first to those nearest to the individual in need: the person's immediate (then extended) family. Failing that, responsibility has historically fallen to the local church parish or voluntary associations, then to professional or occupational associations, and only then to the municipality (or, later, the state) as such.

While this seems primarily a matter of assigning charitable duties, those duties are themselves assigned to corporate entities, from the family up. In that sense, corporatism is a theory about how on-going groups of people take care of one another. As such, it naturally involves a notion of 'mutual aid' more akin to mutual insurance than reciprocal charity.

That is to say, corporatist-style mutual aid is first and foremost a matter of 'risk pooling' – of people within some well-defined group providing one another with insurance and assurance against untoward eventualities that might befall any of them. The primary role of the state, in this connection, would simply be to underwrite and facilitate essentially private and self-governing group-based schemes of insurance and assurance.

Even in corporatist societies, however, there will be some individuals who for one reason or another fall outside any group's purview. In addition, there may be whole groups of people whose risks prove unbearable, even when pooled. So, secondarily, the corporatist state must also arrange residual risk pools for those who are (or are in effect) attached to no other. And it must arrange to reinsure and underwrite risks of whole social groups that find themselves collectively at risk.[24]

The basic *goal* of corporatist welfare policy is security and stability. The fundamental objective is 'no nasty surprises'. On the one hand, that seems generous: everyone will be taken care of, everything will go on just as before. On the other hand, however, that seems mean and miserly: no whole social group will ever be any better off, relative to any other whole social group, than before.[25] It is for this reason that the corporatist welfare regime is generally characterized as 'conservative'. Its basic goal is to preserve the existing social order, and the existing pattern of distributions within it – in stark contrast to the social democratic welfare state's frank intention to alter that existing pattern through redistribution.

The fundamental *threat* to corporatist systems of welfare provision is simply 'individualism'. Corporatist arrangements are predicated upon the assumption that people are embedded in social groups of one sort or another. They would be undermined by free-floating individuals 'shopping around' among the various groups with which they might choose to affiliate, looking for the best deal they can get. Since under corporatism insurance is organized on the basis of such groups, such 'shopping around' poses a threat akin to 'adverse selection', familiar from other insurance contexts. Those who are 'better risks' would opt out of risk pools in which the average risks are worse (and hence rates are higher and/or benefits are lower) and into pools in which the average risks are better (and hence rates are lower and/or benefits higher) (Barr 1987; 1989). Such behaviour would not only undermine corporatist ideology, based as it is on the fiction that there is some natural and immutable association between each individual and the group to which s/he belongs, it would also undermine the very financial viability of mutual insurance arrangements within the worst risk pools.

[24] By virtue of its emphasis upon 'National Insurance', Beveridge's (1942) blueprint for the postwar British welfare state thus looks much more corporatist than social democratic, for example.

[25] At least not by the state's hand: economic growth can of course advantage groups differentially, and in ways that cannot be anticipated ahead of time.

4 National embodiments

In what follows, we will exemplify each model of welfare regime by reference to the institutions of one particular country. The United States will be taken to represent the liberal welfare regime, Germany the corporatist and the Netherlands the social democratic.

We will say more to justify each of those ascriptions in the course of this chapter. While the first two will generally be seen as utterly unproblematic, the third might initially seem more problematic. As already explained in chapter 1, the choice of the Netherlands to represent the social democratic welfare regime has been forced upon us by the available data. But that said, we nonetheless think it is not a bad example of the general class, for reasons also given there. Indeed, as argued in section 1.5, these three might be the 'best cases' of each regime.

4.1   Ideal types and actual countries

Naturally, no particular example can ever embody any particular ideal type perfectly. Each country has its own unique historical experience, its own distinctive economic setting, its own peculiar social dynamics. All of that inevitably overlays, and to some extent confounds, the workings of any theoretical 'internal logic' underlying each sort of welfare regime. However, examples are needed, and these are the best that can be found certainly within the limits of the panel data presently available.

Country specialists are inevitably sceptical of all these sorts of classifications. They are accustomed to fixating, quite rightly given their interests, on the singularity of their chosen country's specific historical experiences and institutional arrangements. They are naturally suspicious of generalizations and scornful of 'models' and 'typologies', the whole point of which is to abstract away from the particularities and peculiarities that they as country specialists make their own stock in trade.

Such micro-analytic work has much to teach us. Social scientists in search of sweeping generalizations have recently been reminded of the many ways in which social institutions, shaped by particular events at particular points in time, exert continuing influence across time (Steinmo, Thelen and Longstreth 1992). They have come to appreciate how those institutions embody not just historical accretions but complex intentions.[1] Over time, too many people have helped shape them, to too many different ends, for us sensibly to ascribe any single intent or simple logic to anything so complicated as a nation's welfare regime as a whole.[2]

Our plan is to pay homage, in some small way, to some of these real-world complications in this chapter, in order that we may in subsequent chapters largely ignore them. The aim of this book is not to tell the full story about any particular country's welfare regime, exactly what it is like or how exactly it came to be that way. Its aim is instead to build on, but transcend, the experiences of these particular countries in the hope of telling a more general story.[3] We want to ask what basic options there are for promoting social welfare, and how well each of them matches up to the sorts of moral goals we set for such regimes.

Any given country, in trying to implement any given option, will naturally do so in its own very special way. But such a multiplicity of surface variations does not change the scarcity of basic structural options. Of course we can only empirically examine those basic options in their embodied forms, and of course we must respect the peculiarities of those particular embodiments. In doing so, however, we must not lose sight of our deeper interest in exploring their underlying functional forms.

4.2 The United States

4.2.1 Policy history: a thumbnail sketch[4]

The rich history of US social policy can, for our purposes, be boiled down to the very few highly salient propositions that follow.

Historically, central government was heavily involved in the nation-building project from independence forwards. That importantly impinged on social affairs, albeit most often incidentally and almost

---

[1] Jurists despair of finding the 'legislative intent' underlying any particular piece of legislation: there were just too many people involved, doing what they did for too many different reasons, to ascribe any single coherent 'intention' to the legislature as a whole (MacCallum 1966). The same is all the more true for social institutions more generally.

[2] The postwar British welfare state was an amalgam of William Beveridge's flat-rate national insurance, Nye Bevan's National Health Service and Rab Butler's Education Act. The first was a Liberal, the second a socialist, the third a Tory.

[3] Esping-Andersen (1987b, pp. 6–7; 1990, pp. 28–9) discusses the tensions between ideal types and particular cases in similar terms.

[4] This section is based largely on: Rimlinger (1971, ch. 6); Orloff and Skocpol (1984); Skocpol and Orloff (1986); Orloff (1988); Quandango (1988a, b); Skocpol (1992; 1995); Williamson and Pampel (1993, ch. 5). For further details see Abbot (1940); for a good short overview, see Heidenheimer, Heclo and Adams (1990, ch. 7).

unintentionally. When laying out the framework for national territorial expansion in the Northwest Ordinance of 1787, for example, one section of each township was set aside to house and fund free public education. In providing a national infrastructure of canals, the National Road and the intercontinental railway, the federal government initiated large-scale public works projects. In the backwash of the civil war, the first war of mass mobilization, the federal government found itself paying war pensions to a substantial portion of the northern population (Skocpol 1992).

Activist though the American state was on those fronts, and important though the incidental social policy by-products of that activism may have been, the basic ethos of US social policy has long been dominated by rugged *laissez-faire* individualism and liberal notions of self-help. The old poor laws, combined with private charity, provided the dominant mode of relief for the old and destitute (including widows and orphans) throughout the first third of the twentieth century, fully two or three generations after most other industrialized countries had enacted public old age pensions.[5]

The Social Security Act of 1935 was indeed a watershed in policy terms.[6] It provided Old Age, Survivor's and Disability Insurance to a substantial number of citizens, thereby doing much to ease the problems of poverty in old age. Nonetheless, that enactment was initially, and long remained, drastically limited in the proportion of the population it covered.[7] The levels of benefits were also quite low.[8] The combination of

---

[5] Katz (1986). Poor laws themselves were a standard feature of developed societies across Europe for centuries. Charlemagne signed one in 779, Holy Roman Emperor Charles V in 1543, and so on (Netherlands Ministry 1990, p. 2). The American colonies, later states, borrowed their own statutes from the Elizabethan Poor Law of 1601 (14 Elizabeth I, c.5); for details see Abbot (1940). Even one of the key precursors of the modern US welfare state – 'mother aid' (Skocpol 1992, ch. 8) – retained the same means-tested and indeed character-tested, stigmatizing form as the poor laws.

[6] A description conceded even by scholars who have made much of its precursors: see most especially Skocpol (1995, p. 152) and Orloff (1988, p. 76).

[7] The original enactment excluded not only farm workers, casual workers, domestic workers and the self-employed but even the contributor's own immediate dependants (spouses, parents and under-aged children). All those exclusions were soon remedied, albeit not necessarily for the noblest of motives (Williamson and Pampel 1993, p. 98; Quandango 1988a, b). Other exclusions remained, however. The upshot was that in 1983 only 56 per cent of American employees were covered by public or private occupational retirement arrangements (OECD 1988b, p. 136), fully 20 per cent below the OECD average (Palme 1990b, p. 45).

[8] As late as 1949, the average claimant of means-tested Old Age Assistance received almost twice that paid to the average claimant of the insurance-based old age Social Security pension (Williamson and Pampel 1993, p. 96). Of course, old age social insurance programmes had historically started with similarly low rates elsewhere (they have been calculated at two-thirds the prevailing rate of public assistance in Munich in 1905, and at half subsistence needs in Britain in 1919: Myles 1988, pp. 266–7). The only surprise is that this remained true in the US as late as 1949, rather than the US, as a latecomer to public old age pensions, leapfrogging this stage and moving straight to a conceptualization of old age pensions as a 'retirement wage'.

low coverage rates and low benefit levels left a large residual population which, even after the New Deal social insurance reforms, had to rely upon means-tested public assistance of a traditional poor-law sort.[9] Means-tested assistance takes several forms, ranging from state-by-state 'social assistance'[10] to federal programmes like Medicaid[11] and Supplemental Security Income.[12] Furthermore, almost uniquely in the industrialized world, the US lacks any universal 'family allowance' or child benefit, in its place offering instead only stringently means-tested Aid to Families with Dependent Children (as it was then called).[13]

While the bottom tier of US welfare provision remains firmly rooted in the classically liberal traditions of means-tested poor relief, the top 'social insurance' tier is also defended in classically liberal terms of 'self-help'. What the Social Security Act provided, in the words of one staff member

Much was done to Social Security pensions during the first Nixon Administration, most particularly in indexing pension levels to the cost of living (Myles 1988). By the mid-1980s the US social insurance pensions had just about caught up with the OECD average in the proportion (around 50 per cent) of earnings they replaced for average wage-earners. However, the minimum pension paid to the lowest income earners replaced under 30 per cent of previous earnings, placing the US third from the bottom of the 18-nation OECD league table – only Japan and Italy being lower (Palme 1990b, pp. 50–1). And what is true of pensions is true across the range of other Social Security schemes, which in the US operate on much the same basis.

[9] In the US, the proportion of its public social expenditures which takes a means-tested form are three times the OECD average (18.2 per cent, compared to an OECD mean of 5.9 per cent, which is nearly two and a half standard deviations in excess of the OECD mean); only Canada (at 15.6 per cent) is in remotely the same league (Esping-Andersen 1990, p. 70). For another perspective on the same phenomenon, in the US the average manufacturing worker's public old age pension replaces about 50 per cent of previous earnings, but that is composed of earnings-related and means-tested portions in equal measure (Palme 1990b, p. 77): again, that heavy reliance upon means-tested Supplemental Security Income supplements to earnings-based Social Security entitlements for workers earning average (much less below average) wages marks the US as a strikingly residualist pension regime.

[10] Or 'general assistance' or 'public assistance', as it is more often called.

[11] A supplement to Medicare, and enacted in the same year, Medicaid provides reimbursement of health expenses on a means-tested basis to claimants of all ages.

[12] Enacted in 1974, Supplemental Security Income (SSI) provides supplementary assistance to qualified Social Security claimants (the aged, blind, disabled, widow/ers and spouses) on a means-tested basis out of federal general fund revenue. That system of Supplemental Security Income replaced the state-federal system of Old Age Assistance, contained in the 1935 Social Security Act, under which states were responsible for setting benefit levels (Quandango 1988a, b). Notably, it was enacted in 1974 in lieu of Nixon's more ambitious Family Assistance Plan, which would have abolished Aid to Families with Dependent Children (discussed below) and, in effect, instituted a guaranteed income on a nationwide basis (Moynihan 1973) – although also enacted at the same time was an 'earned income tax credit' to help the 'working poor', which grew from a modest $2 billion to $12 billion tax expenditure between 1980 and 1992, and is set for still further increases (Myles 1996, pp. 123–4).

[13] Ironically, 'when Aid to Dependent Children (ADC, later retitled AFDC) was established in 1935, its planners conceived of the programme mainly as a protective measure of deserving widows and their children, a small group who, it was believed, would shortly disappear from the public-assistance rolls through absorption into the social security system under the provision for survivors' insurance' (Gilbert 1995, p. 30).

of the Committee on Economic Security drafting it, was 'a mechanism whereby the individual could prevent dependency through his *own* efforts' (Brown 1956, p. 3; emphasis added). A worker's contributions were conceptualized as an 'insurance premium', giving rise to a strictly liberal 'matter of contractual right'.[14]

In the ideological gloss that its founders preferred, and which persists to this day, US Social Security is a matter of people taking care of themselves and their families (compulsory though their contributions to that may be). In the phrase of some of its most persuasive defenders, what the US has is not so much a 'welfare state' as an 'opportunity-insurance state' (Marmor, Mashaw and Harvey 1990, ch. 2). In classically liberal fashion, public assistance is regarded as a 'residual' programme offered on a means-tested basis to those incapable of taking care of themselves and their families through the ordinary market mechanisms and associated social insurance (Titmuss 1974).

4.2.2   Policies and programmes

The basic structure of US social welfare programmes at the beginning of the period (1983), which persisted unaltered during our study, is described in table 4.1. The table summarizes information on social security programmes under five headings – old age, disability and death programmes; sickness and maternity programmes; work injury programmes; unemployment programmes; and family allowances – in the survey of *Social Security Programs Throughout the World*, compiled by the US Social Security Administration (1983). The US Social Security Administration's summaries are far from perfect, in various respects.[15] Recognizing that, we nonetheless reproduce them here as the most authoritative brief synopses available.

As is evident from table 4.1, the US system of social security is a mixture of programmes operating on a combination of different principles. Most of the core programmes – old age, invalidity and death; work injury; and unemployment – are insurance-based in form, funded by contributions from the employer and often employee as well, and paid in an earnings-related form to those experiencing the insured-against contingency. All that is standard enough across the OECD world.

Standard though the forms of its social welfare programmes may be,

---

[14] In the phrase favoured by Frances Perkins, President Roosevelt's Secretary of Labor and chair of the Economic Security Committee (quoted in Rimlinger 1971, p. 229; see further Skocpol 1995, p. 214).

[15] In particular, they are not always completely accurate, and they contain no systematic account of provisions for general social assistance unconnected to insurance-based social security.

Table 4.1. *US social welfare programme structure, circa 1983*

Programme (year enacted: programme type)	Coverage	Funding	Qualifying conditions	Cash benefits	Administration
Old age, invalidity and death (1935: social insurance)	Employed persons	Contributory (employer + employee); income capped	Contributory work history + age / invalidity / death	Earnings-related (with min. and max.); means-tested supplement	Federal gov't through district offices
Sickness and maternity (medical benefits 1965: social insurance) (also cash benefits in five states)	Medicare: pensioners aged 65 +; Medicaid: recipients of other federal means-tested benefits, any age	Medicare: contributory (employer + employee); income capped; Medicaid: general tax revenue	Treatment in covered category; Medicaid: means-tested	Expenses per fee schedule	Federal gov't through private providers
Work injury (1908 federal, 1911 states: compulsory insurance, public or private carriers)	Employees. Industry and commerce; most gov't employees	Contributory (nominal from workers, most from employer)	Work-related injury	Earnings-related (usually 66.7%), capped; usually indexed to wages of state employees	State gov't oversight, often insuring with private insurance carriers; federal gov't for own employees
Unemployment (1935: compulsory insurance)	Employees of firms in industry and commerce, gov't employees	Employer payroll tax; federal gov't pays state programme; income capped	Unemployment; history of previous employment / earnings; available for work; unemployment not voluntary or due to industrial dispute	Earnings-related (usually 50% previous earnings) for 26–34 weeks, extendable by half that again in areas of high unemployment	Federal / state gov'ts
Family allowances (1935: social assistance)	Families with dependent children	General taxation	Means-tested	Flat-rate per child	Federal / state gov'ts

the US is nonetheless unusual in that coverage rates, the proportion of people meeting the qualifying conditions, and the proportion of earnings replaced are all relatively low. Tellingly, even those drawing the old age pension might still qualify as poor (hence the means-tested supplement available under that scheme). Unemployment benefits are paid at most for one year, far less than elsewhere in the OECD. Almost uniquely within the OECD, the US has no universal family allowance or child benefit, only the means-tested Aid to Families with Dependent Children.[16] Sickness benefits are available only to pensioners and to the indigent on a means-tested basis.

Anyone who does not qualify for assistance under any of these headings – and many would not – is forced to fall back upon general public assistance. That is provided by states on a means-tested basis under state poor laws and their legislative successors. In absolute terms, means-tested social assistance may seem small beer: less than a fifth of total US government expenditure on social protection takes a means-tested form. In international comparative terms, however, the point nonetheless remains that this is three times the OECD average (Esping-Andersen 1990, p. 70).

4.2.3   Policy changes, during and after our period

President Reagan, in office at the beginning of our period, waxed lyrical about 'rolling back the welfare state'.[17] Despite such heady rhetoric, though, Reagan effected little change. In his first budget he scored certain modest successes in cutting back social security expenditures.[18] In the course of those struggles, however, Reagan came to learn that Social Security was politically sacrosanct and treated it accordingly in subsequent years.[19]

---

[16] As it was called in the period covered by our study: the programme has since been retitled Temporary Assistance to Needy Families.

[17] Echoing the words of President Franklin Roosevelt's 1939 State of the Union message, President Reagan's 1986 message attacked welfare as 'a narcotic, a subtle destroyer of the human spirit' and suggested that the true measure of the success of welfare programmes ought to be how many of its recipients become independent of welfare (quoted in Goodin 1988, p. 335).

[18] His 1983 Social Security Amendments did bring modest cuts to real future benefit levels (principally by making some portion of benefits taxable) and modest increases in social security taxes on employers (OECD 1988b, p. 111; Williamson and Pampel 1993, pp. 101–4).

[19] When Republicans tried to enact a one-year moratorium on cost-of-living adjustments through the Senate in 1985, Reagan 'cut a deal with [Speaker of the House] Tip O'Neill preserving Social Security in return for higher defense authorizations' (Pierson 1994, p. 68). Later, when calling a 'budget summit' to try to restore public confidence after the October 1987 Wall Street crash (when the Dow Jones lost a quarter of its notional value in

Throughout the 1980s and early 1990s, in consequence, total federal spending on social programmes persistently hovered around 12 per cent. Social Security accounted for the bulk of that, of course. But the sort of means-tested benefits that are the hallmark of the liberal welfare regime persistently accounted for about a fifth of US social expenditures (Pierson 1994, pp. 144–5).

It was only with President Clinton that any real welfare reform came, in the form of the 'Personal Responsibility and Work Opportunity Reconciliation Act of 1996'.[20] That legislation restricted recipients of AFDC (tellingly relabelled 'Temporary Assistance to Needy Families') to two continuous years, or five years over their whole lifetimes. Senator Moynihan complained bitterly that this marked 'the first time in the history of the nation that we have repealed a section of the Social Security Act' (Moynihan 1995: 71). The truth of the matter is worse, still. In the wake of the 1996 reforms, not even *means-tested* assistance will any longer be available for those with long-term needs.[21] That constitutes a renunciation, not only of some small section of the Social Security Act of 1935, but of traditions of poor relief dating back to 1601 and beyond.

The significance of those reforms is, as we have said, not to be underestimated. But all of that, of course, lies outside the period here under consideration.

4.3 The Netherlands

4.3.1 Policy history: a thumbnail sketch[22]

The Netherlands, too, has a long and rich social history. Once again, however, for purposes of our study this can all be boiled down to a very few salient points.

From the days of the early Republic, the United Provinces of the

a single day's trading), 'Reagan excluded only one possible target for deficit reduction: Social Security. In a press conference on October 20, he announced that he was "putting everything on the table with the exception of Social Security, with no other conditions"' (Pierson 1994, p. 68).
[20] Public Law 104–193 [H.R. 3734] August 22, 1996, 110 Stat. 2105. A start had been made in that direction by the Family Support Act of 1988, but as regards its impact on AFDC it turned out to be largely a false start owing to financial pressures then being experienced by the states (Bane and Ellwood 1994, p. 25).
[21] From the federal government anyway. Of course, poor relief had historically been a local responsibility in Anglo-American law.
[22] The discussion in this section is based upon: Daalder (1966); Berben and Roebroek (1986); van Kersbergen and Becker (1988); Therborn (1989); Netherlands Ministry of Social Affairs and Employment (1990, esp. ch. 1; 1996a, b); de Jong, Herweijer and Wildt (1990); de Vroom and Blomsma (1991); Cox (1993); and Dirven, Fouarge and Muffels (1998). For an engaging popular elaboration of similar themes, see van der Horst (1996).

Netherlands operated on the basis of Althusian consociationalism, a system of 'sovereignty from below'. Prerogatives were divided and devolved among many co-equals who, in the absence of any strong central authority, obviously had to cooperate to get anything done.[23]

Nineteenth-century controversies over religious-based schools forced consociationalism into a 'confessional' form which long dominated Dutch politics. Political parties associated with the confessional pillars captured an absolute majority in virtually every parliamentary election between 1918 and 1963. Everyone was supposed, presumptively and prescriptively, to be a member of one and only one of those pillars; all of one's associations were supposed to be within one and the same pillar; all of one's needs were supposed to be catered for within the institutional structure of that pillar. In the Netherlands in this period, for example, what is internationally known as the Red Cross was trifurcated between three distinct 'Cross associations': Yellow-White for Catholics; Orange-Green for Calvinists; and Green for seculars.[24] And so on.

Traditions of 'sovereignty from below' (Calvinist 'sovereignty in one's own circle'; Catholic 'subsidiarity') dictated that any function which could be performed by lower-level associations should be performed by them.[25] The upshot for social policy was that each pillar was held to be primarily responsible for taking care of the welfare needs of its own members, leaving only a very residual role for the state.[26]

When 'pillarization' finally broke down in the early 1960s, there ensued a competitive bidding for the political allegiance of workers newly liberated from confessionally constrained trade unionism. Social democrats 'owned' the issue of social welfare, thanks to their association with Prime Minister Drees' enormously popular universal old age pension, enacted in 1947 during Labour's brief period in power.[27] Confessional parties

[23] Blom (1995); Lijphart (1975). Althusius himself coined the term 'consociationes' to describe the arrangement (Daalder 1966, p. 191).

[24] Therborn (1989, pp. 202, 196, 205, 208).

[25] Therborn (1989, p. 206); van Kersbergen (1995). Such notions are finding a wider audience nowadays, of course, in European Union applications. See, e.g., Delors (1991); Bermann (1994); Føllesdal (1998).

[26] Thus, while the 1815 Constitution declared that 'the care of the poor is a constant concern of the Government', the way that was operationalized legislatively in 1818 and in the Poor Laws (of 1854, 1912 and 1947) was that 'care for the poor was primarily the responsibility of church and lay charity, and that the municipality was only the last resort' (Therborn 1989, p. 207). Indeed, under the terms of those statutes, 'A pauper could expect assistance from the authorities only if his family did not support him or he had been turned away by church and private charity institutions.' In the draconian language of the 1854 Poor Law, the public authorities were empowered to provide assistance only where that was 'absolutely unavoidable' (Netherlands Ministry 1990, p. 93).

[27] The Invalidity Act of 1913 (coming into effect in 1919) provided a meagre old age pension for a sub-set of the population. In the immediate aftermath of World War II and German occupation, the plight of the elderly was sufficiently dire to prompt the government to

countered by sponsoring increasingly generously funded social welfare programmes organized along new, more statist lines.

The transformation from the *nachtwakersstaat* to the *verzorgingsstaat* – from the Nightwatchman State to the Caring State – was effected through the National Assistance Act, enacted in 1963, taking effect in 1965. That enactment abolished the Poor Law, and with it the subsidiarity principle implicit within it. The state assumed primary rather than merely residual responsibility for social welfare. Poor relief became an 'entitlement', a right of citizenship rather than an act of charity.[28] The 'social minimum' thereby introduced was set at the same level as the minimum wage itself, 50 per cent of average earnings.

Throughout the 1960s came a spate of other social legislation, much of it initiated by a progressive Catholic, G. M. J. Veldkamp, who served as Minister of Social Affairs in a variety of short-lived conservative coalitions over that period. Those enactments created the full panoply of modern social welfare programmes, instituting, restructuring, broadening and dramatically increasing children's allowances, old age pensions, unemployment benefits, invalidity pensions, minimum wages and long-term medical benefits.[29]

This expansion of the range of programmes was accompanied by increasingly generous funding. State welfare expenditure used to be constrained by scruples of 'subsidiarity', holding that general tax revenue should only be used to fund residual social assistance for those who were desperately poor and had nowhere else to turn (Therborn 1989, p. 213). That ended with the collapse of the pillars, while certain carry-overs from those older traditions of social administration tended to make expenditures needs-based and cost-led.[30]

bring in an Old Age Pensions (Emergency Provisions) Act 'to secure a basic level of subsistence for the elderly' (Netherlands Ministry 1990, p. 21). Discussions on how to regularize those emergency provisions into a scheme of compulsory social insurance proceeded across the next decade. They eventually culminated in the Old Age Pensions Act, which introduced, starting in 1957, a regular scheme of compulsory social insurance providing a universal, flat-rate pension to everyone in the Netherlands. On the phenomenon of parties 'owning' issues, see Budge, Robertson and Hearl (1987).

[28] In the words of Klompé, the minister responsible for shepherding the Act through parliamentary debate, 'Everyone must be able to hold his head high while making a claim under this act' (M. Klompé, quoted in Netherlands Ministry 1990, pp. 93, 95).

[29] Therborn (1989, pp. 210–13). Netherlands Ministry (1990, ch. 1); Schuyt (1997, pp. 24–8).

[30] First, 'the classical confessional conception of public social policy ... was the idea of a "just" or "necessary" wage, capable of ensuring the livelihood of a family even in times of sickness, invalidity and old age', which led to high levels of income support and earnings replacement (Therborn 1989, p. 212; see also Netherlands Ministry 1990, p. 5; van Kersbergen 1995). Second was the 'financially open-ended' character of 'the idea and practice of [those] self-governing administrations of social insurance' which served as the institutional embodiments of 'basic confessional principles of subsidiarity and cor-

All this happened against the background of general affluence, fuelled by wage restraint, international trade and dividends from North Sea gas.[31] With these constraints on expenditure also relaxed, new social programmes came to acquire the high coverage rates and high benefit levels that are characteristic of interventionist social democratic welfare regimes' tax-transfer policies.[32]

Ideologically, too, the sort of solidarity implicit in the older consociationalism tended to generalize into the sort of solidarity across society as a whole which is the ideological hallmark of social democracy. Under the old pillars, there used to be 'solidarity within one's sphere', within the pillars and their respective employment-based associations. With the breakdown of the old pillars, those traditions of mutual solidarity naturally generalized to society as a whole.[33]

Thus, the Netherlands (like Sweden itself) was a late bloomer among welfare states. As late as 1960, its social expenditures as a percentage of GDP were towards the bottom of the OECD league table (as were Sweden's). By 1980, however, the Netherlands topped the OECD in this regard (bettering Sweden itself).[34] Although still lacking the sort of highly active labour market policies and high female labour force participation characterizing the Swedish welfare state, the Dutch welfare state was moving strongly in these directions from the 1980s (Kloosterman 1994;

poratism'. Rather than being financially capped in any sense, those consociational associations simply 'set premiums to cover costs', however high or low claims against them happened to be in any particular period (Therborn 1989, p. 213).

[31] Wage restraint characteristic of the immediate postwar period (Therborn 1989) was restored by the 1982 Wassenaar Accord: trade unions promised wage restraint in exchange for a shorter working week from business and high replacement rates in social benefits from government; and a central bipartite corporatist institution, the Stichting van de Arbeid, was established to cooordinate subsequent rounds of wage negotiations (Hemerijck and van Kersbergen 1997: 265–9).

[32] 'This extended economic growth and especially the profits from natural gas operations enabled considerable expansion of the government's area of responsibility and of the range and scope of the facilities provided by the welfare state. The auspicious economic climate undoubtedly influenced the calculation of the rate to be awarded in benefits pursuant to the Disability Act of 1967: while the Minister of Finance did not object to 80 per cent at the time, the Minister of Social Affairs would have settled for 75 per cent' (Schuyt 1997, p. 26; see similarly Bussemaker and van Kersbergen 1994, p. 20).

[33] de Jong, Herweijer and de Wildt (1990, p. 3); Netherlands Ministry (1990, p. 24). Socialists had, since the late nineteenth century, been struggling similarly but less successfully to universalize the solidarity manifest in the corporatist welfare systems of Germany, Austria and Italy (Esping-Andersen 1987a, p. 90).

[34] From its 1956 position among the West European countries spending least on social security, the Netherlands rose by 1980 to the top of that league, spending some 40.2 per cent of Gross Domestic Product on public social expenditures. As of 1960, Swedish social expenditure as a percentage of GDP was still only about on a par with that of the UK. By 1980, though, it was spending 37.9 per cent of GDP on social expenditures – second only to none other than the Netherlands, among the countries of Western Europe (Therborn 1989, pp. 209, 193).

Van Berkel and De Graaf 1998); and in other respects it was not radically different from the Swedish one from the 1980s onwards (Esping-Andersen 1996a, pp. 10–11). Whereas in Sweden that transformation came about through the political power of organized labour, the parallel transformation of the Netherlands into a high tax-transfer welfare regime came through the particular way in which old consociational politics fractured in the presence of an economic surplus generated through wage restraint, international trade and North Sea gas (Therborn 1989). By these very different routes, they ended up with similarly social democratic-style tax-transfer policies.

4.3.2 Policies and programmes

For the purposes of outlining the basic structure of social security programmes in the Netherlands, we will rely once again upon the authoritative survey of *Social Security Programs Throughout the World* (US SSA 1983), supplemented by reports from the Netherlands' own Ministry for Social Affairs and Employment (see table 4.2).[35]

As elsewhere in the OECD, many of the core elements of the Dutch social security programme take the form of social insurance. Where the Dutch system differs is in the breadth of its coverage and the generosity of its benefits.[36] At the beginning of the period under study, sickness and unemployment benefits paid 80 per cent of people's previous earnings, up to a relatively high income cap. Although unemployment insurance dropped to 75 per cent of previous earnings after six months and cut out altogether after another two years, the disability benefit at the beginning of this period replaced 80 per cent of previous earnings until age sixty-five (de Jong, Herweijer and de Wildt 1990, p. 4).

Like most countries of the OECD (with the notable exception of the US), the Netherlands offers a universal, flat-rate child benefit.[37] Unlike most OECD countries, the basic Dutch old age pension (AOW) is also

---

[35] de Jong, Herweijer and de Wildt (1990, especially table 2.1, pp. 4–5); Netherlands Ministry (1990).

[36] Its own Ministry of Social Affairs and Employment describes what is distinctive about the Dutch social welfare system in similar terms: 'the generosity of its replacement rates, the leniency of its eligibility rules, the length of its benefit periods, and the comprehensiveness of its safety net' (de Jong, Herweijer and de Wildt 1990, p. 1).

[37] That rate rises with the number of children: at its minimum, it pays families with a single child under three years old some 4 per cent of the minimum wage; at its maximum, it pays some four times that to families with eight or more children aged twelve to seventeen. (Although payment ordinarily ceased, in this period, when the child turned sixteen, it continued to be paid until eighteen if an invalid or twenty-seven if a student.) The family allowance (like student benefits, for example, as well) is subject to further means-tested supplements.

Table 4.2. *Netherlands social welfare programme structure, circa 1983*

Programme (year enacted: programme type)	Coverage	Funding	Qualifying conditions	Cash benefits	Administration
Old age, invalidity and death (1913): social insurance (special supplement for public employees)	Old age: all residents; invalidity: all residents 18 +	Contributory (employer + employee); income capped	Contributory work history + age / invalidity / death	Old age: flat rate; disability: earnings-related (80% of previous earnings, up to cap)	National gov't and industry assoc'ns with tripartite membership
Sickness and maternity (1913): social insurance (separate systems miners, railway workers, seamen and public employees)	All wage-earners and salaried employees (for cash benefits: medical insurance compulsory for low-to-moderate earners, voluntary for self-employed and pensioners)	Contributory (employer + employee); income capped	Cash benefits: fully incapable of doing one's own work; medical benefits: membership in approved sickness fund	Earnings-related; sickness benefit 80% of previous earnings, up to cap; maternity benefit 100% for 6 wks before and 6 wks after + daily payment for 10 days	National gov't and industry assoc'ns with tripartite membership
Work injury (1901; folded into sickness and invalidity, above, in 1967)					
Unemployment (1916, 1949: dual industry and general compulsory insurance) (separate system for public employees)	Employed persons	Contributory (employer + employee); income capped	Employment history; available for work; unemployment not voluntary or due to dismissal for misconduct or industrial dispute	Earnings-related (80% previous earnings, capped), up to 26 wks; thereafter 75% of earnings up to 2 yrs (7 yrs if aged 58 +)	National gov't and industry assoc'ns with tripartite membership
Family allowances (1939: dual, universal and employment related)	All residents with 1 + children	Employer payroll tax (income capped)	Child under 16	Flat-rate per child (rising with no. of children); adjustments linked to minimum wage for 2 + children	National gov't and industry assoc'ns with tripartite membership

universal and flat-rate in form, rather than being work-tested and earn-ings-related.[38] The qualifying condition is formally a 'contributory work history', but those without market income are excused from making contributions and 'this does not reduce their pension rights' (Netherlands Ministry 1990, p. 26).

Finally, the fall-back for anyone not qualifying for assistance under any of those headings is the public assistance 'safety net' alluded to above. The 'social minimum' – 'defined as the amount of money necessary to provide for one's basic needs' – is taken to 'depend on age and household status' and is specified in terms of 'the after-tax statutory minimum wage'.[39] Under the National Assistance Act of 1965, anyone whose income falls short of those levels is (subject to a further assets test) entitled to receive, for an unlimited period of time, a benefit sufficient to bring their income up to (or, given certain 'disregards', sometimes actual-ly above) those levels.[40] These 'social provisions' are financed by general revenue and administered by local and provincial government.

4.3.3   Policy changes, during and after our period

In the Netherlands, as across the OECD, the oil crisis and ensuing recession led to a questioning of the affordability of generous social provisions. In the assessment of the Netherlands Ministry of Social Affairs and Employment (1990, p. 6):

Towards the end of the 1970s, it was generally accepted that social security covered all possible areas and was of a high quality. Benefits were index-linked, and the net minimum benefits actually equalled the minimum wage... But ... economic growth started to stagnate leading to mass unemployment and drastic increases in the national debt. It was gradually realized that this was caused not only by external factors, such as the oil crisis, but also by the basic socio-economic

[38] Within the OECD, purely flat-rate schemes are found only in Denmark, Ireland, New Zealand and Australia, in the latter case in means-tested form (OECD 1988b, pp. 114–37). In the Netherlands, these flat-rate public pensions are supplemented by earnings-related occupational pensions which are publicly insured but privately provided, except in the case of public servants for whom they are publicly provided as well (Esping-Andersen 1996b, p. 69; see further van Gunsteren and Rein 1985).

[39] For 'a two-partner household, with or without children', the social minimum is set at '100 per cent of the net minimum wage; 90 per cent for single parents; 70 per cent for singles'. These levels are reduced step-wise for every year under twenty-three (de Jong, Herweijer and de Wildt 1990, p. 5; Netherlands Ministry 1990, pp. 97–101).

[40] Furthermore, under the National Assistance Act of 1965 the statutory minimum wage to which these 'social minimum' payments was linked itself increased faster than real wages in the early 1970s as an austerity measure (sic!). It was then indexed to real wages throughout the rest of the decade – a practice which ended in 1983 (de Jong, Herweijer and de Wildt 1990, p. 6). These provisions were cut back even further later in the period under study; see section 4.3.3 below.

structure of the Netherlands. There was talk of a crisis in the social state with recognition of the problems in social and economic support. The high collective burden associated with the social state appeared to be out of control, with damaging consequences... The state-organized solidarity seemed to have over-stretched itself ... Consequently a start was made in the early 1980s on a widereaching reform of various legislation.[41]

Early attempts at reforms were largely ineffectual, though.[42] A new push commencing in 1982 eventually led to a series of enactments taking effect in 1987. One tightened eligibility rules for unemployment benefits and lowered its replacement rate from 80 to 70 per cent.[43] Another restricted the generous use of 'labour market considerations' in awarding disability benefits to partially disabled persons, and lowered replacement rates for sickness and disability benefits from 80 to 70 per cent (de Jong, Herweijer and de Wildt 1990, pp. 8–11, 57–61; Hemerijck and van Kersbergen 1997: 269–78; Visser and Hemerijck 1997).[44]

The abuse of sickness and disability benefits as, in effect, an early retirement scheme continued to prove problematic even after those reforms.[45] Proposals for further legislation to close that avenue occasioned stiff resistance, including a million-person march on The Hague in 1991 and a serious rift within the Labour Party (PvdA). Further reforms were eventually legislated in an Act on the Reduction of the Number of Disablement Benefit Claimants, which set in place bonuses for employers hiring partially disabled workers and imposing a financial penalty upon employers whose workers entered the rolls of the 'disabled'. Benefit rates were reduced and the duration of benefit was shortened; more stringent medical recertifications of disability were instituted; and beneficiaries were required to accept any 'normal' job offered to them (Netherlands Ministry of Social Affairs and Employment 1996b, p. 12). The upshot of

---

[41] For a rather different perspective, see Therborn (1986, pp. 151–63).

[42] 'There were simply no instruments and no institutional framework to respond efficiently to the rising unemployment figures' (van Kersbergen and Becker 1988: 493).

[43] It also reduced the second-tier benefit, payable when entitlement to that first-tier benefit was exhausted, to 70 per cent of the statutory minimum wage (Heisler 1996: 175).

[44] Other changes pushed in the direction of increasing generosity, if only at the margins. For example, the Supplementary Benefits Act increased the generosity of 'social minimum' income guarantees by waiving its assets test for the sick, disabled or long-term unemployed (de Jong, Herweijer and de Wildt 1990, pp. 8–11, 57–61). And 1985 changes to family allowance policy allowed payment for any child under eighteen, rather than sixteen as under previous legislation; counterbalancing that, family allowances were no longer paid to families of students eighteen to twenty-seven (US SSA 1993, p. 232; cf US SSA 1983, p. 178).

[45] 'A scheme that originally was meant to support no more than 200,000 people was paying more than 900,000 benefits in 1990. By 1986 in the 55–64 age group those who received a disability benefit outnumbered those with a job' (Hemerijck and van Kersbergen 1997: 271; see further de Vroom and Blomsma 1991).

these reforms was to reduce disability benefit claimants from a peak of 925,000 in 1994 to 861,000 just one year later (Hemerijck and van Kersbergen 1997: 270–4).

In addition to these changes in sickness and disability benefits, the General Social Assistance Act was also revised, with effect from 1996. New workfare requirements ('activation obligations') were legally imposed;[46] and the 'social minimum' payment was marginally reduced (Netherlands Ministry of Social Affairs and Employment 1996b, p. 13; Hemerijck and van Kersbergen 1997: 274). And various other reforms are in the offing, directed at increasing participation levels by inculcating the general sense that it is a social duty to engage in paid labour whenever you possibly can (van der Veen 1998b).

In many important ways, those socio-economic reforms have clearly had a great impact on Dutch life. A much larger proportion of men and particularly of women are now in the paid labour force, albeit often only in part-time labour.[47] But those effects came without any great changes to the Netherlands' basic social welfare arrangements, certainly in the period here under study. Even where initiatives undertaken during our period did have real effects (as in the case of the dramatic reduction in disability benefit claimants), those by and large came only after the end of our study in 1994.

4.4   Germany

4.4.1   Policy history: a thumbnail sketch[48]

Twentieth-century Germany has more history than most. But, again, for the more specific purposes of this book, a few salient points about the background to contemporary German social policy will have to suffice.

Germany industrialized late. When it did, it did so rapidly and without developing a substantial bourgeoisie or, consequently, any very strong liberal traditions. Instead there were influential medieval residues – feudal Junkers on the one side (Moore 1967), and on the other strong guilds (especially among miners and printers) organized as powerful mutual benefit societies with a strong paternalistic ethos and organicist self-conceptions (Esping-Andersen 1987a, p. 81).

---

[46] Although, so far, imperfectly enforced (Heisler 1996: 183).

[47] OECD (1984–95, Statistical Appendices).

[48] The discussion in this section is based on: Moore (1967, ch. 8); Rimlinger (1971, chs. 4–5); Esping-Andersen and Korpi (1984); Alber (1986); Baldwin (1990); Williamson and Pampel (1993, ch. 2); Classen and Gould (1995); and Leisering and Leibfried (1998), ch. 7. For further details see W. Mommsen (1981); for an excellent brief sketch see Heidenheimer, Heclo and Adams (1990, ch. 7, esp. pp. 230–2).

When Bismarck set about unifying Germany under a strong central state, the imperialism of his foreign policy was matched at home by a policy of 'corn and steel', placating Junker agricultural interests with high tariffs while industrializing and urbanizing. In his social insurance initiatives, Bismarck tried to make the state, in the person of the monarch, the protector of the emerging working classes from the consequences of industrialization.[49] That ran up against the power of those older corporate groups, which succeeded in defeating his social insurance proposals when first presented to parliament and which insinuated themselves as administrators of the social insurance system when it was finally enacted several years later.[50]

The basic premise of the system of social insurance as finally enacted was one of *Soldaten der Arbeit*, of social integration and mutual solidarity among employers and workers within the same workplace and, ultimately, the same industry (Esping-Andersen 1987a, pp. 79–80; Steinmetz 1991). That manifests itself, operationally, in the 'mutual solidarity' of those who find themselves sharing the same 'risk pool' constituted by occupationally based mutual insurance arrangements.[51]

The basic structure of those social insurance programmes survived through the Weimar Republic, the Third Reich and Allied Occupation into the Federal Republic and unification.[52] For example, in the interwar years the Social Democratic Party urged a universal state unemployment insurance programme, only to find that one of its principal opponents was none other than the General Federation of Trade Unions (the ADGB) itself, anxious not to lose control of funds, eligibility rules and benefits policies governing the schemes it administered (Esping-Andersen 1987a, p. 81). And 'not even the Nazis could prevail against the well-entrenched

---

[49] Building on Lorenz von Stein's ideas of 'social monarchy' (Offe 1996; 1998: 4; Koslowski 1997).

[50] Rimlinger (1971, pp. 113–14). The original bill, for accident insurance, was defeated in 1881. The Kaiser's message to the opening session of the new parliament held later that year signalled the concession in the following terms: 'The closer union of the practical forces of this [Christian] national life and their combination in the form of corporate associations, with state patronage and help, will, we hope, render possible the discharge of tasks to which the executive alone might prove unable' (quoted in Rimlinger 1971, p. 114). After further hard bargaining with those corporate associations over the administration of the schemes, health insurance was enacted in 1883, accident insurance in 1884 and old age and invalidity insurance in 1889. Contrast the power of the German guilds with the relative weakness of the British 'friendly societies', which physicians and insurance companies systematically outmanoeuvred in negotiations over the 1911 National Insurance Act (Green 1985; 1993, p. 99).

[51] Thus German social insurance was from the outset a model of 'industrial achievement and mutual insurance' (Titmuss 1974).

[52] Indeed, 'in light of the vast upheavals in twentieth-century Germany', this continuity in 'the basic social insurance structure' truly is 'remarkable' (Heidenheimer, Heclo and Adams 1990, p. 231).

power of bureaucrats and social groups defending the traditional social insurance system' their 'promises of a tax-financed, noncontributory system of pensions for all citizens eventually shrivel[ling] into yet another separate plan of compulsory contributory insurance for artisans, [i.e.] independent workers in skilled trades.'[53]

The foundations of the postwar German 'social state' (*Sozialstaat*) laid by the Economic Council (a proto-Bundesrat) and its Economic Director, Ludwig Erhard, were premised on Müller-Armack's notion of a 'social market economy' (*Marktwirtschaft*).[54] Adopted as the official policy of the Christian Democratic Union in 1949, the 'social market economy' framework echoed in Social Democrat calls for a 'socialist market economy'.[55]

In practical terms, this mixture of 'social' and 'market' principles manifested itself primarily in arrangements for corporatist economic management. Himself a Christian Democrat, one of Adenauer's first acts as the first Chancellor of the new Federal Republic was nevertheless to form an on-going compact with the trade unions to establish a system of industrial conciliation which persisted (albeit with notable interruptions) throughout the period here under review. Peak-level corporate intermediation was matched, lower down, by formal schemes of 'co-determination', first in the steel and coal industries, and eventually extended in the mid-1970s to require a highly participatory Works Council for every workplace (Dahrendorf 1990, p. 89; Streeck 1984; 1997). This cooperative, corporatist approach to industrial relations was seen on all sides as crucial to German economic recovery, which in turn was widely seen as crucial to the further amelioration of social problems.[56]

---

[53] Heidenheimer, Heclo and Adams (1990, p. 231). Senior National Socialist Party functionaries did propose schemes which would have radically restructured unemployment, sickness and old age benefits, but Hitler deferred resolution of all those issues until after the war (Heidenheimer, Heclo and Adams 1990, p. 231; see also Rimlinger 1987, pp. 70–4).

[54] In its original version, the 'social' side of that package did not 'make a very impressive list'. It amounted just to saying, 'Employees must be treated humanely without restricting the responsibility of entrepreneurs. Competition must be regulated by certain rules ... Only when he came to housing and social insurance did Müller-Armack show signs of going beyond the pure doctrine of the invisible hand' (Dahrendorf 1990, p. 88).

[55] The finer points of difference between Christian Democrat and Social Democrat versions of the 'social(ist) market economy' are recounted by Rimlinger (1971, pp. 140–8).

[56] Even 'the trade unions were forced to pin their hopes on the future full-employment dividend of economic growth, financed by low wages and high savings' (Esping-Andersen and Korpi 1984, p. 195). Increases in real wages lagged behind productivity growth for fully a decade. The Bundesbank imposed a tight monetary policy, Christian Democratic governments levied high taxes and characteristically ran budget surpluses. All of this led to high rates of capital accumulation and investment, leading in turn to impressively high growth rates. See Esping-Andersen and Korpi (1984, p. 207 n. 18) and sources cited therein.

That same corporatist impulse also manifested itself more directly in a broad consensus on social welfare policy.[57] Social Democratic pressure for a universal flat-rate pension in the early postwar years eventually waned, and a broad cross-party consensus was finally consolidated with the 1957 Adenauer pension reforms.[58] That consensus has remained remarkably robust faced with changes in economic circumstance and to the party in power.[59]

The basic premises of that consensus were that nearly everyone in industrial society is economically at risk, so (contrary to liberal means-testing) protection should not be confined to those presently in distress. The German corporatist consensus further holds (contrary to social democratic levelling) that social protection should be aimed at sustaining people's economic status as set by the labour market, and whenever their market earnings are interrupted people's incomes should therefore be maintained at their previous levels. Finally, the German corporatist consensus emphasizes, and rewards, both the economic importance of full employment for heads of households and the social importance of home-makers not in the formal labour market.[60]

4.4.2   Policies and programmes

For a sketch of the basic structure of German social security programmes, we rely once again on the authoritative survey of *Social Security Programmes Throughout the World* (US SSA 1983) (see table 4.3).

As we see from table 4.3, German social security relies particularly

[57] Kircheimer (1966) talks of the 'vanishing opposition' among parliamentary parties in the Federal Republic over this period more generally (cf. Offe 1998).

[58] Although early in the postwar period the SPD was still campaigning for a Beveridge-style universal old age pension, by the mid-1950s it had become clear that politically this was a non-starter (Baldwin 1990, ch. 3). When drafting its *Sozialplan* in 1957, the SDP ended up endorsing decentralized, occupationally based schemes of social insurance in terms that effectively echoed Erhard's own: 'Through self-administration the awareness is kept alive of the relation between cost and extent of benefits and of the nature of responsible collective self-help' (quoted in Rimlinger 1971, p. 177).

Adenauer's own motives in this reform, it should be said, may well have had more to do with his desire to win over the working classes for rearmament, then on the cards, and to prevent the SPD from casting that issue in the form of a 'guns-or-butter' trade-off (Esping-Andersen and Korpi 1984, p. 197).

[59] When the Social Democrats finally came to power in their own right in 1969 they brought only marginal changes to existing social insurance arrangements: income ceilings for compulsory insurance were lifted; sickness benefits were improved for workers and were extended to farmers and the self-employed; a universal pension was finally initiated, although occupational segregation remained. But all attempts to consolidate and harmonize various existing pension schemes ('abolishing the remaining corporatist vestiges') met with 'massive resistance from the CDU, the employers, and private insurance companies', and 'the SPD's goal of a major reform resulted only in a compromise' (Esping-Andersen and Korpi 1984, p. 198).

[60] Loosely summarizing Rimlinger (1971, pp. 177–8) and Offe (1996; 1998).

heavily on social insurance. Across the whole range of core programmes – old age, invalidity and death; sickness and maternity benefits; work injury benefits; and unemployment benefits – people's entitlements to social insurance benefits are vested through work-based contributions from themselves and their employers, with their dependants acquiring entitlements through the breadwinners' contributions.[61] Administration of these social insurance schemes was traditionally and to some extent still is through a patchwork of agencies of an occupationally based or geographically based sort. Both contributions and benefits are earnings-related, thus preserving income and status differentials.[62]

According to conventional wisdom, all that makes the German welfare state highly 'conservative'. Linking contributions and benefits to prior earnings is explicitly designed to be 'status-preserving', underwriting existing social hierarchies; linking the administration of these schemes to one's occupation or locale further reinforces existing social bonds. According to conventional wisdom, too, 'the state's emphasis on upholding status differentials means that its redistributive impact is negligible' (Esping-Andersen 1990, p. 27; see also 1994, p. 719) – apart of course from its notorious bias in favour of large families.[63]

There are, of course, exceptions to this basic German pattern of (apparently) non-redistributive mutual insurance. Within the German social insurance system, work injury insurance is wholly funded by employer contributions with no matching contributions from employees themselves. There are also certain weakly redistributive elements embedded in the methods of calculating contributions and benefits for other social insurance programmes.[64] The family allowance is a universal flat-rate

---

[61] Making Germany a classically 'male breadwinner's welfare state' (Sainsbury 1996; Esping-Andersen 1996c).

[62] Pensioners with fifty years of contributions to their credit, for example, receive 75 per cent of their previous earnings (Esping-Andersen and Korpi 1984, p. 197). Furthermore, pensions are, almost uniquely within the OECD, indexed to average wages in the three previous years, giving pensioners a proportion of the growth of the economy as a whole rather than merely a cost-of-living adjustment.

[63] Or, as Esping-Andersen and Korpi (1984, p. 198) put it, it serves as a 'bar to any major redistributive advances. The heavy reliance on direct employee contributions to the financing of social insurance, coupled with the highly income-differentiated benefit structure, severely restricted the possibilities for redistribution via wage policies.' See similarly Titmuss' (1974) more sociological discussion of the conservatism underlying the 'industrial achievement' model; public finance economists talk similarly of 'fiscal churning' (Palda 1997) – taking with one hand and giving back to the same people with the other – the principal effect being just a deadweight loss.

[64] The ceiling on income used in all these schemes to calculate both contributions and benefits is one such element (albeit a modest one given that the ceiling is approximately twice the average annual income). Perhaps more important is the practice of weighting up low-income workers with twenty-five years' worth of contributions to 75 per cent of the average annual wages 1957–72 for the purposes of calculating their old age pensions (see US SSA 1983, pp. 94–5).

Table 4.3. *Germany's social welfare programme structure, 1983*

Programme (year enacted: programme type)	Coverage	Funding	Qualifying conditions	Cash benefits	Administration
Old age, invalidity and death (1889: social insurance) (special systems for self-employed, miners, public employees and farmers)	Employed persons, apprentices and unemployment recipients; separate scheme with identical provision for salaried	Contributory (employer + employee); income capped, top and bottom	Contributory work history + age / invalidity / death	Earnings-related, linked to number of years insured; adjusted annually in line with national wage levels	Federal / state gov't + 2 special insurance institutes
Sickness and maternity (1883: social insurance) (special scheme for miners, public employees and self-employed farmers)	Wage and salary earners; apprentices and some self-employed; unemployment recipients and disabled; pensioners and students covered for medical benefits	Contributory (employer + employee); income capped; gov't subsidy for specific groups	Membership in sickness fund; for maternity benefits, work history	Earnings-related (employer pays 100% of previous earnings for 6 weeks, sickness fund 80% up to 78 wks in 3 yrs); maternity benefit 100% 6 wks before and 6 months after birth, with max. and min.)	Federal / state gov't + special insurance institutes; sickness funds organized by locality / occupation / enterprise
Work injury (1884 work accidents, 1925 occupational diseases: compulsory insurance with semi-private carriers) (special scheme for public employees)	Employed persons, most self-employed, students, apprentices, children in kindergarten	Employer payroll tax; gov't subsidy for certain groups; income capped	Work injury	As for sickness; employer pays for first 6 wks, thereafter accident insurance fund; permanent disability: 66.7% of last year's earnings	Federal / state supervision of accident insurance funds, managed by employer / employee reps

	Coverage	Financing	Qualifying conditions	Benefits	Administration
Unemployment (1927: compulsory insurance)	Employed persons, including home-workers, agricultural workers, trainees and apprentices	Contributory (employee + employer); gov't subsidy for certain groups; income capped	Work history; available for work; unemployment not voluntary or due to misconduct or industrial dispute	Earnings related (69 to 41% previous earnings, depending on wage level), for max of 52 weeks; thereafter means-tested supplement, paying 60 to 35% previous earnings indefinitely	Federal gov't through regional / local offices managed by tripartite board / committees
Family allowances (1954: universal) (special scheme for foreign workers with children living abroad)	Residents with 1 + children	General taxation	Child under 16 (or under 18 if unemployed and in training; or under 27 if student; no limit if invalid); income test for students and trainees over 16	Flat-rate per child (rate rising with number of children, up to 4)	Federal gov't through local offices

benefit strongly biased toward large families.[65] There is a means-tested extension of unemployment benefits, which comes into play after a year and continues paying people an earnings-related benefit, in principle indefinitely. Certain favoured social groups (conspicuously among them civil servants, – *Beamte*) have pension arrangements all their own, organized on different bases altogether.

Alongside social insurance there is also a scheme of general social assistance. Germans have a statutory right to social assistance, and some 3.5 per cent of the German population in one way or another availed themselves of it in 1980 (Alber 1986, vol. IV, p. 281).[66] Fully a quarter of those social assistance recipients, however, were elderly people in nursing homes (Alber 1986, vol. II, p. 28);[67] and in terms of overall social expenditure the sums involved were small.[68]

4.4.3   Policy changes during and after our period

With the onset of the recession of the mid-1970s, German unemployment began to rise, spurred on by tight fiscal and monetary policies. Pressures of globalization on an increasingly open economy further exacerbated unemployment throughout the 1980s and 1990s. Managing unemployment, reducing working hours and encouraging early retirement became the top policy priorities over that period (Esping-Andersen 1996a, b; Streeck 1997; Hinrichs 1998; Offe 1998).

Social transfers were also affected, of course. Index-linked pension increases were delayed, and sickness benefits and health expenditure were reduced. The most notable among these cutbacks was the 1989 change indexing pensions to 'net' rather than 'gross earnings'.[69] Various

---

[65] The sums are modest for small families but add up quickly for large ones: payments to a family with a single child in 1983 amounted to under 3 per cent of average monthly earnings; but payments to a family with four children would have amounted to almost 33 per cent of average monthly earnings (calculated from US SSA 1983, pp. 94–5).

[66] Indeed, German pension provisions stipulate a lower threshold below which earnings are deemed 'insignificant' (*geringfügig*), and people earning such insignificant incomes are both excused from social security contributions and also excluded from social security benefits, forcing them to fall back on general social assistance instead (Offe 1998: 6–7).

[67] In 1996 a social insurance scheme was introduced to cover nursing home residents as well. But this, of course, is well outside our period of study.

[68] The DM 3 billion spent on social assistance in 1980 amounted to less than 1 per cent of GDP. Expenditures on pensions were sixteen times that, on sickness benefits seven times that, on unemployment 2.5 times that (Alber 1986, vol. II, pp. 22–9).

[69] Which is expected to have surprisingly large consequences for the long-term affordability of pensions as dependency ratios increase. 'The effect of this seemingly minor adjustment will be to progressively reduce the growth rate of benefits as social security contributions rates increase' (Heidenheimer, Heclo and Adams 1990, p. 260; see further Williamson and Pampel 1993, pp. 32–3; Hinrichs 1998).

other specific programmes were targeted for modest cutbacks.[70] Various specific groups suffered differentially from those cutbacks, guestworkers notably among them, according to conventional wisdom.

Even German unification – the single most dramatic event in any of the countries here under discussion – had, at least in the period here under study, minimal impact on social welfare arrangements. Operationally, existing social security arrangements continued in force in the two halves of Germany for two and a half years after unification, with full merger of the GDR system into the FRG's coming on 1 January 1993. Structurally, the two systems were strikingly similar anyway, as one might expect given their shared ancestry (US SSA 1993, pp. 125–9). The main effect of the change was simply that the Federal Republic's benefit levels were substantially more generous, partly in keeping with higher wage rates there; thus, for example, when the FRG old age pension was introduced into the territory of the former GDR in 1991, payments there went up some 60 per cent.[71] At the same time, of course, workers in the former GDR lost the sorts of industrial protection that they used to enjoy (Standing 1996; 1997) and came to experience labour-market precariousness and consequent dependency on social assistance in unprecedented numbers (Leisering and Leibfried 1998, chs. 8 and 9).

There was, of course, a major impact on the German economy overall from the union of currencies at full parity, from the heavy investment in renewing infrastructure and retooling human capital in the former GDR, and so on (Streeck 1997; Offe 1998). Inevitably that must eventually reflect upon the country's capacity to sustain high levels of social security, particularly when financed in a way (through employer contributions) that directly increases the already high costs of labour.

None of this had impacted in any serious way on the basic patterns of German social welfare policy over the period here under study or in the years immediately following. But the proposals for 'remodelling' the welfare state through some combination of lowering labour costs by reducing mandatory social security contributions, lowering wages and reducing tax-financed social expenditures are ominous signs of what might be yet to come (Offe 1998; Hinrichs 1998).

---

[70] For example, replacement rates of the top tier of unemployment insurance were dropped from 69 to 68 per cent of previous earnings for heads of households with children, and in the means-tested second tier from 60 to 56 per cent of previous earnings (Heisler 1996: 175).

[71] There was also heavy borrowing from West German social insurance funds to finance those new expenditures, which might pose further problems both of legitimacy and finance further down the track (Gaßmann 1983: 86; Clasen and Gould 1995: 193; Hinrichs 1998).

4.5   Fitting cases to kinds

These brief historical and institutional sketches serve to show how much richer the real situation is, in every country, than can be depicted in the bare bones of any ideal type or general classification. That further detail is not unimportant. For the broader purposes of this book, however, the higher level of generalization is of greater importance. In concluding our discussion of particular countries and their welfare regimes, therefore, we shall attempt to situate our countries in these more general classificatory schemes.

4.5.1   Public expenditures

For the purpose of classifying welfare regimes, we take as canonical Esping-Andersen's (1990) typology of regime types and his placement of these three countries within it. The basic idea of these three distinctive types of welfare regime was not originated by him, though. Well before Esping-Andersen, comparisons had long been made between welfare states and clusters observed in them.

Those earlier comparisons had traditionally been based simply on public expenditure levels. The standard cross-national measure of 'welfare effort' is simply the percentage of GDP a nation devotes to social expenditure.[72]

That measure is of course flawed in a great many familiar ways. Differences in programme structure and accounting conventions cause some countries to appear artificially low or high in these league tables (Castles 1985; 1997; Esping-Andersen 1987b, p. 7; Castles and Mitchell 1993; 1997). Such statistics wrongly equate 'welfare effort' with simply spending money, neglecting other possibly more effective policy instruments (Gilbert and Moon 1988). Such statistics equate inputs with outputs, simply assuming that the more money you spent on an objective the more of it you achieved. All those and many other objections to social expenditure league tables are well taken.[73]

Despite all of those well-taken objections, though, there remains something of importance which is captured by crude public expenditure statistics, particularly when the differences are as dramatic as table 4.4

---

[72] See, e.g., Cutright (1965); Jackman (1972); Wilensky (1975); Hicks and Swank (1992); Hofferbert and Cingrinelli (1996); Heidenheimer, Heclo and Adams (1990, pp. 226, 257).

[73] Disaggregating component programmes is also clearly something which any fuller study should do, as many people have urged. See, e.g., Flora and Heidenheimer (1981); Korpi (1989: p. 310); and Esping-Andersen (1990, pp. 106 ff.). For a more detailed breakdown of expenditures on component social programmes, see OECD (1996c).

Table 4.4. *Social spending as percentage of GDP (1985, 1993)*

	1985	1993
Sweden	23.62	31.81
Netherlands	**23.11**	**23.44**
Belgium	22.40	19.80*
Denmark	21.18	25.37
France	20.25	21.45
Germany (W)	**19.12**	**18.63**
Austria	18.81	19.65
Finland	17.85	28.49
Ireland	16.84	14.93
Italy	16.18	18.73
UK	16.13	17.67
Norway	14.61	22.50
New Zealand	14.16	16.65*
Switzerland	12.66	14.86*
Canada	10.25	12.56
US	**8.83**	**9.79**
Australia	8.45	10.65*
Japan	7.07	7.37*
OECD mean	16.20	18.58

Sources: Total non-health social expenditure, as percentage of GDP, from OECD (1996c, Table 1.23, p. 20). Asterisk indicates 1992 statistics (1993 being unavailable).

shows them to be between the three countries here under study.

From table 4.4, we see that of our three countries by far the largest social transfers were made in the Netherlands. Germany spent about four-fifths as much. The US spent about two-fifths as much.

Not only does table 4.4 show sharp differences between the three particular countries under study, it also shows that the differences between our particular countries are representative of similar differences between whole groups of countries across the OECD. Countries do indeed tend to cluster together in their social expenditure patterns. Of course high expenditure alone does not make a country social democratic, any more than low expenditure alone makes it liberal.[74] But in the

[74] Distinctly illiberal authoritarian regimes have similarly low social expenditures, and high expenditures can betoken high levels of social problems rather than highly successful social policies.

expenditure league table the US does indeed sit at the bottom, together with other countries like Canada, Australia and Japan whose welfare regimes are ordinarily cast in the 'liberal' camp. The Netherlands sits in the top league, together with the classically social democratic welfare regimes of Sweden and Denmark.[75] Germany sits in the middle group. Its company there is slightly more mixed, but included there are other definitely classical corporatist regimes such as Austria, France and Italy.

The groupings in table 4.4 have been done on the basis of expenditure levels at the beginning of the period under study, in 1985. However, the final column in table 4.4 shows those categories to be broadly constant across the years under study. None of the three countries here under study would have moved from one group to another over that time, and only a few of the others would have done so.[76]

4.5.2   Decommodification

To supplement such standard rankings of welfare regime based of social expenditure levels alone, Esping-Andersen adds two new and quite distinct indicators. His index of 'decommodification' is clearer and in many ways more persuasive. In this measure, Esping-Andersen (1990, ch. 2) blends information about the generosity of programme benefits and the extent to which recipients have 'paid' for those benefits through workplace contributions over the course of their own working lives. The more generous and the less 'privatized' the benefit, the greater its degree of decommodification and hence 'socialization'.

The classification of countries is done on the basis of information on the 'benefits', 'funding' and 'qualifying conditions' of the sort contained in tables 4.1 to 4.3 above. Through a scoring procedure which is inevitably somewhat arbitrary at the margins, Esping-Andersen (1990, p. 50) produces indices reflecting the degree of decommodification found in each country's pension, sickness and unemployment benefits.[77] Table 4.5 reproduces these programme-specific decommodification scores, alongside Esping-Andersen's (1990, p. 52) own summary score reflecting how decommodified each country's welfare regime is across all three programmes.

Decommodification measures the degree of 'socialism' found in a

[75] By 1993, furthermore, the social democratic cluster had consolidated itself, with Belgium dropping into the next group and Norway and Finland rising to the top group.

[76] By 1993, Finland and Norway would have entered the top ('social democratic') tier, Belgium would have dropped into the middle ('corporatist') tier, and Switzerland would have moved up into it.

[77] Details of that scoring procedure are contained in an appendix (Esping-Andersen 1990, p. 54).

Table 4.5. *Decommodification of social welfare programmes,* circa *1980*

	Pensions	Sickness	Unemployment	Combined index
Sweden	17.0	15.0	7.1	39.1
Norway	14.9	14.0	9.4	38.3
Denmark	15.0	15.0	8.1	38.1
Netherlands	**10.8**	**10.5**	**11.1**	**32.4**
Belgium	15.0	8.8	8.6	32.4
Austria	11.9	12.5	6.7	31.1
Switzerland	9.0	12.0	8.8	29.8
Finland	14.1	10.0	5.2	29.2
Germany	**8.5**	**11.3**	**7.9**	**27.7**
France	12.0	9.2	6.3	27.5
Japan	10.5	6.8	5.0	27.1
Italy	9.6	9.4	5.1	24.1
UK	8.5	7.7	7.2	23.4
Ireland	6.7	8.3	8.3	23.3
Canada	7.7	6.3	8.0	22.0
New Zealand	9.1	4.0	4.0	17.1
United States	**7.0**	**0.0**	**7.2**	**13.8**
Australia	5.0	4.0	4.0	13.0
OECD mean	10.7	9.2	7.3	27.2
standard devia.	3.4	4.0	1.9	7.7

Source: Esping-Andersen (1990, pp. 50, 52).

country's social welfare system. Social democrats would want their social programmes to be fully socialized, both generous and redistributive. Corporatists agree with half of that, favouring high replacement rates but insisting that these should be primarily funded by contributions paid over the recipient's own working life. Liberals disapprove not only of redistribution but also of generosity, for fear that high replacement rates would undermine work incentives. Esping-Andersen's decommodification index should thus serve to bracket the three basic types of welfare regime, with social democrats at the top, corporatists in the middle and liberals at the bottom.

Inspecting table 4.5, we find that the decommodification index does indeed serve that regime-differentiating function. Liberal welfare regimes like the US (together with other classically liberal regimes, Australia and Canada) are firmly at the bottom. Corporatist welfare regimes like that of Germany (together with, among other classically corporatist regimes

France and Italy[78]) constitute a clear middle cluster. At the top of the decommodification ranking sits a clear cluster of classically social democratic welfare regimes (Sweden, Norway and Denmark). The Netherlands is among the several countries that occupy intermediate positions, in between those clear clusters. Although intermediate, the Netherlands is nonetheless much nearer the social democratic than the corporatist pole – much more so, for example, than the other Scandinavian country (Finland) that also sits in that intermediate category.

4.5.3   Welfare regime clusters

Esping-Andersen (1990, ch. 3) goes on to construct a second set of indices of welfare regime clusters, combining various other indicators. Omitted from this second set of indicators, however, is the decommodification index. Hence this second set of indices really does constitute an independent ordering. Still, the basic conclusions come out much as before, at least as concerns the three welfare regimes of concern to us. We reproduce his results in table 4.6, with 'cumulative index scores' for each country in parentheses.

These rankings are based, as we have said, on a blend of other more specific information about each country's welfare programmes, some but by no means all of it information about programme structures of the sort contained in tables 4.1 to 4.3. Indicators of social democracy are 'average universalism' (the proportion of the population covered, across pensions, sickness and unemployment benefits) and 'average benefit equality' (the differential between basic and maximum benefits across those three programmes). Indicators of liberalism are: means-tested benefits as a proportion of total public social expenditures; private pensions as a proportion of all pensions; and private health spending as a proportion of all health spending. Indicators of corporatism are the number of occupationally distinct public pension schemes and expenditure on pensions for government employees (as a percentage of GDP). Some of these indicators are of dubious relevance or reliability, and the procedures Esping-Andersen (1990, pp. 77–8) employs for blending them into composite indicators are inevitably somewhat arbitrary at the margins. Nonetheless, the ordering he produces on the basis of them has considerable surface plausibility.

Table 4.6 shows only two countries qualifying as completely pure on this ranking of welfare regime types. The US scores a perfect twelve on

---

[78] The only anomaly is Japan, which Esping-Andersen (1990, p. 74) ordinarily regards as a liberal welfare regime, sitting squarely within the corporatist cluster on the basis of the decommodification rankings.

Table 4.6. *Welfare regime clusters*, circa *1980*

Liberalism (cumulative index scores 0–12)	Social democracy (cumulative index scores 0–8)	Corporatism (cumulative index scores 0–8)
Strong		
Canada (12)	Denmark (8)	Austria (8)
Switzerland (12)	Norway (8)	Belgium (8)
United States (12)	Sweden (8)	France (8)
Australia (10)	Finland (6)	**Germany (8)**
Japan (10)	**Netherlands (6)**	Italy (8)
Moderate		
France (8)	Australia (4)	Finland (6)
Netherlands (8)	Belgium (4)	Iceland (4)
Denmark (6)	Canada (4)	Japan (4)
Germany (6)	**Germany (4)**	**Netherlands (4)**
Italy (6)	New Zealand (4)	Norway (4)
United Kingdom (6)	Switzerland (4)	
	United Kingdom (4)	
Low		
Austria (4)	Austria (2)	Canada (2)
Belgium (4)	France (2)	Denmark (2)
Finland (4)	Ireland (2)	New Zealand (2)
Ireland (2)	Japan (2)	Australia (0)
New Zealand (2)	Italy (0)	Sweden (0)
Norway (0)	**United States (0)**	Switzerland (0)
Sweden (0)		United Kingdom (0)
		United States (0)

Source: Esping-Andersen (1990, p. 74).

the liberalism dimension and zeros on both others; and Sweden scores a perfect eight on the social democracy dimension and zeros on both others. The German welfare regime shows some traces of both liberalism and socialism, but its predominant character is clearly that of a corporatist welfare regime (scoring a perfect eight on that dimension and only middling scores on the other two).[79] While Sweden constitutes the purest case of a 'social democratic welfare regime', judging from table 4.6, the Netherlands nonetheless sits squarely in the 'strongly social democratic'

[79] In terms of table 4.5, only Austria could credibly claim to be a purer instance of the type, scoring as it does equally high on corporatism, but rather less on liberalism or social democracy.

cluster (scoring six out of eight on the social democratic dimension and only in the 'moderate' range on the other two).[80]

[80] Were we to include 'decommodification' on the same basis as table 4.5's other two indicators of social democracy, then the Netherlands – together with Denmark, Norway and Sweden – once again constitute the clear core of the social democratic cluster. Sweden and Denmark would top the revised list, with twelve points. But the Netherlands would tie with Norway on ten. Their nearest rivals would be Finland and Belgium, scoring eight; and after that comes a group of four countries scoring six points, which clearly constitutes the core of the 'moderate' cluster along the social democratic dimension.

5 Background expectations

The aim of this book is essentially to rank-order Germany, the Netherlands and the United States – and the welfare regimes that they represent – in terms of how successful they are in achieving the various social and economic welfare goals ordinarily associated with welfare regimes. Based on our theoretical models of welfare regimes (chapter 3) and what we know about the specific countries taken as representatives of them (chapter 4), we are now in a position to set out some background expectations in that regard.

This chapter's discussion is merely meant to sketch the background, the received wisdom, against which our study is set. The full implications of the alternative regime logics will be elaborated, and tested, in chapters 7 to 16. However, a sample of what might ordinarily be expected on the basis of existing theories and evidence might helpfully set the scene for those more detailed analyses that follow.

In explicating that received wisdom, we will essentially be following Esping-Andersen's *The Three Worlds of Welfare Capitalism* (1990). But as we said before, those models are not uniquely his own. They are common currency among most cross-national welfare-state researchers. Esping-Andersen's is simply the clearest and most authoritative statement of a broader theoretical structure which he shares with many others.

5.1 Policy priorities

In many ways, welfare-capitalist regimes all harbour similar normative goals and just prioritize them differently. Presumably, though, priorities matter. Whether that presumption is correct – how much difference different priorities actually make to the performance of alternative welfare regimes – is of course precisely the question which our study is designed to address. There may well be important differences between what regimes say and what they do. Still, professed priorities undeniably exert a powerful influence in shaping preliminary impressions and background expectations.

The liberal welfare regime assigns priority to economic growth and efficiency. Within its specifically social welfare sector, the liberal regime ostensibly strives to avoid work disincentives and 'welfare dependency', and to alleviate poverty by targeting welfare benefits narrowly on those in greatest need. The corporatist welfare regime also seeks strong economic performance. But it gives priority to social stability (particularly in the form of households' income stability) and to social integration. The social democratic welfare regime values all these goals too. But it attaches relatively higher priority to reducing poverty, inequality and unemployment.

These varying priorities in turn give rise to expectations about differential performance. Assuming each welfare regime does what it says it is going to do (which is of course a dubious assumption), we would naturally assume that some regimes will achieve some goals better than others. Here we will elaborate the expectations for differential regime performance to which those differing priorities give rise.

5.1.1   Economic performance and efficiency

Successful economic performance is the top priority of liberal capitalist regimes, but it is also a high priority (or anyway a major constraint) for all others. In liberal regimes, the overall aim is to achieve high economic growth rates. As a means to this, liberal regimes want to maintain high levels of employment (these days for both women and men) and, more generally, a flexible labour market in which wages rise and fall in different sectors and labour is reallocated according to demand. In framing tax and transfer policies (income tax, welfare benefits and so on), liberal regimes are anxious to avoid creating work disincentives and welfare dependency that would get in the way of any of that.

The liberal economic worldview goes something like this. 'High replacement rates' (people receiving pretty much the same from social benefits when not working as they would have done from working) give rise to large work disincentives. Those in turn encourage 'welfare dependency' and discourage labour force participation. The combined result of too many wealth-takers and too few wealth-makers is a lower rate of economic growth. Lower growth of course normally means that people in general enjoy less of an increase in their material standard of living (disposable income) than they would in a high-growth regime.

That classically liberal economic worldview is not totally rejected by corporatists and social democrats. Instead, they tend mainly to question the magnitude of work disincentive effects ('Do many people really choose to remain on welfare, even if replacement rates are high?') and

Expectation 1: The United States would be expected to provide lower income
replacement rates through public transfers (social insurance and social
assistance) to people of prime working age (25–59) than Germany and
the Netherlands.

Expectation 2: Over ten years the United States would be expected to have
higher employment rates than Germany and the Netherlands.

Expectation 3: Over ten years the United States would be expected to have
lower welfare dependency rates (i.e. a lower percentage of households
headed by people of working age whose main source of income was
public transfers) than Germany and the Netherlands.

Expectation 4: The United States would be expected to achieve a higher rate
of economic growth per capita than Germany and the Netherlands.

Expectation 5: In the ten year period, more Americans would be expected to
have experienced an increase in their material standard of living
(disposable income) than Germans or Dutch.

Expectation 6: In the ten years, the average increase in the material standard
of living of Americans would be expected to be higher than of Germans
or Dutch.

Expectation 7: In the United States welfare benefits (social assistance) would
be expected to be targeted more tightly than in Germany or the
Netherlands.

Figure 5.1. Expectations regarding economic performance and
efficiency.

whether policies pressuring low-skill, low-income people at the bottom
end of the labour market – forcing them to take paid work – make much
contribution to overall economic efficiency and growth (Flora 1986;
Korpi 1985; Therborn 1986; Gregory 1996).

Given all that, we would naturally expect that the United States, as a
liberal welfare regime, would have lower replacement rates, lower rates of
welfare dependency, higher employment rates and higher economic
growth than Germany and the Netherlands. (As between the other two
countries we have no particular expectations along any of these dimensions.) If the liberal economic worldview is correct, we would further
expect that the material standard of living of Americans would be both

higher and grow more quickly than that of either the Germans or the Dutch.[1]

Liberal welfare regimes also aim to achieve a high level of 'target efficiency' in delivering welfare benefits. This means delivering benefits only to the poor, and then only paying enough to bring people up to the poverty line but not above it (Beckerman 1979a, b). Thus we would expect the liberal US regime to achieve higher target efficiency than Germany and the Netherlands. Neither a social democratic nor a corporatist regime accords high priority to targeting, so we would have no particular expectation as to how Germany and the Netherlands would compare on this dimension.

5.1.2   Poverty, income inequality and unemployment

Social democratic welfare regimes claim to give higher priority to reducing poverty, inequality and involuntary unemployment than do corporatist or liberal regimes. Hence it is reasonable to expect that the Dutch government would achieve lower poverty rates, lower income inequality and lower unemployment than the German and American governments. We would would also expect to find evidence not just of more egalitarian outcomes in the Netherlands but also of greater redistributive impact of government through the tax-benefit system there.

It is not clear *a priori* how one would expect corporatist regimes like Germany and liberal regimes like the US to compare with one another on poverty and inequality measures. On the one hand, a corporatist regime aims as a matter of priority to maintain social stability and the social status of families, which plainly implies a commitment to maintaining relativities between families in circumstances where government intervention is needed (during illness, old age, unemployment and so forth). Reflecting on this, Esping-Andersen (1990) writes: 'the state's emphasis on upholding status differences means that its redistributive impact is negligible'. On the other hand, if an upper-middle class breadwinner falls unemployed, a large injection of funds is required to maintain the financial standing of his or her family. Thus, in order to maintain status differences when families (especially high-status families) fall on hard times, the state would need to do a lot of redistributing, in the sense of shifting a lot of money to people who are presently (though were not previously) poor.[2]

---

[1]   Much of the interest in testing these expectations will lie in seeing whether all links in the chain connecting replacement rates to high economic growth hold good. If any of those links fail, then the whole sequence of reasoning is destroyed. To foreshadow what comes later, chapter 7 will show this to be the case. This confirms, perhaps, the economic superiority of more cooperative social democratic or corporatist-style solutions to the economic problem (Soskice 1991; Goldthorpe 1994; Visser and Hemerijck 1997).

[2]   Of course this point bears only on the redistributive impact of government, not on how one

Liberal regimes intend to target welfare benefits, particularly second-tier benefits, on those in greatest need. In itself, that would be expected to have redistributive, egalitarian outcomes. But the liberal concomitant is an enthusiastic embrace of capitalism and market forces, which could be expected to lead to comparatively high levels of poverty, inequality and involuntary unemployment, since in many respects capitalism is a doctrine of failure: it says, in essence, 'let the strong succeed and devil take the hindmost' (Thurow 1996).

On balance, we would expect to find that corporatist regimes are more effective in reducing poverty and inequality than liberal ones. In their anxiety to reduce work disincentives, liberal regimes tend to provide low coverage rates and particularly low replacement rates. Corporatist regimes, in contrast, typically offer earnings-related benefits which offer substantially higher replacement rates to all (or nearly all) households.

Ideal-typical social democratic regimes, as described by Esping-Andersen, are committed to minimizing involuntary unemployment, in part through active labour market (job training) programmes. From our discussion in section 4.3.3, we know that active labour market policies have become a major emphasis in Dutch political rhetoric only in more recent years.[3] Nevertheless, Dutch expenditures on active labour market policies have been relatively high (albeit nowhere near as high as in Sweden) throughout this period.[4] And in any case, consistent with our approach of evaluating regimes in terms of their normative goals, we expect that the Netherlands should have the lowest level of involuntary unemployment among the three countries.

A corporatist welfare regime, too, emphasizes the labour market attachments of the head of household. It is through the household head's labour market attachments that the family is integrated into the larger society, and it is on the basis of the household head's labour market attachments that the family is entitled to corporatist welfare benefits. But in the corporatist regime, of course, it is only the household head who needs to be employed, whereas in the liberal regime it is much more a case of 'everyone for him or herself'. Thus, we make no prediction as to unemployment rates between Germany and the US.

The expectations set out in figure 5.2 refer to short-term (one-year), medium-term (five-year) and long-term (ten-year) poverty and inequality. For the sake of clarity, we list these expectations in detailed and somewhat repetitive fashion, with apologies for the inevitable inelegance.

The reasoning behind the first five expectations (8 to 12) listed in figure 5.2 has already been stated. Expectation 13 addresses issues of cumulat-

might expect poverty and inequality to compare in corporatist and liberal regimes.
[3] See also: Kloosterman (1994); Hemerijck and van Kersbergen (1997).
[4] OECD (1996c, table 2.9, p. 30).

ive inequality. People are excluded from the possibility of a normal 'mainstream' lifestyle if they are at the bottom of the heap in terms of many or all of the resources which are valued in that society (Runciman 1966; Sen 1973; Townsend 1979; Walzer 1983). The United States, as a liberal capitalist regime, endorses equality of opportunity but not of outcomes. We would therefore expect it to rank highest on cumulative inequalities.[5] A social democratic regime like the Netherlands is of course concerned to reduce social inequality across the board; and while that does not necessarily entail a specific commitment to reducing the cumulativeness of those inequalities, we would nonetheless expect it to turn in a strong performance in terms of reducing cumulative inequalities. Germany, as a corporatist regime, aims to promote social integration, and insofar as cumulative inequalities signal the existence of an unintegrated underclass we might expect it too to make major efforts to reduce cumulative inequality. Thus we would have no firm expectations as to how Germany and the Netherlands might compare along this dimension.

The rationale for the final four expectations listed in figure 5.2 is just this: in all Western countries there are considerable fluctuations in people's annual market incomes, so that inequality of market (especially labour) incomes is less in the long term than in the short term. This implies that even if governments did absolutely nothing, poverty rates and inequality would be lower in the long term. Supposing governments had target levels of poverty and inequality, they would need to do less redistribution to meet those targets in the long term than in the short term.[6] Researchers in both government and academia who conduct computer simulations of the effects of government taxes and benefits routinely build assumptions of diminishing redistribution into their simulations (Falkingham, Hills and Lessof 1993; Harding 1993b). The panel data enable us to assess whether this is justified.

5.1.3   Social stability and social integration

Social stability and social integration are the primary welfare goals of corporatist regimes. The social stability here in view pertains primarily to three domains: income stability; family stability; and stability of attachment to the labour force for men of working age.

[5] The panel studies provide measures of only a few dimensions of inequality. In this book we deem that people suffer from cumulative inequalities – they are socially excluded – if they are in the lowest quintile (20 per cent) of the population in each of three dimensions: post-government income, annual hours of paid work and years of education.

[6] Several of those assumptions might of course be dubious (not least that governments have implicit but unpublished targets for poverty and inequality). But hopefully our evidence might shed light, however indirectly, on those issues.

---

(1) <u>Poverty</u>

<u>Expectation 8</u>: Short-, medium- and long-term poverty would be expected to be lower in the Netherlands than in Germany, and lower in Germany than the United States.

<u>Expectation 9</u>: The short-, medium- and long-term redistributive impact of government through taxes and benefits would be expected to achieve more poverty reduction in the Netherlands than Germany and more in Germany than the United States.

(2) <u>Income inequality</u>

<u>Expectation 10</u>: Short-, medium- and long-term income inequality would be expected to be lower in the Netherlands than Germany, which in turn would have less inequality than the United States.

<u>Expectation 11</u>: The redistributive impact of government on income inequality would be expected to be greatest in the Netherlands, in between in Germany and least in the United States.

(3) <u>Unemployment</u>

<u>Expectation 12</u>: The Netherlands would be expected to have lower rates of short-, medium and long-term involuntary unemployment than Germany and the United States. (No prediction is made as between the latter two countries.)

(4) <u>Cumulative inequality</u>

<u>Expectation 13</u>: Over ten years the US would have the highest percentage of working-age people who suffered cumulative inequalities, being in the bottom quintile of post-government income, annual hours of paid work and years of education. (No prediction is made as between the latter two countries.)

(5) <u>Differences over time: poverty and inequality</u>

<u>Expectation 14</u>: In all three countries long-term poverty rates would be expected to be lower than medium-term, which in turn would be lower than annual poverty rates.

<u>Expectation 15</u>: In all three countries long-term income inequality would be expected to be lower than medium–term, which would be lower than annual inequality.

(6) <u>Differences over time: government redistribution</u>

<u>Expectation 16</u>: In all three countries the effects of government redistribution on poverty rates would be expected to diminish over time; long-term redistribution would be expected to be less than medium-term, which in turn would be expected to be less than short-term.

<u>Expectation 17</u>: In all three countries the effects of government redistribution on income inequality would be expected to diminish over time; long-term redistribution would be less than medium-term, which would be expected to be less than short-term.

Figure 5.2. Expectations regarding poverty, inequality and unemployment.

A corporatist welfare regime aims to maintain household incomes at a fairly stable level – both in normal times and, more particularly, when adverse events (ill-health, unemployment and so on) interrupt or end the ability of the (usually) male breadwinner to earn market income. The corporatist regime also promotes family stability, viewing as ideal a family in which a working-aged male head works and the wife stays at home with dependent children. Family instability (of which we take the change of household head to be a powerful indicator[7]) is thus something which corporatists would clearly wish to avoid. So too is instability of labour force attachment (intermittent employment, punctuated by bouts of non-employment), at least as regards men of prime working age. Clearly, then, we would expect that the German corporatist regime would rank highest on social stability.

We would expect the Dutch social democratic regime to rank second. A social democratic regime, through its redistributive tax-benefit arrangements, intends to stabilize incomes in hard times and, through active labour market programmes, seeks to maintain high male (and female) employment levels and hence labour income in normal times. Because of its corporatist past (discussed in section 4.3.1), we would also expect the Netherlands to rank quite highly on measures of family stability, in a way that a more archetypical social democratic regime might not.

We would expect that the United States, as a liberal regime encouraging individualism, opportunity and social mobility, would have low levels of social stability. Social mobility and social stability are, of course, almost opposites of one another.

Social integration and social stability are obviously closely related goals. Indeed, all our expectations about stability can equally well be read as expectations about social integration. Two more integration-specific expectations ought to be added, however. The traditional corporatist norm for an integrated family requires not only that the male breadwinner be in full-time work, but also that the female partner stay at home if there are dependent children.[8]

Thus, we would expect that Germany had the highest percentage of female partners who stayed at home. The Netherlands would be expected to rank second: as a social democratic regime, of course, it should aim to create conditions under which both women and men can choose whether to do paid work or stay at home (Esping-Andersen 1990); but due to its corporatist past, and a cohort of middle-aged women whose non-working

---

[7] The change of household head is often a signal of some adverse event, such as marital separation or death; and even when the precipitating event is favourable or perhaps neutral in character (marriage, repartnering, a young single person leaving home) it certainly indicates family instability.

[8] For our purposes 'staying at home' will be defined as doing paid work for less than ten hours a week.

---

(1) Income stability

    Expectation 18: Over a ten-year period, stability of household market (pre-government) incomes would be expected to be highest in corporatist Germany, second-highest in the Netherlands and lowest in the United States.

    Expectation 19: Over ten years, stability of post-government (post-tax, post-transfer) income would be expected to be highest in Germany, second-highest in the Netherlands and lowest in the United States.

    Expectation 20: For individuals whose head of household changed one or more times in ten years, post-government income stability would be expected to be highest in Germany, second-highest in the Netherlands and lowest in the United States.

(2) Family stability

    Expectation 21: Over ten years, changes of head of household would be expected to be fewest in Germany, in between in the Netherlands and highest in the United States.

    Expectation 22: Divorce rates would be expected to be lowest in Germany, in between in the Netherlands and highest in the United States.

(3) Stability of labour force attachment

    Expectation 23: Among working-age males (25–29) the highest percentage would be expected to be in full-time work (thirty hours or more) in Germany; the Netherlands would be expected to have the second-highest percentage, and the United States the lowest percentage.

(4) Social intergration and social exclusion

    Expectation 24: Germany had the highest percentage of female partners in families with dependent children (under sixteen) who stayed at home, the Netheralnds had the second-highest percentage, and the United States the lowest percentage.

Figure 5.3. Expectations regarding social stability and integration.

habits were formed in that past period, it is only to be expected that more partners would stay at home there than in a less mixed social democracy such as Sweden or a liberal regime like the United States. As a liberal capitalist society which intends to minimize work disincentives and promote high employment levels, the United States is expected to have the lowest rate of partners staying at home.

5.1.4   *Autonomy*

In chapter 3 we discussed autonomy, which is a goal of most welfare regimes if a priority of none. While the panel surveys contain no data about subjective perceptions of autonomy ('feeling free'), they do enable us to estimate people's autonomy measured in terms of leisure time and, of course, of their disposable incomes. We can therefore measure autonomy in resource terms, with people being considered autonomous if they have both sufficient leisure and sufficient money to be free to make a wide range of choices.

We desist from formulating any formal expectations about the relative rankings of our three countries on autonomy, though. That is simply because we have been deriving those formal expectations from the internal logic of regime types, and of course none of these three countries explicitly proclaims itself to be aiming to facilitate those sorts of autonomy for people.

Still, 'time and money' sorts of autonomy might be an accidental by-product of various other things that various other sorts of welfare regimes intentionally do. For example, a liberal regime, by promoting individualism, opportunity and social mobility, might be thought to promote autonomy of a sort. Or an ideal-typical social democratic regime might promote autonomy by enabling women as well as men to have an unfettered choice between paid work and home duties, or by allocating benefits to individuals rather than to households. Or a corporatist regime might promote autonomy through its tolerance of high rates of non-employment, particularly among homemakers and early retirees. We will leave all that as an open question and simply investigate how the countries rank on autonomy.

5.2   Comparisons in the round

Having formulated all those specific propositions, we hasten to add that we will not be undertaking any formal statistical hypothesis testing relating to them. (With a sample of only three countries, that would hardly make sense.) Nevertheless, those constitute the sorts of propositions that we will be exploring in chapters 7 to 12 below. Those are the sorts of 'background expectations' that anyone steeped in the existing literature on comparative welfare regimes is bound to have internalized and bring to bear on these issues. On the evidence we shall be presenting below, many of them are perfectly correct, but many of the more important among them quite clearly are not.

Beyond generating those more specific sorts of expectations, the theoretical models in chapter 3 also conjure up certain more general images. Each of these different models represents a whole worldview – a view about what things are important for us collectively to do, and about how it is possible and appropriate for us collectively to do them. The more general expectation to emerge from discussion of such theoretical models is that these worldviews, and the activities and accomplishments associated with them, will indeed be found empirically to hang together.

The larger expectation, then, is that each welfare regime will have the distinctive 'profile' which its underlying theory would lead us to expect. Each should be expected to aim especially at certain sorts of results; each should be expected to try to achieve those results through certain mechanisms. Other regimes may, of course, achieve some of the same results and may even use some of the same tools. But looking at them in the round, the overall profile presented by each welfare regime is predicted to be different, in ways picked out by its theoretical underpinnings.

That is the second and larger test of the theories we will mount, in chapters 13 to 16 below. There, we will be looking at the goals which each welfare regime explicitly sets for itself. Our aims there are twofold. Firstly, we want to see, in vaguely absolute terms, whether regimes achieve the results that their underlying theories predict. Secondly, we want to see in vaguely comparative terms whether the welfare regimes that are theoretically predicted to be particularly concerned with certain goals actually are more concerned with them (or anyway more successful in attaining them) than other welfare regimes theoretically predicted to be less concerned with those goals.

In those chapters, we will also be looking at the particular mechanisms which each welfare regime theory adopts as its preferred instruments for pursuing those goals. The theoretical underpinnings of each model lead us to expect that agents working within such a welfare regime would push and pull certain policy levers in certain ways, that they would aim at certain intermediate goals, that they would leave characteristic footprints in the side-effects that their policies produce. Again, agents working within other welfare regimes may sometimes accidentally or incidentally hit the same levers. But our prediction would be that those whose theoretical self-understanding enjoins them to implement these programmes of action will do so systematically rather than sporadically, intensively rather than intermittently. Both in absolute and in comparative terms, our theoretical models therefore lead us to expect each welfare regime to be associated with a disproportionately high devotion to the peculiar bundle of instrumentalities associated with that regime.

6   Testing the theories with panels

In the chapters that follow, we analyse the 'real worlds' of welfare capitalism through the lens provided by socio-economic panel data from the US, Germany and the Netherlands. Furthermore, we analyse those worlds of welfare capitalism through the evidence of these panels alone. We resist the temptation to supplement our panel data with further information compiled from elsewhere.

There is of course much evidence from other sources which could be woven into these analyses. But the selection from among all that material, and the choice between methods for incorporating it, would inevitably be matters on which people's judgments would naturally differ. We have few illusions that our conclusions will be utterly uncontroversial. But we hope that by sticking tightly to the panel data we can avoid gratuitously introducing other sorts of controversy. Whether or not it is the whole story, ours is – if not quite indisputably, anyway minimally disputably – the story that these panel data tell.

The panel studies upon which we draw have, of course, been organized by other scholars, with rather different issues and emphases in mind. For many of the propositions of interest to us, therefore, the tests we concoct using these panel data are inevitably not the very best imaginable. All we would care to claim is that the indicators we identify are the best that can be found within the data sets before us.

6.1   Panels and their alternatives

6.1.1   The power of panel data

Evaluations of welfare states ought be based on the real experiences of real people. There are many different ways in which welfare-state studies might misrepresent the real experiences of real people. One classic way is by taking the legal formalities too seriously. Many previous studies, when judging the coverage or generosity of social programmes, literally read their results off the statute books, assuming just because the regulations stipulate that certain benefits should be paid at certain levels under certain circumstances that this is what actually happens on the ground.[1] Assumptions such as these need only to be stated in order to be discredited.

Just as we cannot simply assume government programmes work the way they are supposed to work, neither can we simply assume that what is true of a person at one moment in time is true at all moments in time. Real people's lives are temporally extended, in ways that are only very imperfectly captured by the freeze-frame annual 'snapshots' of the sort found in ordinary cross-sectional reports based on episodic surveys or government statistics.

Our aim in this book is to use panel analysis to assess the 'real' worlds of welfare capitalism – regime performance over ten years – rather than relying on snapshots or accepting government programmes at face value. Here we will mention, briefly, three crucial ways in which the use of panel data is an immensely powerful tool in studying the sorts of questions with which welfare-state studies ought to be centrally concerned.

6.1.1.1 The longer term matters more   Panel studies are ideal – in certain ways virtually indispensable – for assessing the achievements and failures of welfare states. All of the goals that welfare states standardly pursue are basically medium- to long-term goals. Some make almost literally no sense in a short-term perspective, others just matter a lot more in the longer term.

Take poverty, for example. Short-term poverty can certainly be unpleasant, but in the larger scheme of things it might sometimes matter hardly at all. Many of us have been temporarily poor as students or in between jobs. It is no fun to be forced to use up savings, borrow and tighten your belt, but it is not life-threatening (provided of course you have slack, savings or wealthier friends or family from whom to borrow). Medium- and long-term poverty on the other hand often causes serious distress, detaching people from their normal social contacts, leisure pursuits and 'mainstream' lifestyles.

Or, for another example, take the objectives of social stability and integration. To say that 'a welfare state should provide effective income maintenance to see families though hard times', or that 'individuals in society should be effectively integrated into family life, voluntary organisations and the labour force' is to take at least a medium-term perspective on society. To say those desiderata were satisfied is to say that

---

[1] Almost all calculations of 'replacement rates' suffer that difficulty, for example. See, e.g., Korpi (1989); Esping-Andersen (1990); Palme (1990a, b); Whiteford (1995); OECD (1996e).

we had actually observed, for a period of years, that most family incomes were stable and that most individuals were integrated rather than excluded from social institutions and opportunities. To describe a society as stable or integrated 'in the short term' would be almost literally meaningless.

6.1.1.2 Tracking individuals through time A second reason for using panel data is to enable us to track the same individuals through time. When we do, the world turns out to be much less stable than it seems, seen through the prism of successive cross-sections.

Recall in this connection the central finding of the University of Michigan Panel Study of Income Dynamics (Duncan *et al.* 1984), which was alluded to in chapter 1 and which turns out to be replicated surprisingly well even in what had long been presumed to be the more stable economies of continental Europe (Duncan, Gustafsson *et al.* 1993):

- Just looking at cross-sectional snapshots, it seemed as if earnings in America were pretty stable over time. The top 10 per cent of American earners get roughly the same proportion of national income, year in and year out (and indeed decade in and decade out); and so on down the earnings ladder.
- The natural inference from that aggregate-level stability in earnings was that individual-level earnings were similarly stable. One tended to presume (but from aggregate-level data, one could only presume) that people received more or less the same income year in and year out simply because the same proportion of the population received more or less the same proportion of national income year in and year out.
- But when the University of Michigan team followed the earning patterns of 5,000 American families, going back to the same individuals every year for ten years to ask them what they actually earned each year, it turned out that this presumption was radically in error. Many people's earnings went up from one year to the next, while many others' went down.
- There was considerable stability in the gross aggregates, despite major fluctuations at the individual level, simply because those fluctuations largely offset one another. But while the overall aggregates remained the same – roughly the same percentage of national income went to the top 10 per cent of earners, year in and year out – it turned out to be wrong to infer, as one naturally had been doing, that this was because the same people occupied the same positions year in and year

out. The overall pattern of distributions – the aggregates – remained much the same. But the individuals occupying the various slots in the income league table differed dramatically from year to year.[2]

These differences really do matter, not just (obviously) for the people themselves but also for social scientists trying to understand what has been happening to them. We used to assume, from the stability of the aggregate statistics, that we have a more or less permanent socially excluded underclass reliant upon welfare, and a more or less permanently fixed group of producers with more or less reliable earnings.

If that were so, welfare-state policies would invariably take from the former and give to the latter. There would be permanent winners and permanent losers in such a stable pattern of redistribution, and only certain sorts of moral values – and only certain sorts of political strategies – which would in turn be able to sustain that practice. But if, as the Michigan Panel Study of Income Dynamics suggests, earnings fluctuate so dramatically that virtually anyone might need to fall back on welfare benefits at least occasionally, then one year's benefactor may turn into next year's beneficiary. A much broader range of moral values and political strategies might be able to sustain transfer policies, on that basis.

The substantive point is an important one, and one to which we shall be returning in subsequent chapters. It is the more methodological point which we want to emphasize here, however. The point is just that important substantive findings like these can only emerge through panel studies tracking particular individuals through time – re-interviewing the same people year in and year out. It is an important fact about the world which could be (and, as it happened here, would be) obscured, were we to confine our attention to aggregate statistics about overall distributions or general patterns alone.

6.1.1.3 Linking before and after   Finally, by tracking the same individuals through time, panel studies also allow us to link our images of people 'before' and 'after' key events, in a way that is impossible using cross-sectional data alone.

Thus, for example, panels enable us to assess the impact of major life events and experiences on people's incomes. We can estimate the impact of divorce, remarriage, unemployment, birth of children and so on, on pre- and post-government incomes. Clearly such estimates only become

[2] See similarly Duncan, Hill and Hoffman (1988); Levy (1977); Ruggles (1990, ch. 5); Bane and Ellwood (1986; 1994, esp. chs. 2–3).

possible with panel data which record people's income before and after these major life events.

For another example alluded to at the outset of this section, panel data enable us to calculate *actual* replacement rates of public benefits, at the extent to which state benefits really do (or do not) replace previous market income for individuals or households whose earning capacity has been impaired. Using panel data, we can compare a person's income in a period when he or she was working with the same person's income in an immediately subsequent period when he or she relying instead on state benefits. The capacity to calculate actual replacement rates, rather than just reading nominal replacement rates off the statute books, is once again a significant gain in evaluating welfare-state performance.

6.1.2   Alternatives to panels

Prior to panel studies, we had little recourse but to rely upon successive waves of cross-sectional 'snapshot' information. Those snapshots can be sequenced, one after the other, to form the basis of 'longitudinal, time-series' analyses. But despite all the enormously sophisticated ways these cross-sectional snapshots can be mathematically manipulated, snapshots they ultimately remain.

Great strides have been made in recent years toward collecting such cross-sectional snapshots on a comparable basis cross-nationally. The Luxembourg Income Study aims to collect unit-record level income data on a comparable basis across a range of countries in successive waves (roughly five-yearly, though many countries are falling badly behind).[3]

The LIS file has many virtues, not least of which is its individual unit-record data on genuinely comparable items across countries. Although the data represent individual unit records, however, they are not necessarily the same individuals in each wave of the study. There is no way, in the standard LIS file, to track particular individuals across time.[4] That is the great advantage of panel data of the sort we shall be using here.

In the absence of actual panels, the best that could traditionally be done was to construct computerized 'micro-simulations'. This involves constructing large synthetic samples of national populations, attributing known population characteristics to sample members,

[3] Smeeding, O'Higgins and Rainwater (1990); Atkinson, Rainwater and Smeeding (1995).
[4] Ironically, the data supplied to the LIS study for some countries actually comes from national socio-economic panels, stripped for LIS deposit of the on-going individual or household identifiers (or, more precisely, assigned new non-matching ones for the purposes of LIS deposit). The new PACO (Panel Comparability project) attached to LIS promises eventually to provide cross-national data on a genuinely comparable basis.

and then 'aging' the sample in ways estimated to be normal for that population.[5] 'Aging' the sample involves, for example, having sample members marry, divorce, become ill, recover or die at the rates usual for the nation as a whole.

Such micro-simulation is highly useful in estimating the short- and long-term benefits and costs to different sections of the population of introducing alternative taxes and benefits. For that reason, micro-simulation is now routinely used in Western countries as an aid to budgeting, where equity or distributional effects are a significant concern. Invaluable though such micro-simulations obviously are for policy advice, these estimates can of course be no better (and may well be worse) than the historical data upon which they are based (including cross-sectional studies and, occasionally, panel data). Furthermore, micro-simulations can of course only project forwards present patterns: within such methodologies, there is no way to anticipate such genuine discontinuities as might occur.

While micro-simulation is useful for estimating alternative futures, panel studies are clearly the most valuable resource for evaluating the performance of welfare states in the recent past. Micro-simulations are essentially predictions of what will occur. The evidence of socio-economic panel studies testifies to what actually has occurred. Thus, where the real-life evidence of panels diverges from the results of mere simulations, the evidence of the panels is decisively to be preferred.[6]

6.2   The structure of the panel data

The basic structure of panel data is a file tracking the same people through time.[7] The same people are re-interviewed, year in and year out.[8]

[5] See, e.g., Galler and Wagner (1986); Falkingham, Hills and Lessof (1993); Harding (1993a); Falkingham and Hills (1995); Sutherland (1995).

[6] One example, already on the record, concerns estimates of the long-term redistributive impact of the German state (cf. Galler and Wagner 1987; Headey and Krause 1994, p. 148). Other findings generalizing that proposition will emerge in the course of subsequent chapters.

[7] The fullest introduction to panel studies is through the annual publication of the US Panel Study on Income Dynamics, *Five Thousand American Families* (Duncan and Morgan 1973 *et seq.*). See further Atkinson, Bourguignon and Morrisson (1992, section 3).

[8] Comparing annual panel results with those of the US Census Bureau's Survey of Income and Program Participation, which compiles its statistics monthly, provides some measure of how much information might be lost through yearly rather than monthly surveys. The results of that US Census Bureau survey suggest that *circa* 1984 poverty spells lasting four months – long enough to be genuinely problematic, but short enough to be masked in annual income statistics – might have affected fully a tenth of Americans (calculated from Ruggles 1990, Table. 5.2, p. 97; see more generally pp. 90–103). Thus we must always recall that, in addition to whatever inter-year volatility annual panels reveal, there is also considerable intra-year volatility which they mask.

They are assigned a unique identifier, which stays with them through time; and the information they supply each year is recorded under their personal identifier number.

6.2.1   The nature of the panels

Before describing the three panels separately, it is good to note important features they have in common. They are all based on very large national representative samples, and they are all official or semi-official studies funded by government. They all began with samples of 10,000 people – very large indeed by survey research standards – and these people have been re-interviewed every year for at least ten years. There are now about 26,000 individuals on file for the Dutch and German surveys and over 30,000 in the United States.

National panels begin with the selection of large representative samples, drawn according to a well-understood, reliable set of procedures for 'national stratified probability sampling'. These procedures yield samples which appear to be broadly accurate demographic miniatures (in terms of sex, age, income, education, ethnic background and so on) of the nation as a whole.[9] Women are easier to contact than men, and a little more willing to give interviews, while young mobile people are hard to catch up with (they are never at home!). Neither are the homeless represented in standard panels.[10] In general, though, checks comparing the demographics of large national samples with census data show the samples to be highly reliable.

Over the years the representativeness of panels is maintained by adding the families of 'split-offs'.[11] Split-offs, in this jargon, are individuals who leave the home of the family to which they belonged when first interviewed and set up their own household. Thus when a young person leaves home to get married, or a couple separates with one of them leaving the marital home, the split-off and his or her entire new household join the panel. The consequence is that the number of panel members in these already large national surveys increases over time.

Panel members thus need to be given two identifying numbers by

[9] These panels are reweighted, as discussed below, towards known population attributes such as age, sex, marital status and (in the US and Germany but not the Netherlands) racial or ethnic background.

[10] A major effort by the Bundesarbeitsgemeinschaft Wohnungshilfe (1994, p. 115) to enumerate the West German homeless in 1990 produced an estimate of some 130,000. Adding that number to the rolls of the poor would have increased the 1990 German poverty rate from 7.5 to 10 per cent. Obviously, homelessness of that magnitude is a non-trivial issue for poverty research, but other ways must be used to track the homeless: it cannot be done through panels.

[11] Additional samples also add immigrants and other newcomers to the population.

survey managers. As we have already said, each person has a unique individual identifier, which remains the same over the years; but because people can and do change households, they are given a separate household identifier, which they share with other members of the same household, and which of course changes if they change households.

The idea behind including split-offs is to maintain a sample which is demographically representative of the nation. Checks comparing the characteristics of panel members with census data show that the procedure works very satisfactorily. In general terms, panel sampling procedures mirror birth, marriage and death in the population at large. Individuals join the panel if they are born into an existing panel household, or if they marry or cohabit with a panel member. They leave only at death, or if they decline to continue serving as respondents, or if they cannot be traced by survey managers.[12]

In all panels, drop-out rates (technically, 'panel attrition') pose something of a threat to sample representativeness.[13] Drop-out rates are always worst in the second wave (second year) of a panel, when initially reluctant respondents decide not to continue. Typically around 8 to 10 per cent of first-wave panel members drop out at wave two. After that, panel attrition rapidly declines, with typically 2 to 3 per cent dropping out each subsequent year. As noted, these people are numerically more than compensated for by split-offs and their new households.

Attrition rates differ, however, among different sections of the population. Young residentially mobile people (especially young men) and poorer people both tend to drop out of panels at higher rates than others. To adjust for this, panel results – including all the results in this book – are routinely weighted to bring each sample sub-group back to its correct proportion in the population as a whole.

The principles behind weightings are straightforward. Suppose the population is exactly 50 per cent male and 50 per cent female, and the panel's initial sample was originally designed to reflect that fact. But suppose that panel attrition has been such that, in year six, the panel has 53 per cent women and 47 per cent men. Then to produce accurate results for the population as a whole it is necessary to multiply the women's results by $47/53$ and the men's results by $53/47$.

Simple though weighting might be in principle, in practice it can become quite a complicated business. The American, German and Dutch survey managers work out weights each year for each individual

---

[12] Or, less commonly, if they emigrate or are institutionalized.
[13] The steps described below have, however, been very successful in preventing any known biases from creeping in due to panel attrition in the American PSID (Becketti, Gould, Lilliard and Welch 1988; Atkinson, Bourguignon and Morrisson 1992, section 3).

and each household, based on multiple individual (or household) characteristics (such as the individual's age, the age of the head of household, the household's income, the level of education and so on). We routinely employ those weights in analysing these data.[14]

6.2.1.1 The American panel   The American Panel Study of Income Dynamics (PSID) was initially funded in 1968 by the Office of Economic Opportunity, the government agency coordinating President Johnson's 'War on Poverty', and run by the Survey Research Center of the University of Michigan under the leadership of James N. Morgan.

Initially the PSID study was based on 'five thousand families'.[15] Unlike the German and Dutch panels, there is in the American panel just one respondent per household, with the head or the head's partner answering on behalf of the whole family.

For the purposes of our study, we use the panel surveys for 1983 to 1992. While the data from the other two countries is later by two years (1985–1994), the 1992 data was simply the latest American data available at the time of writing. There are about 32,000 respondents on file for the 1983–92 period.

Since the PSID was initially commissioned by the Office of Economic Opportunity, which had a particular interest in studying poverty, poor people (including blacks) were deliberately oversampled. This suits us, since we are also especially concerned to study poverty and income inequality: the oversampling ensures that there are sufficient respondents in each cell, even of highly complex breakdowns of the population. But the oversampling of the poor also means that it is especially important in reporting the American results to use the appropriate 'weights' to bring the panel results back into line with the overall American population.

6.2.1.2 The German panel   The German Socio-Economic Panel (GSOEP) is funded by the federal government and is now run by the German Institute for Economic Research Panel Group, headed by Gert G. Wagner in Berlin. That Institute is one of the leading economic 'think tanks' required to provide joint economic reports to the federal government.

---

[14] Specifically, we employ the cross-sectional weights provided when analysing one-yearly data; and we employ the longitudinal weights provided when analysing data across more than one year. In analysing the Dutch panel data, we used only the cross-sectional weights provided by the survey managers and calculated longitudinal weights ourselves because of differences between the longitudinal weights provided by the Netherlands CBS and those employed by managers of the US and German surveys.

[15] Hence the title of the annual compilation of research reports emanating from the project (Duncan and Morgan 1973 *et seq*).

The GSOEP began in 1984 with a sample of 13,919 individuals in 5,921 households. In 1990, after the fall of the Berlin Wall but before re-unification, the panel was extended to East Germany. In this book, however, we restrict our analysis to the West German sample alone, and we use the last ten years of data available – 1985–94. For these years, there are about 26,000 respondents on file.

In the German panel, all household members aged sixteen and over are interviewed separately. An additional household interview form is also completed by the head of household or partner. This enables detailed cross-checks to be made on household income data, labour force partici-pation and other matters on which family members sometimes give slightly differing reports.

To cater for the particular interests of government and academics, there was also deliberate oversampling in the German panel. The five main immigrant (guestworker) groups in the country – Italians, Greeks, Yugoslavs (Serbs and Croats), Turks and Spaniards – were each initially represented by about a thousand respondents, so that their economic and labour force experiences could be analysed. Again, therefore, it is import-ant to use appropriate weights to compensate for this deliberate sample bias.

In the German case, the procedure of using split-off households to augment the panel has not been as effective in maintaining representa-tiveness as in the United States and the Netherlands. The principal reason is that since 1989 large numbers of immigrants, many of German background, have streamed in from Russia, Kazakhstan and Eastern Europe. Because these groups were not represented in the original panel, it was decided in 1995 to add a special new immigrant sample to the main panel. Of course, 1995 is just outside the period covered by this book, but we ought nevertheless to take note of the slightly higher figures for poverty and other small changes which can be observed when the extra sample is included.[16]

6.2.1.3 The Dutch panel The Dutch Socio-Economic Panel (SEP) is the most 'official' of the surveys, being run directly by the Netherlands' Central Bureau of Statistics. The SEP also began in 1984 with over 11,000 respondents. As in the German panel, all household members

---

[16] When in 1995 the new immigrant sample was added in order to catch the large numbers of immigrants who had come to Germany from Eastern Europe since 1989, preliminary analysis suggests that the difference in the poverty rate for Germany overall was some 0.7 per cent greater including that 'new immigrants' sample than it would have been without it. No doubt our estimates of German poverty rates are similarly slight underestimates for the last few years under study. But such small changes certainly would do nothing to change the comparative rankings of our three countries overall.

aged sixteen and over are interviewed separately. Initially, interviews were carried out twice a year (in April and October), but in 1990 it was decided to switch to once-a-year interviews.

For the purposes of our study, we use results of the panel surveys for 1985 to 1994. Again, the choice of years was dictated purely by data availability.[17] As in the German file, the total number of panel respondents for these years is close to 26,000.

In the Dutch panel no groups were deliberately over or undersampled, so weights there simply correct for panel attrition. Although Dutch weights do not make so much difference to the overall results as the American and German ones, we routinely use them nonetheless.

Certain other manipulations are also required to render income data from earlier years fully comparable with income data collected on a slightly different basis in later years.[18]

6.2.2   Bringing the three panel data files into line

In the early 1990s the German Institute of Economic Research (under Gert G. Wagner) and the Centre for Demography and Economics of Aging at Syracuse University (under Richard V. Burkhauser) began work to make the German and American data files as comparable as possible.[19]

This involved some redefinition of concepts and measures, including measures of household income and labour force participation, in order to bring the two sets of data into line. New variables had to be constructed which identically reflected those new definitions for the two countries. The latest available PSID–GSOEP Equivalent File which was available at the time of writing our book was that issued in 1997, covering the years 1980–92 for the United States and 1984–95 for Germany.

[17] As of 1990, income reporting in the Netherlands is done a year in arrears, with 1994 income not being collected until the 1995 survey. Hence 1994 was the last year for which complete data were effectively available, even though our results are based on an analysis of the 1995 survey.

[18] In panel survey methodology, there are two approaches to finding out what has happened to people over the past year. One, the so-called 'monthly' method, focuses primarily on what happened to respondents in the 'last month' and extrapolates to the whole year from that information (adjusted by rather more cursory information also collected about 'major changes' in people's employment, income, family circumstances and so on over the whole year). The alternative, the 'annual' method, asks people to provide the income figures they reported on their last year's tax return. The latter method is now preferred, and the Dutch data-collectors moved over to it in 1990. For 1989, they actually collected data in both ways, however; and comparing the results of the survey done in both ways reveals that reported incomes were marginally lower, particularly in low-income households, using the annual rather than the monthly method. We have used the 1989 differential to produce a regression equation for adjusting pre-1989 incomes to what they would have presumably been, had that data been collected in the new 'annual' way.

[19] For a brief description see Wagner, Burkhauser and Behringer (1993).

We had then to construct a ten-year Dutch file, using the same concepts and variables as in the latest PSID–GSOEP Equivalent File. Where items of particular interest had for some reason been omitted from the official Equivalent File, we also supplemented that with matching items from the larger original 'underlying' files for all countries. Among the important additions we made to the official Equivalent File were the particular programme headings (old age pension, child benefit, unemployment insurance, and so on) coded together in the official Equivalent File as 'public transfer payments'. In supplementing the Equivalent File in these ways, we have of course taken the greatest care to ensure that genuinely comparable data were drawn from each national data set.

Thus, the three panels are as internationally comparable as possible. Some small, ineliminable differences remain, as will be mentioned below. But we are reasonably confident that the international comparisons we report on poverty, inequality, income stability, social integration and so on are based on fundamentally valid and comparable measures.[20]

6.3 The variables: definition and operationalization

Many of the more specific indicators and measures we will be using will be introduced more fully as they first appear in the text, and we allude to them here only briefly, if at all. But there are certain other variables which recur throughout the text, for which it will be convenient to have a clear definition from the start.

6.3.1 Components of income

In assessing income, we are trying to judge people's material standard of living, or rather the potential level of consumption that their income affords them.[21] The components of household 'pre-government income' (which is mostly market income) are:

---

[20] Among many minor adjustments, one in particular merits special mention. People who simply fail to report whether or not they received income under too many headings are omitted from the files, and hence from our analysis. In the file released by the Dutch Central Bureau of Statistics, however, these incomplete returns were still included. Evidence from a much larger Dutch income survey (the Income Panel Survey) shows that the original SEP data has too many extremely low incomes, most likely for this reason. Judging also from the US and German experience, the effect of this is to disregard any respondent with a post-government income below the equivalent of Hfl. 2,000; hence, we have merely omitted from our analysis anyone with post-government equivalent income below Hfl. 2,000.

[21] If they choose not to spend all their income, their actual living standard will be below the potential afforded them by that income stream (Ringen 1988).

- labour income;[22]
- asset income (for example, income from rents, royalties and dividends);[23]
- private transfers (gifts; child support from ex-partners); and
- owner-occupiers' imputed net rent.

This last 'imputed net rent' item represents the 'rental income' which owner-occupiers notionally receive, *qua* owners, from themselves, *qua* tenants of the home in which they live (net of repairs and maintenance). While this element of owner-occupiers' imputed net rent is reported in the American and German files, it is not available in the Dutch panel. Rather than remove this component from American and German pre-government incomes, we decided simply to use the best measures available for each country. (This decision was made, we should add, only after calculating that omitting imputed rent in the United States and Germany would make only slight differences to poverty, income inequality, income stability and all other measures based on pre- or post-government income.)

What we shall call 'post-government income' (and others call 'household disposable income') is defined as pre-government income minus direct taxes plus government payments.[24] Those government payments (which we shall call 'public transfers') include both social security payments made from contributory social insurance funds and payments like family/child allowances and means-tested social assistance (welfare) payments funded by general taxes. Our measure of post-government income takes no account of indirect taxes (such as sales taxes or GST/VAT). Neither does it take any account of the value of non-cash benefits and services provided by government (only the value of US food stamps is included).[25] We further confine our own analysis to people with positive post-government incomes, again on grounds of presumed data unreliability in other cases.[26]

Labour income is recorded on an individual basis. To get total house-

---

[22] Comparing self-reported annual earnings to employer records shows these statistics to be highly reliable, at least in the early years of the American PSID (Duncan and Hill 1985).

[23] Information on net wealth, as distinct from the income stream flowing from it (asset income) appears only intermittently in some of these panels (and not at all in others).

[24] The Dutch data contain no direct evidence on taxes actually paid by individuals or households. In calculating post-government incomes, we have simply estimated how much would be owed in taxes by people, given their reported income.

[25] That omission is non-negligible, but its omission does not alter the relative rankings of the three countries here under study (Smeeding *et al.* 1993).

[26] Given all the components included in pre- and post-government income – which are supposed to include, for example, the income of the self-employed, income from assets and savings and private transfers from, e.g., family, friends and private charities – it is hard to see how anyone could have zero or less post-government income and remain alive.

hold labour income we aggregate across all individuals who are members of that household. Income under all other main headings – including asset income and transfer income from both public and private sources – is only ever ascribed to the household as a whole. The panel data themselves provide no direct information on how income is shared within households. (In calculating 'equivalent incomes', discussed below, it is simply assumed that all income coming into the household is pooled and shared equally among all members of the household.)

Finally, all income statistics have been adjusted for using the consumer price index. Thus, all incomes are expressed in terms of inflation-adjusted national currency units.

6.3.2   Equivalence scales

Cash incomes per household need to be adjusted by means of 'equivalence scales' reflecting household composition, in order to reflect the economies of scale that come from sharing larger households.

Many different equivalence scales have been used over the years. For certain purposes, the choice among these various equivalence scales seems to matter; for others it does not seem to make much difference.[27] We follow the recent OECD International Experts' recommendation in taking our 'equivalence scale' to be the 'square root of household size' (so, for example, the equivalence scale for a household of four would be two).[28]

In calculating 'equivalent income' for each household, we first add up all the incomes of all individuals in that household. We then divide that sum by the equivalence scale, as above. That 'equivalent income' is then imputed equally to every member of the household.[29]

[27] At the level of national aggregates, using different equivalent scales does not seem to make much difference to a nation's overall ranking in inequality league tables. But here, as elsewhere, what is sometimes of interest is precisely what national aggregates gloss over: using different equivalence scales will make different households appear poor (an equivalence scale weighting children relatively high, compared to adult members of the household, will make larger families appear poorer, for example). See Atkinson, Rainwater and Smeeding (1995); Buhmann et al. (1988); Hagenaars (1991); Coulter, Cowell and Jenkins (1992).

[28] Atkinson, Rainwater and Smeeding (1995). This procedure yields results which are close to the older 'modified OECD equivalence scale', which involved a weighting of 1.0 for the first adult, of 0.5 for the other adults, and of 0.3 for children aged fourteen or less (Atkinson 1998b, p. 27).

[29] We take 'households' as reported in the panel data as our units of analysis, although there are important distinctions which in principle ought be drawn within them between 'spending units', 'family units' and indeed 'inner family units' (Atkinson 1998b, pp. 59 ff.). Just as in developing countries there might be several separate family huts in the same family compound (Deaton 1997, pp. 23–4), so too in the three countries here under study there might be several distinct family units sharing the same roof.

That is to assume that every member of the household has the same standard of living. To some extent that is ensured by joint consumption: they share the same house, they eat off the same table, and so on. But not all of a household's income is spent on such joint consumption goods; and insofar as there is anything left over after those joint consumption goods have been bought, the imputation of equal equivalent income to each member of the household implies that each has equal drawing rights on the household's income. That assumption is open to challenge, given what we know about the actual patterns of income-sharing within households.[30] So far, however, that research has not yielded any robust predictions of how income actually will be shared within the household. We therefore adopt the default assumption – conventional in all such studies – that income (or more precisely, the same standard of living) will be shared equally by everyone within the household.

6.3.3   Employment variables

Official statistics categorize people according to their employment status. According to the standard conventions, people are deemed 'non-employed' if they are not in paid labour, for whatever reason. 'Unemployed' is standardly seen as a sub-set of that category, referring to those who are involuntarily non-employed. The ordinary way of ascertaining whether a person is unemployed in a conventional labour-force survey is to ask whether that person has taken active steps to find work in the last four weeks (for example, written letters to potential employers, gone for interviews and so on) and has found little or no work. Only active seekers who have performed almost no paid work in the period are classified as unemployed.

Such a definition helps serve to keep the official unemployment figures down. In other respects, however, it is obviously highly debatable. It excludes anyone who finds more than some arbitrarily low number of hours of work each week. Also, and more importantly, it excludes 'discouraged workers' who would take work at a reasonable wage but who have given up the search as hopeless. (Such a definition also of course errs in the opposite direction, including as unemployed those people who are only going through the motions of seeking work which they do not genuinely want and would avoid taking if they possibly could.) Because of these obvious flaws in the concept of unemployment, and because of the unreliability of self-assessed reports of unemployment (which are of

---

[30] Atkinson (1998b, pp. 60–2). See further evidence in intra-family distributions surveyed in chapter 3 above.

course the only kind the panel data contain), we do not try to tease any unemployment statistics as such out of our panel data.[31]

The more reliable employment indicators to be found within the panel data concern the number of hours respondents report working per week.[32] According to the standard convention, people are deemed to be in 'full-time employment' if they work thirty or more hours per week. They are deemed to be in 'part-time employment' if they work between ten and thirty hours a week. If they work between zero and ten hours a week, they are said to be in 'casual employment'.

For some purposes, we can content ourselves with traditional labour force participation rates – the percentage of people, in various categories, who are engaged in either full- or part-time paid labour. But for many purposes it matters exactly how many hours people are working.

Toward that end, we propose in section 7.2 a measure which combines full-time, part-time and casual work into a single overall measure of the 'person-year employment rate' for the country as a whole. Such a measure blends together the measures of annual working hours which panel surveys provide for each respondent.

6.3.4 Demographic variables

Panel data also include information on the age of members of the household. We use this as a surrogate for 'stage in the lifecourse', as follows. When we talk of people of 'prime working age', that will refer to those aged twenty-five to fifty-nine.[33] People of 'retirement age' will be taken to refer to those aged sixty-five or over. 'Children' will ordinarily be taken to refer to people aged under sixteen.[34]

Those categorizations deliberately exclude 'transitional' age groups altogether. Some of those aged sixteen to twenty-five will have left school

---

[31] As background to our other discussions, though, it might be useful to note – for what it is worth – that the *Handbook of US Labor Statistics* (Jacobs 1997, p. 295) reports unemployment (calculated according to the US definition) as averaging 5.2 per cent per year in Germany, 6.3 per cent in the Netherlands and 6.1 per cent in the US over the decade under study (1983–92 in the US, 1985–94 in the other two countries).

[32] These self-reports should be treated with caution, however. At least in early waves of the American PSID these reports proved relatively unreliable when compared to employer records of hours worked (Duncan and Hill 1985).

[33] For certain purposes we also give statistics on people of 'working age' more broadly, aged 16–64. We sometimes also refer to 'households of working age', defined as those with a head of household who is under age sixty. Wherever one of those other groups is under discussion, the age bands will be specifically mentioned.

[34] Certain equivalence scales, as noted earlier, differentially weight adults and children, and when doing so typically count as children anyone under eighteen. But in the form of the equivalence scale we use adults and children are not distinguished.

and be in the labour market; others will still be at school or in higher education. Some of those aged sixty to sixty-four will have retired, others will still be at work. Thus we confine our attention to 'core' groups of each category, and ignore these transitional age groups as potentially confounding factors.

Where no specific demographic group is singled out, we will of course be talking about everyone, whatever their age. But ordinarily we will confine our attention to some specific age group, typically the prime-working-age group. The reason is simply that in all countries there are very specific (and sometimes very distinctive) social programmes of income support for the elderly; and, what is worse for the purposes of comparative analysis, programmes that have the same practical effect are organized in ways that cause them to be coded differently in different countries.[35]

To avoid those potentially confounding effects, we ordinarily try to focus our analyses principally upon people of prime working age, examining impacts on the elderly separately. That is not always possible, and it is not always desirable. (Poverty rates are ordinarily given first for the whole population, and only then are they broken down for specific sub-groups; and we must obviously follow those reporting conventions here, as well.) But given the very different policy regimes to which they might potentially be subject, we will try wherever possible to focus primarily upon people of prime working age, and report what is happening to the elderly separately.

6.3.5 Programme variables

As already mentioned, panel data categorize government transfer payments under certain broad headings. These categories distinguish programmes (such as social assistance or child benefits) which are standardly funded from general tax revenues from other programmes (such as old age pensions, first-tier unemployment insurance and so on) which are standardly funded from contributions paid by employers and employees. In our discussion, we will refer to these as 'non-contributory' and 'contributory' programmes, respectively.[36]

---

[35] For a good synopsis of the range of 'retirement income packages' across countries, see Rein and Turner (1997). Differences in arrangements for sickness benefit (particularly the way it is paid by employers rather than government, for the first few days or weeks in some places) might create similar problems for cross-national comparisons even as regards working-aged people to some lesser extent (particularly in the period here under study).

[36] The panels' codebooks unhelpfully dub the first 'public transfer' programmes and the second 'social insurance' or 'social security' programmes. We prefer the more standard terminology, which brings the distinctive features of each group into sharper focus.

We will also distinguish, from time to time, between 'mean-tested' and 'non-means-tested' programmes.[37] The defining feature of a means-tested programme is that payment is conditional on some test of income or assets. In the countries under study, non-means-tested benefits include the basic old age pensions, first-tier disability and unemployment insurance and child benefits (in the two countries that have them). Means-tested benefits include social assistance, the American AFDC and SSI programmes, and in most places a second-tier of unemployment insurance available on a means-tested basis to those who have exhausted their first-tier entitlements.

6.3.6   Measures of effects over time

The great advantage of panel studies is that they allow us to track people to see what happens to them over time, and through that to determine the longer-term effects of various factors on people's lives. Both methodologically and substantively, we are anxious through this study to find out what difference these differing time perspectives make to people's lives and to our assessment of public policies.

Thus, we report separately on short-term, medium-term and long-term effects, along various dimensions. By 'long-term' effects, we mean just the effect over the full ten years under study. By 'medium-term' effects, we refer to the effect over five years. We provide information separately on both the first and second of the two five-year periods into which our study naturally divides.

By 'short-term' we mean single-year effects. As evidence of this, we provide information on single-year effects for two particular years (1987 and 1992 for the Netherlands and Germany; 1985 and 1990 for the US). These years are chosen to be around the midpoints of each of the two five-year periods.

Fortuitously, those single-year reports – and all the more strongly the five-yearly reports – capture countries at different points in the economic cycle. The first period corresponds to something of an economic 'boom' for each country and the second something of an economic downturn (which was of course worse in some countries than others). By comparing how regimes performed over those two periods, we can compare how well each does in good times and bad, as well as of course comparing how they do relative to one another.

Our measure of one-yearly effects is the familiar one. It aggregates

---

[37]   There is a general tendency for non-contributory programmes to be means-tested, and for contributory ones not to be. But the correlation is far from perfect. Child benefits, for example, are non-contributory but not means-tested.

people's income over the entire year in question, and we then examine how their whole year's income compares to some benchmark (such as the poverty line, likewise defined on a whole-year basis). Inevitably, such whole-year aggregates obscure much of what is going on in people's lives day to day, week to week or even month to month. Living below the poverty line even just for a few months is a non-trivial hardship, even though your income may then pick up and your whole-year income rise above the whole-year poverty line. Non-negligible numbers of people experience just that pattern.[38] But transient poverty of that sort is elided in the sorts of 'annual poverty rates' which are so standard among government statisticians and poverty researchers – and rightly so, they might say, on the assumption that longer-term poverty does matter more.

Our calculations of five- and ten-yearly effects mimic that same method, aggregating people's incomes over still longer periods. One-yearly effects (annual poverty rates and such like) are assessed by aggregating each person's weekly and monthly incomes into a whole-year income for that person. In like fashion, we assess five-yearly effects by aggregating each person's income over each of the five years in question into a five-yearly income for that person, and so on for ten-yearly effects. Those longer-term aggregations elide what is happening to individuals year to year in just the same way that annual aggregations of whole-year income elide what is happening to them month to month. But the rationale in each case is the same: the longer term simply matters more.

We employ two other techniques, beyond merely aggregating incomes over longer periods, to assess effects over time. 'Hit rates' calculate the number of years, out of the ten years under study, in which poverty (or welfare dependency or full-time employment or whatever) 'hits' a person. That is a measure of 'recurrence'.

The other technique – 'spell analysis' – provides us with information about duration. In its original demographic application, this technique was used to calculate 'life tables' built around literal 'survival': the proportion of people still alive after fifty, sixty or seventy years. Poverty researchers have adapted these techniques to examine how long 'poverty spells' last. In the chapters that follow we further adapt them to examine the duration of 'welfare spells'. Across all these applications, though, the basic technique remains the same: you just calculate the proportion still persisting after one, two or however many years.[39]

---

[38] As section 8.4 will show, in all three countries fully a third of pre-government poverty spells (and in Germany and especially the Netherlands, a substantially larger proportion of post-government poverty spells) last less than a year.

[39] These techniques pose familiar problems of both 'left' and 'right' censoring. Left censoring involves treating all poverty spells as if they ended in the same year as our study ended, ignoring the fact that some will continue for some years after our study. Here we

Note that hit rates and spell analysis have a subtly but importantly different focus. In spell analysis, the unit of analysis is the spell, not the person. The issue under study there is how long, once a spell of poverty has commenced, it takes for it to end. With hit rates, the unit of analysis is the person and how that person fares over time. The issue there is how often poverty hits any given person, over the course of the ten years under study. Hit-rate analysis would be unable to distinguish a person who was poor every other year (five out of ten) from a person who was poor for five years running and then got out of poverty for good. Spell analysis would be unable to distinguish a situation in which five different people were each poor for only one year from a situation in which the same person was poor every other year for five years out of the ten under study. Thus these two techniques are important complimentary ways of examining effects over time.

6.3.7   Outcome measures: poverty, inequality and redistribution

In the chapters that follow, we will be deploying a wide array of more specific measures of policy outcomes, touching upon issues of poverty, inequality, stability, integration, autonomy and efficiency. For the most part, we will simply introduce the measures as we come to them in the ordinary course of our discussion. But it might be useful to provide some preview here of the sorts of measures we will use in discussing some of the more recurring concepts.

Primary among them is the notion of 'poverty'. Among academics and social policy-makers, poverty has come predominantly to refer to 'relative deprivation' (Runciman 1966; Townsend 1979) or, more recently, 'social exclusion' (Jordan 1996). Survey research has confirmed that people do indeed see themselves, and are seen by others, as being poor and excluded from a mainstream lifestyle if their incomes are below about 50 per cent of median income in the society in which they live (Hagenaars 1986; Muffels 1993; Rainwater 1974; Van Praag et al. 1982). Thus we take as our main measure of relative poverty the conventional OECD standard, according to which a person is defined as poor if that person's post-government equivalent household income is less than 50 per cent of median equivalent household income.[40]

Another key concept is income inequality. Here we will deploy three

follow the conventional practice of eliminating left-censored cases (since we do not know how long they had been going on before the study started) but of including in our spell analyses right-censored cases (which are still continuing at the end of the study) (Bane and Ellwood 1986).

[40] To highlight differences between countries, key results are also given for 40 per cent ('very poor') and 60 per cent ('near poor') poverty lines.

measures: the Gini coefficient, the mean logarithmic deviation (Theil-0) and the decile ratio. Gini, the best known of these measures, ranges between zero (perfect equality) and one (complete inequality: one person or income group having all the income of society). Despite its widespread use, however, Gini has various familiar limitations.[41] The Theil-0 coefficient is the alternative now preferred by most economists, in part because of its nice mathematical properties and in part because it actually seems most sensitive to what matters most to policy-makers concerned with inequality.[42] The simple decile ratio – the income of people at the ninetieth percentile of the distribution divided by the income of people at the tenth percentile – is attractively straightforward and captures much of what we need to know for international comparisons (Atkinson and Micklewright 1992).

Finally, for many purposes we want to estimate the 'redistributive impact' of government (or 'the welfare state') on various variables under discussion. What difference do taxes and transfers make to poverty, inequality, income stability and so on? The general formula we will employ across all those domains is:

Governmental redistribution =
$$\frac{((\text{pre-government income}) - (\text{post-government income}))}{(\text{pre-government income})}$$

This formula can be adapted to a variety of contexts.[43] For example, governmental reduction of the poverty rate (the percentage of people who are poor) is simply the poverty rate based on pre-government incomes (pre-government poverty: the percentage who would have been poor on the basis of their market incomes alone) minus the poverty rate based on post-government incomes (the percentage actually poor after taxes and transfers), all divided by pre-government poverty. The government reduction in income inequality can be calculated, similarly, as the inequality in post-government incomes minus inequality in pre-government

---

[41] The most serious of which is that it is more sensitive to changes in the middle of the income distribution than at the bottom and top ends, which are usually of more interest to policy-makers and social scientists.

[42] In our analysis, we use the Theil-0 variation on the standard Theil coefficient because it is particularly sensitive to changes at the bottom end of the distribution (which is to say, it is responsive to increases or reductions in the income of the poor); and given that sensitivity, in calculating Theil-0 we trim the top and bottom 1 per cent of the sample. Theil coefficients, this one included, also have the desirable property of being mathematically decomposable, which means that one can say how much income inequality is due to, say, inequality between men and women or between ethnic groups, and how much inequality is reduced by, say, direct taxes or means-tested benefits (Theil 1967; Shorrocks 1980).

[43] We borrow it from Kakwani (1986) and Ringen (1991).

incomes, all divided by pre-government inequality.[44] The government reduction in income instability can be calculated, in like fashion, as the instability in post-government incomes minus the instability in pre-government incomes, all divided by pre-government instability, and so on.

[44] Strictly speaking, these 'reductions' will always be negative numbers. But in reporting them we will omit the repetitive use of minus signs, taking all 'reductions' to be implicitly negative. (Where a minus sign does very occasionally appear in such tables, it will reflect the opposite of a reduction – i.e. an actual increase in inequality, or whatever, due to government interventions.)

Part II

One standard of success:
external moral criteria

There are various moral values, identified in chapter 2 above, which welfare regimes might be supposed to serve. Among them are:

- promoting efficiency;
- reducing poverty;
- promoting equality;
- promoting social integration and avoiding social exclusion;
- promoting social stability; and
- promoting autonomy.

In the chapters that follow, we identify some indicators within the panel data bearing on each of those social concerns. Those indicators then serve as standards against which we will measure the performance of the 'best exemplars' of each of the alternative types of welfare regimes.

In the main text of chapters 7 to 12, we confine ourselves to summary statements and graphic presentations of that information. Associated with each chapter, however, is a set of appendix tables where each of the indicators is defined more precisely and all of the data to which the text refers are set out in full.

In the nature of things, very few of the indicators that we will be using here directly tap what is morally of most concern to us. Most of these indicators are more or less indirect, bearing somewhat obliquely upon what really matters from a moral point of view. When we find an imperfect link between welfare regimes and the ends they are supposed to serve, it will therefore always be something of an open question whether the fault lies with the welfare regime or with the indicator.

Furthermore, some of those indicators are themselves causally (and in some cases, even logically) linked with one another. We will attend to issues of causal linkages, particularly in chapters 13 to 16 below. But it is worth noting that, from a moral point of view, we may well care about some of those factors independently of any further causal consequences they might have. We may, for example, think it socially important to equalize educational attainments across the community as an end in itself, whether or not that actually makes a further contribution toward equalizing incomes.

Some of those interrelationships between the variables in view are positive. In so far as they are causally connected at all, equalizing education presumably does indeed equalize income. But some of those interrelationships are negative, even within one realm (for example, it is standardly thought that equalizing opportunities necessarily entails creating opportunities for unequal eventual attainments) and certainly so across realms. Sometimes that is analytically true: the tight social integration that corporatists cherish, for example, is precisely what champions of autonomy eschew; and this is reflected in the fact that some of the indicators we propose for those values are actually identical in form but opposite in sign. At other times the tension between values is of a more contingent and empirical sort: as it happens, for example, one major source of long-term equality in earnings across the community as a whole is short-term instability in each person's earnings from year to year; so if we promoted short-term security and stability of the sort corporatists cherish in people's earned income, we would undermine society-wide long-term income equality of the sort social democrats demand.

Finally, it is important to recall from chapter 3 above that each particular type of welfare state is embedded in a larger political-economic regime. That larger regime seeks to promote people's welfare, not only through transfer payments made by the explicitly social-welfare sector, but also through the distribution of earnings generated through the productive sector of the economy. Thus, in subsequent chapters we will be applying these criteria to both the pre-fisc and post-fisc (both the pre- and post-tax and public transfer) income distributions generated under each regime.

The best welfare state, after all, might well be one which is embedded in a larger policy regime which leaves little for it to do. If our goal is to eliminate poverty or to ensure income equality, for example, a policy regime which achieves that by the way in which it distributes earned income is no less successful in that task than a regime which achieves the same result through a system of taxes and transfers. We may not credit 'the welfare state' as such with the accomplishment, because we tend to reserve that term for the system of transfers alone. But that amounts to parcelling out the credit too finely to be of any real interest to any real people; it is a distinction without a difference to anyone living under any given regime or to anyone trying to choose between them. The credit which is due to the 'welfare-producing regime' (or whatever one wants to call it) would be identical, either way.

7   Promoting efficiency

Efficiency means many different things, as chapter 2 has shown, and not all of them are well captured in the panel data.[1] Nevertheless, these data do directly and effectively address the two key components in the classic 'equity versus efficiency' critique of the welfare state.

Arthur Okun (1975) offers the image of the welfare state as a 'leaky bucket'. Some of the benefits we try to deliver to the poor simply seep away before reaching them. One source of leakage is 'work disincentives'. Suppose that, for every dollar transferred by welfare programmes to the poor, the poor themselves work fewer hours, thereby reducing their earned income by half a dollar; then in Okun's terms half the dollar we were trying to transfer to them has seeped away. A second source of leakage, in Okun's classic account, is 'target inefficiency': if half the money we transfer to people through welfare programmes goes to people other than those we were trying to help through the programmes in question, then again half the money has seeped away.[2] Both of those more specific efficiency issues can and will be addressed through panel data, presented in sections 7.4 to 7.6 below.

When economists, and politicians influenced by them, talk of the 'economic inefficiency' of the welfare state, however, they often refer to nothing so specific as that. What they mean to say is simply that the welfare state somehow or another constitutes a drain on national resources and a drag on economic growth. And, these critics would be the first to remind us, a smoothly functioning economy is after all the

---

[1] Even many of the more important senses of efficiency, economically understood, cannot themselves be properly addressed through these data. The panel data tell us only a little about allocative efficiency (whether resources are used most productively) and virtually nothing about people's material standard of living (how income flows translate into consumption goods and thence into 'utility') or their subjective senses of well-being (how satisfied they are with their lives).

[2] Lindbeck (1995: 10) agrees that these factors – which he dubs 'moral hazard' and 'benefit cheating' respectively – are indeed the two principal sources of 'hazardous adjustments' in response to generous welfare states. Lindbeck goes on to develop his 'basic hypothesis . . . that such hazardous adjustments tend to be stronger in the long run than in the short and medium term'.

principal mechanism by which most people's welfare needs are most powerfully served. In so far as the welfare state really does undercut the functioning of the economy, then, it would be importantly counter-productive to its own welfare goals.

Whether the welfare state really does hinder economic performance – and if so, how badly – is of course a much debated topic.[3] We cannot hope to settle it conclusively within the scope of our present study. But that, too, is a topic on which our panel data do importantly bear. To show how, we will first set out (in section 7.1) the 'efficiency critique' rather more formally than do many of those themselves deploying it. We then proceed to show that there is no real difference between these three countries in terms of economic growth and prosperity (section 7.2). That, note, is despite significant differences in terms of various other things – employment rates, work disincentives and target and programme inefficiencies (sections 7.3 to 7.6) – which according to the stylized neo-classical economic model of the world would lead us to expect growth rates to differ.

7.1   The neo-classical economist's world

The neo-classical economic critique of the welfare state has taken firm root, not only within the OECD (1981; 1988a, b; 1990a; 1994; 1996e) but also within the policy discourses of most advanced industrial countries themselves (Gilder 1981; Murray 1982; 1984; Lindbeck 1995; 1997; Lindbeck et al. 1994; cf. Marmor, Mashaw and Harvey 1990, ch. 3; Saunders 1994, ch. 5; Atkinson 1995a, ch. 6; 1995c; 1999).

That critique can be represented in the form of a 'hypothesized chain of causation' linking micro-economic causes to macro-economic consequences.[4] Key components of that critique are represented, in only slightly stylized form, in figure 7.1.

The principal idea behind the neo-classical economic critique is that social programmes with high replacement rates pay people about the same amount as they would have earned from paid labour, and that constitutes a powerful disincentive for them to bother working. Those

---

[3] Useful surveys of this large literature include: Danziger, Haveman and Plotnick (1981); Atkinson (1985, section 5; 1995a, c; 1999); Moffitt (1992); Esping-Andersen (1994, pp. 720–6); and Saunders (1994).

[4] There is also a claim that welfare programmes, particularly pay-as-you-go pensions, depress private savings and hence investment in productive sectors of the economy (Feldstein 1980; 1996; Feldstein and Pellechio 1979; cf. Danzigar, Haveman and Plotnick 1981: 1005; Okun 1975, p. 99). We omit discussion of those issues both here and in our subsequent analysis, purely on the grounds that the panel data contin no reliable information on the size of (as opposed to the income stream derived from) people's assets or wealth or, hence, private savings (see section 6.3.1).

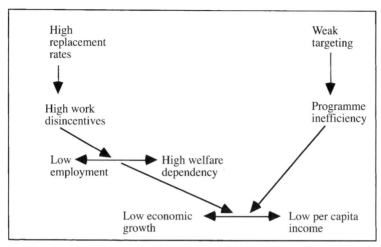

Figure 7.1. The hypothesized neo-classical economic chain of inefficiency.

disincentives are expected to be reflected in low employment rates and high rates of welfare dependency, which in turn constitute a drag on economic growth, thus reducing per capita national income. In a second and independent link in the neo-classical chain of causation, poorly targeted benefits being paid to needy and non-needy people alike are seen as both inefficient and economically costly, in so far as there are deadweight losses associated with the 'fiscal churning' involved in collecting tax revenues and distributing them back to the very same people (Browning 1993; Tanzi and Schuknecht 1995; Palda 1997).

That neo-classical economic critique depicting the welfare state as a hindrance to economic growth has in its turn been subject to widespread and challenging critiques. A full survey of that large literature is obviously beyond our scope here. Instead, we shall simply present the results of our panel surveys as they bear on those familiar controversies.

7.2   Promoting economic growth

In analysing that hypothesized chain of causation, it pays to start at the bottom and work our way back upwards. After all, the bottom line is what really matters. The principal reason that champions of economic efficiency give us for worrying about the inefficiencies of social welfare programmes is that they lower economic growth and our material standard of living. If it turns out at the end of the day that they do not, then those purported inefficiencies are of no consequence – or anyway they do not have the principal consequence that their critics claim.[5]

To foreshadow what comes later, the three countries under study turn out to be very different on many of the measures that neo-classical economists use to measure the efficiency of social welfare programmes. Despite their differences on all those measures, though, these three countries nonetheless manage to produce strikingly similar economic growth rates.

There are of course many different ways to assess economic growth. Judged in terms of the growth in real (inflation-adjusted) GDP, the German economy grew 26.7 per cent over the decade under study, the Dutch 26.5 per cent and the US 27.8 per cent.[6] But a better measure of economic welfare is the rate of growth in real GDP *per capita* (it is the well-being of *persons* with which we are concerned, after all). As figure 7.2 shows, growth in real GDP per capita over that decade was 19.1 per cent in the Netherlands, compared to 17.4 per cent in Germany and 17.2 per cent in the US. (The data underlying figure 7.2, and all others appearing in this chapter, will be found in appendix table A1, at the end of this book.)

Judging from those GDP statistics, then, it would seem that these three countries are broadly similar in their economic performance over the decade. Contrary to popular mythology, the US economy did not decisively outperform the other two economies over this period, no matter how you look at these GDP growth rates. And looking at growth in GDP per capita, which is arguably the better measure of welfare, it is actually the Netherlands that is the best performer over this period. How each of these countries achieved what it did, economically – and what it might have achieved, had it pursued other policies instead – is beyond the remit of this book.[7] What matters for our present purposes is just the economic bottom line.

The only reason we care about the bottom line of the national econ-

---

[5] There may, of course, still be a case to be made for targeting benefits more tightly on those in need of them, so more needy people can be helped with the same levels of public expenditure (Barr 1985; Le Grand 1990).

[6] Calculated from OECD (1996g; 1998). Annual growth rates for each of these countries for each of the ten years are given in OECD (1996f, annex table 1, p. A4). The 'decade under study' to which these statistics refer is 1985–94 for Germany and the Netherlands, and 1983–92 for the US, to correspond with the results reported in the rest of the book. Taking exactly the same years for the US as the other two countries, the growth both in GDP and in GDP per capita would have been marginally lower than the rates reported in the text, as shown in appendix table A1, Eff 1B.

[7] The US engaged heavily in deficit spending (OECD 1996b, pp. 45, 53, 283, 407), while the Netherlands under the Wassenaar Accord engaged in wage restraint (ILO 1984–96, tables 16 and 23).

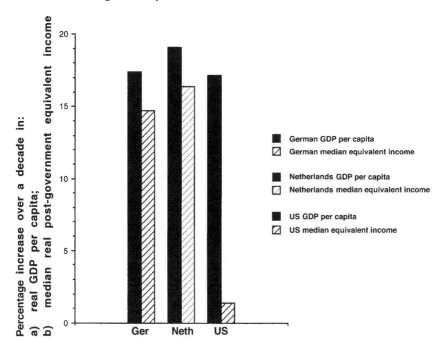

Figure 7.2. Increase in average income over ten years (based on appendix table A1: Eff 1A and Eff 1B).

omic ledger, though, is because of its impact on the lives of people living in those countries. 'Equivalent income', taking account of people's household circumstances in ways described in section 6.3.2, is the best available indicator of people's real standard of living. Interrogating the socio-economic panel data before us, we can discover what proportion of people in each country had a higher real (inflation-adjusted) equivalent income at the end of the decade than at the beginning. When we do that, we find that only just over half of people in the US were better off at the end of the decade than the beginning, compared to around two-thirds of people in the Netherlands and even more in Germany.[8]

Interrogating those same socio-economic panel data, we can ascertain by how much the median individual's real equivalent income increased over the course of the decade. Those results are displayed in figure 7.2. There we see, in striking fashion, that while the fruits of economic growth

[8] Larger proportions were made better off over the first five years, smaller proportions over the second, in all three countries – reflecting the effects of the economic downturn that hit all three countries in the second half of the decade under study.

were passed on to middle-income people in Germany and especially in the Netherlands, this did not happen to anything like the same extent in the US. Thus, while median equivalent income increased by between 15 and 16 per cent in Germany and the Netherlands respectively, it increased only just over 1 per cent in the US.[9]

The bottom line, in terms of the average person's standard of living, is just this. Not only does the social democratic welfare regime of the Netherlands top the league in terms of all the standard welfare-related goals, it also tops the league in terms of the economic well-being of the average citizen. Conversely, the liberal welfare regime of the US not only comes bottom of the league in terms of welfare-related goals but also does far worse at promoting economic well-being for average citizens. Official US government ideology over this period was that further wealth bestowed upon the rich would 'trickle down' to the poor (Gilder 1981; Murray 1982; cf. Goodin 1988, ch. 9), but on the evidence of these panels it seems that the trickle did not even reach median income earners.

Note that the strong economic performance of the Netherlands comes despite its considerably higher level of social spending.[10] And it is also despite considerable differences on the various other indicators of the 'economic inefficiency' of these countries' welfare sectors, to which we now turn.

7.3   Promoting high employment

There are many reasons to try to get everyone who wants to go out to work a job in the paid labour market. The most obvious one in the context of the present chapter is that doing so increases the productivity of the economy overall and, in so doing, makes us all better off financially. To that classically liberal way of putting the point, corporatists would add that there are also social advantages which come from having people well

---

[9] Again, the growth in median equivalent income was higher in all three countries over the first five years, and lower (in the US, negative) over the second five years due to the economic downturn affecting them all in that period. These basic findings are in line with the vast array of other evidence surveyed by Levy and Murname (1992) and they are confirmed by Schluter's (1998) more sophisticated 'stochastic kernel' analysis of US and German income inequalities in these panels over the same period.

[10] The Netherlands devotes over twice as much of its GDP to social spending as the US (OECD 1996c, table 1.23, p. 20; reproduced in section 4.5.1 above), but the Netherlands' economic growth rate seems not to suffer to any great extent in consequence. That finding is in line with much existing cross-national evidence suggesting that the level of government spending does not much affect economic growth (Saunders 1985; Castles and Dowrick 1990; Alesina and Rodrik 1991; Esping-Andersen 1994, pp. 720–6); for a survey of this and conflicting evidence see Atkinson (1999, ch. 1).

integrated into their workplaces; and social democrats would add that work can also be personally satisfying, a good in itself. And of course all of them would concede the plain financial fact that the nearer we are to 'full employment', the higher the ratio of wealth-makers to wealth-takers in our society, and hence the more 'affordable' social welfare programmes will be.

The most familiar measure of success in employment policy – unemployment rates – is not particularly useful for these purposes, counting as it does only people who report themselves as 'available for work'. All those who are not looking for work, ranging from housewives to 'discouraged workers' who have given up trying to find work, are not counted among the unemployed for official statistical purposes. That renders unemployment rates an inadequate measure of 'full employment'.[11]

Rather than 'unemployment rates', a better measure for these purposes would be 'employment rates' or 'labour force participation rates'. But as we remarked in section 6.3.3, although conventional reports of labour force participation rates do distinguish between people in full- and part-time employment, they do so only in very broad-banded categories.[12] Furthermore, different countries define part-time employment differently, and OECD statistics characteristically make no effort to standardize across them.

From the economic point of view it does matter exactly how many hours people are working overall in each country. To try to get at that issue, we have constructed a measure to supplement the standard international battery of measures which might be called the 'person-years employment rate'. This is defined as:

Person-years employment rate =

$$\frac{\text{(total annual hours worked by all persons aged 16–64)}}{\text{((potential working hours) multiplied by (number of persons aged 16–64))}}$$

where 'potential working hours' $= 52 \times 40$.

The idea behind this measure is that the potential number of available hours of work across any given country in a given year is the number of people of potential working age (aged sixteen to sixty-four inclusive) multiplied by fifty-two weeks in the year multiplied by the forty hours

---

[11] For what it is worth, the US Labor Department reports that over the years 1985–94 rates of unemployment, defined according to the US conventions, averaged 5.2 per cent in Germany, 6.3 per cent in the Netherlands and 6.4 per cent in the US (Jacobs 1997).
[12] 'Full-time' is anything over thirty hours, conventionally; 'part-time' is conventionally anything between ten and thirty hours.

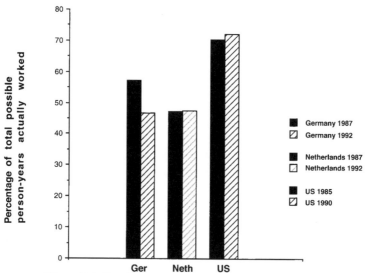

Figure 7.3. Employment rates (person-years, for all persons aged 16–64) (based on appendix table A1: Eff 2A).

available in a working week.[13] The 'person-years employment rate' is then simply the number of 'person-years' actually worked in the country, relative to a situation in which all eligible people work forty hours a week every week of the year. The advantage of this measure for international comparisons is that it standardizes national employment rates, relative to a maximal potential working year.

Figure 7.3 reports employment rates, in this person-year fashion, for all people of working age (16–64) across the three countries under study. There we see that the US made by far the fullest use of its potential workforce, with the other two countries far behind – and in the case of Germany, actually dropping.[14]

[13] The forty-hour week standard is a matter of international law, under the 1935 'Convention concerning the reduction of hours of work to forty a week', which came into force in 1957 (ILO 1996, vol. I, pp. 261–3). Of course, in some places the standard working week is substantially less than forty hours, and many people in most places work more than that; and most people in most places take a few weeks' holidays, rather than working all fifty-two weeks of the year. None of that information is lost through our standardization. Quite the contrary, the whole point of standardizing as we do is to highlight those differences. Our procedure is similar to the 'full-year-full-time-work' standard used by Haveman and Berkshadker (1998) to calculate earnings capacities.
[14] The *Handbook of US Labor Statistics*' (Jacobs 1997, pp. 294–5) report of 'employment status of the working-age population, approximating US concepts', similarly shows employment rates for persons aged sixteen and over to be roughly on a par in Germany and the Netherlands and substantially lower in both places than in the US.

That drop in the person-year employment rate in Germany is largely a reflection of the economic slump in the second half of our period, which hit there particularly hard. The primary way in which that economic pressure impacted on employment was to exacerbate a tendency, already well underway in both Germany and the Netherlands, for older men increasingly to retire early (Kohli *et al.* 1991). Were we to focus on the experiences of prime-age workers (aged 25–59) alone, that drop in the German person-year employment rate might disappear.[15] However, retiring people prematurely represents underutilization of economic resources which, in terms of the neo-classical economic critique, ought to be taken into account. Thus it is indeed the larger group of all working-aged people, aged from sixteen to sixty-four, with which we should be concerned.

Thus we see that it is indeed the liberal regime, which purports to care most about economic efficiency, which actually makes most use of available labour. The corporatist and social democratic regimes under study here make substantially less use of the labour time potentially available to them.

7.4   Reducing work disincentives and welfare dependency

In the neo-classical economic worldview sketched in figure 7.1, low employment rates are expected to be associated with – causing and being caused by – high rates of welfare dependency. Both are expected to constitute a drag on economic growth rates. The economic sustainability of the welfare state is undermined, neo-classical economists would insist, if there are relatively too few wealth-makers and relatively too many wealth-takers in the community at large.

These neo-classical economists also have a further account causally linking welfare-state transfers to those high rates of welfare dependency. Macro-economic allocative inefficiencies result from people who could have made productive contributions to the economy through paid labour being tempted instead to live non-productively (in an economic sense, anyway) off welfare benefits. The micro-economic cause of that is the 'work disincentives' that are created by generous welfare programmes, which tempt people to live off the state rather than earning their keep in the labour market. That micro-economic account of 'work disincentives' is supposed to predict and to explain the macro-economic phenomenon of high welfare dependency and low employment rates.

[15] Indeed, for that age group Dutch and German person-year employment rates might even have been rising, given the further fact that over this period substantially more women were entering the labour market on at least a part-time basis.

In discussing these issues, we will first look (in section 7.4.1) for evidence of the macro-economic phenomenon of 'welfare dependency' before turning (in section 7.4.2) to examine further evidence bearing on the credibility of the 'work disincentive' explanation of it.

7.4.1   Welfare dependency

Let us look first, then, for evidence of widespread 'welfare dependency'. 'Dependency' of course means different things to different people. Often it refers to a character trait or a cast of mind rather than an objective state of affairs (Goodin 1988, ch. 12; 1998b; Fraser and Gordon 1994; Gibson 1998, ch. 10). Here we will be using the term in its more objective sense. When talking about rates of 'welfare dependency', we will be talking about the proportion of the population who rely upon public transfers as their principal source of post-government equivalent income in any given year.[16]

Welfare dependency, thus defined, necessarily constitutes a drain on the productive sectors of the economy, in the sense that money spent subsidizing consumption on the part of welfare beneficiaries is money that is not available to invest in other productive endeavours. (In other respects, of course, putting money into the hands of consumers serves to stimulate the economy.)

Over and above that, welfare dependency, thus defined, sometimes also constitutes an allocative inefficiency within the larger economy. That will be the case if – but only if, and only to the extent that – the recipients of welfare could have made a productive contribution in the market for paid labour, had they not been subsidized through welfare payments not to work. It is inefficiencies of this latter sort to which talk of 'work disincentives' points, and it is accordingly this sort of inefficiency that will concern us in this section.

Of course, it is not necessarily the case that everyone who lives off welfare benefits could always have made a valuable contribution in the paid labour market. The old and the young are not only excused from paid labour; traditionally, they have been statutorily prohibited from engaging in it. The sick and disabled, likewise, are excused from paid labour – partly on humanitarian grounds, but presumably also in part on the economic grounds that the market value of their contribution would be relatively lower anyway.

---

[16] This would be much higher, of course, were we talking about just the percentage of people who received some benefits, regardless of the size of the sum; on this see the discussion in section 9.5 below. For a discussion of alternative conceptualizations and measures of welfare dependency, see Gottshalk and Moffitt (1994).

All that is merely to say that there are no good economic grounds for expecting any country to have, literally, a zero rate of welfare dependency. A certain amount welfare dependency is not only socially understandable but economically excusable.

What exactly those levels might be need not detain us here, however. Our enterprise is an essentially comparative one. And for these purposes we can use the welfare dependency rates of one country as a benchmark for others. Of course, demographics differ across these three countries: Germany and the Netherlands have higher proportions of elderly people in their populations, and the US has a higher proportion of children. But confining our attention to people of prime working age, there is no reason to think that there should be any great variation in the proportion of the populations that should (on grounds of allocative efficiency) be excused from paid labour. Insofar as we find substantially different rates of welfare dependency across these three countries, that would constitute *prima facie* evidence of some allocative inefficiencies in the labour market – evidence of potentially productive labour being siphoned off into a non-productive life on welfare instead.

The evidence from the panels does indeed indicate substantial cross-national variation in the proportions of people who depend upon welfare benefits as their principal source of income. Whereas fully a quarter of Dutch people of prime working age depend upon public transfers as their principal source of income sometime over our ten-year period, less than half as many Germans do (with the American figures being halfway between those two).[17] Furthermore, as figure 7.4 shows, the frequency with which people depend on public transfers as their primary source of income is persistently (albeit decreasingly) higher in the Netherlands than the US and Germany.

Across all three countries, however, welfare dependency is not a particularly recurring phenomenon over time. As figure 7.4 shows, only half as many people depend upon public transfers as their principal source of income in three or four years as they do in one year across all three countries. The proportion depending upon public transfers in eight or more years is halved yet again.

Another, more sophisticated way of analysing these data is to look at

[17] Of course, the elderly depend both more heavily and more frequently upon public transfers (e.g. old age pensions) as their primary source of income across all three countries – more so in Germany and the Netherlands than in the US (see appendix A1, Eff 3B). Before chalking that US performance up as a triumph for the free market, however, we would have to investigate just how 'free' US workers are to contribute or not to their private occupational pensions: often US workers are (or anyway were, in this period) required to contribute, and required to contribute to some specific pension plan (or to one among a short-list of alternative pension plans) by the terms of their employment.

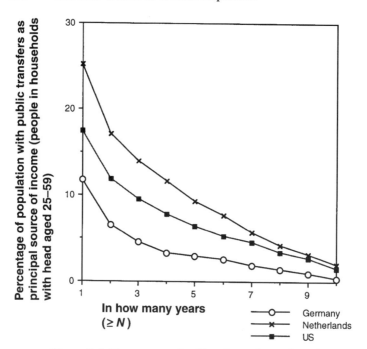

Figure 7.4. Recurrence of welfare dependency (based on appendix table A1, Eff 3A).

the duration of 'welfare spells', using the same techniques as traditionally employed to analyse 'poverty spells'.[18] (We will use the term 'welfare spell' as shorthand for 'periods of depending upon public transfers as one's principal source of income', making no distinction between social insurance and social assistance.[19]) In spell analysis, the question is how long a 'spell' – here, a spell of depending upon public transfers as one's primary source of income – will persist, once initiated.

Figure 7.5 shows that 'welfare spells' in that particular sense are rather shorter in Germany and the US and rather longer in the Nether-

[18] See sections 6.3.6 above and 8.4 below.
[19] Spells of relying upon social assistance – 'welfare', strictly speaking – would be far fewer and shorter. Leisering and Leibfried (1998, ch. 3) report that only 6 per cent of people claiming any social assistance in one German town (Bremen) continue doing so for more than five years. Duncan et al. (1995, p. 77), analysing 'social assistance spells' cross-nationally, find that spells last longer in the US (and especially longer in the UK) than in Germany. Neither of those other two studies focuses, as we do here, upon depending upon public transfers as one's primary source of income, though: both Leisering and Leibfried (1998) and Duncan et al. (1995) focus simply upon people receiving social assistance in any amount.

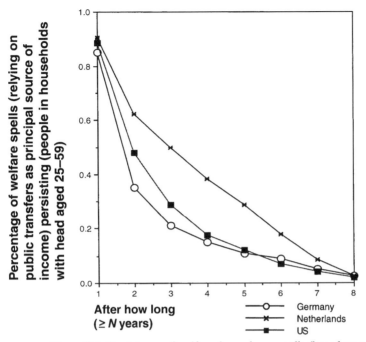

Figure 7.5. Persistence of welfare dependency spells (based on appendix table A1, Eff 3C).

lands.[20] Again, however, note the similarities as well as the differences. None of these countries end dependence on welfare swiftly. Welfare spells last a year or more in over 85 per cent of cases in all three countries. By the same token, all these countries do end welfare spells eventually, with 97 per cent of welfare spells ending everywhere by the eighth year. In between, welfare spells tend to last rather longer in the Netherlands. Half of welfare spells end inside two years in Germany and the US, but not for another year in the Netherlands; two-thirds of welfare spells end by the third year in Germany and the US, but not until the fifth in the Netherlands. Eventually, though, the Netherlands catches up, and by the eighth year only the same stubborn 3 per cent of welfare spells persist there as elsewhere. Everywhere, it seems, people who do come to depend upon public transfers as their principal source of support tend to depend upon them for some little time – but the vast majority of them do

---

[20] There are obviously variations across programmes here. Looking just at lone mothers, Duncan and Voges (1993) report that they remain on social assistance benefits no longer in Germany than the US, despite the benefit being substantially more generous in Germany than the US (see further Leisering and Leibfried 1998, pp. 197–8).

eventually get back on their own feet, in all three welfare regimes.

On issues of welfare dependency, then, our conclusions are mixed. The social democratic welfare regime does indeed seem to invite the largest proportion of people to depend upon public transfers as their primary source of income. Contrary to our ordinary expectation, however, it is not the liberal welfare regime but rather the corporatist one which minimizes such welfare dependency.[21] The proportion of people relying upon welfare declines over time in all countries, though. There is not much evidence of a permanent 'welfare class' in any of these countries: the proportion of the prime-working-age population relying upon public transfers as their principal source of income for all ten years was minuscule in Germany and very small in both the other two countries.[22]

7.4.2   Work disincentives

Whereas the macro-economic story is couched in terms of welfare dependency, the micro-economic explanation is supposed to be couched in terms of work disincentives. According to that telling of the tale, the reason people do not engage in productive paid labour when they could have done is that they are better off relying on welfare benefits instead.

The extent to which welfare payments discourage work effort has been studied many times in many ways by economists concerned with these topics, most famously through various Negative Income Tax Experiments. These worked by experimentally manipulating the levels of income support provided, and then comparing the hours worked by those receiving such income supports to the hours worked by randomly selected control groups.[23]

In our panel data, there is no way of replicating that experimental design. All we can do is to look at the number of hours worked by people when they are in receipt of public transfer payments, compared to when they were not. The 'work disincentive' hypothesis predicts, first and foremost, that households will work far less when on welfare than when not.

In that respect, the 'work disincentive' hypothesis turns out to be

---

[21] Although rather fewer people depend upon public transfers under the corporatist regime, those who do tend to depend upon them for as long or longer. That might mean that corporatist regimes pick out for public transfers those who really are unfit for ordinary service in the labour market, and who inevitably remain dependent upon public transfers for a more protracted period. In so far as that is true, any 'allocative inefficiencies' associated with welfare dependency (the productive potential of getting welfare dependants back to work) would be relatively low.

[22] Under 0.5 per cent in Germany and only 1.5 per cent to 2 per cent in the US and the Netherlands respectively, as figure 7.4 has shown.

[23] Timpane and Pechman (1975); Rivlin (1971); Danziger, Haveman and Plotnick (1981); Moffitt (1992).

substantially confirmed. In none of the three countries do we find the average person who depends primarily upon public transfers for support putting in many hours of paid labour. Cause and consequence are hard to disentangle here, though. One interpretation would be that people do not work hard because welfare benefits are high. Alternatively, perhaps people do not engage in much paid labour when they are dependent upon public transfers for the same reason they are dependent upon public transfers – they are sick or injured or have just had a new baby, for example. Or perhaps people might not engage in much paid labour simply because the rules governing public transfers do not permit them to do so: they dare not earn too much (reportable) money through paid labour for fear of being removed from the public transfer programme altogether or for fear of seeing their welfare benefits taper off too sharply.

Another way of looking at the micro-economic story underlying the work disincentive explanation of welfare dependency is in terms of 're-placement rates'. What proportion of one's previous earnings can one achieve by claiming welfare benefits instead? Or, conversely, by how much can one improve on one's welfare benefits by going out to work? Previous studies have simply read replacement rates off the formal statutes and administrative regulations alone.[24] But of course the law is one thing, the practice another. Vagaries of administrative application of the law combine with vagaries of take-up on the part of beneficiaries to ensure that the formal rules are not necessarily representative of actual practice.[25] Here we report what actually happens to people, as opposed simply to what should officially happen to them according to the law of the land.

When looking at replacement rates in that more behavioural way, what we find is this. People of prime working age who shift from the private sector to public transfers for their primary source of income get around 75 per cent of their previous earnings in Germany and the Netherlands but 67 per cent in the US.[26] By the same token, when people of prime working age who had been depending primarily upon public transfer income shift

[24] That is the basis upon which Esping-Andersen (1990, ch. 2) calculates one key element of his decommodification index, for example. See similarly Palme (1990a, b); Duncan *et al.* (1995, pp. 95–6); Whiteford (1995); OECD (1996e).

[25] Comparing the Family Expenditure Survey with actual number of Supplementary Benefit claimants, Atkinson (1989b) estimates that only about 75 per cent of people entitled to public assistance claim it in the UK, for example. Similar, or lower, results have been reported for means-tested benefits in West Germany and the US (Atkinson 1985, section 4.2; Atkinson 1998b, p. 101). In the early 1980s take-up rates for German means-tested social assistance and for the means-tested supplement to the Dutch unemployment benefit were both around 66 per cent (Atkinson 1998b, p. 182; see also van Oorschot 1991: 18–19; Eardley *et al.* 1996).

[26] These replacement rates are broadly consonant with the pattern of official rates the OECD (1996e, p. 31) reports for all three countries for a couple with two children in the first month of unemployment benefit. The US rate reported there is 68 per cent, the German 71 per cent and the Dutch 77 per cent.

into paid labour, they get fully 43 per cent more money on average in the US; in Germany they get 37 per cent more; and in the Netherlands they get only 14 per cent more.[27] In terms of work disincentives, then, the social democratic welfare regime is clearly worst and the liberal welfare regime is clearly best.

Micro-economists, as we have said, fixate upon that fact. But it is a fact that fits imperfectly with the macro-level phenomenon which it is supposed to explain. True, the social democratic welfare regime, which creates the most disincentives to work, alsoas the highest rates of welfare dependency. But it is not the case that the welfare regime that provides the strongest incentives to work (the liberal regime) actually achieves the lowest rates of welfare dependency. These, as figure 7.4 has shown, are found in the corporatist regime.[28]

Of course, one never knows just how high welfare dependency rates would have been in the US had it not been for the stronger incentives to work provided there by relatively less generous welfare provisions. But rather higher replacement rates have proved consistent with lower welfare dependency rates in Germany. Only a strong believer in American exceptionalism could, in such circumstances, resist the conclusion that there must be more to the explanation of welfare dependency than the disincentives to work created by high replacement rates.

7.5   Promoting target efficiency

Turning next to the bundle of issues surrounding 'target efficiency', we must once again begin by acknowledging the inevitable imprecision in our indicators. For a start, there is the ambiguity in the notion of

---

[27] These are proportions of the individual's previous year's 'individual labour income plus public transfer income'. Note that 'public transfer income' to the household is a function of the status of other members of the household as well as the individual upon whom we are, for these purposes, focusing; and even where public transfers can be reliably attributed to particular individuals within the household, how much one member of the household gets in public transfers is often a function of the status of other members of the household as well. The only alternative, however, is to express those proportions in terms of the individual's 'total household equivalent income', which is even more contaminated in these ways (it is especially affected by the labour income of other members of the household). Appendix table A1 (Eff 4A) reports both measures, which as it happens yield broadly similar results.

[28] True, the social democratic welfare regime is the one which has the highest work disincentives and the lowest employment rate and the liberal welfare regime is the one which has the lowest work disincentives and highest employment rate; but the mechanism which is supposed to be linking those two variables, according to the causal hypothesis sketched in figure 7.1, is missing (i.e. the liberal regime's lowest work disincentives do not translate into the lowest rates of welfare dependency).

who exactly is supposed to be the 'target' group for each programme.[29]
Ideally, we ought to assess target groups – and hence target efficiency –
strictly according to the internal standards set in the programme's legislative charter and formal administrative apparatus. What would count in
those terms as 'target inefficiencies' arise principally in two ways. One is
through administrative error – the misclassification of cases under the
operative rules of the programme. The other is through the behaviour of
individuals wrongly claiming benefits to which they are not really entitled
or of individuals failing to take up benefits to which they are rightly
entitled. Within the scope of a study such as ours, however, it is obviously
impossible to conduct any detailed assessment of whether or not particular claimants formally qualify for a benefit under the terms of detailed
legislative and administrative regulations. Socio-economic panels just do
not provide information adequate to that task.

Instead, as a crude indicator, we propose to assess 'target efficiency' in
terms of the extent to which welfare payments go to the poor and only the
poor – where 'the poor' are defined as those with an equivalent income of
less than 50 per cent of the median equivalent disposable (post-government) household equivalent income nationwide.[30] That amounts to assuming that the ultimate aim of all social welfare programmes is to
alleviate poverty, and that alone, which is obviously untrue, both for some
welfare regimes as a whole and for many (non-means-tested) welfare
programmes within every regime. Still, this focus on 'the poor and only
the poor' really does seem to capture at least something of what liberal
critics at least are complaining about when they talk of the 'target inefficiency' of social welfare programmes.[31]

---

[29] There are many different ways of construing this group. Is it the group that the initiators of
the programme intended to help when setting up the programme? Or is it the group of
persons formally entitled to receive the benefit under the programme's legislative charter
and administrative regulations? The two are not necessarily the same. Some unspecified
proportion of alleged target inefficiencies will simply be due to sloppy drafting of
legislation or to administrative subversion of legislative intentions.

[30] As explained in section 6.3.7 above, and elaborated in more detail in section 8.1 below.
Once again, none of this should necessarily be taken as conclusive evidence that
programmes fail in their *own* terms, even in so far as these programmes aim at succouring
the poor and only the poor. Standard though our definition of poverty is among academics
and within the OECD, it is not necessarily the same standard as is implicit in the legislative
charter or administrative regulations of particular countries' welfare programmes.

[31] When complaining of the 'inefficient targeting' of the sorts of programmes characteristically enacted by social democrats, for example, what liberals often seem to be saying is not
that those programmes are failures by their own standards but rather that they are not
targeted on the poor and should be. Within liberal welfare regimes, at least, a large part of
what some of the major non-means-tested welfare programmes were supposed to do was
alleviate poverty. And although old age pensions are rarely targeted, even in the most
liberal welfare regimes, the whole point of them at the time of their enactment was, even
there, supposed to be to alleviate poverty in old age.

In assessing target efficiency, we need to be sensitive to both directions in which targeting might err. Statisticians standardly distinguish 'type I' and 'type II' errors – confirming a hypothesis which is in fact false, and disconfirming a hypothesis which is in fact true. In social welfare policy both sorts of errors can also occur. One type of targeting error occurs when we pay benefits to someone who does not deserve them, the other when we deny benefits to someone who does (Goodin 1985; Atkinson 1995a, ch. 9; 1998b, pp. 224–30).

Statisticians suppose there is an inevitable trade-off between type I and type II errors in any statistical procedure. There is reason to believe that the same is true in the administration of social welfare programmes as well (Lipsky 1984; Goodin 1985). Whatever procedures we establish to reduce the number of people wrongly granted benefits will also tend to increase the number of people wrongly denied them. In what follows, we discuss each type of targeting error in turn, concluding with a discussion of trade-offs between them.

7.5.1   Overpayments

Discussions of targeting inefficiencies ordinarily focus upon people receiving benefits that they do not deserve. Those are the sorts of errors which are said to involve a 'waste of public funds'. Assuming that the standard of deservingness is poverty and that alone, we shall here use the term 'overpayments' to refer to cases of people receiving public transfers even though they are not poor.

Focusing on people of prime working age, there is considerable variation in the rates of overpayments across the three countries here under study.[32] Figure 7.6 shows that the US is very substantially better at minimizing overpayments than either Germany or the Netherlands. On a one-yearly basis, fully two-thirds of the recipients of public transfers are not poor, whereas in the US only about one-sixth are. Figure 7.6 shows that the rate of overpayments diminishes sharply over time in all countries. However, over a third of those who have received public transfers every year out of ten were never poor in any of those ten years in the Netherlands and especially Germany, whereas in the US that rate was only 2 per cent.[33]

Many programmes of course make no attempt to restrict themselves to

---

[32] We impose that age restriction on our analysis here primarily to avoid the confounding effects on the old age pension, which everywhere would increase the rate of overpayments and decrease the amount of variation across countries.

[33] All those results are essentially identical if we restrict our focus to 'serious overpayments', understood as those made to people who were nowhere near poor (i.e. having equivalent incomes more than 60 per cent of the national median).

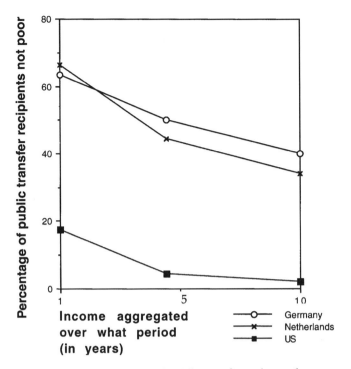

Figure 7.6. Proportion of public transfers going to the non-poor (based on appendix table A1, Eff 5A).

succouring the poor, and it should come as no surprise that programmes which are not means-tested pay benefits to people who are not poor. Of course, that failure to target the poor is precisely what critics of the target inefficiency of welfare regimes are complaining about: from the perspective of their critique, paying welfare benefits to the non-poor is what is economically problematic, and it is the rate of such payments overall that ought to concern us. From that perspective, furthermore, it ought to be regarded as a point of pride that in the liberal US welfare regime even officially non-means-tested programmes make strikingly few payments to non-poor people of prime working age.

For those who are inclined to judge welfare regimes more in terms of their own internal criteria, however, it might be useful to disaggregate overpayments by programme type. Confining our attention to means-tested programmes – which are after all the ones which self-consciously strive to target their payments on the poor – the rate of overpayments drops dramatically across all welfare regimes. The one-yearly rate of overpayment of means-tested benefits remains substantially higher in the Netherlands than elsewhere, averaging 17 per cent there compared to 7 per cent in Germany and 3 per cent in the US.[34] But literally no one in any of these three panels receives means-tested benefits in each of the ten years despite being poor in none of those years. And even over just five years, the rate of overpayment of means-tested benefits has dropped to 3 per cent in the Netherlands (and to 1 per cent in the US and 0.5 per cent in Germany).

7.5.2   Underpayments

If social welfare programmes are supposed to be targeted on the poor and only the poor, it is as much a failure of targeting for people who are poor not to receive benefits as it is for those who are not poor to receive them. In examining that second sort of targeting error, therefore, we will be looking at issues of underinclusiveness. We will examine cases of benefits not being paid to people, despite the fact that they were poor and hence presumably deserving of them. Those targeting errors we dub 'underpayments'.

Still focusing just on people of prime working age, we once again find considerable variability in those error rates across the three countries under study.[35] As shown in figure 7.7, around 35 per cent of the poor in the US receive no public transfers on a one-yearly basis, compared to around 15 per cent in Germany and 5 per cent in the Netherlands.[36] Over time, that proportion declines in the Netherlands whereas it rises (at least on a five-yearly basis) in both Germany and the US. Virtually no one who was poor in all ten years received public transfers in none of those years in the Netherlands. In the US, in contrast, almost 40 per cent of those who were poor in each of the ten years never received public transfers in any of them.[37]

[34] The same general patterns (although sometimes different percentages) are reported in Rainwater, Rein and Schwartz's (1986, pp. 197–8) analysis of means-tested benefits in the US, UK and Sweden and in Mitchell's (1991, p. 86) analysis of Luxembourg Income Study data *circa* 1980.

[35] Once again, the age restriction is designed primarily to avoid the conflating effects of the old age pension. Were old age pensioners to be included, these error rates would decrease across all countries and the differences between them would not stand out so clearly.

[36] Both the percentages and patterns here are substantially at variance with Mitchell's (1991, p. 90) analysis of Luxembourg Income Study data *circa* 1980. Although her results for the Netherlands in 1983 are virtually the same as ours for 1984, her results for both other countries are very different. Whether that divergence derives from different periods or different data bases is unclear.

[37] Comparable ten-yearly comparisons could not be done for Germany, because the number of individuals who were poor in all ten years was too small to permit further analysis. Confining our analysis to cases of underpayments to the 'seriously poor' (i.e. those with

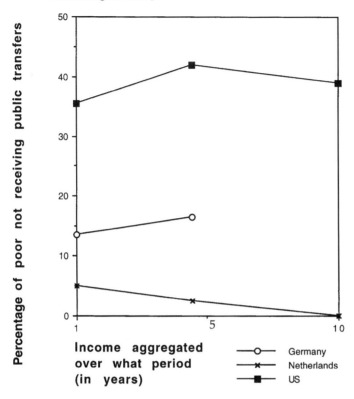

Figure 7.7. Proportion of the poor not receiving public transfers (based on appendix table A1, Eff 5C).

In the case of underpayments, it makes little sense to disaggregate means-tested and non-means-tested programmes. True, it is only means-tested programmes that explicitly take into account the income of beneficiaries. But social programmes can benefit all the poor without taking explicit note of anyone's income (universal benefits paid to everyone are paid to all the poor, along with all others). And in any case (and more importantly in terms of the design of the present study), means-tested benefits are typically paid to people on the basis of their income, net of all other (non-means-tested) public transfers. Many of the pre-government poor receive no means-tested benefits, precisely because they receive enough non-means-tested public transfers to bring them above poverty

incomes of less than 40 per cent of median equivalent income nationwide), the US underpayment rates would be only about three-quarters those reported in figure 7.7, while those for the other countries would be about the same.

without any means-tested supplements.[38] In assessing underpayments, then, we really have to look at total public transfers: it would be dangerously misleading to look at means-tested ones alone.

7.5.3   Trade-offs: over- versus underinclusiveness

The pattern thus traced for these three countries confirms the speculation that there may indeed be a trade-off to be made between errors of underpayment and errors of overpayment, errors of underinclusiveness and errors of overinclusiveness. The country with the highest rate of the first sort of error (the Netherlands) has the lowest rate of the second; and the country with the lowest rate of the first sort of error (the US) has the lowest rate of the second.

This is shown graphically in figure 7.8. There we map the rate at which each of these three countries has traded off errors of overpayment for errors of underpayment, at each of the various points in our study.[39] Naturally, we cannot know whether each of these countries got the best 'rates of trade' that they could have done; and we cannot necessarily infer anything about the exact shape of the 'feasible set' or the 'possibility frontier' from so few points. Still, from this general pattern it does look suspiciously as if there may indeed be a necessary trade-off of some sort between one sort of error and the other.

Where each welfare regime locates itself on the graph – how many errors of one sort it is prepared to trade for one sort of error of the other – tells us much about the nature of those regimes. For example, on a one-yearly basis the social democratic Netherlands is on average prepared to trade around twelve errors of overpayment for every error of underpayment; corporatist Germany is prepared to tolerate around five; and the liberal US is prepared to tolerate only around two. Thus, the social democratic welfare regime truly is prepared to 'err on the side of kindness' (overpayment rather than underpayment) much more than the liberal or corporatist regime – six times more, by that count.

---

[38]   The impact of this differs across welfare regimes of course. Both corporatists and social democrats prefer (for different reasons) to work through non-means-tested benefits instead of means-tested ones. Consequently, the proportion of the pre-government poor receiving no means-tested benefit appears very high in both Germany and the Netherlands, though the proportion receiving no public transfers of any sort is gratifyingly low. In the liberal US, the difference is less marked. Rainwater, Rein and Schwartz (1986, pp. 197–8) find broadly the same pattern comparing Sweden and the US in respect of the proportion of the poor receiving means-tested benefits.

[39]   Thus, there are two one-yearly points, two five-yearly ones and one ten-yearly one for each country (except that there were too few cases of people who were poor in all ten years to calculate a ten-yearly underpayment rate for Germany).

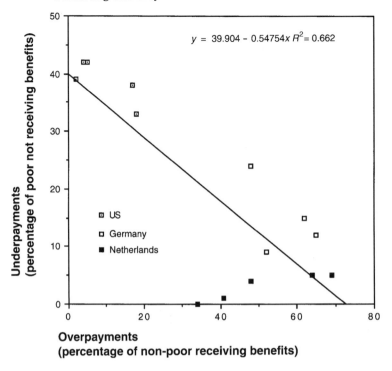

Figure 7.8. Trade-off between errors of overpayment and underpayment (based on appendix table A1, Eff 5A and Eff 5C).

7.6   Promoting programme efficiency

Where discussions of target inefficiency deal in terms of the proportion of people paid welfare benefits in error, discussions of 'programme efficiency' deal in terms of the proportion of monies spent in error. Once again, it is assumed that the poor are the target of all social welfare expenditures. Social welfare programmes are then said to be efficient, in this sense of 'programme efficiency', in so far as expenditures made through them go only to the poor.

For a formal index of 'programme efficiency', thus construed, we employ the 'poverty reduction efficiency' measure originally proposed by Beckerman (1979a, b) and which has now become standard across welfare-state studies.[40] According to this measure:

[40] E.g. Mitchell (1991, chs. 5, 8); Saunders (1994, ch. 4); Atkinson (1998b, pp. 207 ff.).

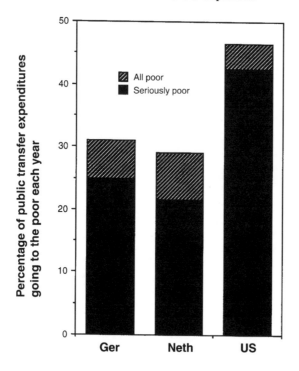

Figure 7.9. Programme efficiency of public transfer expenditures on poor and seriously poor (based on appendix table A1, Eff 6B).

Programme efficiency =
   (the proportion of programme expenditures going to persons who are poor) × (1 – the 'spillover'),

where the 'spillover' is the proportion of benefits in excess of what would be required to lift people out of poverty.[41]

Looking at the programme efficiency of public transfer payments over-all, we again find considerable variation across our three countries. Figure 7.9 shows the proportion of public transfer expenditures going to the poor each year, taking the average of the two one-year point estimates for each of our panels. As we see there, only around 30 per cent of transfers go to the poor in Germany and the Netherlands, whereas half as much again goes to the poor in the US.[42]

---

[41] For any given individual, this 'spillover' is of course just 'public transfers' minus the 'poverty gap' for that individual.

[42] Mitchell (1991, p. 82) reports broadly similar results based on Luxembourg Income Study data (Germany 1981, Netherlands 1983, US 1979).

The darkened portions of figure 7.9 represent the proportion going to the 'seriously poor', defined as those with pre-government equivalent incomes of less than 40 per cent of the national median. There are marked differences across the three countries in that respect as well, with a much larger proportion of US expenditures going to the seriously poor than in Germany or especially in the Netherlands.

Figure 7.10 examines programme efficiency in a cross-time perspective. The issue there is what proportion of public transfer expenditures goes to people who are poor on the basis of their one-yearly income, compared to the proportion going to people whose pooled five- or ten-yearly income is below the poverty line. From figure 7.10, we see that that proportion drops sharply with those longer time perspectives (albeit rather less sharply in Germany than the other two countries). Even in the most programme-efficient welfare regime (the US), less than 30 per cent of public transfers go to people who were poor on the basis of their ten-yearly pooled pre-government equivalent incomes.

As in section 7.5.1 above, judging programmes in terms of the efficiency with which they target expenditures on the poor is more appropriate when applied to means-tested programmes than it is to non-means-tested programmes which do not (formally, at least) even try to do so. Were we to confine our analysis to means-tested programmes alone, the same broad patterns traced in figure 7.10 would emerge in even more exaggerated form.[43]

Clearly, the liberal welfare regime is most successful at achieving programme efficiency and the social democratic regime least successful. How the liberal welfare regime achieves that programme efficiency is clear from section 7.5. Liberal regimes minimize the number of errors of overpayment, at the cost of maximizing the number of errors of underpayment. While liberals thus succeed in not squandering welfare benefits on the non-poor, that success comes at the cost of frustrating the purposes of welfare policy in other respects, by denying welfare benefits to people who are poor and deserve them. The social democratic welfare regime is more successful at succouring a larger proportion of the poor, precisely because it is prepared to run the risk of benefiting the non-poor

---

[43] With average one-yearly German programme efficiency for means-tested programmes being just under 40 per cent, for Dutch means-tested programmes just over 10 per cent and for American means-tested programmes an astounding 86 per cent. Five- and ten-yearly rates drop off in a similar way to figure 7.10, though in the US especially they remain even at the ten-yearly point, extremely high (63 per cent). Rainwater, Rein and Schwartz (1986, p. 197) similarly report that in liberal welfare regimes like the US and Britain around 80 per cent of money spent on means-tested public assistance goes to the pre-transfer poor, whereas in social democratic regimes like Sweden only 36 per cent does, all on a one-yearly basis.

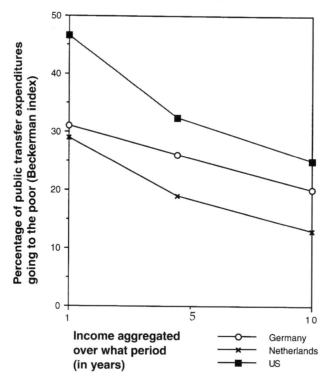

Figure 7.10. Programme efficiency of public transfer expenditures over time (based on appendix table A1, Eff 6A).

as well: in so doing, it arguably serves the purposes of welfare policy better than the liberal regime, but not in ways that the Beckerman index of programme efficiency is designed to detect (Weisbrod 1970).

7.7   Hypothesized inefficiencies versus the real world

Thus there are a great many ways in which welfare programmes might be thought to be *prima facie* inefficient. But there is an important difference, here as always, between *prima facie* and on-balance assessments.[44] And

---

[44] There are various other considerations an on-balance assessment would have to take into account. Among them are these:

(1) Though inefficient in themselves, they may nonetheless constitute importantly compensating components of a 'second-best' set of arrangements, where first-best conditions cannot all be met (Lipsey and Lancaster 1956).

(2) Complaints about target inefficiencies presuppose that there is some mechanism available for targeting benefits more precisely without greater administrative costs or target-efficiency costs (discouraging from claiming or wrongly disqualifying deserv-

there are many more factors at work producing economic growth than those in the chain of causation traced in figure 7.1.

The upshot of our discussion in this chapter is that some welfare regimes do indeed conduct their affairs in more efficient ways than others. By most of the standards picked out in the neo-classical economist's hypothetical chain of causation, the liberal welfare regime ought indeed to be deemed more efficient than either the corporatist or especially the social democratic one. At the end of the day, though, those intermediate inefficiencies do not really seem to matter in so far as the bottom line is economic growth and prosperity. All these welfare regimes seem to produce about the same sort of economic growth and prosperity for their citizens.

How exactly they manage to do so is a mystery that is beyond the scope of our study. The simple fact that they do so is sufficient for our present purposes. 'Incentives are not behaviours', in the terms of one wise maxim of policy analysis (Marmor, Mashaw and Harvey 1990, pp. 219–22).

> ing claimants); both are typically involved in tighter means-tests (Goodin 1985), and on balance it might be most efficient even in the narrow sense towards which 'target efficiency' points simply to accept some over-inclusiveness as the inevitable cost of including all who should be included (Goodin, Le Grand *et al.* 1987).
>
> (3) Complaints about 'work disincentives' rightly point out that the poor are not *financially* as well off as they would have been had they continued to work the same number of hours: but money is only part of people's welfare, and poor people who work fewer hours are in other respects (leisure) clearly better off; so the leak here is from money to leisure, rather than 'waste' pure and simple, and the overall effect of the transfers on people's welfare more comprehensively assessed is thus indeterminate just on the basis of financial calculations.

8   Reducing poverty

What poverty 'really means' is a vexed question. As it is actually experienced by those who are poor, poverty may well be more a matter of social conventions than objective conditions. Poverty is arguably relative rather than absolute, socially determined rather than reflecting fixed natural necessities, requisites of sociability rather than material necessities. Were we constructing indicators *de novo* we might wish to take all those considerations on board. The data available to us in the panel studies, however, have little bearing on more subjective aspects of the social experience of poverty.

What the panel surveys provide in abundance is information about people's command over cash resources. By anyone's reckoning, that is largely what poverty is all about. The analysis of panel data provides insights into poverty, its duration and recurrence, which are unavailable in any other way.

8.1   Measurement issues

In assessing the adequacy of a family's income, among the first things we must do is to take into account how many mouths must be fed. Hence we must adjust for household size, which is conventionally done through 'equivalence scales' of the sort discussed in section 6.3.2 above.

The next step in addressing the adequacy of people's incomes is to specify what level of income, thus adjusted, constitutes poverty. Relying upon 'official' poverty lines would be impossible. Even if every country in the world recognized an official poverty line, different countries applying different poverty lines would confound any genuinely comparative research. But in any case, among all the countries of the OECD, only the US recognizes an official poverty line, and one which is much disputed at that (Orshansky 1965; Ruggles 1990; Citro and Michael 1995).[1]

---

[1] Beyond the period here under study, the Netherlands has come close to accepting an official poverty line very similar to our own in its November 1995 report on *The Other Side of the Netherlands* (*De andere kant van Nederland*) (Dirven, Fouarge and Muffels 1998, pp. 158 ff.).

Here we shall adopt, with slight amendment, the practice which is conventional among OECD poverty researchers of taking '50 per cent of median national equivalent disposable (i.e., post-government) income' as our measure of 'poverty'.[2] When speaking of the proportion of the population falling below the 'poverty line' or the 'poverty threshold' in the discussions that follow, what we mean is simply 'the proportion of individuals in the population who have less than 50 per cent of median equivalent disposable (post-government) income'.

Using that measure, we calculate 'poverty rates' for the countries under study over various different periods. Annual poverty rates – the percentage of people in the country who are poor in any given year – are the sorts of statistics which are familiar from cross-sectional studies of the more standard sort. Using our panels to track the same individuals though time, however, we can also calculate the extent to which people are poor over the longer term. That is a condition more serious, and surely more demanding of policy intervention, than short-term poverty. We therefore distinguish short-term (one-year) poverty from medium-term (five-year) and long-term (ten-year) poverty. First, we look at poverty in two specific years: one in the late 1980s, another in the early 1990s. Then we look at poverty over two five-year time slices: one over the late 1980s which is an unbroken boom period in all these economies; another over the early 1990s, which contains a slump for all these countries. Finally, we look at poverty over the entire ten-year period, from the mid-1980s to the mid-1990s. As explained in section 6.2.6, we calculate longer-term poverty simply by aggregating all of an individual's income over the period in question (five or ten years); and an individual is then said to be poor on a five- or ten-yearly basis if that individual's N-year income, added together, would have been below the poverty threshold for all those years.[3]

[2] See, e.g., Atkinson, Rainwater and Smeeding (1995). European Union reports tend to use as their standard of poverty '50 per cent of *mean* equivalent disposable (post-government) income' (O'Higgins and Jenkins 1990; Atkinson 1998b, p. 23; cf. Muffels 1993). But that measure is unduly sensitive to outliers in the sample – especially inappropriately, to the rich getting richer (thus raising mean income, and with it the poverty threshold). Intuitively, how many people are deemed poor ought not to be sensitive to what is happening at the very top end of the income distribution. Calibrating the poverty threshold in terms of median income helps to mitigate the risk of that.

Of course, no poverty measure is utterly without its problems. Ours is subject to the problem, pointed out by Ringen (1988: 359), that 'if a dictator overnight chops off the heads of the richest 10 per cent [of the population], there will automatically be less poverty'. (Strictly speaking, what would happen is just that the poverty line would drop, and with it the absolute number of people who fall below it: but whether that is a larger or smaller percentage of the depleted population depends on how exactly income is distributed.) Conversely, if we exclude from the sample everyone with zero income, the poverty line will automatically rise (Atkinson 1998b, p. 23n).

[3] That is, below 50 per cent of the median equivalent income aggregated over those five or ten years for the nation as a whole.

Finally, as explained in section 6.3.1, we distinguish 'pre-government' and 'post-government' income. 'Pre-government income' consists principally of 'market income' (including both labour and asset income); it also includes typically small amounts of 'private transfer income': alimony from ex-partners; gifts from family or friends or private charities; and so on.[4] 'Post-government income' is just 'pre-government income' adjusted for government taxes and transfers (that is, adding transfer payments to that individual from the government, and subtracting the taxes that individual pays to the government).

8.2   Reducing the extent of poverty

The basic facts on the extent of poverty across our three countries are as simply stated as follows:

- In all three countries pre-government poverty is surprisingly high – in the neighbourhood of 20 per cent. Furthermore, it remains stubbornly high, at least over the medium term, reducing only slightly over the course of a full decade. As is to be expected, pre-government poverty is marginally higher in the second period (containing an economic slump for all countries) than the first (which was a boom period in all countries); but again, even those factors make much less difference than might have been expected to overall national pre-government poverty rates.

- Post-government poverty, however, varies dramatically across these countries. Even just on an annual basis, the proportion of the population of post-government poor in the US is on average around 18 per cent, whereas it is less than half that in Germany and less than half that again in the Netherlands. Significant though they are, those differences are magnified further still over time. Dutch poverty rates drop to around 1 per cent over a five-yearly period, whereas American rates remain around 15 per cent and German ones around 6. And whereas post-government poverty virtually disappears (dropping to 0.5 per cent) in the Netherlands over a ten-yearly

---

[4] In Germany and the US, but not the Netherlands, it also includes a component of 'imputed rent' representing the benefits to private homeowners of living rent-free in their own homes. Calculations on earlier Dutch data suggest that including this variable makes virtually no difference to the overall distribution, so this difference between the three data sets is unlikely to alter our basic findings very much.

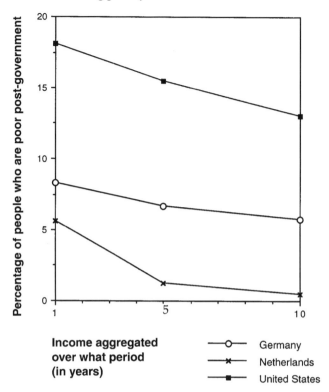

Figure 8.1. Extent of poverty, post-government (based on appendix table A2, Pov 1A).

period, it remains stubbornly stuck at just under 6 per cent in Germany and at 13 per cent in the US.

These post-government poverty results are presented graphically in figure 8.1. (A full account of the data underlying this figure and all other findings discussed in this chapter will be found in appendix table A2.) Figure 8.1 presents poverty rates in the form in which cross-national poverty researchers are most accustomed to seeing them – for the whole population. In many respects, old age is different in all these countries (both in the sense that people's working years differ importantly from their non-working years, and also in the sense that provision for old age differs in different countries), and given those differences it might be more fruitful to focus separately on the poverty of the aged and among people in working-aged households. Poverty among the aged, specifically, is further discussed below. Suffice it for now to say that, if figure 8.1 were redrawn to represent poverty just among people in working-aged households, it would look essentially just the same.[5]

The clear conclusion is that, while the labour markets of these three countries are performing similarly in terms of the pre-government poverty they throw up, their governments are very different in the extent to which they ameliorate that pre-government poverty through taxes and transfers. The social democratic welfare regime of the Netherlands and the corporatist welfare regime of Germany do far better at alleviating poverty through taxes and transfers than does the liberal welfare regime of the United States, with the social democrats somewhat outperforming the corporatists even in the short term and very substantially outperforming them in the longer term.

Aggregate poverty rates for the nation as a whole, however, mask the very different experiences of different groups within the population. Some groups are more likely to be pre-government poor in some countries than others. From earliest times, the aged and children have constituted 'vulnerable' groups upon which policy-makers focus (Palmer, Smeeding and Torrey 1988). Latterly, that focus has come to include racial minorities and, more recently still, single mothers. And there is clear evidence of higher rates of poverty among all those groups in our panels. Blacks and hispanics in the US and guestworkers in Germany are substantially more likely to be poor, and to stay poor for longer. So too are single mothers and female-headed households.[6]

Pre-government poverty rates among the aged vary in misleading ways across countries. In some countries, workers depend primarily upon state old age pensions to support them in old age, whereas in other places the aged rely more typically upon private occupational superannuation which is coded as pre-government income even where participation is legally mandatory (Rein and Turner 1997). What really matters, though, is of course post-government poverty – and there some very real differences among the three welfare regimes do stand out.

Aged poverty rates, post-government, are five times greater in corporatist Germany and ten times greater in the liberal US than they are in the social democratic Netherlands, even on an annual basis. And once

---

[5] To confirm that, just compare the poverty rates reported in appendix table A2 for items Pov 1A (the whole population) and Pov 1B (people in households whose head is under age sixty).

[6] All those results are essentially the same as reported in our preliminary presentation of these findings for the first five years (Headey, Goodin, Muffels and Dirven 1997, table 5).

again those differences – great though they already are – are even more greatly exacerbated over five- and ten-yearly periods. Post-government aged poverty remains at about 25 per cent in the US and at about half that in Germany, across all periods, whereas in the Netherlands it starts far lower (around 2 per cent) and virtually disappears over ten years.

Much the same story can be told about the three welfare regimes' performance with respect to child poverty and poverty among single-parent families. Pre-government poverty rates among those groups are somewhat higher in the US than in Germany or the Netherlands. But post-government poverty rates are dramatically so. And again, the social democrats in the Netherlands do far better at reducing (indeed, virtually eradicating) child poverty over the longer periods than do corporatists in Germany (where even on a ten-yearly basis child poverty remains at 5 per cent).

Another group of particular policy concern is the 'working poor'. Pre-government poverty among those in full- or part-time employment is low (around 2 per cent) in the Netherlands and only a little higher (just under 5 per cent) in Germany, on an annual basis; and while it is substantially higher in the US (around 12 per cent), annual poverty among the US working poor is only about half as high as among the population at large. Little can be said about the comparative performance of these different welfare regimes over longer periods (the number of individuals in these cells of the tables becomes too small). A striking fact about the working poor nevertheless does seem to emerge. Among those in work, poverty seems to be essentially unaffected by government taxes and transfers in all the countries under study. Post-government poverty rates among those in full- and part-time employment are essentially the same (indeed in the US they are systematically higher, if only slightly so) as pre-government poverty rates. Perhaps the explanation is that governments are reluctant to assist the working poor, for fear of reducing work incentives.

8.3   Reducing the depth of poverty

In addition to our concerns with the extent of poverty, we are also concerned about the *depth of poverty*. It is not just a matter of how many people are poor: it is also a matter of how poor they are. A country's having 5 per cent of its population below the poverty line would be bad. But its having 5 per cent of the population only just below the poverty line is not nearly as bad as it would be to have more than half those in poverty living way below the poverty line.

Formally, the standard way of measuring the depth of poverty is in terms of 'poverty gaps'. This measures how far below the poverty line the average poor person falls[7] – a calculation which can only meaningfully be done on post-government incomes.[8] Our data suggest that the average individual whose post-government income is below the poverty line falls below it by about 30 per cent across all three countries under study on an annual basis. In the US, that remains true on a five- and ten-yearly basis as well. But in both Germany and the Netherlands five-yearly poverty gaps are only about half the annual ones, reducing by half (or, in Germany, more) again on a ten-yearly basis.

Another and in many respects better way of getting an intuitive grasp on the depth of poverty is to look at the percentage of the population in deep poverty. Recall that our poverty line is 50 per cent of median income. So anyone with an income of less than 40 per cent of median national income can be considered to be in 'deep poverty'. In terms of their pre-government incomes, about a fifth of the population across all three countries is in deep poverty on an annual basis, and about a seventh of them remain so even on a ten-yearly basis.

In terms of post-government incomes, though, the real differences between welfare regimes emerge. More than 10 per cent of Americans remain in deep poverty annually even after government transfers, whereas in the other two countries the numbers are only half that (even less in the Netherlands). Furthermore, over time the proportion of Americans in deep poverty reduces only slightly (to around 8 per cent on both a five- and ten-yearly basis). In Germany longer-term rates of deep poverty hover around 2 per cent, whereas in the Netherlands deep poverty drops to 1 per cent on a five-yearly basis and literally disappears on a ten-yearly basis. As with the extent of poverty, so too with the depth of poverty: the social democratic welfare regime seems best, and the liberal welfare regime decidedly worst, at reducing it; and the differential between them increases over time.

Although we are mostly concerned with the poor and the very poor, we ought also to spare a thought for those on the edge of poverty. The same sorts of analysis can be conducted of the fate of the 'near poor' by looking at those just over our poverty line, whose income is under 60 per cent of national median income. In terms of people's pre-government income,

[7] Mathematically, the poverty gap, G, is expressed as:

$$G = ((0.50 \ Y_m) - (Y_p)) \ / \ Y_p$$

where Y_m = the median equivalent disposable (post-government) income among the population as a whole; $(0.5 \ Y_m)$ = the 'poverty line'; Y_p = the median equivalent disposable (post-government) income among all households with equivalent disposable (post-government) incomes below 50 per cent of Y_m.

[8] Given the fact that a substantial proportion of the poor rely exclusively on public transfers, and have essentially zero pre-government incomes, pre-government poverty gap calculations are not terribly meaningful.

well over 20 per cent of the population of all three countries would be 'poor or nearly poor' on an annual basis, reducing only slightly over time. But in terms of annual post-government income only about half as many would be 'poor or nearly poor' in the Netherlands (and about two-thirds as many in Germany), whereas in the US almost the same proportion would remain 'poor or nearly poor' after government taxes and transfers as before them. Over longer periods, once again, the US does little to reduce rates of 'near poverty', Germany does a little more and the Netherlands substantially more. On the basis of ten-yearly income, just under 20 per cent of Americans would be 'poor or nearly poor', whereas only half as many Germans would be, and only just under 3 per cent of Dutch people would be.

Varying the poverty line to allow us to look at people who are both 'deeply poor' or who are 'poor or nearly poor' thus tells us important things about the different welfare regimes. The methodological point of such an exercise is to check to what extent our findings might be altered by adopting an alternative poverty line. The upshot of that sensitivity analysis is that, while the exact numbers of people in poverty would of course differ, the general patterns would not. And that in turn points to a conclusion of substantive importance: the three different welfare regimes here under study differ not only in *how many* people they make and leave poor; they differ, too, in *how poor* they make and leave those people.

8.4   Reducing the duration of poverty

There is also a temporal dimension to poverty which is separate from questions of depth and extent. Bad though it is to be in poverty for one year, it is far worse to be in it for several. It is this issue which panel studies are peculiarly able to explore, in ways that standard cross-sectional profiles are not.

We explore issues of the duration of poverty through the technique of 'spell analysis', described in section 6.3.6 above. Basically, this involves calculating the proportion of poverty spells still going on after one, two or however many years. The 'duration of poverty' is thus measured as the unbroken period of time an individual's total income remained below the poverty line. Both pre- and post-government incomes can be analysed in this way, but it is of course post-government poverty which is of principal concern to us.[9] The results of just such an analysis of the

---

[9] For what it is worth, about a third of pre-government poverty spells disappeared before the end of the first year across all three countries; but whereas in the US two-thirds of pre-government poverty spells had ended by the fourth year, in both Germany and the Netherlands it took fully eight years for them to do so.

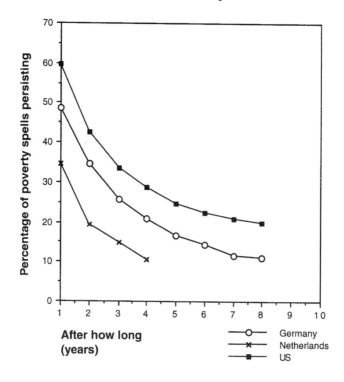

Figure 8.2. Duration of poverty spells, post-government (based on appendix table A2, Pov 3A).

duration of post-government poverty spells appear in figure 8.2.

From Figure 8.2 we see some striking differentials in the duration of post-government poverty spells. In the Netherlands, only just over a third of such spells last over a year. In Germany, almost half do. In the United States almost 60 per cent do. Whereas almost three-quarters of post-government poverty spells have ended by the third year in Germany, that takes two more years in the US. And so on.

The clear conclusions are that the social democratic Dutch welfare regime is highly adept at curtailing the length of poverty spells through its public transfer programmes, as well as at minimizing the number of such spells in the first place. Corporatist Germany's tax-transfer system does well, but rather less well than the social democratic Netherlands, in both respects. The liberal United States generates far more poverty spells than either of the other welfare regimes and does far less than either of the other two to reduce them through its tax-transfer system.

8.5 Reducing the recurrence of poverty

Panel data also allow us to assess, in a way cross-sectional data do not, the frequency with which poverty recurs, hitting the same people time and again. As explained in section 6.3.6, this is a separate issue from the duration of poverty spells. It is perfectly possible for any given household's poverty spells to be short in duration but for them to recur frequently. Imagine a situation in which no household remains in poverty for more than a year at a time, but the same households take it in turns being in poverty every other year. Such a pattern would obviously be of far more concern than a pattern in which different households are in poverty every year, with no one household ever having to suffer poverty more than once.[10]

For a measure of recurrent poverty which speaks to those concerns, we might examine 'hit rates', understood as the total amount of time over ten years that a person's equivalent income has been below the poverty line. Again, these statistics can be calculated for both pre- and post-government incomes, though it is once again post-government poverty which is of principal concern.[11] These post-government poverty recurrence rates are graphed in figure 8.3.

In all three countries, of course, a sizeable majority of people are never post-government poor at any time over the ten years. But even then, the size of that majority varies considerably across the three countries, from just over 60 per cent in the US to 76 per cent in Germany and 81 per cent in the Netherlands. The more striking differences, however, come in how frequently post-government poverty strikes the same people in those different countries.

As we see in figure 8.3, in the Netherlands only just under 8 per cent of the population experiences post-government poverty in two or more years out of ten. In Germany, almost twice as many do, and in the US three times as many do. Virtually no one experiences post-government poverty in seven or more years out of ten in the Netherlands, whereas in the US fully 10 per cent do, and even in Germany almost 3 per cent do.

In terms of poverty recurrence, then, it is once again the social democratic Netherlands whose public transfers are best at reducing the number of times post-government poverty strikes the same persons, time and

---

[10] What is of concern here is not, strictly speaking, 'recurrence' – the number of times the household falls back into poverty, having previously escaped it – but rather the number of years overall that the household has spent in poverty. What we ought to try to minimize is that total number of 'poverty years'.

[11] For what it is worth, once again, about 60 per cent of people are never pre-government poor across all three countries, and in all three countries only a quarter are pre-government poor three or four times.

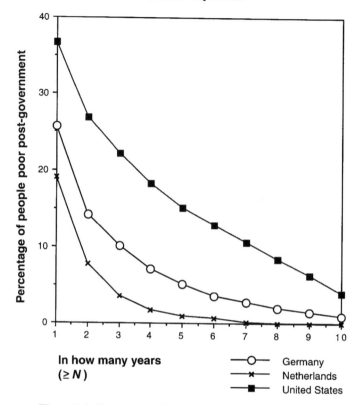

Figure 8.3. Recurrence of poverty, post-government (based on appendix table A2, Pov 4A).

again. Corporatist Germany does notably worse, and the liberal US very dramatically worse, on this score.

8.6   Government poverty reduction

Brute facts about poverty are fascinating in themselves. At the end of the day, however, our concern with poverty is a public policy concern. We want to know not only how much poverty there is, and how deep, long-lasting and recurring it is; we are also vitally concerned with what governments can do about it.

8.6.1   The need for government intervention

Throughout this chapter, we have been focusing primarily upon post-government poverty. We do so on the grounds that what really matters, at the end of the day, is how many people are poor (and how poor they are, how often and for how long), taking account of both the income they receive through the market and of assistance they receive from the government.

In assessing the extent to which government action is needed at all, though, it is people's pre-government incomes upon which we must focus. Pre-government income, after all, represents how well off people would be in the absence of government interventions.[12] And how many people would be poor on the basis of their pre-government incomes alone thus provides a measure of the 'need' for government intervention to alleviate poverty.

Told in terms of government performance and post-government poverty, the story of this chapter has been one of great variability across different countries and different welfare regimes. Told in terms of market performance and pre-government poverty, the story is one of substantial uniformity.

If they had to live on their pre-government incomes alone, almost a third of the population in all three countries would be poor for two or more years out of ten. In any given year, pre-government poverty would strike about 20 per cent of the population in all three countries, and pre-government poverty would remain around 15 per cent even on a ten-yearly basis even in the best-performing country. Furthermore, three-quarters of the pre-government poor in each country would be deeply so, with incomes below 40 per cent of median national income; that too remains true across all countries even on a ten-yearly basis. And even after eight years more than a third of pre-government poverty spells would still be continuing in the Netherlands and Germany, and a quarter in the US.

In short, a very substantial proportion of the population in all countries would be at serious risk of falling into poverty, at some time or another, if they had to live off their market incomes alone. And in the absence of government interventions, that would often be grinding poverty: deep, persistent and recurring. Taking pre-government income as a measure of the need for government interventions to alleviate poverty, then, it would

---

[12] The real situation is much more ambiguous than that simple sentence makes it seem, since many of the government interventions in view impact, positively or negatively, upon the performance of economic markets, and hence 'pre-government' incomes. These interactions are so complex that we might never be able to disentangle them and rigorously specify the counterfactual of what the income distribution would really look like in the absence of any government interventions at all. Given those complications, 'pre-government income' seems as good a rough approximation as any other. For the classic discussion of these issues, see Ringen (1987; 1996b: 20–1).

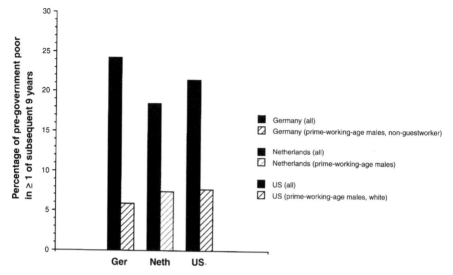

Figure 8.4. Risks of pre-government poverty among those in the top half of the income distribution in the first year under study (based on appendix table A2, Pov 5A).

seem that that need is substantial and substantially uniform across all countries and all welfare regimes.[13]

Furthermore, the risk of poverty and the need for government assistance to alleviate it is widespread across the population. Certainly the risk of poverty is not uniform: some people are clearly more at risk of pre-government poverty than others. But the proportions of people who fall into poverty at some time or another are surprisingly high, even among the most privileged groups in society.

To illustrate that proposition, let us focus on those people who started the decade in the top half of the income distribution in the first year under study, and then ask what proportion of them fell into poverty over the course of the next nine years. Figure 8.4 shows the proportion of the economically advantaged who fell into pre-government poverty at some time or another over the decade to be surprisingly high – around 20 per cent (a little less in the Netherlands; a little more in Germany, and more again in the US).

To some extent, these results are driven by people falling into pre-

---

[13] And, judging from these panel results, across swings in the business cycle: pre-government poverty rates are not substantially larger in the second half of the period (which corresponds to an economic downturn in all countries) than in the first half (which was a boom period in all countries). For details, see appendix table A2, Pov 1A.

government poverty simply because they retired and no longer had any substantial pre-government income. It is a point nonetheless well worth noting, that even the relatively well off are at substantial risk of poverty upon leaving the workforce. But old age and retirement is a more predictable sort of risk, from which mid-career people might imagine themselves to be effectively insulated.

To show what sorts of really unpredictable risks that even mid-career people run of poverty, then, the second bar for each country in figure 8.4 focuses purely upon people of prime working age (25–59). Furthermore, to show that the risk of poverty is far from negligible even among the more favoured sectors of the labour force, we focus there upon prime-working-aged males in the dominant ethnic groups (white in the US, non-guest-worker in Germany[14]) in each of these countries. Again, we turn our attention to people who were in the top half of the income distribution in the first year under study, and ask what proportion of them fell into poverty in one of the subsequent nine years.

As the second bar for each country in figure 8.4 shows, that most privileged sub-set of the population is less at risk of falling into pre-government poverty at some time over the decade. That is only to be expected. The more striking finding is that there remains a very real risk of falling into poverty, even among those favoured by income, gender, age and (in two of the three countries) race. Across all countries, this group stand a better than one in eight chance of falling into pre-government poverty, at some time or another over the course of the decade.

The upshot is that no one is effectively immune from falling into pre-government poverty. It certainly helps to be well off, to be middle-aged, to be male and to be white or non-foreign. But none of that constitutes anything like a guarantee that one will not fall into poverty at some point or another. People in those privileged categories ought to realize that one in eight people just like them fell into poverty sometime or another in each of these three countries, over the decade under study.

8.6.2   The effectiveness of government interventions

We have been reflecting upon different welfare regimes' respective performances throughout this chapter. Perhaps the most striking graphic representation of those differences is shown in figure 8.5.

Clearly, judging from figure 8.5 there is much that governments can do

---

[14] The Dutch panel contains no information on the corresponding category (immigrants) in that population: the statistics we report on the three countries are therefore not strictly comparable in that respect, but they are near enough, given the modest percentage of immigrants in the total population of prime-working-age Dutch males.

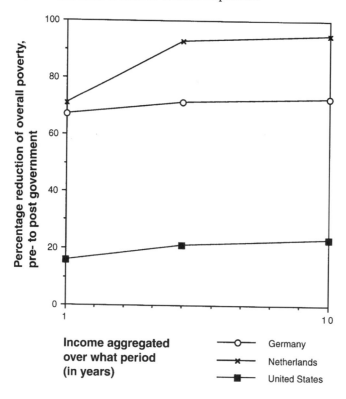

Figure 8.5. Government reduction of poverty overall (based on appendix table A2, Pov 6A).

– and that the social democratic Netherlands, in particular, does do – through public transfers to reduce the incidence of poverty. From our discussion throughout the rest of this chapter, it is equally clear that there is much that governments can do – and that social democrats do do – to reduce the depth, duration and recurrence of poverty.

Figure 8.5 shows corporatist welfare regimes to be almost as effective as the social democratic regime in reducing poverty on an annual basis, although less so on a five- and ten-yearly basis. As our discussion in the rest of the chapter has shown, the corporatist regime is also rather less effective at combating poverty in all those respects as well. That is broadly in line with our background expectations, perhaps. What is surprising, against that background, is instead that the corporatists' performance comes as close as it does to the social democrats' in so many dimensions. Across all the dimensions we have surveyed here, the corporatist welfare regime seems broadly in the same league as the social democratic one in combating poverty.[15]

Liberal welfare regimes, in contrast, are strikingly bad at combating poverty in every respect. In one way that is odd, given that it is liberals who are so utterly fixated upon the question of 'what do they do for the poor' (Lampman 1974) as the litmus test for their welfare institutions, and who refuse to brook any other policy goals for those institutions. But while it is true that liberals want their welfare state to help the poor and only the poor, it is also true that they want it to do so in the most efficient way possible and at least cost to the overall macro-economic performance of the country. That is the 'big trade-off' which liberals constantly confront, and that is what causes liberals to temper their pursuit of social equity and poverty alleviation. That was the subject of the last chapter.

The comparative performance of welfare regimes at reducing poverty over time is also of interest. From figure 8.5 we see that liberal and corporatist welfare regimes eradicate only a very little bit more poverty in the long and medium term than in the short term. The social democratic welfare regime, in contrast, not only reduces poverty more than the other two regimes but reduces it even more over five years and ten years than over a single year. It is a good performance that gets even better over time.

These general patterns stand out more starkly still when we shift our attention from the whole population (which was the focus of figure 8.5) to working-aged households alone. Figure 8.6 graphs the same statistics as Figure 8.5, but just for people living in households whose head was under age sixty. Comparing figures 8.5 and 8.6, we can clearly see that the only sort of poverty the liberal US welfare regime removes is poverty among the aged (and it removes only about half that, compared to Germany and the Netherlands which remove some 90 per cent of it). The impact of US government taxes and transfers on working-aged households is either nil (on a ten-yearly basis) or negative, actually pushing more of them into poverty. The same is true, in less extreme fashion, of corporatist Germany: the bulk of its anti-poverty efforts are confined to the elderly, with its overall poverty reduction rates around 70 per cent, dropping to nearer 20 per cent (and declining over longer periods) for households of working age. The same is even true of the social democratic Netherlands in the

---

[15] Both of them, it ought also to be noted, are rather less effective at reducing poverty in economic downturns than they are at reducing it in economic boom times. That is evident in the poverty rates based on one-year income aggregates reported in appendix table A2, Pov 1A. But as we also see there, that differential performance was substantially eradicated in both countries in the poverty rates based on five-yearly income aggregates (even though the economic slump extended across several of those five years). There is no such pattern of differential boom/bust performance in reducing poverty in the US, which reduces poverty so much less anyway.

short and medium term; but the social democratic welfare regime very substantially reduces long-term working-aged poverty (by over 90 per cent) in a way that the other two regimes most clearly do not.

Let us close this discussion by looking at the different policy instruments through which different welfare regimes attack poverty. Figure 8.7 displays the step-wise reduction in pre-government poverty, made first by social insurance pension payments, then by other public transfer payments, then by taxes.[16] In that figure, we once again confine our attention to the population aged under sixty, and we examine government policy performance in alleviating poverty on the basis of incomes aggregated over one, five and ten years.

Figure 8.7 shows Germany and the US as having about the same profile, no matter which aggregation we consider. Both remove about the same proportions of people under age sixty from poverty by social insurance pensions and by other public transfers, and then both tax about the same proportion of people whom public transfers have rescued from poverty back into poverty. Similar though their profiles may be in that respect, however, the crucial difference is of course that Germany starts (and thus also ends up) with a much smaller proportion of its under-sixty population poor than the US; and that, too, is true no matter which aggregation we consider. The social democratic Netherlands, in contrast, removes a relatively smaller proportion of pre-government poor from poverty through social insurance pensions, but it eradicates a very much larger proportion of poverty through other public transfers, and (especially in the ten-yearly aggregated incomes) does not tax nearly such a large proportion of people back into poverty.

Two aspects of that finding are particularly surprising in terms of our background expectations about the policy instruments characterizing each type of welfare regime. First, Germany removes about the same proportion of the population from poverty through other public transfers as it does through the contributory social insurance pensions which are the corporatist regime's hallmark. Second, within the liberal US welfare regime we would expect heavier reliance on public transfer-style public assistance for the relief of the working-aged poor; but the US actually achieves no more poverty reduction through that route than it does through social insurance schemes for that same age group. Only the Netherlands runs true to its regime form. The Netherlands achieves far

---

[16] In the University of Syracuse matching file upon which our work is based, 'household social security pensions' includes old age pensions, widows' and orphans' pensions and disability pensions in the US and Germany. 'Public transfer programmes' include everything else. Given that categorization, Dutch old age and disability pensions (funded as they are primarily out of general tax revenues) are more like public transfers than social security pensions, and we categorize them accordingly.

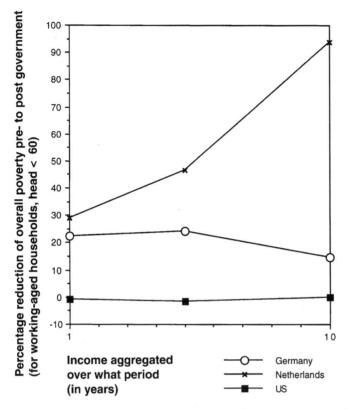

Figure 8.6. Government reduction of poverty among working-aged households (based on appendix table A2, Pov 6B).

more working-aged poverty reduction through tax-funded public transfers of a social democratic sort than it does through social insurance[17] – and the absolute amount of poverty reduction it achieves in those ways is very substantial indeed.

What figure 8.7 also shows is that all three welfare regimes tax a certain proportion of people back into poverty, to some greater or lesser extent. That is true even of the Netherlands in respect of one-yearly income aggregates; and while it essentially ceases being true of the Netherlands on longer-term aggregates, it remains powerfully true of the US and Germany on all income aggregates.

In a way, this should come as no surprise. After all, tax policy is quite

---

[17] This is less because they rely on different programmes than because they organize broadly the same programmes (disability pensions, etc.) on a different basis, relying more on public funding and less on insurance contributions.

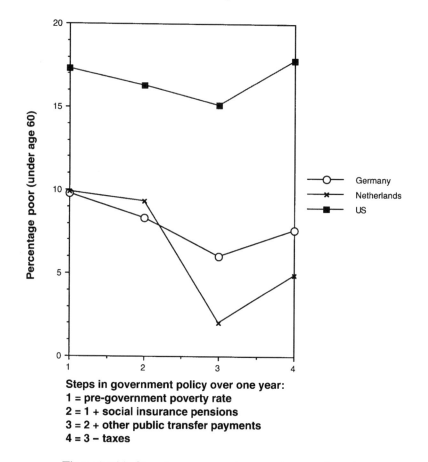

Figure 8.7(a). Steps in government poverty interventions, incomes aggregated over one year (based on appendix table A2, Pov 6F).

separate from social welfare policy, pursuing substantially different goals through altogether different instruments. Still, figure 8.7 provides graphic evidence of the extent to which liberal and corporatist governments, especially, are undoing through their tax policies what they have done through their welfare policies. On the face of it, that figure would seem to suggest the need for improved harmonization of tax and transfer policies, particularly in those welfare regimes.

The combination of inadequate transfers and punitive taxes on the working poor in the US, in particular, seems to have disastrous effects on the incentives for the most privileged segments of the workforce to

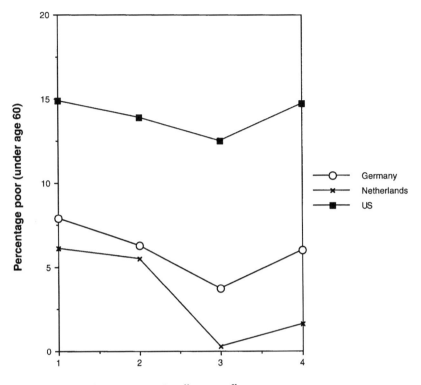

Steps in government policy over five years:
1 = pre-government poverty rate
2 = 1 + social insurance pensions
3 = 2 + other public transfer payments
4 = 3 - taxes

Figure 8.7(b). Steps in government poverty interventions, incomes
aggregated over five years (based on appendix table A2, Pov 6F).

support anti-poverty policies there. In both Germany and the Netherlands, government interventions reduce the numbers of well-off, prime-
working-aged males who fall into poverty over the course of a decade.
The numbers of those people falling into post-government poverty at
some time over the decade is about a sixth less, in each of those two
countries, than the number who would have been poor on the basis of
their pre-government incomes alone. In the US, in stark contrast, government interventions actually increase the numbers of such people falling
into post-government poverty by almost a third again.

It is not as if the more privileged groups in the US need government

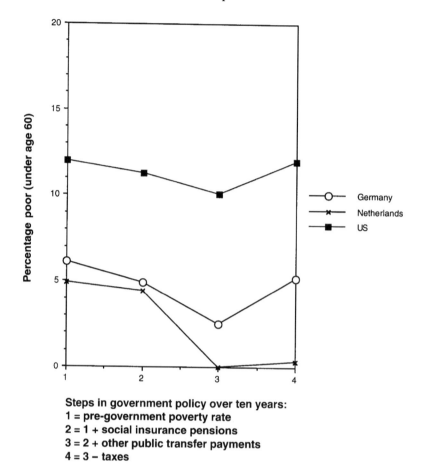

Steps in government policy over ten years:
1 = pre-government poverty rate
2 = 1 + social insurance pensions
3 = 2 + other public transfer payments
4 = 3 – taxes

Figure 8.7(c). Steps in government poverty interventions, incomes aggregated over ten years (based on appendix table A2, Pov 6F).

interventions any less than their counterparts abroad. If anything, they need them more: their rates of falling into pre-government poverty at some time over the course of the decade are higher than those of their counterparts abroad. The point is simply that the inadequacy of US benefits and the harshness of US taxes on the working poor make this most privileged group net losers from the operation of the US tax-transfer system. They stand at real risk of needing government help, but what the US government gives them hurts rather than helps.

9   Promoting equality

The real meaning of social equality is much disputed, as is evident from chapter 2. Some say that we should be concerned primarily with equality of social status, with things like 'equal respect', 'equal consideration' or 'equal concern' being prime goals in view. While acknowledging these as important goals too, other commentators say that we should first and foremost be concerned instead with equality in the distribution of material goods and services. And even within that realm further disputes arise. Some would want us to pick out certain centrally important goods and services where equality seems to matter more than elsewhere. Or again, some say that we should be primarily concerned with equality of 'welfare' (or 'happiness' or 'well-being'), and that worrying about equality in the distribution of resources amounts to fetishizing what are merely means towards those other more important ends; others insist that what really matters is equality in the distribution of opportunities, and that looking at the distribution of resources is part (but only part) of that.

Were we constructing our empirical indicators *de novo*, we might want to try to capture some of those further distinctions. Within the existing panel data there is little that bears on many of those more subtle issues. But what the panels offer in abundance is a wide range of reliable and internationally comparable economic indicators: information about respondents' command over cash resources and how many hours they worked to get them. With those indicators, we can analyse people's material standard of living.[1] That is an immensely important part of the story that anyone would want to tell about equality, even if it is only part of that story.[2]

---

[1] Or, anyway, what level they could have, if they actually chose to spend their income: a distinction rightly emphasized by Ringen (1988).

[2] As emphasized by, for example, Rainwater (1974).

9.1   Measurement issues

There are many ways of measuring inequality, each of which tends to bring out slightly different aspects of the phenomenon. Mathematically the most subtle of these is the mean logarithmic deviation index of inequality, owing to Theil (1967). The formula for calculating this 'Theil-0' index is relegated to a footnote.[3] Suffice it to say, here, that the Theil-0 index is particularly sensitive to variations at the lower end of the distribution. The lower the Theil-0 statistic, the more equal is the distribution.

The Theil-0 index has a number of mathematically attractive properties. Not least of these is that it is 'decomposable', which is to say that Theil-0 indices can be meaningfully added and subtracted from one another, in a way that most other indices of inequality cannot (Theil 1967, pp. 94–6; Sen 1973, p. 35; Shorrocks 1980). Decomposability is highly useful in determining how much inequality between the sexes or races or whatever contributes to overall inequality. For such reasons the Theil-0 index is the preferred inequality measure among many, if not most, contemporary economists working in this field.

The Theil-0 index poses certain problems for these purposes as well. For one thing, it presupposes a log-normal distribution. That is approximately true of post-government equivalent income, but it is strikingly untrue of pre-government equivalent income: a substantial proportion of the population (up to 20 per cent in the case of the Netherlands, for example) has zero pre-government income. The Theil-0 index proves not at all robust against violations of that magnitude to its log-normal assumptions. Various adjustments can be made to overcome such difficulties, of course, but those adjustments are imperfect correctives.

Among non-economists, the Gini index is perhaps the most familiar index of inequality. Again, the formalities will be relegated to a footnote.[4] Suffice it to say, once again, that the smaller the Gini index the more

---

[3] The Theil-0 (T_0) index is defined as follows:

$$T_0 = \frac{1}{n} \sum_{i=1}^{n} \log(\mu/y_i)$$

where i = individuals in the population (1 to n); y_i = the share of income going to the ith individual and μ is the mean. In calculating Theil-0 we follow the conventional practice of omitting the top and bottom 1 per cent of the sample to increase the stability of the statistic.

[4] Calculation of a Gini index starts by plotting a Lorenz curve, with a proportion of the population on one axis (poorest to richest) and a proportion of the nation's income (or wealth or whatever) on the other. The Gini coefficient is then calculated by taking the area between that curve and the 45 degree angle line of 'perfect equality', as a fraction of the entire area below that line.

equal the distribution. And given the way it is calculated, the Gini index is particularly sensitive to what happens in the middle of the distribution. That, in turn, constitutes the Gini's greatest drawback for the purposes here in view. Those concerned with social inequality are concerned primarily with the fate of the poor, or perhaps the very rich and the very poor. The relative standing or fluctuating fortunes of moderately comfortably-off people in the middle is of comparatively little concern to those concerned with overall social inequality. Yet it is precisely in this middle range of the distribution that the Gini index is most sensitive.

A simple measure that captures those concerns far better is the '90/10 ratio': that is, just the income (or wealth or whatever) of the ninetieth percentile, divided by that of the tenth percentile. The larger the 90/10 ratio, the richer the rich are compared to the poor, and hence the more unequal the distribution.[5]

One great virtue of the 90/10 ratio is its utter simplicity, which makes it intuitively easily accessible to the lay reader. Simple though it is, the 90/10 ratio arguably best captures what is of most concern to us when talking about social inequality (Atkinson, Rainwater and Smeeding 1995). True, that ratio focuses exclusively on the fate of the fairly rich and the fairly poor and ignores whatever might be going on in the middle. But so too, perhaps, do social reformers worried about inequality in the first place. Of course, 90/10 ratios cannot be used for all purposes: sometimes (as in the Netherlands again) the person at the tenth percentile of the income distribution has no pre-government income; and of course ratios cannot be calculated with zero in the denominator. For a great many purposes, however, 90/10 ratios provide a revealing insight into social inequality.

In appendix table A3, we report all three of these indices, as appropriate. In the text, however, we confine ourselves to talking in terms of more familiar and accessible measures: Gini coefficients, 90/10 ratios or, more straightforwardly still, the proportion of the population in particularly disadvantageous circumstances.

Here as in chapter 8's discussion of poverty, we distinguish between pre-government and post-government income distributions and the equality found within them. Looking at those distributions on an annual basis generates the sort of results familiar from traditional cross-sectional studies. But here again, we shall also take advantage of the unique opportunities afforded by panel data to pool each person's income over five or ten years, and look at the inequality of those distributions as well.

Note, finally, that all the measures to be reported in this chapter will be

[5] Occasionally we will use a '75/25' ratio, calculated in essentially the same way.

concerned with inequality across the community as a whole. Another way of interrogating these same data, and one which takes particular advantage of the peculiar strengths of panel data, is to look at inequalities in each person's income *across time*. Evening out income over the lifecourse is, of course, a very important function of the welfare state. Equalization of that sort will, however, be reserved for our discussion of 'social stability' in chapter 11.

9.2   Promoting income equality

As with poverty so too with equality, there is little difference across the three countries in the levels of pre-government income inequality thrown up by the market. In Germany and the United States the Gini coefficient of inequality of pre-government incomes is around 0.43 on an annual basis, and a bit lower in the Netherlands. Like poverty, inequality in pre-government income distributions reduces over time in all these countries, ending up between 10 and 15 per cent lower in the distribution of ten-yearly income than in that of annual income. But across all these countries the Gini coefficient of inequality in market income would, even on a ten-yearly basis, remain between 0.334 (in the Netherlands) and 0.389 (in the US).

Government taxes and transfers do much – but very much more in some places than in others – to alter the income inequalities thrown up by the market.[6] As shown in figure 9.1, the Gini coefficient of inequality in post-government incomes remains at 0.37 in the US on an annual basis, dropping only to 0.327 among incomes aggregated over ten years. But it drops to around 0.27 in Germany and the Netherlands, even just on an annual basis. On a ten-yearly basis it drops further still, to 0.222 in Germany and 0.196 – six-tenths of the pre-government rates – in the Netherlands.[7] (The data underlying figure 9.1, and all others in this chapter, will be found in appendix table A3, at the end of this book.)

The 90/10 ratio tells the same story even more strikingly. In the US, the post-government income of the ninetieth percentile is almost six times that of the tenth percentile's, on an annual basis; and even over ten years it still remains 4.6 times that. In Germany, post-government income inequalities are lower. There, the ninetieth percentile gets around 3.5 times the post-government income of the tenth percentile annually, drop-

[6] It also seems true that government taxes and transfers do less to equalize incomes in times of economic downturn (the second half of our period) than in economic booms (the first half of our period), across all three countries. See appendix table A3, Eq 1A.
[7] Analysing the same panel data using Shorrocks' (1978) more sophisticated techniques, Burkhauser and Poupore (1997) likewise find greater 'permanent income inequality' in the US than Germany.

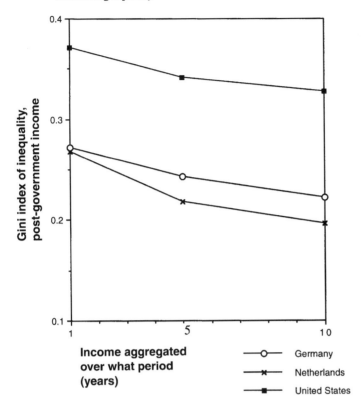

Figure 9.1. Inequality in post-government income (based on appendix table A3, Eq 1A).

ping to 2.8 times that over ten years. In the Netherlands, post-government income inequalities are lower still. Even on an annual basis, the ninetieth percentile's post-government income is only around three times that of the tenth percentile's, dropping to under two times theirs over ten years. In short, the 90/10 ratio is twice as high in the liberal US as in the social democratic Netherlands on an annual basis, and is even more than that on a ten-yearly basis, with corporatist Germany coming in between but much nearer the Dutch than the American performance.

9.3   Promoting social equality

Social inequality represents another important dimension of inequality which equalitarians would want to see reduced. There are of course many aspects of that phenomenon, and once again only a few of them are captured in panel data which are primarily devoted to the study of income dynamics. There is nothing in them that even remotely bears upon inequalities of social status, for example; information on health and housing was collected from some countries' panels but not others; and so on.

There are essentially just two dimensions of social inequality we can explore at all systematically through the use of these panels: one is educational inequality; the other is inequality in the distribution of paid employment.

9.3.1   Inequality in education

Within these data, the only way to adduce educational inequality is from differences in people's reported 'levels' of education. In all three panels, information was collected from the panels on the respondent's level of educational attainment. The countries have very different educational systems, however, confounding any attempt at straightforwardly adducing comparative statistics on educational inequality from 'level of educational attainment' data. The one thing that does seem broadly comparable across all three countries is what it means to complete secondary school – and, by extension, what it means to have further education beyond that point.

Thus we can get a small and imperfect glimpse into the extent of educational equality in these three countries by asking what proportion of the population has no more than a secondary-school education. In both Germany and the Netherlands that proportion is high (around 87 per cent), whereas in the US it is substantially lower (just under 60 per cent). Now, in certain obvious respects it is good to have more people with more education, as in the US. But insofar as educational *equality* is concerned, the German and Dutch pattern is decidedly more equal. There, most people have completed secondary school, and few have proceeded beyond that – which is a much more equal distribution of educational advantage than that found in the US, where the top 40 per cent go on to further (in non-negligible proportion, much further) education.

We have to content ourselves with that rather informal ranking of the three countries, rather than trying to measure educational inequality through any fancier statistics. The various higher qualifications that people pursue are hard enough to render cross-nationally comparable; locating them on anything like an interval scale is more daunting still. But the differences between Germany and the Netherlands on the one hand, and the US on the other, are sufficiently great for this measure to be telling, despite its relative informality. Educational attainment is higher in the US, but it is also much more unequal there than in the other two countries under study.

9.3.2   Inequality in employment

There is another area of socio-economic inequality on which the panel studies provide substantially richer and apparently reliable data. That concerns the number of 'hours worked' in paid labour.[8]

As our measure of inequality in employment, we take the ratio of the number of hours worked by the seventy-fifth percentile of households, divided by the number of hours worked by the twenty-fifth percentile. We use a 75/25 ratio rather than the 90/10, because the tenth percentile of households sometimes has no hours in paid labour, and it is of course impossible to calculate the ratio with zero in the denominator. We aggregate the total number of hours of paid labour of everyone in the household, rather than basing our calculations on individual labour hours alone, precisely because households characteristically try to compensate for the unemployment of the primary earner by increasing the work hours of secondary and tertiary earners. Finally, we focus on households headed by a person of prime working age to prevent our results being confounded by the sorts of variation in working hours that come with the movement from school into the labour market and from the labour market into retirement.

The dominant dimension of inequality in the distribution of paid employment is of course that of gender. Thus, we will look first at inequalities in working hours among prime-working-aged men alone; and then we will look at inequalities in employment status between prime-working-aged men and women together.

From figure 9.2 we see that inequality in hours worked by households is lowest in the Netherlands and greatest in Germany. Furthermore, those inequalities diminish across time. In the Netherlands and the US, those rates decline at about the same rate, and the inequality between households in the number of hours worked over ten years is only about five-sixths the inequality in hours worked over one year. Inequalities in employment declined at about the same rate in Germany on a five-yearly basis, but then dropped much more precipitously on a ten-yearly basis. The final result is that inequality between households in the number of hours worked over the whole ten years is identical to that found in the US

---

[8] In the panel data, there is a separate self-reported measure of 'employment status' which seems to produce much less reliable results. Hence we prefer to report instead on people's apparently more reliable (or anyway internationally more comparable) reports of hours worked.

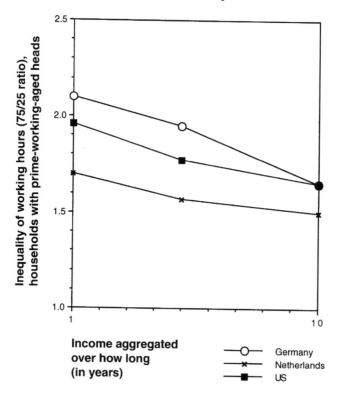

Figure 9.2. Inequality in employment among households
(based on appendix table A3, Eq 2A).

on a ten-yearly basis as well. The Netherlands, however, has lower rates
of employment inequality than either of the other two countries, regardless of the period over which labour hours are aggregated.

9.3.3   Cumulative inequality

In looking at inequalities in the distribution of all these various social
goods, we should be concerned not only with how unequally each of them
is distributed, but more especially with how cumulative those inequalities
are, looking across the distributions of all these goods taken together.
From the point of view of the equality principle, however it might be
construed, it would be far worse for people who get little of one good to
get little of all others as well. It would be far better, from an egalitarian
point of view, that those who get little of one good get lots of some other.

Michael Walzer (1983, ch. 1) speculates that there might be different 'spheres of equality', with different things being allocated according to distinctive principles, each very different from the ones governing other spheres. In such circumstances it is easy to imagine how a form of 'complex equality' might emerge, with everyone getting more of some things and fewer of others in a way that roughly balances out.

We address this question of the cumulation of inequalities across spheres more fully in our discussion on 'social exclusion' in section 10.4 below. To foreshadow this, we report there evidence of modest levels of multiple deprivation across three spheres (income, employment and education).[9] These levels are high enough to be of genuine policy concern, but they are low enough to provide substantial support for the hypothesis of 'complex equality'. Broadly speaking, social and economic inequalities really do seem to constitute separate spheres, and inequalities really do seem to balance one another across them.

9.4   Promoting equal citizenship

There is a political dimension to equality as well as a socio-economic one. Of course political interventions of an egalitarian sort are supposed to impact directly upon social and economic equalities as well. But above and beyond the material difference political interventions might make is the sheer fact of 'equal citizenship', which is itself a value of considerable importance.

Again, that notion has many connotations that are not easily cashed out in terms of the sorts of socio-economic variables contained in our panel data. Equal citizenship is essentially a status concept. It is essentially a matter of 'equal respect'. Its earliest and still primary connotations are equality in the rights and duties of citizens: equality before the law, equality in voting rights, equality in duties to bear arms in defence of one's country and to serve on juries judging one's peers. Obviously, none of the variables in our panel data remotely bear on any of that.

There is, however, one clear way in which the panel data do touch upon issues of 'equal citizenship' . Equal citizenship might be taken to imply, among other things, universality in the distribution of state benefits. If welfare benefits are indeed 'rights of citizenship', as Marshall (1949) would have it, then clearly every citizen should receive them – or at least some of them, some of the time.

The universal payment of a flat-rate, basic income, paid to every adult

---

[9] Those levels would be substantially more modest, yet again, if we did the calculations on an individual rather than household basis. The latter is of most concern to integrationists, the former perhaps to advocates of equality.

in the community, is everywhere still just a dream. But in many places there are some entitlement programmes, such as old age pensions or child benefits, which are paid on a flat-rate, universal basis. The income streams that those categorical programmes generate flow differentially to households, depending upon age structures and family circumstances, of course. But it is not beyond the bounds of possibility that a patchwork of such programmes might end up paying some monies (maybe even broadly the same amount of money) to nearly everyone in the community, under some heading or another.

Across all three of the countries under study, old age pensions are indeed a nearly universal benefit for the age group in question. So too are child benefits for families with benefit-aged children, at least in the two countries that have child benefits as such. (The US is atypical within the OECD world for lacking them: its only analogue is Aid to Families with Dependent Children, as the programme was called in the period under review, received by only 7 per cent of families with children.)

Setting those two explicitly universalistic programmes aside, there are further questions about the universality of the other benefits that each welfare regime has to offer. This is displayed in figure 9.3. There we see that between a quarter (in the US) and a third (in the Netherlands) of people receive some public transfers other than old age pensions or child benefits from government in a single year. The proportion that receives some such benefits over longer periods rises in all countries, but much more dramatically in the Netherlands than in either of the other countries. Some 60 per cent of Americans and Germans receive some public transfer payment other than old age or child benefits from their governments at some time over the course of ten years. In the Netherlands, it would seem from this panel, literally everyone does.

Ensuring that everyone gets something from the welfare state can be politically important in building a political support base for the welfare state (Goodin, Le Grand et al. 1987, ch. 1). It may be morally important in signalling the state's equal concern and respect for all its citizens. That may amount to a largely empty gesture, though. Despite the fact that everyone gets something from the state, some people might get very much more than others; and despite the fact that everyone gets the same thing from the state, that might just amount to everyone getting the same paltry sums.[10] Still, the symbolism of equal citizenship matters alongside the money.

[10] That seems to be the case in the US: benefits there are lower, but more equal (see appendix table A3, Eq 3E).

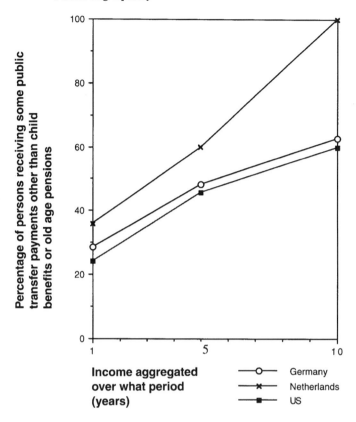

Figure 9.3. Equal citizenship: benefit universalism (based on appendix
table A3, Eq 3D).

9.5   Government reduction of inequality

Interesting though brute facts about social inequality may be in themselves, our principal concern here is with what difference government
might make.

9.5.1   The need for government intervention

Most of the discussion in this chapter has, once again, been framed
around post-government income distributions and the equality found
within them. That is only right. The lived reality of inequality is after all
the post-government distribution. But in assessing the need for government intervention – in assessing what inequality would be like in the

absence of government intervention – it is the pre-government income distribution to which we should look.

In so doing, however, we are handicapped by the fact that the most intuitively accessible indicator of inequality, the 90/10 ratio, is undefined for pre-government distributions. The reason that is so (the tenth percentile has zero pre-government income, and you cannot divide by zero) in itself reveals something about inequality, of course. But for more systematic assessment of the extent of pre-government inequality we are forced to rely on indicators with less immediate intuitive significance.

We can nevertheless get something of an intuitive grasp on what is and is not an acceptably low Gini coefficient of income inequality by using our intuitive assessments of post-government inequalities as benchmarks. Annual Gini coefficients for the post-government US income distribution are around 0.37 – and most of us who are concerned about inequality at all would regard post-government income inequalities in the US as unacceptably high. By contrast, annual Gini coefficients for post-government Dutch income are around 0.27, and most of us concerned with inequality regard those as impressively low.

With those benchmarks in place, we can now go back to assess pre-government income inequalities in light of them. Two facts stand out, when inspecting pre-government income inequalities:

- Income inequality is everywhere substantially higher pre-government than post-government. Even in the Netherlands, annual pre-government Gini coefficients are on average some 8 per cent higher than the US post-government Ginis of 0.37, which we deem unacceptably high. Annual German pre-government Ginis are fully 16 per cent higher than that, on average, and American ones a little higher still.
- Furthermore, pre-government income inequalities do not reduce much over time. The ten-year pre-government Gini is only 11 per cent lower than the annual in the US, and the German and Dutch only around 16 per cent lower.

In short, in the absence of government intervention, inequality in all three of these countries would be higher than the highest levels we observe even in the least egalitarian of them, post-government; and in the absence of government intervention, those high levels of inequality would persist over time. Those who are concerned with equality at all would clearly find that an intolerable state of affairs.

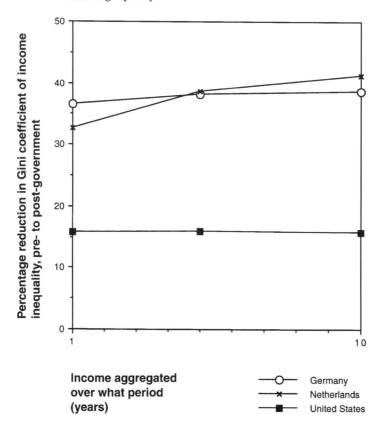

Figure 9.4. Government reduction in income inequality (based on appendix table A3, Eq 4A).

9.5.2 *The effectiveness of government interventions*

Let us look, now, at the difference that different governments, and the different types of welfare regimes that they represent, make in reducing income inequality. Figure 9.4 plots the percentage reduction in Gini coefficients of income inequality, pre- and post-government.

From that figure we see that on average German and Dutch government interventions reduce income inequality by between 30 and 40 per cent, with the Germans doing rather better than the Dutch on an annual basis. This rises towards (and in the Dutch case exceeds) 40 per cent, on a ten-yearly basis. The US government interventions apparently reduce income equality by fully less than half that on either a one-, five- or ten-yearly basis.

Clearly, different welfare regimes do perform very differently when it comes to reducing income inequality. In social democratic countries like the Netherlands, the market generates rather less income inequality to start with, and their welfare regimes do much more to reduce it both in the short and especially in the long term than do liberal welfare regimes like the US. In corporatist countries like Germany, the market may generate almost as much income inequality as the liberal US regime, but corporatist welfare regimes do much more (in the short term, proportionately more even than social democratic regimes) to ameliorate that income inequality through public transfers. Still, over time it is the social democrats who achieve the lowest levels of income inequality.

10   Promoting integration

Social integration, too, has the many facets already discussed in chapter 2. Some commentators see it primarily as a matter of psychological attachment: as 'belonging' or some such, as the opposite of feeling 'alienated'. Others think of it more in terms of social networks and 'caring communities'. Yet others think of it primarily in terms of 'normative integration' – of people internalizing the values and codes of conduct of their larger community.

Many of these concerns can be captured only very imperfectly in the panel data available to us. There are no indicators of 'civic participation', 'group joining' or 'voluntary memberships' common across all the panel surveys; there are no measures of residential mobility; and so on. While the measures we concoct of those other aspects of social integration will necessarily have to be indirect and imperfect, it is surprising how many good indirect measures of social integration can be concocted out of this very differently oriented data set. And of course, specifically economic aspects of integration – which is a central aspect of integrationist concerns – are captured very well indeed in these data.

10.1   Promoting integration into households

The family is conventionally characterized as the building-block of society. Conservative politicians concerned to promote social integration are therefore concerned, first and foremost, to promote strong and stable family ties. They are anxious that people accept the responsibilities attending to the extended family: grown children caring for their parents and siblings, as much as for their own offspring. They bemoan the rise of the 'nuclear family'. And they bemoan still more the breakdown of even nuclear families through separation and divorce. Social integrationists thus internalize centrally among their goals those of maximizing the number of people living in family units and of minimizing the number of family breakdowns.

The panels are invaluable when it comes to tracking the consequences of separation and divorce over time. For judging the frequency of separation and divorce itself, however, ordinary cross-sectional data is perfectly adequate (and in certain respects preferable).[1] Those studies consistently show the divorce rate to be substantially higher in the US than the other' two countries under investigation. Indeed, US divorce rates tend to be more than twice those of Germany and the Netherlands across most of this period. Even in the final year under study, by which time German and Dutch divorce rates had caught up a bit with the American, 2.04 per cent of German marriages ended in divorce in 1994 and 2.35 per cent of Dutch marriages did likewise, whereas fully 4.57 per cent of American marriages ended in divorce that year (UN 1997, table 25).[2]

Household integration in the simpler sense of the number of adults living in shared households is more reliably adduced from our panel data. Several caveats need nevertheless to be entered about that variable. Ideally we would like to know the number of *related* adults living together: but some of these surveys omit to query the adults' relationship to the head of household or other household members. Thus we are forced to rely on an imperfect measure which picks up lodgers alongside members of the extended family. Nor does the 'shared household' variable tell us what members of the household do to, for or with one another. All the 'household' variable tells us is whether you share a roof with other adults, which is substantially less than the sort of 'integration into households' that those seeking it would want.[3]

Even with these caveats duly entered, the 'shared household' data still

[1] The panel data imply that, over the course of ten years, only around 4.0 per cent of married couples ever divorced in the Netherlands, whereas 9.5 per cent did in Germany and 16.6 per cent did in the US. Those results seem hard to reconcile with the cross-sectional statistics reported in the text.

[2] Extrapolating from the current year's divorce rate, we can (after the fashion of demographic 'life-tables') project the proportion of marriages in each country likely to end in divorce. The proportion of marriages that would be expected to end in divorce, on the basis of 1985 divorce rates, would have been 54.8 per cent in the US but only 30.2 per cent in West Germany and 34.4 per cent in the Netherlands (Guibert-Lantoine and Monnier 1997: 1210). That is the last year for which information is available for the US, so comparison across all three countries for subsequent years is impossible. Dutch and German projections wobble around over the next ten years, dropping to just over 29 per cent in each case at the midpoint of our study (1990) and ending up at 36.5 per cent for Germany and 39.0 per cent for the Netherlands in the last year of our study (1994).

[3] Neither of course does the sheer fact of sharing a marital bed necessarily imply sharing a life, still less sharing equally in household tasks; so this is a problem which plagues other more standard ways of operationalizing social integration as well.

A better indicator of what household members do for one another might be given by the 'private transfers' variable, if only it specified (as in the panel data it does not) from whom the transfer has come, whether a member of the same household or not. Private transfer income is in any case small in all countries (as evident from appendix table A6, Aut 3A).

provide an important insight into something that is of significance to advocates of social integration. Sharing a house (on whatever basis) with other adults (whatever their relationship) knits you into the social fabric in a way that living alone does not. Thus it is telling evidence, from a social integrationist point of view, that fully 10 per cent more adults live in households they share with other adults in the Netherlands than in Germany or the US, with Germany actually having the lowest rate of shared households among these three countries.[4] It must of course be said that even in Germany the proportion of adults sharing households is high (76 per cent in Germany, rising to 85 per cent in the Netherlands). But the fact remains that the unintegrated tail is greatest in corporatist Germany, where corporatist values are supposed to prioritize social integration as a central goal.[5]

10.2   Promoting integration into the labour force

For those concerned with social integration, the integration of individuals into households is only a first step. Those households should be integrated, in turn, into larger social structures.

Perhaps the most important way in which households are integrated into the wider society, certainly in modern capitalist societies of the sort under study here, is through the household head's attachment to the paid labour force. On that aspect of social integration the panel data do afford good information. We can say that individuals (and through them, their households) are relatively well integrated into the labour market if they are stably engaged in full-time employment. Conversely, those who are not employed or who are employed only intermittently or part-time are relatively less well integrated.

In all three countries, well over 90 per cent of heads of household of prime working age (under sixty years old) are in full-time employment in at least one year of the ten under study. But integration, in its fuller sense, implies 'stably integrated'. And as figure 10.1 also shows, the proportion of household heads who are in full-time employment over the whole decade drops off in all countries, but much more precipitously in some countries than others.[6] Even just confining our attention to people of

[4] See appendix A4, Integ 1A. The average size of households is marginally greater in the US, having in the mid-1980s some 2.6 persons per household, compared to 2.3 in Germany (no data for the Netherlands). But that is just because Americans have a higher birth rate and hence more children in their households (UN 1997, table 27).

[5] The results remain much the same if we restrict the analysis to people aged under sixty-five, suggesting that these findings are minimally affected by people's partners dying and leaving them living alone in old age.

[6] Broadly the same pattern is found if we confine our attention to males of prime working age.

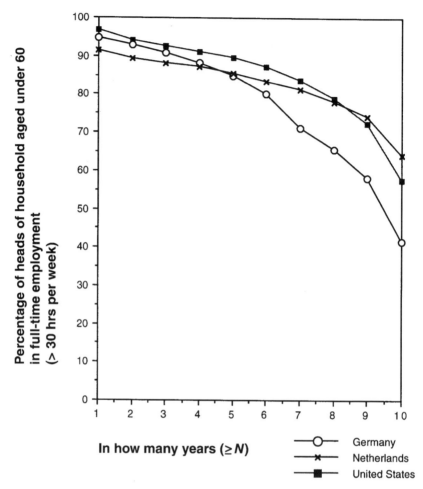

Figure 10.1. Integration of households into labour market (based on appendix table A4, Integ 2A).

prime working age, across all three countries less than two-thirds of heads of household were in full-time employment for all ten years under study. In corporatist Germany, which among the three countries under study should in theory accord highest priority to the integration of household heads into the workforce, the proportion in continuous full-time employment is lowest among the three countries, falling to a paltry 42 per cent in full-time employment for all ten years. In the decade-long perspective, the Netherlands, which started out being (by a slight margin) the lowest on this dimension, ended up being (by about the same margin) the highest.[7] (The data underlying figure 10.1, and all others in this chapter, will be found in appendix table A4, at the end of the book.)

10.3   Promoting economic integration

Beyond integration into the workforce in a social sense, those concerned with social integration would also be interested in the extent to which everyone in the community shares a common fate. If the community is economically tightly integrated, everyone's fortunes will rise and fall together.[8] If some prosper while others suffer then that is a sure sign the community is not tightly integrated, economically.

In trying to operationalize this notion of a 'shared financial fate' using the panel data before us, we can look at the extent to which changes in people's incomes rise and fall together or independently of one another. If people's fortunes rise or fall together, then no one's place should change in the rank ordering of incomes across the country as a whole. If we find that substantial numbers of people do change places in that rank ordering, then that is evidence that people's economic fates fluctuate relatively independently of one another in that country.

Figure 10.2 displays the proportions of people in each country who have moved more than one quintile in the nationwide rankings of income, pre- and post-government, over the ten years under study. There we see that people share more nearly the same economic fate (or at least they do post government taxes and transfers) in corporatist Germany than in the social democratic Netherlands. But surprisingly enough once again, people share more fully still in the same economic fate – both pre- and especially post-government taxes and transfers – in the insistently non-solidaristic US than in the other two countries.

That finding may to some extent be just a statistical artefact, of course. Where the income distribution is substantially more dispersed, as it is in the US, a person has to earn substantially more dollars to move a quintile within that distribution. Where the distribution is less dispersed, as in Germany and especially in the Netherlands, it takes a correspondingly smaller change in real cash terms to move a quintile (Björklund 1993).

---

[7] Although derided as a 'male breadwinner' model, the more general (and generous) way to phrase the corporatist ideal would indeed have us focus on integrating heads of household into the workforce, whatever their gender. Were we to focus on the integration of prime-working-age males rather than on heads of household, Germany would continue to have the lowest proportion of that group in full-time continuous employment over longer time periods (with the other two countries reversing position, and the US enjoying about as much of a ten-year advantage over the Netherlands as the Netherlands does over the US in figure 10.1).

[8] A similar thought underlies Danziger and Haveman's (1978) 'economic concept of solidarity'.

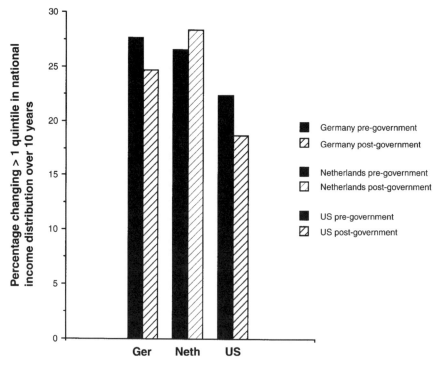

Figure 10.2. Shared economic fate (based on appendix table A4, Integ 3A).

That thought leads us to suspect that our measure might overstate the extent of a truly 'shared economic fate' where the income distribution is relatively unequal and, conversely, to understate it where the income distribution is relatively more equal. Thus we would have clear grounds for suspecting the ranking of the US compared to both the other countries, both pre- and post-government. But as section 9.2 has shown, income equality both pre- and post-government is more nearly the same in the other two countries; so there are fewer grounds for suspecting those countries' rankings relative to one another.

In both Germany and the Netherlands, however, post-government income is distributed substantially more equally than is pre-government income. Following the logic sketched above, that (combined with the possible bias in our measure) might explain why there seems to be less of a 'shared economic fate' post-government in the Netherlands than pre-government. But the same is true in Germany. Despite that bias in our measure, figure 10.2 nevertheless shows more 'shared economic fate' post-government than pre-government. The conclusion that German government taxes and transfers work to increase the extent to which people share the same economic fate ought thus to be regarded as all the stronger.

Something similar could be said about the evidence in figure 10.2 suggesting that there is more of a 'shared economic fate' post-government taxes and transfers in the US as well. Section 9.5.2 has shown that the US does far less to make the post-government income distribution more equal than the pre-government one. But certainly the post-government income distribution, even in the US, is no more unequal than the pre-government one; whereas figure 10.2 shows that, judged in terms of the proportion of the population that jumped a quintile in the income distribution, there is more of a 'shared economic fate' in the US post-government distribution than in its pre-government distribution. That result is not quite so dramatic as in Germany, where a similar result emerged despite the possible measurement bias pushing in the opposite direction. But certainly the US result, here, cannot be explained away by that possible measurement bias either.

Thus we can be moderately confident that the tax and transfer policies of corporatist Germany do promote social integration, in the sense of promoting a 'shared economic fate'. They do not necessarily do so uniquely among the three countries under study, though. While possible measurement biases stand in the way of any strong comparison across all three countries, we have almost as good reason for supposing that US tax and transfer policies induce an increased 'shared economic fate' as well – and if the measurement biases are not too severe, it would seem that liberal US policies actually promote more of a 'shared economic fate' than corporatist German ones.

10.4 Avoiding social exclusion

Finally, concern with social integration gives rise to concern with its opposite, 'social exclusion'. Integrationists fervently hope to avoid creating what has been variously known over time as 'two nations' (Disraeli 1875), 'Other Americans' (Harrington 1962) or an 'underclass' (Wilson 1987) – whole groups of people's being systematically and persistently left out of social life, right across the board.[9]

---

[9] Social exclusion sometimes refers, instead or additionally, to individuals (paradigmatically, the homeless: Jencks 1994) who are socially alienated, outside ordinary social networks and have no one to whom they might turn for help. In terms of French policy discourse, which has done so much to shape European Union discourse on social exclusion, these people constitute the problem for which insertion seems the obvious solution (Favell 1998, ch. 3). Such individuals are not well captured in the panel data available to us, however.

We can get at least a partial handle on the problem of social exclusion by looking at the cumulation of disadvantages across key social arenas. Suppose we found that the same people were at the bottom of the distribution of income as were at the bottom of the distribution of education and the bottom of the distribution of employment. And suppose, furthermore, we found those people at the bottom of all three of those distributions not just briefly but in the long term. That would constitute clear evidence of a 'socially excluded' group in society. If instead we found different people occupying the bottom tiers of those different distributions, then while we would still have social inequalities, at least we would not have cumulative inequality of the sort talked of as 'social exclusion'.

Thus, our measure of social exclusion will be a variation on familiar measures of 'multiple deprivation'.[10] We look at whole households rather than individuals within them, restricting our attention to households with a head of prime working age.[11] We aggregate the post-government equivalent incomes and the hours in paid labour of all individuals to get the household's total; and then we aggregate each household's total income and work hours over the whole decade under study, to yield the total ten-yearly income and employment for each household. The educational attainment variable for each household will be taken just to be the head of household's level of educational attainment. Having thus defined each of the three variables under consideration, we then identify which households fall in the bottom quintile (bottom 20 per cent) of each one of those three distributions. Finally, we identify households which fall in the bottom quintile of all three of those distributions simultaneously. Those are the households which we will call 'socially excluded'. Whether or not that measure captures everything that worries us about social exclusion, it certainly captures three central aspects of cumulative inequality that preoccupy people concerned with social exclusion.[12]

The percentages of households in each country which can be said to be

---

[10] Ringen (1987, p. 241) uses a similar procedure to ours here to assess 'accumulated deprivation', counting what proportion of people were in the bottom decile of all three distributions (of income, housing and personal capacity or efficacy). Atkinson and Sutherland (1989, p. 84) also construct a similar measure of 'multiple deprivation' (housing, income and family status), finding that rather fewer people in Britain suffer multiple deprivation across all three dimensions rather less often than would be statistically expected purely at random.

[11] The first, because otherwise housewives and other non-working members of well-off households would conflate our findings; the second, because household heads who are retired or still in school would similarly conflate our findings.

[12] Note that in Rogers' (1995, pp. 254–9) 'Design of policy against exclusion', the principal prescriptions are for interventions in precisely these three sectors: labour markets (to integrate marginalized members of the workforce); education and training; and social security and assistance (for income support).

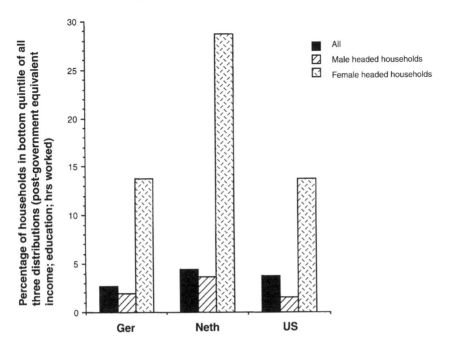

Figure 10.3. Social exclusion (based on appendix table A4, Integ 4A).

socially excluded, on that definition, are shown in figure 10.3. Among all households, social exclusion stands at 2.7 per cent in Germany, compared to 3.8 per cent in the US and 4.4 in the Netherlands. These percentages are somewhat lower than the percentages standardly discussed, but they are very much in the same ballpark.[13] Remember, too, that many of the 'socially excluded' – the homeless, the institutionalized and illegal immigrants, for example – are excluded almost by definition from a panel study. Taking account of all of them would bring the numbers up, perhaps to something much nearer ordinary expectations.

If the percentages of households we estimate as being socially excluded seem small, it pays to bear in mind what a 'random sort' of household would have yielded here. We are looking at the percentage of households in the bottom 20 per cent of three distributions simultaneously. If

[13] René Lenoir, when coining the term in 1974, 'estimated that "the excluded" made up one-tenth of the French population' (Silver 1995, p. 63; see also Atkinson 1998c, p. 11). In the US, Levy's (1977) initial estimate of the size of the 'underclass' – which he defined as people with incomes persistently below the poverty line – ran at around 5 per cent of the total US population; others using different methodologies have of course reported very different numbers there (see Ruggles 1990, pp. 103–15 for a survey).

households were randomly sorted, we would statistically expect only 0.8 per cent ($0.2 \times 0.2 \times 0.2$) of households to end up in all three bottom quintiles at once. We find three (in Germany) to five (in the Netherlands) times that number socially excluded. The percentages may seem small, but they are real: they are far from random.

In assessing social exclusion, most especially, it proves important to distinguish between male- and female-headed households. Among households headed by a male for the entire ten years, social exclusion was rather less (in the US, substantially less) than for households as a whole. Among households headed by a female for the entire ten years, social exclusion was substantially greater – seven (in Germany and the Netherlands) to nine (in the US) times greater than for male-headed households.

10.5   Summing up social integration

We have in this chapter examined social integration from several different angles. Here it turns out that the countries under review look rather different depending upon what aspects of social integration matter most to you.

In terms of integrating people into households, the Netherlands seems best and the US seems worst. In terms of integrating households into labour markets, the picture is more mixed: the US does better at integrating households at some point or another, but the Netherlands seems best at integrating households in the long term. In terms of ensuring that everyone across the community shares a common economic fate, the US might actually do best, though German government taxes and transfers most clearly do operate in the desired corporatist direction. And in terms of avoiding social exclusion, the Germans clearly do best. The overall conclusions are thus somewhat mixed. Depending upon which indicators are accorded highest priority, any of these three countries might be said to promote social integration best.

11   Promoting stability

People value security and stability in their lives, and they look to their governments to safeguard them in all sorts of ways. Many of the ways in which governments do so have little or nothing to do with social welfare policy. Defence and dikes contribute as much to the security and stability of people's lives as do old age pensions and unemployment insurance. Even within the distinctively social welfare realm, there are many more aspects to security and stability than are readily represented by data from panel studies primarily concerned with income dynamics.

Still, income stability is an undeniably important aspect of social stability. Furthermore, it is something which is uniquely well explored through panel data, which have heretofore been all too little utilized for that purpose. We will examine those issues, alongside a few more sociological ones, after a few brief remarks on the sorts of indicators we will be employing in this chapter.

11.1   Measurement issues

Some indicators of social instability are relatively simple and straightforward. We can get a perfectly good handle on some aspects of the phenomenon simply by counting the frequency of destabilizing events like divorce and unemployment. But for other purposes, particularly assessing income instability, something more complex than sheer frequency counts is required.

In this chapter we will employ two such measures of instability within a distribution (of employment or income or whatever). One of them is mathematically unassailable. First is the 'coefficient of variation', which is simply the standard deviation divided by the mean of the distribution. The larger the coefficient of variation, the more the variation within the distribution – and if what it is a distribution of is 'income over time', then the more variation within that distribution the greater the instability of the distribution over time.

A measure that might be more intuitively accessible to the lay reader is the 'min-max ratio'. That is calculated simply by taking each person's worst-year's income over the ten years under study, and dividing it by that same person's best-year's income. The lower the min-max ratio, the lower the worst year's incomes are and/or the higher the best year's incomes are – which is to say, the more variation and hence instability there is in incomes over those years.

Of course, the min-max ratio concentrates on only two years, the worst and the best, out of the ten years under study. The min-max ratio captures the variation in those two extreme years, but about the other eight years it says nothing. The coefficient of variation picks up variation across the whole range, and thus provides fuller information on the distribution as a whole. For that reason, it is mathematically preferable. But the min-max ratio is more intuitively accessible, and by and large it seems to track that other more formal measure tolerably well.[1]

We take the median individual's coefficient of variation or min-max ratio to represent the country's as a whole, for the purpose of most of the baseline reports that follow. But in section 11.4 below we also explore the distribution of income instability by looking, more specifically, at those measures of income instability for people in the bottom half of the equivalent income distribution.

11.2   Promoting stability in social life

Before turning to issues of income stability, let us reflect briefly upon issues of social stability more broadly. After all, the sort of stability that is probably most important to people is stability in their personal lives.

Of course, certain sorts of household instability are inevitable. You leave the family home upon coming of age; your own children grow up and leave home; in old age, one partner dies before the other. Such household changes are as unsettling as they are inevitable. But more disconcerting still, perhaps, are the unexpected sorts of household instability associated with things like separation and divorce.

Our panel data afford us a good window on many of those issues, insofar as they involve household breakdowns. Figure 11.1 graphs the number of changes of heads of household experienced by what percen-

---

[1] Both measures are imperfect in various ways. Suppose, for example, that your income is subject to a high but constant rate of growth (or decline); then your income would be deemed 'highly unstable' on both these measures, even though having your income grow (or decline) by a steady 20 per cent per year is stability of a sort. Or again, suppose that your income fluctuated a great deal from year to year, but that at least it never dropped in any year below your income in the previous year; then again your income would be deemed 'highly unstable' on both these measures, even though having your next year's income always at least as high as last year's once again provides stability of a sort.

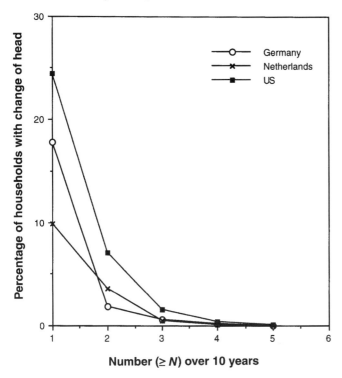

Figure 11.1. Instability of households (based on appendix table A5, Stab 1A).

tage of the population, country by country, across the ten years of our study. The data underlying figure 11.1, and all others in this chapter, will be found in appendix table A5, at the end of this book.

In reflecting upon that figure, the first thing to say is of course that the vast majority of people in all three countries experienced no household breakdown at any point over these ten years. But here again, the size of that majority differs considerably across our three countries – ranging from a high of 90 percent in the Netherlands through 81 percent in Germany down to 75 percent in the US.

Looking at these statistics the other way around, fully a quarter of Americans experienced at least one household breakdown over the course of ten years, whereas only a tenth of the Dutch did (with Germans being in between, two-thirds of the way towards the American pattern). Turning next to the percentage of people suffering multiple household breakdowns, the US continues to be well ahead of both the other countries. Between those other two countries, the results are mixed. Although fewer people in the Netherlands experience one household breakdown than in Germany, more people there experience two breakdowns; thereafter the numbers are essentially the same in the two countries.

Thus the corporatist welfare regime, despite trumpeting most loudly values of security and stability, is actually only a middling performer on that score when it comes to stability of households. Corporatist Germany sees substantially more households break down at least once over the course of ten years than does the social democratic Netherlands. And that finding is mitigated only by the fact that more households break down twice in the social democratic exemplar than in the corporatist one, their patterns thereafter being essentially identical.

11.3   Promoting employment stability

In addition to security and stability in their personal lives, people also value security and stability in their working lives. What matters crucially in that connection is how many different jobs a person has had and how long they have lasted.

The Equivalent Files contain no direct indicators of job turnover. What they do contain (as discussed in section 10.2 above) is information on working hours. From that information, we can infer facts about the stability of full-time employment across time. That is not necessarily to say that people have the same job for all those years. The panels' information on number of hours worked do not allow us to say in which job those hours were worked. But at least those data provide information of a sort on the stability that comes from having a full-time job of some sort or another.[2]

When discussing these data in section 10.2 above, our concern was with the integration of people – primarily heads of households – into the workforce. There, accordingly, our attention was focused primarily upon maximizing the proportion of heads of household in full-time employment. In the present chapter, our concern shifts to the stability of people's employment. That is a concern that applies to everyone of prime working age, not just heads of households. And, in terms of figure 10.1, it implies a concern not so much with how high the lines are but instead with how 'flat' they are. That is to say, employment stability is less a matter of how many or how few people are employed and more a matter of

---

[2] Changing jobs is clearly destabilizing, in a personal and psychological sense, whatever the circumstances. But another sort of stability, and a materially more important sort, is provided by being able to step directly from one full-time job into another. The continuity of full-time employment that is reported in figure 11.2 would therefore be all the more reassuringly stable, if it comes in the face of multiple job changes.

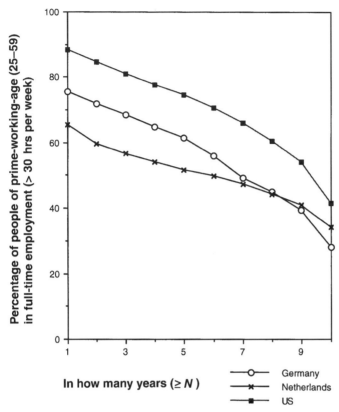

Figure 11.2. Stability of employment (based on appendix table A4, Stab 2A).

how long each of those employed remains in full-time employment. This is shown in figure 11.2. There we see most stability of employment – the flattest line – is achieved by the Netherlands. The lines for Germany and the US start higher than that for the Netherlands, reflecting the fact that a larger proportion of the prime-working-age population is in work for at least one year out of the ten in Germany and the US than in the Netherlands. But the lines for Germany and the US drop off more steeply than that for the Netherlands, reflecting the fact that larger proportions of the people employed in some years are not employed in others in Germany and the US than in the Netherlands. Ironically, it is Germany – whose corporatist ethos would lead us to expect it to place highest priority on employment stability – that has the smallest proportion of its prime working-aged people in full-time employment for nine or more years.

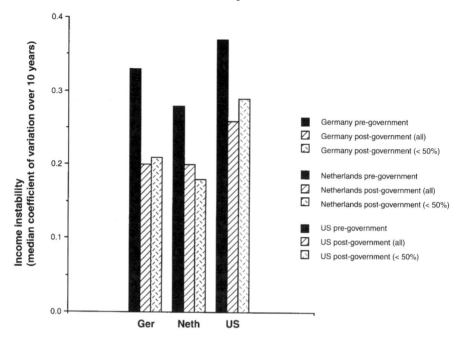

Figure 11.3. Income instability, pre- and post-government (of people in households whose head is under age sixty) (based on appendix table A5, Stab 3A).

11.4   Promoting income stability

People are concerned with secure and stable employment for a whole range of reasons, some more social than economic. But the principal reason most people worry about secure and stable employment, no doubt, is for the secure and stable incomes that flow from it.

Figure 11.3 presents data on coefficients of variation in both pre-government and post-government income over the ten-year period in all three of the countries. (In all cases, analysis is restricted to people living in households headed by persons under age sixty, to avoid movement into retirement conflating our results.) More will be said about the instability in pre-government income in section 11.6 below. Suffice it to say, for now, that pre-government incomes were more stable in Germany than the US, and still more stable in the Netherlands by about the same margin again.

Looking at the middle bar of figure 11.3 for each country, we see that government taxes and transfers do much to damp down those instabilities across all three countries. In all countries, post-government income stability for people overall is only about two-thirds its pre-government levels. The instability of post-government incomes for Americans in general is lower than that pre-government in the Netherlands; and among Germans in general, post-government income instability is identical to that of the Dutch in general.

What is striking in figure 11.3, however, is how unstable even post-government incomes remain in the US compared to the other two countries. Post-government income instability for Americans in general is more than a quarter greater than it is for the Germans or the Dutch in general. Putting that difference in terms of min-max ratios: in Germany and the Netherlands the median person's post-government income in his or her worst year was 53 per cent of that in his or her best year; in the US, by contrast, the median person's post-government income in his or her worst year was only 44 per cent of that in his or her best year.

Fluctuating incomes matter more to the less well off, who presumably have fewer savings to cushion themselves against such fluctuations. Thus we display, as the final bar for each country in figure 11.3, the instability in post-government incomes of people in the bottom half of the distribution of post-government equivalent incomes. As we see from the final bars in figure 11.3, in Germany and the US poor people's post-government income is actually more unstable than that of the population at large (by between 5 and 10 per cent, in Germany and the US respectively).[3] In the Netherlands, by contrast, the coefficient of variation representing the instability of post-government incomes of prime working-aged people is actually around 10 per cent lower for people in the bottom half of the income distribution.

The conclusions to be drawn regarding the comparative performance of welfare regimes are fairly clear. The liberal welfare regime of the US generates considerable income instability in people's market income; and although it does a fair bit to mitigate that income instability through its government's taxes and transfers, instability in post-government income remains substantially higher under the liberal US welfare regime than under the other two. The corporatist welfare regime of Germany generates rather less income instability in market incomes than the US and does rather more to counteract it through government taxes and transfers. The social democratic regime of the Netherlands generates less instability in pre-government incomes than does Germany; but it also

---

[3] Schluter's (1996a, b; 1998) more sophisticated 'stochastic kernel' analysis suggests that income mobility is particularly high at the bottom of the German income distribution, compared to the American.

does less, through its government's taxes and transfers, to mitigate it than Germany. The upshot is that post-government incomes are equally stable in the Netherlands and in Germany, with both being far more stable than the US. Furthermore, in the social democratic Netherlands (unlike both the other countries), post-government income is actually more stable among below-average earners than among the prime-working-aged population as a whole.

11.5   Promoting income stability across the lifecourse

In many important respects the welfare state redistributes income across the lifecourse of any given individual at least as much as it redistributes income across individuals. As Rowntree's (1901, pp. 169–72) pioneering work showed, and as much research has confirmed since, it is part of the normal lifecourse that people's earnings start slowly, peak in their middle years and then drop off again in old age.[4] One important function of the welfare state is simply to redistribute income from our high-earning middle years to our low-earning youth and old age.[5] Insofar as that is all it does, then any redistribution associated with the welfare state looks much more like the upshot of an ordinary insurance (or assurance) policy (Goodin and Dryzek 1986; Barr 1989; 1992; Ringen 1996a, pp. 24–5). That, of course, would cast the case for the welfare state in a very different light politically and morally as well.

Much income instability is indeed strongly associated with ordinary lifecourse events. In addition to those traditional lifecourse events alluded to above, people now have increasingly to cope with new ones such as separation and divorce and early retirement.

Governments keen to reduce insecurities and instabilities engendered by such lifecourse events have basically two options. Either they can try to reduce the number of such events that occur, or else they can try to mitigate the effects of such events if and when they do occur. Policy interventions of the former sort by and large lie outside the scope of the data collected by our panel studies. But information is available within them on the extent to which government taxes and transfers either mitigate or exacerbate the economic disadvantages associated with things like separation and divorce, when they do occur.

These data are presented in figure 11.4. What is depicted there is the extent to which one particular (but particularly important) lifecourse

[4] See, e.g., Lydall (1955); Morgan (1965); Atkinson (1975, pp. 36–40); Layard (1977); Björklund (1993); Falkingham and Hills (1995); Leisering and Leibfried (1998).
[5] For dramatic evidence of that happening in Sweden, see the Swedish Central Bureau of Statistics' graph reproduced in Heidenheimer, Heclo and Adams (1990, p. 358).

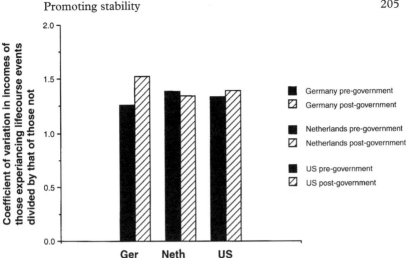

Figure 11.4. Income instability due to separation and divorce, pre- and post-government (based on appendix table A5, Stab 4A).

event – separation and divorce – induces instability in people's incomes, first pre- and then post-government. From that figure we see that instability in the pre-government income of divorcees is around 25 per cent greater than that in the pre-government incomes of those not experiencing any such events, across the three countries in question. The difference is that the Netherlands mitigates slightly (and the US exacerbates, but only slightly) those disadvantages attending divorce and separation, whereas Germany substantially exacerbates them, so much so that those experiencing separation and divorce in Germany suffer fully half again more post-government income instability than do those not suffering those events.

Of course one interpretation of these results might be that corporatist Germany, in its quest for social stability, deliberately engineers economic disincentives to marital dissolution. Maximizing the economic disadvantages of divorce might be part and parcel of a larger strategy for minimizing the numbers of divorces overall. But if that is the strategy, then it is simply not working: as we pointed out in section 10.1, German rates of separation and divorce are still relatively high, almost as high as the Dutch even though the Germans are much less generous to divorcees.

This general pattern of findings is confirmed by figure 11.5, which displays the overall level of post-government income instability as a function of the number of household breakdowns that a person has experienced over ten years. Unsurprisingly, it is everywhere the case that the more breakdowns you suffer the more unstable your income. Figure

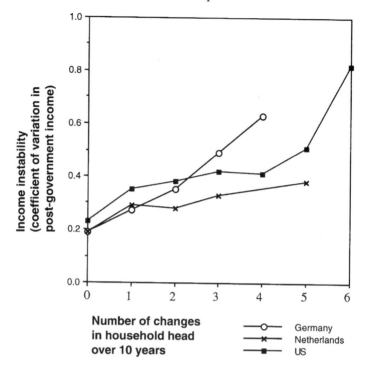

Figure 11.5. Instability in post-government income due to household breakdown (based on appendix table A5, Stab 4B).

11.5 shows that post-government income instability in Germany and the Netherlands is essentially identical for those suffering one or no breakdowns, and it is only just a little higher in each case in the US. But differences in the three welfare regimes emerge fairly dramatically the more household breakdowns people experience above that, with the Netherlands providing clearly the most stability in the income of people with two or more breakdowns and, beyond that, Germany actually providing by far the least.

The social democratic welfare regime, once again, provides most security and stability in the post-government incomes of people suffering destabilizing lifecourse events. And corporatists, who profess those values most vociferously, actually deliver on them no better and sometimes far worse. The liberal welfare regime of the US also performs poorly in this regard, though for those suffering multiple disasters it actually performs better than corporatist Germany.

11.6   Government reduction of income insecurity

The basic facts about income security are socially and politically important. They are too little understood, and too little has been done heretofore employing the unique resources of panel data to illuminate them. At
the end of the day, however, our concern here as elsewhere is a public
policy concern. We want to know not only how unstable people's incomes
are, we are also vitally concerned with what governments can do to help
stabilize them.

11.6.1   The need for government intervention

Most of our discussion of income instability in this chapter has focused
primarily upon post-government income stability. That arguably is what
matters most to people. Post-government income is what they have in
their pockets to spend, after all, and pre-government income is relevant to
their lives only insofar as it is reflected in those post-government holdings.

In assessing the need for government action, however, it is pre-government incomes once again that matter. The instability we find in people's
pre-government incomes is the instability that they would actually experience in their incomes, in the absence of any government intervention.

As we saw in figure 11.3, pre-government incomes are much more
stable in some countries than others. They are substantially less stable in
the US than in Germany or the Netherlands. And among the less well off,
who presumably have fewer savings to cushion them against year-to-year
income fluctuations, pre-government labour income is actually somewhat more unstable in both the US and Germany. Only in the Netherlands is pre-government labour income marginally more stable for prime-
working-aged people in the bottom half of the income distribution than
for prime-working-aged people overall.

Similarly, among prime-working-aged males – who are presumably
most households' primary earners, whose incomes should ideally be more
stable than those of households' secondary and tertiary earners – pre-
government labour income tends to be more unstable than that of prime-
working-aged people overall. The coefficients of variation in pre-government labour incomes are actually higher by a tenth (in the US) to a fifth
(in Germany and the Netherlands) for prime-working-aged men than for
the prime-working-aged population taken as a whole.

Taking those two factors together, we find that those whose incomes
should ideally be most stable – primary earners in the bottom half of the
income distribution – actually experience more instability in their pre-
government   labour   incomes   than   does   the   prime-working-aged

population taken as a whole. The coefficients of variation are between 5 and 35 per cent higher in the US and the Netherlands respectively, with Germany coming in much nearer the Netherlands.

The upshot is that government intervention is certainly needed across all countries to help stabilize pre-government incomes, most particularly of those most in need of income stability (households' primary earners and the less well off). But while government action is needed in all countries, it is needed far more in some countries than others. Instability in pre-government incomes is, unsurprisingly, greatest in the liberal US; more surprisingly, it is almost as great in corporatist Germany. And instability of pre-government incomes in the most at-risk groups (primary earners and the less well off) are most severe there as well. In the Netherlands, those at-risk groups also suffer rather more instability in their pre-government incomes than others. But in the social democratic Netherlands, pre-government income instability is substantially lower across the board, and government action to alleviate it is correspondingly lower as well.

11.6.2   The effectiveness of government interventions

How much governments do to reduce pre-government income instability through their taxes and transfers is, naturally, conditioned by how much they need to do. There is substantially less instability in pre-government incomes in the social democratic Netherlands to start with, so we should not be surprised to find that governments there do substantially less to reduce it further.[6] The more interesting comparison is between the other two welfare regimes, where pre-government income instability is more severe and government interventions more needed.

As we have seen in figure 11.3, the liberal welfare regime of the US does quite a bit to stabilize people's post-government incomes. Through its tax-transfer system, the liberal US succeeds in reducing the coefficient of variation in post-government incomes by just under 30 per cent. Corporatist Germany does better still, reducing it by fully 39 per cent.

Welfare state transfers can and do, then, underwrite a measure of stability in people's post-government incomes which is not found in their pre-government ones, especially in liberal and more especially still in corporate welfare regimes. In closing, let us explore the relative effectiveness of the different mechanisms by which this is done.

Some public transfers are flat-rate and unrelated to previous earnings, whereas others are (at least for a time) earnings-related and explicitly

---

[6] Dutch post-government income instability is only 9 per cent lower than pre-government income instability, measured through the coefficient of variation.

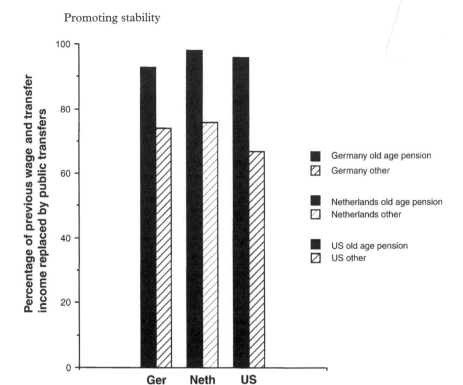

Figure 11.6. Replacement rates of public transfers (based on appendix table A5, Stab 6A and Stab 6B).

geared to replacing people's previous earnings. Countries vary in the extent to which they rely on one or other mode of transfer. They also vary in the proportion of previous earnings they try to replace through their various transfer programmes.

As a measure of that, we calculate the 'effective replacement rate' of public transfers, as follows. Find those people whose principal source of income in one year was market income and whose principal source of income in the next year was public-transfer income. Then calculate their income in the second (public-transfer-dependent) year as a proportion of their income in the first (market-dependent) year. The larger that proportion, the larger the 'effective replacement rate' of public transfer payments in that country.

Our natural expectation would be that corporatist countries like Germany, which are centrally concerned with income stability, should have very high replacement rates. Calculations reveal that effective replacement rates are very high across all countries for old age pensions, as figure

11.6 shows. But even in respect of old age pensions, replacement rates are marginally higher in both the US and especially the Netherlands than in Germany. As regards other public transfers, replacement rates are much lower across all countries, with the differential being greatest (and replacement rates of those 'other' public transfers lowest) in the US. But again, as regards public transfers other than old age pensions, replacement rates are marginally higher in the Netherlands than in corporatist Germany, where corporatist regime logic leads us to expect them to be highest.

In short, people's incomes and many other aspects of their lives are more stable in the social democratic Netherlands than elsewhere. And government interventions are at least partly to credit for that.

12   Promoting autonomy

Autonomy, some may say, connotes a state of mind much more than a state of affairs. Clearly, there is more to being a 'free spirit' than can be teased out of stark socio-economic facts and figures alone. Still, people are certainly not autonomous in any of the relevant senses if they are unable to meet their subsistence needs, or if they must depend upon the arbitrary will of others to do so. So socio-economic status does have an important bearing on questions of 'autonomy', and it is that side of the question that we will be principally exploring through our panel data.

12.1   Issues of conceptualization and measurement

Before addressing those issues directly, however, there are issues of conceptualization and measurement to be canvassed.

At the level of conceptualization, autonomy is essentially a matter of having and exercising free choice; and that is essentially a matter of having viable options between which to choose. Consider the example of a single parent who engages in forty hours a week of paid labour as well as running her household and caring for her young children. Her choice to go out to work as well will look far more autonomous if it had been a viable option for her and her family to rely instead on public assistance – if, had she not gone out to work, she would have had the option of receiving welfare benefits which would have been adequate to meet the needs of herself and her children.[1] If she had no other way to feed herself and her family except to go out to work, then her 'choice' to work forty hours a week in paid labour would look far less autonomous (indeed, it would hardly have counted as a 'choice' at all).

This centrality of such counterfactual conditionals ('what would have happened had she chosen otherwise'), however, poses a serious problem for anyone trying to operationalize notions of autonomy. To assess how

---

[1] Or if she had the option of living off her family, friends, trust account or private charity. Any of those would generate options which, even if forgone, would nonetheless have made her decision to go out to work more autonomous.

autonomous people's choices were, we need to know how viable their alternative options were; and to know that, we need to know what would have happened if people had done something other than they did. But what would have happened in various different counterfactual scenarios – where 'paths not taken' might actually have led – often proves as hard to predict as the future itself.

Important though that may be as a point about operationalizing notions of autonomy in general, however, such difficulties often prove less pronounced in the particular settings here in view. Ordinarily people not working in paid labour would have, as an alternative, received welfare benefits of some sort or another; and if they had chosen to draw a welfare cheque rather than a pay cheque, each of them would presumably have been paid about the same welfare benefits as people on welfare were already drawing.[2] The implication of that would therefore be that welfare regimes which promote the autonomy of welfare recipients by paying them reasonably high benefits can also, at the same time, be said to be protecting the autonomy of non-recipients. Their choice to engage in paid labour will have been rendered more autonomous by their having been given, by the welfare system, a viable option of not engaging in paid labour.

A second difficulty in the conceptualization of autonomy surrounds the issue of thresholds. Just how 'viable' do the alternative options have to be for one's choice to be considered 'fully autonomous'? In reality, of course, these things are always matters of degrees. Options are more or less viable, and people are more or less autonomous by virtue of them. No one is ever completely autonomous, completely beyond the reach of natural necessities of one sort or another. But virtually no one is ever totally lacking in autonomy, either (suicide is almost always an option).

Even if autonomy itself is rightly conceived as a continuous variable, however, it still makes sense to talk in terms of a threshold of 'minimal autonomy'. This ought be regarded as a 'social minimum', dictated by the standards of society rather than by any analytic or natural necessity. And like our standards of 'poverty', this 'social minimum' too ought be seen as relative to the levels of autonomy enjoyed by others in that society.[3]

Where that threshold should be set is a disputed question. Some, inspired perhaps by Veblen's *Theory of the Leisure Class* (1925), might be

---

[2] Were all, or even very many, of those in paid labour suddenly to opt for welfare instead, there is of course every reason to suppose that financial pressures would eventually force welfare payments down.

[3] And for the same reasons: in bargaining games, how much your freedom of manoeuvre buys you depends on how much freedom of manoeuvre others have (Goodin 1990a).

tempted to set the threshold quite high.[4] On that sort of view, only the landed gentry and their contemporary equivalents (company directors, tenured academics[5] and such like) would qualify as autonomous. By that standard, autonomy would inherently be a privileged position which not many people in any given society could ever expect to achieve.

An alternative, which we pursue in this chapter, is to set the standard low. We talk about 'minimal autonomy', defining it in such a way that it can and should be seen as a realistic aspiration for all members of a society and a realistic goal for social policy. With the more specific measure of 'combined resource autonomy' proposed in section 12.6 below, we effectively set a 'minimal autonomy' line which is akin to (indeed, which incorporates) the 'poverty line' itself. In both cases, we really can hope and expect welfare regimes to try to ensure that everyone is above the threshold on those minimal standards of autonomy as well as income.

12.2   Personal autonomy

Before turning to those more economic aspects of autonomy, though, let us consider in passing a couple of more sociological ones. The first is a notion of 'personal autonomy', understood broadly as the capacity to live our lives as we please under conditions of our choosing. A crucial part of that is living with those of your choosing, on terms of your choosing. That in turn has several aspects, two of which will be detailed below.

12.2.1   Independent living

Consider first the option to 'live independently'. This is a cherished goal among young adults aspiring to break free of the family home. But it is also seen as a highly important option among disabled and grey rights activists (Morris 1993).[6]

Living independently does not necessarily mean living alone, of course. Many people who are given a genuine choice in the matter will prefer to form joint households, perhaps even with related others. Some young adults may prefer to remain in the family home for a time. Many prefer to form a family of their own. Many elderly people will prefer to live with relatives rather than in institutions. But it is having a genuine option of living on your own ('independently', in that sense) which makes the choice to do otherwise count as autonomous.

---

[4] Linder (1970), without addressing these specific issues, is clearly writing in that tradition.
[5] Recall the familiar jibes about 'the leisure of the theory class'.
[6] Feminists, too, celebrate the sort of autonomy that can come from escaping a family home run along traditionally patriarchal lines (Elsthain 1981; Barrett and McIntosh 1982).

This is where the measurement problems to which we alluded in section 12.1 arise, though. We know that what actually happened must *ipso facto* have been possible; but it is far harder to know what other possibilities there might have been which were never realized. We know that people who actually chose to live alone had that outcome among their options. But we have no way of knowing, counterfactually, whether people who did not genuinely could have chosen otherwise.

The only way we can know for sure whether or not people in general have that option is to see whether a fair few of them actually take it. That is not to celebrate living alone as ideal; it is merely to say that one's autonomous choice of doing otherwise is predicated upon having that as an option, albeit an option that most of us might not always prefer.

Seen in this light, the relative proportions of people living alone or in households of unrelated others is important (albeit indirect) evidence of personal autonomy.[7] Unfortunately, it is impossible to obtain information (in these panels or indeed in most social statistics) on the exact nature of an individual's relationship to others in the household. But just looking at the average number of adults living in households shared with one or more other adults, it seems that the Dutch are rather less autonomous than either Germans or Americans in this respect.[8]

12.2.2   Reforming households

Further evidence of personal autonomy – the capacity to live one's life as one pleases – is provided by evidence on the forming and reforming of households. No one would care to claim that family breakdown is in itself a good thing, either for the people involved or for the wider society. But neither is being trapped in a household from which one would prefer to escape.

There can be no denying that the 'divorce revolution' brought liberation, of a sort, to women (and men, too) (Weitzman 1985). And it was not only people who actually took the option of getting out of no-longer-desired marriages who found themselves thus liberated. The divorce

---

[7] In shared households comprised of several unrelated adults, we would ordinarily expect more egalitarian, non-hierarchical relations to prevail – and more autonomy for each member of the household, in consequence.

[8] As reported in appendix table A4, Integ 1A, some 76 per cent of Germans and 78 per cent of Americans lived in households shared with other adults, whereas 85 per cent of Dutch people did in this period. According to UN (1997, table 27) statistics – which do not distinguish here between adults and children – the average US household had around 2.6 people in it over this period, whereas the average German one had 2.3 people (no data are reported for the Netherlands). But that presumably just reflects higher birth rates in the US over the period in question, as discussed in section 7.2 above.

revolution also liberated people who, having been given the option of getting out, chose to stay married.

Again, however, it is in the counterfactual nature of 'options not taken' that they are hard to access directly. Once again, we have to approach the measurement problem indirectly. We assume that relatively more of those who chose to stay married had a genuine option of doing otherwise, the more of their compatriots there were who actually pursued the divorce option. Again, that is not to celebrate family breakdowns in themselves; it is merely to celebrate the sort of truly 'voluntary union' that can only exist when dissolving the union is a viable option.

Looking at the frequency of family breakdowns in general, the US has most and the Netherlands least, as has already been shown in section 11.2 above. Those statistics are fine as far as they go: the statistics as presented there do indeed bear upon the 'social integration' concerns central to the discussion of that earlier chapter. But as far as our present concern is with the autonomy of the people involved, some further differentiation is required.

Sometimes people leave their existing households simply because they feel they have to, without reflecting at all upon the viability of that option. And when they have done so, they all too often find that none of the alternative options prove to be particularly viable either. Surely we would not care to call people who are forever shifting between unviable options autonomous, just because they are forever in the process of shifting around between those bad options.

Who has viable options and who does not can hardly be reduced to a simple matter of socio-economics, of course. Poor people as well as rich can often count on assistance from family or friends or new partners.[9] Still, as a rough indicator of the economic viability of separating, socio-economic status is as good as any and better than most. Low incomes are certainly a source of strains and stresses on one side, and high incomes are certainly a source of empowerment on the other.

Let us concentrate, then, on household breakdowns among people who are in the top half of the distribution of post-government equivalent income. In figure 12.1 we find that, while more American and German households than Dutch break down once, fewer German households break down twice or more; the US and Dutch rates of households breaking down twice or more are essentially identical among the more affluent half of the population. What inferences ought be drawn from that depends upon just how heavily multiple as against single instances of household breakdowns ought be weighted, when it comes to assessing

[9] Less often can they count on adequate alimony or child support from ex-partners, it seems (Ellwood 1988).

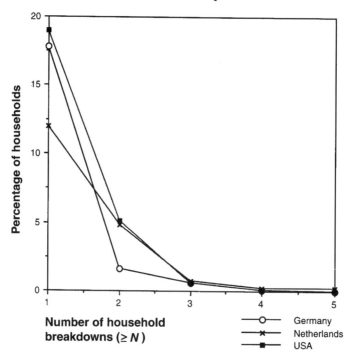

Number of household
breakdowns (≥ N)

—○— Germany
—×— Netherlands
—■— USA

Figure 12.1. Autonomous household breakdowns (occurring in the top half of the distribution of post-government equivalent income) (based on appendix table A6: Aut 1A).

personal autonomy. But however that may be, it is in any case clear that personal autonomy in forming and reforming households is unambiguously higher in the US than in either of the other two countries under study. (The data underlying figure 12.1, and all others in this chapter, will be found in appendix table A6, at the end of this book.)

12.3   Labour market autonomy

Another aspect of autonomy is the extent to which people are free to shape their own working lives. Victorian novelists used to talk (in ways to which we return in section 12.4 below) about persons of 'independent means' – those who did not have to work at all for a living. In similar vein, we might deem someone more autonomous the greater the extent to which they pick and choose their own work patterns to suit themselves. By this standard, those who (voluntarily) change jobs more often or (voluntarily) vary their working hours more would count as more autonomous.

Of course, not all labour market instability reflects autonomous choices. Far from it: people often find their employment involuntarily terminated, or they find themselves involuntarily retired before their time or involuntarily restricted to working reduced hours. Hence nothing about autonomy can necessarily be inferred from the sheer existence of labour market instability.

In looking for evidence of 'autonomy in labour markets', what we are looking for is therefore evidence of *voluntary* non-employment. Of course there is no very good direct evidence of that, in our panel files or elsewhere: it is simply not something that labour economists or national statisticians have any particular reason to measure.

But in the same spirit as our operationalization of 'voluntary household breakdown' in section 12.2 above, we might look at the rates of non-employment among people in the top half of the income distribution. Those people are less likely to have to go to work for a living, at any particular point in time: to some extent, they will have savings and investments that could tide them over, at least for a time; to a much larger extent, people with higher post-government equivalent incomes will be sharing a household with someone else whose earnings could tide them over, at least for a time. People with equivalent incomes in the top half of the income distribution therefore are more likely to have a genuine choice of going out to work in the paid labour force or not. If they choose to do so, their choice is rendered autonomous by the fact that not doing so was, for them, a viable option. People in the bottom half of the income distribution, by contrast, have little choice but to seek paid employment; and presumably they would less often opt out of it of their own volition.[10]

Again, let us emphasize that this is not to celebrate opting out of the paid labour market as such. Nor is it to celebrate the fact that the rich have options that the poor lack. It is, instead, just the best solution we can find to a tricky measurement problem. We simply take the proportion of better-off people who opt out of the labour market as an indirect indicator of the alternative options – and hence relative autonomy– of those who opt in.

Those rates on 'autonomous non-employment', which serve as our measure of 'labour market autonomy' overall, do indeed vary considerably across the countries (and to some extent across the period) under study. As figure 12.2 shows, 'autonomous non-employment' was highest

---

[10] Haveman and Berkshadker (1998) approach much the same problem from the opposite end, calculating the proportion of people which would be poor even if they worked full-time-full-year at a wage rate reflecting the earnings capacity which we could reasonably impute to people with their personal characteristics and human capital. People who have to work full-time-full-year in their most lucrative employment, just to make ends meet, have no scope for voluntarily cutting back their hours in paid labour.

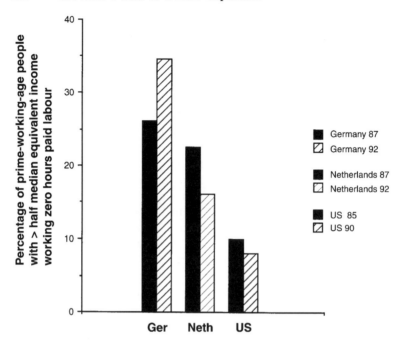

Figure 12.2. Autonomous non-employment (based on appendix table A6, Aut 2A).

in Germany; and, unlike the other two countries, it actually increased in the second half of the period. Autonomous non-employment was lowest and decreasing in the US (at about a third of German levels). Autonomous non-employment in the Netherlands was near the German level in the earlier portion of the period, but fell in the Netherlands while rising in Germany in the later portion. Insofar as our measure of 'autonomous non-employment' is indeed a good indicator of labour market autonomy more generally, it seems that it is highest in Germany and lowest in the US among the three countries under study.

12.4   Economic autonomy

Even those more sociological aspects of autonomy depend, in ways we have been tracing in previous sections, upon economic autonomy. That can be characterized, broadly, as 'command over resources'.[11] This section will be concerned primarily with different ways in which people

[11] Of course, not all people living in rich households will necessarily enjoy much command over the household's resources: the case of non-working wives is a classic case in point (Piachaud 1982; Pahl 1983; 1989).

might exercise 'command' over resources of a narrowly financial sort, with the subsequent section 12.5 turning to consider another important resource (time). Those two sorts of resources will then be blended together in the measure of 'combined resource autonomy' which we propose, and deploy, in section 12.6.

12.4.1 Independent means: asset income

As we have already intimated, 'economic autonomy' has something to do with what Victorians used to call 'independent means'. What the Victorians meant by that was private wealth – having assets sufficient to generate an income adequate to meet your needs, without your having to engage in paid labour.

Indentured servants and arranged marriages are commonly taken to represent the antithesis of autonomy in this respect.[12] Liberals sometimes take the converse phenomena – free markets in labour (and lovers and everything else) – to constitute paradigms of autonomy (Brittan 1988). But 'wage slaves' are slaves, too, as Marxists always used to say.[13]

The Victorian ideal of 'independent means' can be probed, after a fashion, through the panel data's reports of the 'asset income' of households. These data are far from perfect, however. While the reported levels look plausible enough for the US, those for the other countries (Germany, in particular) look implausibly low.[14] Still, for what it may be worth, let us calculate the extent to which people could meet their basic needs (specified by the poverty line) through their reported asset income alone.

In all three of these countries, very few people could escape poverty through their asset income alone.[15] On the basis of one-yearly income, the numbers range between 2 per cent in Germany to over 4 per cent in the Netherlands, with the US in between. Aggregating income over longer (five-yearly or ten-yearly) periods does not change that much. Some 4 per cent of Americans could evade poverty through their asset income aggregated over ten years, compared to some 2 per cent of the Dutch and rather fewer Germans. The point to notice here, however, is not so much

---

[12] And rightly so, assuming the individuals being married do not have any opportunity to give meaningful consent to the arrangements. Sometimes they might, but that is presumably not the typical case.

[13] And so too are sex slaves, who have no choice but to sell their bodies to keep body and soul together. See Pateman (1988b, chs. 5 and 7) on the analogy between wage slaves and sex slaves.

[14] Perhaps, for tax or other reasons, people in Germany invest in assets geared more towards generating capital accumulation than asset income.

[15] For details, see appendix table A6, Aut 3A.

where the countries stand in the comparative rankings, but rather that across all three countries the percentages are pretty uniformly tiny.

12.4.2 Independent means: state support

'Independent means', on the Victorian understanding of the term which we borrow for present purposes, is having guaranteed access to an income stream adequate to meet one's basic needs, without engaging in paid labour. Assets and the income they generate is one source of that. But welfare rights – at least insofar as they do indeed constitute rights, that is to say, non-discretionary entitlements (Reich 1964; Titmuss 1971; Goodin 1988, ch. 7; Van Parijs 1995) – might constitute another.

The crucial factor in making welfare rights autonomy-enhancing is their non-discretionary character. Not being subject to the arbitrary will of any specific other person is the key aspect of autonomy in this realm (Hayek 1960). Thus, the Guardians of the old Poor Law, dispensing poor relief to whomever they thought fit, enjoyed a level of discretionary power over their benefices that genuinely impinged on the autonomy of their recipients. The administrators of most social insurance systems enjoy no such discretion: whether or not any particular person is entitled to an old age pension depends just on that person's age and contributory history. So dependent though pensioners might be upon their pensions as their sole source of financial support in old age, that dependency does not render them non-autonomous. They are just depending upon officials respecting their rights.

There is no good measure, in the panel data or (so far as we know) anywhere else, of the extent to which any given welfare regime's benefits are non-discretionary and hence autonomy-enhancing in these ways. None of the standard ways of categorizing social welfare programmes quite capture this issue in the way we would like.

It is not a matter of whether programmes are universal or categorical, for example. Even 'universal' programmes are universally available only to residents (and sometimes only to legal residents or only to formal citizens) of the country, and some discretionary elements can enter into those determinations; and even categorical programmes can be relatively non-discretionary, if the categories are tightly specified in the rulebooks binding programme administrators. Nor, again, is our distinction quite captured by the familiar difference between means-tested and non-means-tested programmes: some means-tests are framed in such a way as to leave administrators lots of scope for discretion;[16] other

---

[16] As did the old British Supplementary Benefits system, which notoriously allowed caseworkers to demand to see the holes in a claimant's old clothes before paying an allowance for new ones. See more generally Goodin (1988, ch. 7).

means-tests can be almost as automatic as claiming an old age pension vested by one's own workplace contributions (imagine, for example, a means-test that just consisted of presenting your family's income tax return for the previous year). Thus, we are simply unable to rank the three welfare regimes under examination in any systematic way on this one crucial dimension of the extent to which they promote people's autonomy.

There is another dimension to the question, however, upon which the panel data do have obvious bearing. 'Independent means' is a matter of having means which are both independent and adequate; and although the 'independence' with which people can claim their benefits cannot be assessed through the panel data, their adequacy clearly can. Indeed, it already has in chapter 8's assessment of the impact of government taxes and transfers on poverty rates in our three countries. The data presented in section 8.6.2 shows quite clearly that the social democratic welfare regime of the Netherlands provides public transfers adequate virtually to eliminate poverty, that the public transfers of corporatist Germany are almost as adequate to that task, but that the public transfers of the liberal US are pretty inadequate to that task. Translating those previous findings about poverty reduction into the language of autonomy enhancement, we can say that the sort of welfare entitlements provided by the social democratic (and, to an only slightly lesser extent, corporatist) welfare regimes might be adequate to provide people with an 'independent means of living' in a way that those of the liberal regime too rarely do.

12.4.3 Independent means within households

Having 'independent means' is as important within households as across them. Those concerned with autonomy within households are concerned for each adult member of the household to have a sufficient income, in his (or, more especially, her) own right to meet his (and especially, her) needs. People with an income that is sufficient to meet their own needs are economically independent in a way that dependent members of a household clearly are not. And even if one's own resources are not fully adequate to meet one's needs, at least having more resources of one's own gives one more bargaining power and hence autonomy within the household, when it comes to the disposition of the household's economic resources.[17]

We can explore that issue, too, through our panel data. For a first cut, we can look at the income of the non-head of household, as a proportion

[17] See Folbre (1982; 1996); England and Kilbourne (1990); Lundberg and Pollack (1993); Knijn (1994); Young (1952).

of that of the head. The higher the non-head's income is relative to that of the head, the more independent the non-head is, economically. Of course, only people of prime working age (which we take to be twenty-five to fifty-nine) can reasonably be expected to have an independent labour income at all, so we will confine our analysis to that group.

As we have already commented, all three countries are in the midst of something of a social revolution in terms of female labour force participation, which has obvious implications for the earnings of non-heads of household, too. Thus, instead of presenting some summary statistic for the entire decade, we need to look at the situation at three points in time: the first, last and middle years of the decade under study.

This revolution in female labour force participation hit first in the US, where at the beginning of our period the median non-head's labour income was 30 per cent of that of the head of household. By the middle year it had risen to over 40 per cent and by the tenth year to over 50 per cent. In Germany, the median non-head's labour income was 9 per cent at the beginning of our study, rising to over 20 per cent in the middle year, and rising again to over 35 per cent in the tenth year. In the Netherlands, in contrast, the median non-head's labour income was literally zero (and hence zero per cent of the head's) in the first and middle year of our study, and only negligible in the final year.

Assessing the respective welfare regimes in the light of these findings, we would have to say that the liberal welfare regime of the US is – at least for the period under study – by far the best at providing all members of the household with an 'independent income' and the sort of autonomy within the household that comes with it. But with female labour force participation rates changing rapidly across all three countries, that might well be a peculiarity of the period under study rather than a fixed feature of any of those welfare-regime types.

12.5   Promoting temporal autonomy

Though income is the ordinary focus of attention, it is of course time that is the ultimate scarce resource (Zeckhauser 1973). Another important aspect of resource autonomy is, therefore, temporal autonomy: 'free time'. One's leisure time is by definition one's own, to do with as one pleases.

What in practice one can do with one's leisure time is, of course, constrained by various other factors, among them socio-economic ones already mentioned. (We consider those two factors in conjunction in section 12.6 below.) Nevertheless, leisure time is a necessary if not sufficient condition of personal autonomy. It is what provides people with the opportunity, in a temporal sense, to deploy their other resources to ends of their own choosing.[18]

While there is no direct measure of leisure time in any of our three panel surveys, 'time budget' data is contained in the underlying German panel files. Those data are somewhat rough in several respects. They are based on respondents' estimates of how long they spend doing various tasks, rather than on 'daily diaries' of the sort favoured by time-budget specialists;[19] and in the German files, time use is categorized into only four categories ('work time'; 'unpaid housework time'; 'unpaid time caring for children'; and 'unpaid time caring for others'). Obviously, there are many finer distinctions which it would be nice to be able to make. But for the broad purposes here in view, those three 'unpaid work' categories probably capture most of what we need.[20]

Using the German panel's time-use data, we can surmise how many hours of unpaid labour (in housework or caring for children or others) people do, in households of various sorts. To get a measure of 'leisure time' available to people in various sorts of households, we then simply deduct the number of paid and unpaid hours of labour that they do from the number of available hours.

There is no readily available time-use data contained in any of the other panel surveys. To compute 'leisure time' for people in the other two countries, we have therefore just assumed that people in households of the same structure in those other countries put in the same number of hours of unpaid labour (in housework and caring for children and others) as people in the equivalent households in Germany. While there is some cross-national variation in these respects, it seems minimal at least for the broad household types with which we are here concerned.[21]

While our calculations of leisure time are thus based on various assumptions and extrapolations, and ought therefore to be treated with considerable caution, the results set out in figure 12.3 are nonetheless striking. People in the US, across all prime-working-aged groups, have

[18] These issues have been explored in, for example, Linder (1970) and Schor (1991).
[19] For the broad purposes here in view, those two methods tend to yield much the same results: compare, for example, Baxter and Gibson (1991) and Bittman (1992); ABS (1994). In particular, people's reports of the 'number of hours usually worked' seem to correspond relatively closely, on average, to diary-based reports of the number of hours worked on any particular day (Bittman and Goodin 1998, fn. 9).
[20] In the absence of direct evidence from the panels, we will for our 'leisure time' calculations simply assume that 'eating and grooming' take two hours a day, eight hours are spent 'sleeping' and those in paid labour spend a total of one hour a day commuting to work.
[21] As found in an analysis of time-use data for the twenty-eight surveys of thirteen OECD countries (including all three countries here under study) that are contained in the Multinational Comparative Time Budget Data Archive held at the University of Essex (Bittman and Goodin 1998). Compare, also, our German estimates of hours of unpaid labour with the Australian ones reported in ABS (1994, table 10, p. 38).

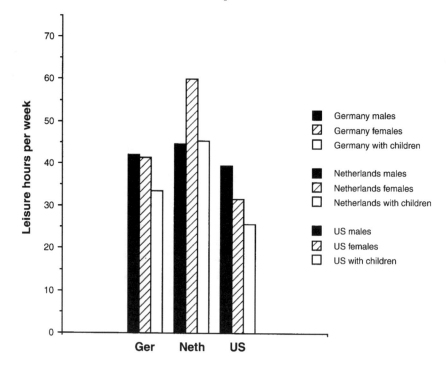

Figure 12.3. Leisure hours per week (based on appendix table A6, Aut 4A).

substantially less free time (largely because they put in more paid work time) than do people in Germany or, especially, the Netherlands. While those differences are evident even for prime-working-aged men, they are far more striking for women of prime working age – again, in large part because not nearly so many women worked many paid labour hours in Germany or the Netherlands, at least in the period under examination here.

The most time-stressed group is, of course, families with children. The demands on the time of a single parent trying to tend both a job and a family are particularly high; so too are the demands on the time of a working wife, who (given the traditional division of household labour) is often in effect doing a 'second shift' after coming home from work (Hochschild 1989; 1997; Baxter and Gibson 1990). That 'second shift' phenomenon is no doubt the reason that prime-working-age women have so many fewer leisure hours than the corresponding men in the US, where such a large proportion of women are in the paid workforce.

Quite apart from the extraordinary demands on the time of single parents and working wives, however, the sheer time costs imposed by young children on parents of both genders are striking. Furthermore, children seem to impinge most on the free time of people in the US, where people have least free time to start with; and they seem to impinge proportionately least on the free time of people in the Netherlands, where people have most of it to start with.

In all these ways, then, it seems that the Netherlands is the welfare regime best suited to promoting temporal autonomy. Across a range of family types, and taking account of both paid and unpaid work demands on people's time, it seems that the Dutch have most time that they can truly call their own and the Americans the least.

12.6 Promoting combined resource autonomy

Both 'time' and 'money' are required, in some suitable combination, for overall resource autonomy.[22] Imagine someone with a very high income but who has to work sixteen hours a day, day in and day out, to earn it. Such a person with no time to enjoy that income, however high it may be, would for that reason rightly be said to lack resource autonomy in some important respect. Conversely, imagine someone who is unemployed: having plenty of free time, but no money with which to enjoy it, that person too would lack resource autonomy in some important respect (Jahoda, Lazarsfeld and Zeisel 1933; Jahoda 1982). Here we attempt to put those two elements together in a composite measure of 'combined resource autonomy'.[23]

12.6.1 Defining 'combined resource autonomy'

Just as it takes both 'labour' and 'capital' to produce any material goods, so too it takes both time and money to produce what we might call 'combined resource autonomy'. How exactly those two variables blend together in that 'autonomy production function' is something we cannot

[22] The way they interact in promoting people's welfare is discussed in Vickery (1977) and Atkinson (1998b, pp. 172–8).
[23] In other attempts to get at somewhat similar issues from a slightly different angle, economists construct a human capital equation to try to estimate the 'earnings capacity' of people who work part-time or not at all in paid labour. The 'income forgone' – the difference between what they did earn and what they could have earned, according to that equation – constitutes for those authors the shadow price representing the value of 'home production' (Becker 1965; Garfinkel and Haveman 1977; Haveman and Buron 1993; Travers and Richardson 1993, ch. 1; Saunders, O'Connor and Smeeding 1994). For us it might be taken to represent the value of labour withdrawn from, and hence 'autonomous' and independent of, the labour market.

specify *a priori*; and the panel data provide us with no information from which any such production function might sensibly be derived.

What we can say, however, is that there are important thresholds along both the 'time' and 'money' dimensions. No one can be said to be autonomous who has so little income she cannot meet basic needs, and that is true regardless of how much leisure time that person might have. Similarly, no one can be said to be autonomous who has so little free time that he cannot make any very effective use of his income, and that is true regardless of how high his income might be.[24] Operationally, let us set the first threshold at the poverty line and the second at forty hours of paid work a week.[25]

We will say that someone has 'combined resource autonomy' if and only if that person meets both of two criteria. First, to have 'combined resource autonomy' a person will have to have an income above the poverty line. Second, to have 'combined resource autonomy' a person will also have to engage in less than forty hours of paid labour per week. In the results that follow, we report what proportion of the population possesses 'combined resource autonomy', assessed according to this two-fold test.

12.6.2 Measuring combined resource autonomy

Our basic results are presented in figure 12.4 showing the proportion of the total population that passes this two-fold test of 'combined resource autonomy' over various periods for our three countries. There we see that over two-thirds of the total population can be said to have 'combined resource autonomy' in the US in any given year, compared to over 80 per cent in Germany and over 90 per cent in the Netherlands. In all countries,

---

[24] In the Cobb-Douglas analogy, those thresholds specify in effect 'zero factor inputs' for each factor. In the standard Cobb-Douglas function, zero labour inputs or zero capital inputs would yield zero output. So too zero money inputs or zero leisure inputs would yield zero autonomy.

[25] Although the standard working week is shorter than that in both Germany and the Netherlands, the forty-hour week serves as a useful benchmark. Indeed, it is a matter of international law, under the 'Convention concerning the reduction of hours of work to forty a week' signed in 1935, eventually coming into force in 1957 (ILO 1996, vol. I, pp. 261-3). People might autonomously choose to work more, of course.

Ideally, we would like to include both paid and unpaid work hours here (after the ingenious fashion, perhaps, of Vickery 1977 for the US). But while hours in paid work are reported in full in all three countries' panels, unpaid work hours are measured directly in only one of the panels. We have, in section 12.5, estimated Dutch and US unpaid work hours on the basis of that German data. But we acknowledge the uncertainties inevitably attaching to those estimates, and prefer to deal for purposes of our 'combined resource autonomy' measure strictly in terms of the more reliable measures of income and paid work hours.

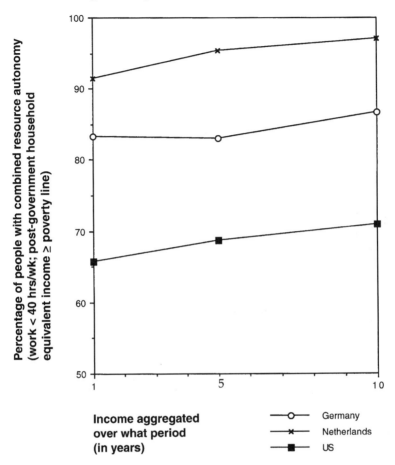

Figure 12.4. Frequency of combined resource autonomy, based on post-government household equivalent income (whole population) (based on appendix table A6, Aut 5B).

those proportions rise slowly as we aggregate more years, so that on a full ten-yearly basis nearly the entire population of the Netherlands would be deemed to have achieved 'combined resource autonomy'.

It is important not only to look at how many people are autonomous but also to look at how often they are autonomous over successive years. Figure 12.4 shows that when individuals' income and work hours are pooled over longer periods they look somewhat more autonomous in all three countries. Figure 12.5 addresses the importantly separate question, 'In how many years out of ten were people autonomous?'

The 'hit rate' calculation in figure 12.5 shows that the vast majority of

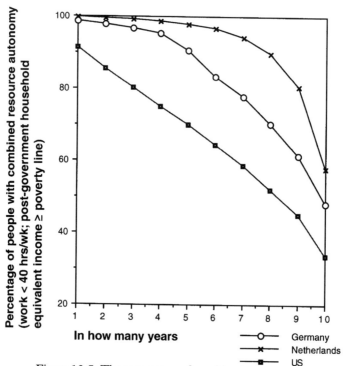

Figure 12.5. The recurrence of combined resource autonomy, based on post-government household equivalent income (whole population) (based on appendix table A6, Aut 5C).

people in every country qualify as autonomous under our standard for at least one year out of the ten (over 90 per cent of Americans, even, and nearly 100 per cent of Dutch people). Those proportions remain impressively high in the Netherlands across pretty much the whole range, but they drop off more sharply in Germany and more sharply still in the US. Only 20 per cent of the Dutch fail to achieve 'combined resource autonomy' in two or more years out of our ten. Nearly half of Americans and nearly a third of Germans fail that standard.

12.6.3 Refining combined resource autonomy calculations

Those baseline calculations are problematic in several respects. For one thing, they are biased upwards because they include the entire population, rather than just those of working age. One component of our 'combined resource autonomy' test, recall, is hours in paid labour. Those who are too young or too old to be in paid labour at all trivially satisfy this criterion, thus artificially inflating (in one sense, at least[26]) the proportion of the population that is said to be autonomous.

Looking just at people of prime working age (ages twenty-five to fifty-nine), however, many the same patterns emerge. The Netherlands has the largest proportion of autonomous people (around 90 per cent on an annual basis, rising toward 95 per cent on a ten-yearly basis); Germany has the next highest proportion (hovering around 80 per cent across all periods); and the US has the lowest (hovering around 60 per cent). In both the Netherlands and Germany almost everyone of prime working age is autonomous in at least one year and even in the US that is true of almost 90 per cent of people. Only about 20 per cent fail that standard in two or more years in the Netherlands, whereas in Germany half and in the US fully two-thirds do.

There is a second respect in which those baseline calculations represented in figures 12.4 and 12.5 might prove problematic. Just as they neglect the fact that some people have lots of 'free' time imposed by force of law, so too those calculations neglect the fact that other people have lots of other demands on their time.

As we have seen from section 12.5 above, people with young children have many more demands on their time than others. And having more mouths to feed imposes more demands on their finances as well.[27] Thus, people with children can reasonably be deemed particularly sensitive on both dimensions which together make up our measure of 'combined resource autonomy'. An income below the poverty line poses particular hardships on people whose flexibility in coping with the problems of a low income are constrained by the inflexible needs of young children; and so too having less time outside of paid labour would impose a particular hardship on those with most need of it in coping with the burden of unpaid labour necessarily associated with coping with the needs of young children.

Let us look, then, at people with young children to see if more or fewer of them enjoy 'combined resource autonomy' (defined in terms of income and paid working hours alone) than do prime-working-aged people in general. If fewer of them have it, under circumstances in which they actually need it more, then that seems to be a particularly undesirable outcome. The evidence of the panels suggests that, while parents have

---

[26] Certainly those in either age bracket who would like to engage in paid labour but are precluded from doing so by child labour laws or mandatory retirement laws cannot be said to have autonomously chosen their leisured state. On the other hand, their leisure time is real enough, and the choice of what they do in other than paid labour is their own (at least for the not too young and not too frail old).

[27] Though extra members of the household of course cost proportionately less than the first, as reflected in equivalence scales; see section 6.3.2.

about the same levels of 'combined resource autonomy' as non-parents in Germany, they actually have less of it (albeit not much less) in both the Netherlands and the US.

There is a third and in many ways much more important respect in which our baseline estimates in figures 12.4 and 12.5 might prove problematic. They lump together males and females, who we know to have very different work and earnings patterns. In fact, those baseline calculations commit that sin in two respects. Not only do they fail to give separate breakdowns for males and females but, more importantly, they focus on 'household equivalent income', which (as explained in section 6.3.2 above) assumes that the household pools all the income coming into the household, from whatever source, with all members of the household sharing it equally among themselves. The effect of this is to ascribe 'combined resource autonomy' to a non-waged wife who is utterly dependent upon her husband's income for her financial support – which is not at all what many people would care to call an 'autonomous' existence.

We can easily remedy the first half of that problem by breaking down our statistics according to gender. We can remedy the second by taking as our income measure 'individual labour income', instead of 'household equivalent income': the former you earn in your own right, the latter you might enjoy merely by the grace and favour of other members of your household.

Breaking results down by gender reveals that, taking 'household equivalent income' as our standard, women invariably enjoy more 'combined resource autonomy' than do men across all three countries. That in itself might not seem surprising. After all, there are fewer women than men in the paid labour market, which means that they have more leisure hours and (on the 'household equivalent income' sharing assumption) the same income as their husbands. That logic, however, would lead us to expect the female lead in 'combined resource autonomy' to be greatest in countries where female labour force participation is lowest (Germany and the Netherlands) and least where it is highest (the US). Surprisingly enough, the results turn out just the opposite.

Of course, taking 'individual labour income' as our standard we would expect far fewer females than men to enjoy 'combined resource autonomy', particularly in countries with lower female participation rates. That expectation is indeed borne out in the data for both Germany and the Netherlands. To be sure, well over a third of women still enjoy 'combined resource autonomy' in both Germany and the Netherlands just on the strength of their own earnings. But that is only about half the number of women who would be deemed autonomous by virtue of an equal share of their household's earnings in those two countries. In the US about as many women as men enjoy 'combined resource autonomy' through their own 'individual labour incomes' alone. That is not, however, because more women are autonomous in the US than in the other two countries: instead it is merely because so many fewer men are autonomous in that respect in the US than elsewhere.

12.6.4 Sources of combined resource autonomy: market, family, government

Finally, let us assess the various mechanisms through which the three countries' different welfare regimes provide 'combined resource autonomy'. First we look at the proportion of the population that would be said to enjoy 'combined resource autonomy' on the strength of 'individual labour income' alone: that can be taken to be the measure of autonomy attributable to the labour market. Next we look at the proportion of people who would enjoy such autonomy on the strength of 'pre-government household equivalent income': that can be taken to be the measure of autonomy attributable to the family. Finally we look at the proportion of people who would enjoy such autonomy on the strength of 'post-government household equivalent income': that can be taken to represent the measure of autonomy attributable to the state. None of those measures captures what we want from it perfectly. Still, each of them speaks tolerably well to some of our underlying concerns in those respects.

Figure 12.6 presents results separately for one-, five- and ten-yearly income aggregations. Looking across these three graphs, we see that 'combined resource autonomy' increases across all countries over longer time spans. We also see that market income does most to promote it, across all countries and all periods; and across all countries and all periods the family makes a substantial further contribution to providing people with 'combined resource autonomy'. The Netherlands is generally ahead of both the other countries in both those respects, and in both respects its lead generally increases over longer periods.

Where the Dutch and German performances really pull away from the American is in respect of the contribution that the state makes to people's 'combined resource autonomy'. Whereas in Germany and the Netherlands state taxes and transfers confer 'combined resource autonomy' on around 14 per cent more people than would have had it on the basis of market or family contributions alone, US government taxes and transfers confer 'combined resource autonomy' on only about 4 per cent more people than would have had it on the basis of market contributions alone. Note, furthermore, that the results presented in figure 12.6 pertain to the

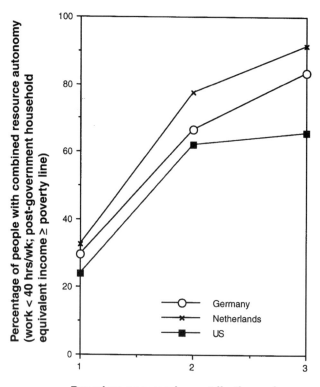

Based on one-yearly contributions of:
1 = market (individual labour income)
2 = family (pre-government equivalent income)
3 = state (post-government equivalent income)

Figure 12.6(a). Sources of combined resource autonomy over one year (based on appendix table A6, Aut 6C).

whole population; and were we to concentrate on the prime-working-aged population alone, the US state's contribution to 'combined resource autonomy' would virtually vanish altogether.[28]

[28] The young and the elderly are both arguably special cases that ought to be treated separately in such calculations. Youngsters living in their parents' households have abundant free time outside paid work and, by virtue of their share of the household's income, money with which to enjoy it; elderly people who have retired again have abundant free time and (at least in most cases) a pension that allows them above-poverty income with which to enjoy it. Including the former in our calculations increases the importance accorded to family; including the latter increases the importance accorded to the state.

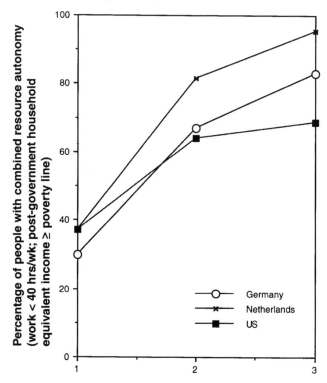

Based on five-yearly contributions of:
1 = market (individual labour income)
2 = family (pre-government equivalent income)
3 = state (post-government equivalent income)

Figure 12.6(b). Sources of combined resource autonomy over five years (based on appendix table A6, Aut 6C).

It bears emphasizing that the government can contribute to people's autonomy, even in our sense of 'combined resource autonomy', in many more ways than can be captured by these indicators. Given the information available in the panel data, our indicators are only capable of registering contributions made through the government's tax and transfer activities. But government can also promote people's autonomy, in our sense, through, for example, hours and wages regulations.

Government-initiated reductions of working hours have indeed occurred in both Germany and the Netherlands during the period under study. Those government initiatives contribute importantly to the proportion of people we deem to have 'combined resource autonomy' in the figures

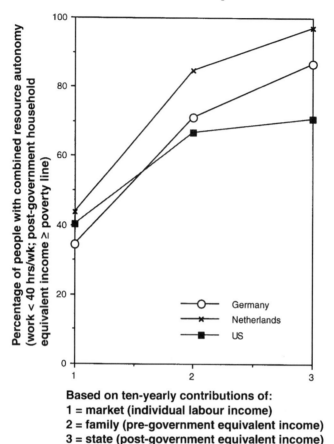

Based on ten-yearly contributions of:
1 = market (individual labour income)
2 = family (pre-government equivalent income)
3 = state (post-government equivalent income)

Figure 12.6(c). Sources of combined autonomy over ten years (based on appendix table A6, Aut 6C).

above, but in a way (because of the limitations of our data) that gets credited to 'the market' rather than 'government'. So too have governments in both places been party to discussions over wage levels, employment rates, part-time working arrangements, and so on. All that, too, might impact on 'combined resource autonomy', but our indicators will misattribute that to the market rather than the government.

How much of the 'combined resource autonomy' apparently generated through the labour market is really owing to the activities of government instead must necessarily remain an open question from the perspective of our panel studies. Nevertheless, it is noteworthy that the country in which the government which is most activist in these other (non-tax-transfer) respects as well – the Netherlands – is credited in figure 12.6 with achieving the highest levels of 'combined resource autonomy' through the labour market, and increasingly so over time. We might therefore reasonably speculate that at least some of these features of the Dutch economy are due to the policies of the Dutch government, beyond the tax and transfer policies on which the panel data provide information.

12.7 Governments' other contributions to autonomy

Governments do many other things that directly or indirectly affect autonomy in all the various other aspects discussed in this chapter. Policies promoting 'family values' reduce it, forcing young people to remain living at home and to depend financially upon their parents for support.[29] Policies encouraging 'flexible labour markets', reduced working hours and part-time labour might promote autonomy, if (but only if) those policies were designed in such a way that they actually gave workers greater choice over their working lives. Alas, there is all too little in the panel data which would help to capture these contributions to people's autonomy.

Once again, these panel data offer us a good window onto the government's contribution to autonomy essentially only in its economic aspects. That is an undeniably important aspect of autonomy, but equally undeniably it is far from the only one. Judging welfare regimes in terms of the resources they provide people for autonomous self-management, the social democratic welfare regime seems to do much more to promote people's autonomy. Social democratic welfare regimes lift more people out of poverty, providing them with the sort of autonomy that comes from economic sufficiency.[30] Social democratic welfare regimes – at least of the

---

[29] Some young people would choose to do that voluntarily, but being forced by law to do so deprives them of the choice to do otherwise and hence makes their action involuntary.

[30] As section 7.4.2 above has shown, more people depend upon the government as their principal source of income in social democratic regimes than others. Commentators preoccupied with neo-classical economic concerns of 'efficiency' would look at those statistics and bemoan the fact that so many people there are 'dependent on the government'. But another way of looking at those same statistics – the way favoured by post-productivists (Offe 1992) – is to say that those people enjoy their incomes 'independently of the market'. The question is just which is the greater threat to a person's autonomy, the market or the government. In the increasingly deregulated world of weak labour law and increasingly exploitative labour practices, it is not unreasonable to suppose that people's autonomy interests might be better served by their depending upon government assistance – particularly if that assistance is given as a matter of right, which is minimally subject to the discretionary judgments of administrators at the point of provision.

sort represented by the Netherlands in our study[31] – provide more people with both the time and the money that form some important (if not the only) preconditions of a truly autonomous life.

[31] A social democratic welfare regime of a more classical sort, with an 'active labour market policy,' would impose stronger obligations to work, and the 'forced labour' that would effectively entail would actually reduce autonomy, albeit in ways not well mapped in our measures.

Part III

Another standard of success:
internal institutional criteria

What we have been discussing, up to this point, constitutes the overall social objectives that welfare states are supposed to serve. Different types of welfare regimes approach those tasks differently. Each different type of welfare regime embodies a different strategy, embedded in different institutions, internalizing different emphases among the goals and setting different standards of institutional success.

Those specific institutional objectives and standards of success, internal to the logic of each type of welfare regime, are what we turn to explore next. It is not enough simply to ask which welfare regimes produce the best results, according to our overall criteria of moral assessment. To do that would be to treat each regime as a 'black box', asking no questions about how exactly each welfare regime works to produce the results it does. But then we cannot be confident what credit, if any, the particular welfare regime actually deserves for any accomplishments with which it is notionally associated.[1] To know with any confidence that welfare regimes work to achieve our social objectives, we need to know how they work. To give them any genuine *credit* for working, we need to know that they work as intended, foreseen and planned.

It is also important to recall (from chapter 3 above) that the mechanisms by which each particular type of welfare regime works to promote people's welfare includes primary as well as secondary, pre-government (family and market) as well as post-government components. One way welfare regimes work is through taxes and transfer payments of the sort associated with the welfare sector as such. Another equally important way is through the distribution of earnings generated through the productive sector of the economy. What we want to assess is the combined success of both strategies – both productive and redistributive – in promoting various social objectives.

In chapters 13 to 16, we present no new data. Instead, we offer summary judgments based on the data already presented as to how our 'best case' representative of each regime fared. We embody our conclusions in a set of tables, trying, in a somewhat impressionistic way, to bring all that evidence to bear on the comparative assessment of welfare regimes. But in those tables we provide explicit references to where in the appendix tables the relevant information can be found in full.

---

[1] In another connection, Aaron Wildavsky (1973) similarly queries whether 'planning' should be deemed a success if, as in Japan over the relevant period, economic growth was always several times what the planners had forecast. In such circumstances, one suspects that whatever the causes of economic growth, they probably had precious little to do with the activity of planning as such.

13 The United States as a liberal welfare regime

Having previously set out the basic theories lying behind liberal welfare regimes (section 3.1), we wish now to test those theories against the actual experience of one liberal welfare regime in particular – that of the United States. The basic institutional structure of the American welfare regime has already been discussed (section 4.2). Our task here is simply to assess its performance in pursuit of its chosen strategies and goals.

This test will essentially be against the liberal welfare regime's own internal standards of success. But to know whether the liberal welfare regime did as well as it could along those dimensions, it helps to know whether others have done better still. Thus in assessing how well the liberal welfare regime accomplishes its chosen goals through its chosen means, we look at the performance of the United States welfare regime alongside that of Germany and the Netherlands.

13.1 Mapping liberal welfare strategy

In terms of its social welfare policy, the ultimate goal of the liberal welfare regime is to promote high economic growth and, within its specifically social welfare sector, to reduce poverty in the most efficient possible manner. As shown schematically in figure 13.1, the liberal welfare regime aims to promote people's welfare primarily through a highly productive capitalist economy and only very much secondarily through a residualist system of social-welfare transfer payments.

In combating poverty, liberal welfare strategy relies most heavily upon the economic sector keeping pre-government incomes high and pre-government poverty low, through some combination of unearned asset income from capital and earned income from the labour market. It relies secondarily on private transfers – gifts from family and friends and private charities.

If those economic and social sectors work as liberals hope, then there will be little need for public sector transfer payments to alleviate poverty. Insofar as they are needed, the liberal welfare strategy is to help the poor

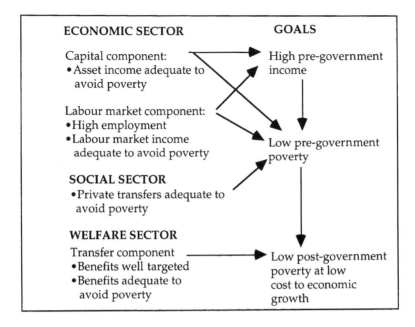

Figure 13.1. Liberal welfare strategy.

and only the poor, and to help them only as much as strictly necessary. The aim is to target benefits tightly, and to tailor them carefully to avoid paying more than strictly required to alleviate the poverty in view.

In this chapter, we address two basic questions. First, does the liberal welfare state do what it says it is going to do? That is to say, does it meet its own internal standards of success? Second, does the liberal welfare state do that in the ways it says it is going to do it? That is to say, does it work effectively through the mechanisms specified in the basic liberal welfare strategy, as set out in figure 13.1 above?

13.2 Does the liberal welfare regime achieve its goals?

Our conclusions as to whether or not the liberal welfare regime achieves its own goals, and how well it does in that respect compared to other welfare regimes, are summarized in table 13.1. In this and subsequent such figures, we will rank countries on a one- to four-star basis. Those assessments, although inevitably somewhat impressionistic, are nonetheless firmly rooted in the panel data. (The final column of each summary table indicates where in the appendix tables to find fuller information upon which our assessments are based.) Our one- to four-star rankings

Table 13.1. *Meeting the liberal welfare regime's goals*

	Liberal (US)	Soc. Dem. (Neth.)	Corporatist (Ger.)	Reference (appendix table)
High and growing incomes	★	★★★	★★★	Eff 1A
Low pre-government poverty	★★	★★	★	Pov 1A
Low post-government poverty	★	★★★★	★★★	Pov 1A

give some sense, in a way that simple rank-orderings could not, of the varying gaps between different countries' performances and of the varying absolute levels of performance across the several dimensions of evaluation.

First let us look at what are, in the context of social welfare policy anyway, intermediate goals towards the liberal regime's ultimate end of least-cost poverty reduction. One such goal – which is also of course an end in itself, for liberal welfare regimes – is to maximize both the level of and growth in people's pre-government incomes. According to conventional wisdom, the liberal regime does exceedingly well at that; but on the evidence presented here, while average incomes might be higher in liberal regimes, average incomes grow very much less rapidly in liberal regimes than in either of the others. The liberal social welfare strategy hopes, secondly, that high average market earnings will translate into low rates of pre-government poverty. In that regard the liberal regime is also substantially a failure in absolute terms, though it must be said that neither of the other regimes do well in that regard, either (and the corporatist regime does even worse).

The upshot is that there remains far more pre-government poverty for public sector transfers to correct than the liberal strategy would wish. And that in turn puts considerable pressure on the bifurcated nature of the ultimate liberal aim of securing low post-government poverty at low economic cost. The liberal welfare regime of the US is much better than the others at keeping the costs down (certainly social expenditure as a percentage of GDP is lowest there). It achieves that, however, at the cost of allowing substantially more poverty to remain post-government than elsewhere. In short, the liberal welfare regime is partly a success, but in larger part a failure, according to its own internal standards of success.

Table 13.2. *Performance of the liberal welfare regime's economic sector*

	Liberal (US)	Soc. Dem. (Neth.)	Corporatist (Ger.)	Reference (appendix table)
Asset income sufficient to avoid poverty	★	★	★	Aut 3B
High employment	★★★	★	★★	Eff 2A
Labour income sufficient to avoid poverty	★★	★★	★★★	Aut 3A

13.3   Does the liberal welfare regime function as claimed?

Having deemed the liberal welfare regime largely a failure by its own self-specified goals, we need next to examine its specific mechanisms to determine where it has gone wrong. To do this, we examine the performance of its economic, social and welfare sectors respectively.

13.3.1   The economic sector

The liberal welfare regime works, first and foremost, through its economic sphere. The liberal strategy is to provide people with high market income, from capital or labour or both.

Table 13.2 shows that, while people's asset income (i.e. income from capital) is negligible in all these regimes, employment rates at least are much higher in the liberal regime than others. It is also the case, however, that substantial proportions of people would be poor on the basis of their labour market earnings alone. But the liberal welfare regime is not unique in that respect: the social democratic welfare regime is no better and the corporatist one is only a bit better.

13.3.2   The social sector

The liberal welfare regime relies, secondarily, upon the 'voluntary sector' as an adjunct to markets. Insofar as people are poor on the basis of their market income, liberals hope that private giving (from family and friends and charitable institutions) will go some considerable way towards relieving their distress.

That turns out to be largely an idle hope. As table 13.3 shows, the vast majority of people who are poor on the basis of their market incomes would still be poor even after taking account of all private transfers they receive; and that seems substantially the same across all three regime

Table 13.3. *Performance of the liberal welfare regime's social sector*

	Liberal (US)	Soc. Dem. (Neth.)	Corporatist (Ger.)	Reference appendix table)
Private transfers sufficient to avoid poverty	★	★	★	Aut 3A

types. Certainly the liberal regime does not evoke substantially more private giving than the other two regime types, in ways that its advocates might have hoped.

13.3.3 The welfare sector

The liberal regime's welfare policy is indeed of a 'residual' sort. The liberal strategy relies primarily on keeping poverty rates down through the workings of capital and labour markets and, secondarily, through private charity. But as has already been seen, the workings of both the economic and social sectors in the liberal regime leave considerably more for the public sector to do, by way of relieving poverty, than the liberal strategy counts on.

The liberal welfare sector is supposed to rely principally on schemes of tightly targeted and only just adequate transfer payments. Whereas other regimes are more 'generous' in both respects, the liberal strategy is to ensure that benefits go only to the poor and that they get only just enough to cover the barest necessities.

Judging from the patterns summarized in table 13.4, the liberal welfare regime rather overachieves in its quest for a 'mean and lean' welfare state. It certainly does not give people more than they need to escape from poverty: instead it errs in the opposite direction, standardly giving poor people less than they need. Nor does the liberal welfare state generally give benefits to many who do not need them: again, it errs instead in the opposite direction, not paying benefits to substantial proportions of those who are in need.

13.4   The liberal welfare regime: an overall assessment

In certain key respects, then, the liberal regime seems to work precisely as claimed. Its economic sector generates moderately high pre-government income and economic growth, mostly benefitting above-average earners; and its welfare sector is tightly targeted to ensure that it does not undermine the market. But contrary to liberal hopes, high incomes on average

Table 13.4. *Performance of the liberal welfare regime's welfare sector*

	Liberal (US)	Soc. Dem. (Neth.)	Corporatist (Ger.)	Reference (appendix table)
Benefits well targeted:				
– on only the poor	★★★	★	★	Eff 5A
– on all the poor	★★	★★★★	★★★	Eff 5C
Benefits adequate to avoid poverty	★	★★★★	★★★	Pov 1A

do not translate into adequate incomes for the poor. The market and private giving leave substantial proportions of people in poverty, and welfare programmes that are over-tightly targeted mean that a substantial proportion of them remain so. The liberal welfare regime succeeds in keeping costs down, but at the cost of allowing poverty to remain comparatively high.

14   The Netherlands as a social democratic welfare regime

The basic theories lying behind social democratic regimes have been set out in section 3.2. We are now in a position to test those theories against the actual experience of one social democratic welfare regime in particular – that of the Netherlands. The basic institutional structure of the Dutch welfare regime has been set out previously (section 4.3). There we have also given our reasons for believing that, despite its chequered past and hybrid character, the Netherlands in this period can indeed be taken as a representative – indeed, arguably the best – of social democratic welfare regimes, at least in respect of its tax-transfer policies. Here we test the performance of the Dutch welfare regime against those social democratic goals and strategies.

This test will essentially be against the social democratic welfare regime's own internal standards of success. But the assessment is by its nature an intrinsically comparative one. We want to know not only how well, in absolute terms, the social democratic welfare regime does at accomplishing its chosen goals through its chosen means, we also want to know whether some other welfare regime beats social democrats at their own chosen game. Thus we assess the performance of that regime alongside the performance of the other regimes along all the dimensions that matter to social democracy.

14.1   Mapping social democratic welfare strategy

The social democratic welfare regime, like the liberal one, is also concerned to promote people's welfare first and foremost through the economic sphere. But while they are not utterly insensitive to overall aggregates, social democrats are much more sensitive to the distribution of well-being across the community. Accordingly, they are much more prepared to manipulate certain key features of the market economy to social ends, in one way or another – even at some cost to overall productivity. And they are very much more prepared, through social-welfare transfers, to readjust market distributions in more egalitarian directions.

246

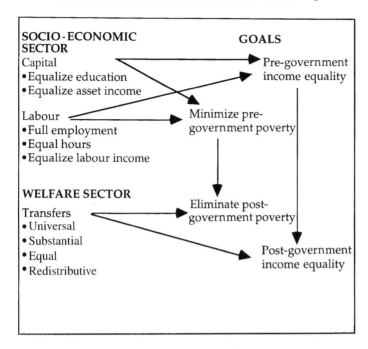

Figure 14.1. Social democratic welfare strategy.

The ultimate aim of social democratic welfare regimes is 'social equality' – a crucial component of which is of course 'eliminating poverty'. There is more to social equality than income equality alone, of course, but that is an undeniably important aspect of it and in any case it is the aspect far and away best represented in the panel data before us.

Social democrats pursue equality in post-government income distributions in two ways. One is through the tax-transfer system, which is designed in such a way as to eliminate the poverty and to reduce the inequality found in the pre-government income distribution generated by the market. But social democrats also strive to arrange the productive sector of the economy in such a way as to promote more equal pre-government income distributions as well.

Thus, as shown in figure 14.1, the ultimate goal of the social democratic welfare regime is equality in the post-government income distribution. It pursues that directly through its tax-transfer system and indirectly by arranging its economic sector so as to promote, as an intermediate goal, the elimination of poverty and the promotion of equality in the pre-government income distribution generated by the market.

This chapter is devoted to assessing the social democratic regime against our two standard questions. First, does the social democratic welfare regime do what it says it is going to do? Does it achieve its own chosen goals (and does it do so better than other welfare regimes do)? Second, does the social democratic welfare regime do what it says it is going to do through the mechanisms it says it is going to employ? Which is to say, does it work through the mechanisms specified in figure 14.1?

14.2   Does the social democratic welfare regime achieve its goals?

Our summary judgments on the first question – whether the social democratic welfare regime achieves its own chosen goals – are contained in table 14.1. As before, these are indeed summary judgments, expressed in rather qualitative one- to four-star form, and once again the last column of this figure identifies the appendix tables containing the quantitative data upon which these judgments are based.

In terms of its ultimate goals, the social democratic welfare regime is really very successful. It virtually eliminates post-government poverty and it promotes a very substantial measure of equality in post-government incomes. Furthermore, it does both very much more so than the liberal welfare regime, and somewhat more so than the corporatist welfare regime (which is, in both respects, a somewhat surprisingly strong second).

The social democratic welfare regime (of the Netherlands, anyway) is rather less successful in reducing pre-government poverty or promoting pre-government income equality in the distribution of market income, as a step towards those other more ultimate aims. While pre-government poverty and income inequality rates are relatively lower in the social democratic welfare regime than in either of the other two, in absolute terms they are nevertheless quite high. (In both cases, they are on a par with the levels of post-government poverty and income inequality which egalitarians find so unacceptable in liberal welfare regimes.)

14.3   Does the social democratic welfare regime function as claimed?

Finding that the social democratic welfare regime is successful in achieving its ultimate goals, despite a rather modest performance in achieving its intermediate goals, suggests that some aspects of the social democratic strategy are (at least in the Netherlands) more successful than others. It is to the assessment of those more specific mechanisms in the social demo-

Table 14.1. *Meeting the social democratic welfare regime's goals*

	Soc. Dem. (Neth.)	Liberal (US)	Corporatist (Ger.)	Reference (appendix table)
Low pre-government poverty	★★	★★	★	Pov 1A
High pre-government income equality	★★	★	★	Eq 1A
Low post-government poverty	★★★★	★★	★★★	Pov 1A
High post-government income equality	★★★★	★★	★★★	Eq 1A

cratic welfare strategy that we now turn, examining the economic and welfare sectors in turn.

14.3.1 The economic sector

The social democratic regime would strive to reduce poverty and increase equality in the market distribution of pre-government income by exercising an egalitarian influence on both capital and labour. Within the capital sector, social democrats would try to equalize both human capital (education and training) and finance capital (and the asset income stream that flows from it). Table 14.2 shows that social democrats do indeed equalize education, but no more so than corporatists. (It ought also to be added that both regimes do so by levelling down rather than levelling up.)

In terms of the labour market, the key to the social democratic strategy is full employment. There are exemptions for people unfit to work and for people engaged in other socially useful activities (education, child-rearing and so on). But the classic social democratic idea is that, apart from them, every able-bodied person of prime working age should be engaged in full-time paid labour which is, broadly speaking, equally remunerative for each of them. Decomposing this strategy into its separate strands, this amounts to a call for: full employment among everyone of prime working age; equal hours worked by all; and equal labour income for all.[1]

As foreshadowed in chapter 4, it is in respect of this sort of 'active labour market policy' where perhaps the Netherlands looks least social democratic. Certainly the archetypical social democratic welfare regime, Sweden, spends a larger proportion of its GDP on such policies. But

---

[1] Or as that strategy has been modulated in the light of the caring commitments of families with young children or dependent elderly people, that everyone should spend equal total hours in paid and unpaid labour, which might entail people with particularly heavy caring commitments at home working only part-time in paid labour.

Table 14.2. *Performance of the social democratic welfare regime's economic sector*

	Soc. Dem. (Neth.)	Liberal (US)	Corporatist (Ger.)	Reference (appendix table)
Equal education	★★★	★	★★★	Eq 2B
Full employment	★★	★★★	★★	Stab 2A
Equal hours worked	★★★	★★	★★	Eq 2A
Equal labour income	★★★	★	★★	Eq 1B

Dutch spending on active labour market policies has been substantially above the OECD mean throughout this period; and only a very disparate group of other OECD countries (Ireland, Denmark, Belgium and Sweden) spend more (OECD 1996c, table 2.9, p. 30; cf. Janoski 1996).

In the Netherlands, as in Germany, active labour market policies were traditionally oriented towards male heads of households. Female labour force participation rates traditionally lagged far behind male ones in both those countries, compared to the US. That changed fairly dramatically over the course of the period under study, however, with increasing numbers of Dutch women entering the paid labour force, albeit often on a part-time basis.

Finally, social democrats would wish to minimize the inequality in the distribution, across all households, of the number of hours worked by members of prime working age. That distribution is indeed rather less unequal in the Netherlands than in corporatist Germany or the liberal US.

Where the Dutch welfare regime does perform very much as social democrats would indisputably wish – and where social democracy, as represented by the Dutch regime, can claim to be a great success – is in generating pre-government labour incomes that are more equal than in corporatist Germany and substantially more equal than in the liberal US. Through its robust wages policy, the social democratic welfare regime of the Netherlands can apparently deliver to people relatively equal pre-government labour incomes, despite the fact that some of them work more hours than others (with still others not working at all) in the paid labour market.

All that helps to explain why the social democratic welfare regime in the Netherlands induces relatively more equality in pre-government income distributions than the other two regimes. The levels of inequality generated by labour and capital markets, and the proportions of the population left in poverty by them, are still disappointingly high in absolute terms, even in social democratic welfare regimes, though. Judging by the Dutch performance anyway, the social democratic welfare regime seems unable to eradicate poverty and inequality through the economic sector alone.

14.3.2   The welfare sector

In addition to working through the economic sector, social democratic regimes are also particularly concerned to reduce poverty and inequality through their welfare sector. However much or little poverty or inequality the market generates, they hope to ensure adequacy and broad equality in people's post-government incomes through their deeply redistributive systems of taxes and transfers.

As we have said in section 14.2 above, the social democratic welfare regime, as represented by the Netherlands, is remarkably successful in that endeavour. Here we shall explore the mechanisms by which it achieves that outcome, concentrating particularly on the workings of public transfer programmes.

Social democrats would want public transfers to be universal (paid to everyone), substantial (involving non-negligible sums of money), equal (the same level of benefit for everyone) and redistributive (shifting money from the rich to the poor). Those various desiderata might or might not be logically or pragmatically in tension with one another: that is something we have already discussed in chapter 2 above. What we want to explore here is the more empirical question of to what extent welfare regimes' transfer programmes actually display those attributes.

The three welfare regimes' performance along all these dimensions is summarized in table 14.3. There we see that, as regards the universality of public transfer payments, the social democratic regime comes out substantially ahead of the liberal one, with the corporatist regime surprisingly close behind. Furthermore, social democrats pay people substantial sums through public transfers and (like corporatists) do so in a heavily redistributive way. The liberal welfare regime may pay more nearly equal sums to everyone, but those sums are so low as not to make much redistributive difference.

All these factors combine to cause the social democratic regime's welfare sector to make a very substantial contribution to the reduction of pre-government poverty and income inequality. The corporatist regime's welfare sector operates surprisingly similarly. The liberal regime's paying small sums to a select sub-set of the population, in contrast, prevents it from making any great impact on poverty or income inequality.

Table 14.3. *Performance of the social democratic welfare regime's welfare sector*

	Soc. Dem. (Neth.)	Liberal (US)	Corporatist (Ger.)	Reference (appendix table)
Transfers are universal	★★★★	★	★★★	Eq 3A
Transfers are substantial	★★★★	★	★★★	Pov 5A
Transfers are equal	★	★★★	★★	Eq 3E
Transfers are redistributive	★★★	★★	★★★	Eq 4A

14.4   The social democratic welfare regime: an overall assessment

The conclusion is that the social democratic welfare regime works broadly as advertised, certainly as regards the equalizing impact of its welfare sector. Its success in manipulating the economic sector so as to reduce pre-government poverty and to equalize pre-government market incomes, although still very real, is rather less dramatic,[2] but no matter, given the redistributive power of the social democratic regime's tax-transfer system.

The social democratic welfare regime's performance is not absolutely unique in that respect. The corporatist welfare regime's welfare sector comes somewhat near to being as equalizing. (The corporatist welfare regime achieves less post-government income equality overall, but only because corporatist pre-government incomes are significantly more unequal to start with.) Similar though their equality statistics might seem, however, it is clear that while corporatists reduce inequality more in the middle of the income distribution, social democrats reduce it more at the top and especially the bottom of the income distribution.[3] Thus, while the corporatist welfare regime turns in a surprisingly strong performance, it nonetheless remains clear that it is the social democratic regime which does most towards eliminating poverty and reducing income inequality.

---

[2] Whether that is a reflection on the social democratic model or on the Netherlands as an exemplar of it remains an open question.

[3] There are two key pieces of evidence for this conclusion. One is found in the greater reduction of poverty by social democratic regimes (appendix table A2, Pov 5A). The other is in the disparity of inequality measures (appendix table A3, Eq 1A): comparing Germany and the Netherlands, the indicator of inequality that is most sensitive to the middle ranges of the distribution (Gini) is broadly similar for the two countries; but those measures which are more sensitive to the bottom (Theil-0) or to the bottom and top (the 90/10 ratio) show Dutch incomes to be much more equal than German ones.

15 Germany as a corporatist welfare regime

Having set out the basic theories lying behind corporatist regimes in section 3.3, we now wish to test those theories against the actual experience of one exemplary corporatist welfare regime – that of Germany. The basic institutional structure of the German welfare regime has already been set out in section 4.3. Our task here is to test its performance, in pursuit of its chosen strategies and goals.

Once again, this test will primarily be against the corporatist welfare regime's own internal standards of success. But there is a comparative element in this assessment as well. We want not only to know whether the corporatist welfare regime does what it says it will do in the way it says it will do it; we also want to know whether it does those things better than the other welfare regimes under review. Hence we will once again look at the performance of corporatist Germany alongside that of the liberal United States and the social democratic Netherlands.

15.1 Mapping corporatist welfare strategy

The crux of the corporatist welfare strategy is to integrate individuals into households through marriage, and households into the economy through the paid employment of the household's head. Through strong social integration on both those fronts, the corporatist regime hopes to achieve its ultimate aim of a stable social and economic order.

Here, as elsewhere, not all of those concepts are easily captured by the sorts of variables available to us in the panel data. But many of the things of greatest concern in implementing that basic corporatist strategy are effectively operationalized though variables which are found in the panel studies. Thus, for example, when saying their ultimate aim is a 'stable system of social stratification', an important part of what corporatists mean by that is income stability. And when talking about 'social integration' as an important intermediate goal toward that ultimate end, at least part of what corporatists mean is what we have called 'economic integration' – everyone sharing a common economic fate. Those, as

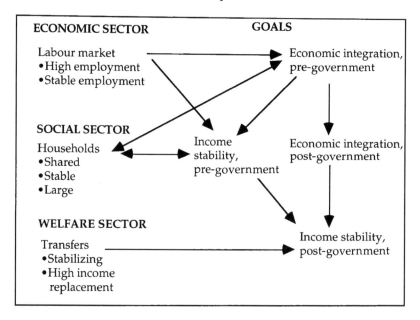

Figure 15.1. Corporatist welfare strategy.

indicated in figure 15.1, are what we will be taking as the goals of corporatist welfare strategy in our discussion in this chapter.

There are several planks in the corporatist welfare strategy for producing stability in people's post-government incomes. One is by working through its social and economic sectors to stabilize their pre-government incomes. Another is by integrating workers into the common economic life of the community. Yet another is by providing public transfers, when they are needed, in such a way as to replace a large proportion of people's previous earnings. The complex interactions between these components of the corporatist welfare strategy are mapped in figure 15.1.

In this chapter, we are concerned firstly with the question of whether the corporatist welfare regime succeeds or fails, by its own self-prescribed standard of success. Does it stabilize people's incomes, and does it do so better than alternative welfare regimes? We are concerned secondly with mechanisms. Does the corporatist regime do what it says it will do in the ways the representation of its strategy in figure 15.1 says it will do it?

Table 15.1. *Meeting the corporatist welfare regime's goals*

	Corporatist (Ger.)	Liberal (US)	Soc. Dem/ (Neth.)	Reference (appendix table)
Economic integration, pre-government	★★	★★★	★★	Integ 3A
Income stability, pre-government	★	★	★★	Stab 3A
Economic integration, post-government	★★	★★★	★	Integ 3A
Income stability, post-government	★★★	★★	★★★	Stab 3A

15.2   Does the corporatist welfare regime achieve its goals?

The ultimate aim of the corporatist welfare regime is, as we have said, to stabilize the social order. And as we have also said, we will be operationalizing that in terms of stabilizing people's post-government income over time.

Judged in those terms, the corporatist regime is indeed moderately successful. That is the summary judgment contained in the last line of table 15.1. But as we also see there, the corporatist achievement on that score is not unique (it is matched by the social democratic welfare regime).

In adducing the sources of those respective regimes' comparative success in this regard, we need only read upwards in table 15.1. There we see that pre-government incomes were not particularly stable under the corporatist welfare regime (they were noticeably more so under the social democrats). And while the liberals seem particularly adept at integrating people into the larger community economically, neither corporatists nor social democrats are as strong on that score.

In short, the corporatist welfare regime seems to have succeeded in achieving its ultimate goal. But it seems to have done so despite a relatively weak performance on all of the intermediate goals set out in the corporatist welfare strategy.

15.3   Does the corporatist welfare regime function as claimed?

That curious result can be explored more fully by examining the specific mechanisms through which the corporatist welfare regime is supposed to work. We now turn to that task, looking at the economic, social and welfare sectors in turn.

Table 15.2. *Performance of the corporatist welfare regime's economic sector*

	Corporatist (Ger.)	Liberal (US)	Soc. Dem/ (Neth.)	Reference (appendix table)
Full employment				
– prime-aged males	★★★	★★★	★★★	Stab 2A
– all heads of household	★★★	★★★	★★★	Integ 2A
Stable employment				
– prime-aged males	★★	★★★	★★★	Stab 2A
– all heads of household	★★	★★★	★★★	Integ 2A

15.3.1   The economic sector

The corporatist welfare regime strives to promote economic integration and income stability, in part by ensuring that every head of household is in stable, full-time paid employment.

As table 15.2 shows, all three welfare regimes – the corporatist regime certainly among them – are pretty successful at integrating prime-aged males and heads of households more generally into the labour market. They are particularly successful at ensuring full employment, even just of all heads of households. However, when it comes to ensuring the stability of employment, the second plank in their economic programme, corporatists actually prove less successful than either of the other two regimes.

15.3.2   The social sector

Corporatist strategy is predicated on conjoining the stable integration of heads of households in the workforce with the integration of everyone else into stable household units, and the income stability enjoyed by the head of household is supposed in that way to flow on to the rest of the household.

Once again, however, corporatists are only moderately successful at ensuring household integration and stability. Not only is their achievement low in absolute terms, as table 15.3 indicates, it is also comparatively poor, with the social democrats enjoying markedly higher scores on both household integration and household stability than the corporatists themselves.

Table 15.3. *Performance of the corporatist welfare regime's social sector*

	Corporatist (Ger.)	Liberal (US)	Soc. Dem/ (Neth.)	Reference (appendix table)
Households are shared	★★	★★	★★★	Integ 1A
Households are stable	★★	★	★★★	Stab 1A

15.3.3 The welfare sector

Within the corporatist welfare strategy, just as within the liberal one, the welfare sector is supposed to play only a residual part. Corporatist regimes count principally on economic and social arrangements to provide everyone – heads of households, and through them the rest of the members of their households – with a stable and secure income.

Corporatists look to the welfare sector only if and when markets or marriages fail. But when they do, the corporatist welfare sector is supposed to be designed in such a way as to replace a sufficiently large portion of breadwinners' lost wages to ensure the maintenance of their previous standard of living – to 'preserve their place in the social order', determined, in part, by income stratification, as corporatists themselves might prefer to put it.

As seen in table 15.4, corporatist welfare regimes do indeed succeed in stabilizing people's post-government incomes. Corporatists do this primarily through high replacement rates, paying people a large proportion of their previous earnings when they shift onto public transfers as their principal source of income. The greater stabilizing effects of corporatist taxes and transfers is what enables corporatist regimes, having started out with higher pre-government income instability, to match the income stability found in post-government incomes in social democratic regimes.

Table 15.4. *Performance of the corporatist welfare regime's welfare sector*

	Corporatist (Ger.)	Liberal (US)	Soc. Dem/ (Neth.)	Reference (appendix table)
High replacement rates	★★★	★★	★★★	Eff 4A
Transfers are stabilizing	★★★	★★	★★	Stab 6C

15.4   The corporatist welfare regime: an overall assessment

The upshot is that the corporatist welfare regime succeeds, but it does so rather in spite of itself. That is to say, any success that it has in ensuring people secure and stable incomes comes not through stability and security in its economic or social sectors, which are its officially preferred mechanisms. Such stability as corporatists produce is achieved instead primarily through the highly stabilizing tax-transfer activities of its state welfare sector, which in corporatist theory ought be purely a subsidiary device.

16   Conclusions

Ours is a book principally devoted to exploring what difference alternative welfare regimes make to people's lives. In previous chapters the discussion of differences has accordingly enjoyed pride of place. In concluding, however, it is only proper to set those differences firmly in perspective. Importantly different though welfare regimes are, in many ways what matters more are features that all of them have in common.

It bears emphasizing, for example, that in all the countries we have studied the vast majority of people are not poor at any given time, and a sizeable fraction of them never will be. In all three countries, most of those who do fall into poverty will not remain poor for long, one way or another. Finally, in all three countries government is a 'force for good', whether defined in terms of reducing poverty, increasing equality, promoting integration, underwriting stability or furthering autonomy.

Some governments promote those goals better than others, to be sure, and they do so more or less efficiently. Discussion of those differences will once again come to the fore later in this concluding chapter. But to set that discussion in proper perspective, it is important to emphasize that choosing between alternative welfare regimes is less a matter of choosing the 'lesser of evils' than of choosing the 'greater of goods'. Any of the welfare regimes under review is better, in any of those ways, than is the uncorrected market.

16.1   Horses for courses?

Comparative policy analysis is acutely sensitive to the fact that different regimes have different priorities. That being so, comparative policy analysts tend to suppose that it is only natural that different regimes should set about tackling their rather different objectives in rather different ways. This leads, equally naturally, to evaluative relativism: since different regimes are trying to do essentially different things, it is only right that we should judge each in terms of its own internal standard of success rather than trying to hold all of them up to any common standard.

259

The upshot tends to be a common presumption among comparative policy analysts that we need 'horses for courses'. If what you care about is equality, then the social democratic regime (which itself attaches greatest priority to that goal) is presumably the welfare regime for you. If instead what you care about is social integration, then the corporatist regime (which emphasizes that goal) is instead presumably the one for you.

Up to this point, we have by and large fallen in with that tradition and organized our discussion along those familiar lines. But we are now in a position to be more conclusive. We foreshadowed in chapter 2 that it might sometimes happen that one welfare regime beats another at its own game, proving superior according to its own internal standards of success; and were that to happen we would then be in a position to say that one welfare regime was decisively superior to another, whichever of those goals you preferred. We foreshadowed in chapter 2 that we might be able to come up with at least a weak 'partial ranking' of welfare regimes on the basis of some such logic. On the basis of the results presented in the foregoing chapters, that is just what has happened.

Far from being a matter of 'horses for courses', it turns out that the social democratic welfare regime is 'the best of all possible worlds'. The social democratic welfare regime turns out to be the best choice, regardless of what you want it to do. The social democratic welfare regime is clearly best on its home ground of minimizing inequality. But it also turns out to be better at reducing poverty than the liberal welfare regime, which targets its welfare policy on that to the exclusion of all else. The social democratic welfare regime is also at least as good at promoting stability (and arguably at least as good at promoting social integration) as is the corporatist welfare regime, which ostensibly attaches most importance to those goals. The social democratic welfare regime is also best at promoting key elements of autonomy, something valued by all regimes if not necessarily prioritized by any. Thus, no matter which of those goals you set for your welfare regime, the social democratic model is at least as good as (and typically better than) any other for attaining it.

Of course, as liberals emphasize and everyone else acknowledges, however grudgingly, the redistributive sector of the economy is necessarily parasitic upon the productive sector of the economy. If there was no one creating wealth, then there would be nothing for government to redistribute. Furthermore, some liberals may well go on to say, if everyone were earning enough for themselves in the market, there would be no need for government to redistribute anything. Be that further proposition as it may,[1] at the very least the requirements of 'economic efficiency' must

---

[1] Government intervention may still be wanted to ensure equality or stability, even if markets provide income adequacy without any government intervention.

be seen to set important constraints upon the operation of all welfare regimes: they must not get too much in the way of economic productivity.

'Efficiency' is of course a complex notion, with its many different indicators often pointing in different directions, as our discussion in chapter 7 has shown. But insofar as our 'bottom-line' concern with efficiency is with the way in which welfare policy might undermine economic productivity, then the crucial fact is simply that the social democratic welfare regime upon which we have focused – the Netherlands – managed to sustain economic growth at a rate certainly on a par with (and in some ways higher than) the other countries under study. And both the social democratic and corporatist regimes passed on much more of that growth dividend to middle-income earners than did the liberal regime under study, at least over this period.

How the social democratic regime managed to achieve such high economic growth must be something of a mystery to neo-liberal micro-economists. They would point to various factors (its relatively low employment levels; its welfare system's high replacement rates and hence large work disincentives; and its high rates of welfare dependency), all of which should, on the standard neo-liberal model of the economy, lead to lower economic productivity. And of course maybe it did: we can never know how much faster the Dutch economy might have grown, had all those welfare recipients been in paid labour.

An equally plausible interpretation of our general pattern of findings, however, is to say that they simply call into question the 'necessary truths' of neo-classical economics. There seem to be several different paths to economic productivity. It seems possible, in certain circumstances, to sustain generous welfare benefits without greatly increasing the numbers of people relying upon them. And it also seems possible, in certain circumstances, to sustain high rates of welfare dependency while at the same time achieving relatively high rates of economic growth. Thus one upshot of our study is to cast doubt upon the necessity of Okun's (1975) 'big trade-off' between equity and efficiency, between social and economic objectives.

According to traditional wisdom, we are forced to choose between the liberal regime (which promotes greater economic efficiency) and the social democratic regime (which promotes greater social justice), with the corporatist regime offering itself as a good compromise between them (coming in a strong second in both respects). According to traditional wisdom, our choice between these regimes will necessarily be dictated by the relative weights we assign to those two sorts of objectives.

At the outset, we only expected the analysis in our book to help to clarify the terms of Okun's 'big trade-off' by putting some magnitudes on the gains and losses in view. The upshot of our analysis, however, has

been to single out the social democratic welfare strategy as strictly dominant over both the others. The social democratic welfare regime is at least
as good as (and usually better than) either of the other welfare regimes in
respect of all the *social* objectives we traditionally set for our welfare
regimes. Furthermore, the social democratic welfare regime is at least as
good as any other on *economic* objectives as well – at least if we assess
economic objectives in terms of 'bottom-line' economic growth rates
rather than in terms of the various things that economists assert (without
warrant in our evidence) to be causally connected to them.

16.2   Time cures all?

A second broad general conclusion arising from our studies – and the sort
of conclusion that can only come on the basis of the sorts of panel studies
upon which we have been privileged to draw – concerns the simple role of
time in overcoming social ills.

Across virtually the entire range of indicators we have here been
examining, social distress tends to wane over time. Those who are poor in
one year will not, by and large, remain poor for long. However unequal
people's incomes are in any given year, those inequalities will by and large
tend to even out over subsequent years. However unstable a person's
income is from one year to the next, those fluctuations tend by and large
to counterbalance one another over the space of several years.

Still, it would be an irresponsible exaggeration to say that 'time cures
all', in any literal sense. Milton Friedman (1962, pp. 171–2) might be
taken to represent the voice of complacency on this score, when he urges:

the need to distinguish two basically different kinds of inequality: temporary,
short-run differences in income, and differences in long-run income status . . .
The one kind of inequality is a sign of dynamic change, social mobility, equality of
opportunity; the other of a status society . . . [C]ompetitive free-enterprise capitalism tends to substitute the one for the other . . . [I]nequality in [non-capitalist
societies] tends to be permanent, whereas capitalism undermines status and
introduces social mobility.

But of course the fact that incomes fluctuate over time for each person
does not necessarily mean that they will eventually end up being equal
across all people (Hills 1998). And while the passage of time certainly
does seem to ameliorate most problems for most people, even at the end
of fully ten years a certain (even if sometimes small) number of people
continue to experience distress across virtually all the sorts of problems
and across all three of countries we have studied.

To say that most people's poverty ends after two years – as half of poverty spells do in the US, for example (Bane and Ellwood 1994, p. 29) – is not to say that everyone could have got out of poverty by the end of two years if only they had tried. The long-term poor might indeed be different in ways to which any decent policy ought to respond: and upon further investigation, those differences may turn out not to be just a matter of education and training and moral character that are either easily resolved or easily blamed on the person concerned. All we want to emphasize here is the fallacy of inferring support for US-style 'two years and you're out' welfare reforms from the evidence contained in panel studies showing that most welfare recipients do indeed manage to get out by the end of two years. To assume that all can, just because some (even most) can, is a simple logical fallacy.

It would be likewise irresponsible to infer that, just because the sheer passage of time eases most social ills, government interventions are any the less required.[2] Certainly public transfers will be needed to tide people over in the short term, and some people in the long term as well. The changes in people's incomes that can be produced through public transfer payments are massively greater than those produced through the passage of time alone. For example, the passage of ten years reduces pre-government poverty in all three countries by about one-fifth; and although the US government's transfers do only about the same again, in Germany and the Netherlands the government interventions reduce poverty by four times that amount. Or, again, the passage of ten years reduces pre-government income inequality in Germany and the Netherlands by about a sixth, whereas government interventions there reduce it by over twice that amount.

Our real conclusion, then, is not so much that 'time cures most things' but rather that 'over time, government interventions can cure most things'. We have shown not only that government interventions help to achieve all the social objectives ascribed to welfare regimes, but also that they help more over longer periods than shorter ones. That is more strikingly true of some regimes and some objectives than others, naturally. But what is more striking still is that it is true to some substantial extent of all welfare regimes and in respect of all their social objectives.

Our closing comment on the 'time cures all' excuse for government inaction is just this. Even if someone's distress is only temporary, distress is none the less distressing for its (probably) only being temporary. It is a wholly appropriate, and not insignificant, function of government to tide people over periods of temporary distress of just that sort. And how many

---

[2] Even advocates of 'two years and you're out' endorse not only short-term public transfer payments but also various other government schemes to 'make work pay' and to make welfare recipients 'work-ready' (Bane and Ellwood 1994).

people need assistance, if only in this brief fashion, might be the more appropriate measure of the real social value of public interventions (Ruggles 1990, pp. 90–103).

Compensating for 'the lumpiness of luck over time' might be a somewhat bland and boring role for the welfare state. But it is one which can be widely embraced, without prejudice as regards deeper principles.[3] Whatever their higher aspirations, and whatever their success (or otherwise) in achieving them, one of the most important things all tax-transfer systems do is to even out the fluctuating fortunes that all too many citizens are bound to suffer over time.

Precisely because their fortunes do by and large fluctuate, though, most people who are welfare beneficiaries in one year will be (and will have been) productive taxpayers in other years. Government assistance in such circumstances is more like 'disaster relief' or a 'bridging loan' which will be repaid many times over through tax contributions once recipients' fortunes have again turned.[4] Redistribution here is not between one person or one social class and another, but between periods of fortune and misfortune across one's own life.[5] Seen in that light – which is the sort of the light powerfully cast by panel studies of income dynamics – the role of welfare state seems almost unexceptionable.

Some people of course do end up being net welfare-state beneficiaries in a big way, even in a whole lifetime perspective. On the evidence of this book, however, that is a much less common phenomenon than we might have imagined.[6] And many more of us benefit than we might have imagined from the sort of insurance against those risks of life that we all, in one way or another, inevitably run.[7]

---

[3] Rowntree (1901). Buchanan and Tulloch (1962, ch. 13); Zeckhauser (1974); Goodin and Dryzek (1986).

[4] On the disaster relief model, see Hirshleifer (1987) and Landis (1998). Leisering and Leibfried (1998, ch. 4) report that over half of German recipients of means-tested benefits (among them some relatively long-term recipients) regarded themselves as using social assistance merely to 'bridge' over some temporary difficulties.

[5] Micro-simulations suggest that, in the UK for example, some 62 per cent of government taxes and transfers are intra-personal – with the transfers being paid for by the same person at some other point in time – and only 38 per cent are genuinely interpersonal (Falkingham, Hills and Lessof 1993). Ringen (1996a, p. 25) rightly emphasizes the importance of such a result for the politics and sociology (and indeed political morality) of the welfare state.

[6] Recall the results discussed in section 8.6.1 above. One in eight (in Germany and the Netherlands; one in six in the US) of the people who were in the top half of the income distribution in the first year under study dropped into poverty at some time over the course of the study. And privilege provides only a very partial protection. The proportion of those in the top half of the income distribution at the beginning of the study who dropped into poverty at some time over the ten years was half that high, even among white (in the US; non-guestworker in Germany) males of prime working age.

[7] Furthermore, that is increasingly so in the post-industrial era (Esping-Andersen 1999).

Appendix table A1   Indicators of efficiency

I   National income

Eff 1A (growth in real income): 'the percentage of people whose real (i.e. inflation-adjusted) post-government equivalent income has increased over N years, and by how much it increased for the median individual'.

Year	Germany		Netherlands		USA	
	Better off at end of period (%)	By how much (%)	Better off at end of period (%)	By how much (%)	Better off at end of period (%)	By how much (%)
1985–89 (83–87)	69.0	9.7	68.7	14.2	57.0	6.0
1990–94 (88–92)	60.3	4.1	55.9	3.8	48.9	−5.4
1985–94 (83–92)	69.9	14.7	66.5	16.4	51.1	1.4

Eff 1B (growth in real GDP over the decade): 'percentage change in real GDP over the decade' (1985–94 for Germany and the Netherlands; 1983–92 for the US).

	Germany			Netherlands			US		
	Real GDP (million DM)	Population (000)	Real GDP per capita (DM)	Real GDP (million H fl.)	Population (000)	Real GDP per capita (H fl.)	Real GDP (billion $)	Population (000)	Real GDP per capita $
1983							4,424.3	234,307	18,882.49
1985	2,055,997	61,024	33,691.61	443,250	14,491	30,587.95	4,793.2	238,466	20,100.14
1992							5,653.2	255,407	22,134.08
1994	2,605,419	65,859	39,560.56	560,590	15,382	36,444.55	6,027.1	260,651	23,123.26
Growth 1983-92							27.8%	9.0%	17.2%
Growth 1985-94	26.7%	7.9%	17.4%	26.5%	6.2%	19.1%	25.7%	9.3%	15.0%

Source: OECD, *National Accounts: Main Aggregates,* vol I, 1960–94 (Paris, 1996) for Germany; OECD, *National Accounts: Main Aggregates,* vol. I, 1960–96 (Paris, 1998) for Netherlands and US; GDP in constant 1990 prices, population estimates at 1 July each year.

II   Employment rates

Eff 2A (employment rate): 'the fraction of possible person-years actually worked in the country, over N years (= number of hours actually worked / (number of people of working age × 52 weeks per year × 40 hours per week))' (for individuals aged 16–64).

Year	Germany (%)		Netherlands (%)		USA (%)	
	All	Female	All	Female	All	Female
1987 (1985)	57.3	31.8	47.4	22.9	70.4	(1983) 46.4
1992 (1990)	46.8	29.4	47.6	25.1	72.2	(1992) 51.6

III   Welfare dependency

Eff 3A (recurrence of welfare dependency): 'total amount of time over ten years that an individual's principal source of income is public transfer payments' (hit rates) (for households with heads of prime working age, 25–59).

	Germany (%)			Netherlands (%)			USA (%)		
	All	Means tested	Non means-tested	All	Means-tested	Non means-tested	All	Means-tested	Non-means-tested
≥ once	11.7	4.4	9.2	25.2	6.9	22.6	17.5	11.8	8.3
≥ twice	6.5	2.1	4.5	17.1	4.0	14.6	11.9	8.7	3.6
≥ 3 times	4.5	1.0	3.2	13.9	2.8	11.4	9.5	6.6	2.6
≥ 4 times	3.3	0.7	2.7	11.6	2.0	9.2	7.8	5.5	1.9
≥ 5 times	2.9	0.6	2.0	9.3	1.2	7.0	6.4	4.4	1.5
≥ 6 times	2.5	0.4	1.8	7.7	0.9	5.6	5.2	3.7	1.1
≥ 7 times	1.9	0.2	1.5	5.7	0.7	4.0	4.5	3.3	0.8
≥ 8 times	1.4	0.1	1.1	4.2	0.5	2.9	3.4	2.4	0.6
≥ 9 times	0.9	0.0	0.6	3.1	0.3	1.9	2.7	1.8	0.4
≥ 10 times	0.4	0.0	0.4	2.0	0.1	1.2	1.5	0.9	0.2

Eff 3B (recurrence of welfare/market dependency among the aged): 'total amount of time over ten years that an individual's principal source of income is (a) public transfer payments or (b) market income, for households headed by people aged over 56' (hit rates) (for households with heads > 56).

	Germany (%)		Netherlands (%)		USA (%)	
	Public transfers	Market income	Public transfers	Market income	Public transfers	Market income
≥ once	89.8	55.5	88.8	68.8	67.8	79.0
≥ twice	86.4	48.3	82.2	58.0	58.6	71.0
≥ 3 times	81.8	42.0	77.4	49.1	52.0	65.5
≥ 4 times	78.6	37.0	70.0	42.2	46.3	60.0
≥ 5 times	72.6	30.4	64.7	37.0	40.9	55.6
≥ 6 times	69.6	27.1	59.0	31.7	35.6	50.4
≥ 7 times	63.0	21.1	51.6	24.3	31.8	45.5
≥ 8 times	57.9	16.5	45.3	17.9	27.0	39.7
≥ 9 times	51.7	13.1	32.0	11.1	22.4	35.0
≥ 10 times	44.4	9.8	20.7	5.3	15.9	26.9

EFF 3C (persistence of prime-working-age welfare dependency): 'the period of unbroken time an individual's principal source of income is public transfer payments' (survival rates, spell analysis) (for households with heads of working age, 25–59; for public transfer programmes other than old age pensions).

Survival after	Germany (%)		Netherlands (%)		USA (%)	
		Unweighted error		Unweighted error		Unweighted error
1 year	85.0	0.006	90.5	0.004	88.6	0.008
2 years	35.0	0.012	62.2	0.010	47.8	0.012
3 years	21.2	0.012	49.8	0.012	28.6	0.012
4 years	15.0	0.012	38.2	0.013	17.7	0.011
5 years	10.8	0.011	28.6	0.013	12.2	0.009
6 years	9.0	0.010	17.8	0.013	7.0	0.008
7 years	5.0	0.009	8.5	0.011	4.3	0.006
8 years	2.7	0.007	2.7	0.007	2.0	0.004
Percentage of cases censored	7.44%		7.89%		8.36%	
Unweighted no. of spells		1,710		1,553		1,679

Eff 3D (magnitude of public transfers): 'the proportion of the prime-work-ing-aged population deriving various proportions of their total post-government income from public transfers' (excluding old age pensions; for individuals aged 25–59).

(a) *Means-tested programmes*

Year	Germany			Netherlands			USA		
	> 25%	25–45%	> 45%	> 25%	25–45%	> 45%	> 25%	25–45%	> 45%
1987 (85)	1.6	1.3	1.8	3.7	2.8	2.9	6.1	6.2	6.0
1992 (90)	1.3	1.3	1.3	1.9	1.5	2.5	5.5	4.2	5.9
1985–89 (83–87)	1.3	1.3	1.3	3.5	3.6	3.1	5.6	5.9	5.6
1990–94 (88–92)	1.1	1.0	1.3	3.5	2.3	5.7	5.4	5.9	5.3
1985–94 (83–92)	1.1	0.9	1.3	3.3	2.8	3.8	5.5	5.9	6.4

(b) *Non-means-tested programmes*

Year	Germany			Netherlands			USA		
	> 25%	25–45%	> 45%	> 25%	25–45%	> 45%	> 25%	25–45%	> 45%
1987 (85)	6.5	6.1	7.2	12.2	11.2	16.9	2.9	2.6	4.6
1992 (90)	5.7	5.2	6.1	16.6	14.4	19.7	3.0	2.5	4.8
1985–89 (83–87)	6.3	6.1	7.0	12.8	12.0	15.0	3.1	2.7	4.4
1990–94 (88–92)	5.5	5.2	6.4	16.5	16.2	17.2	3.2	2.6	5.6
1985–94 (83–92)	5.8	5.4	7.1	14.2	13.2	15.9	3.3	2.7	5.6

(c) *All public transfer programmes*

Year	Germany			Netherlands			USA		
	> 25%	25–45%	> 45%	> 25%	25–45%	> 45%	> 25%	25–45%	> 45%
1987 (85)	6.6	6.4	6.9	15.4	13.9	19.8	6.7	6.3	8.7
1992 (90)	6.5	6.0	6.9	19.5	16.4	24.1	6.6	6.3	7.5
1985–89 (83–87)	7.6	7.5	8.3	16.3	15.7	18.0	8.7	8.3	10.3
1990–94 (88–92)	6.7	6.2	7.6	20.2	18.9	23.0	8.6	8.5	10.8
1985–94 (83–92)	6.9	6.3	8.5	17.6	16.3	19.8	8.5	8.4	11.5

Work disincentives

Eff 4A (replacement rate of public transfer payments, other than old age pensions): 'for individuals whose principal source of income was public transfers in one year and whose principal source of income was not public transfers in another year (the transfer income of that individual in the transfer-dependent year divided by that individual's income in the non-transfer-dependent year) (median individual, median year)' (for households with heads of working age, 25–59; for public transfer programmes other than old age pensions).

1985–94 (83–92)	Germany		Netherlands		USA	
	Wage + transfer income (%)	Total equivalent h'hold income (%)	Wage + transfer income (%)	Total equivalent h'hold income (%)	Wage + transfer income (%)	Total equivalent h'hold income (%)
Moving from earnings to public transfers	74	75	76	83	67	71
Moving from public transfers to earnings	137	132	114	112	143	137

Eff 4B (replacement rate, old age pensions): 'for individuals whose principal source of income was the old age pension in year x and whose principal source of income was not public transfers in year $x-1$ (the transfer income of that individual's income in year $x-1$) (median individual, median year)' (for households with heads over age 56).

1985–94 (83–92)	Germany		Netherlands		USA	
	Wage + transfer income (%)	Total equivalent h'hold income (%)	Wage + transfer income (%)	Total equivalent h'hold income (%)	Wage + transfer income (%)	Total equivalent h'hold income (%)
Moving from earnings to public transfers	93	89	98	74	96	75
Moving from public transfers to earnings	102	121	95	127	98	130

Eff 4C (change in hours worked when receiving welfare): 'among those in receipt of public transfers in some but not all years, the median number of hours a year members of the household worked during years in which public transfers were the household's principal source of income as a proportion of the median number of hours members of that household worked while market income was the household's principal source of income, for the median household in this group (= hours$_{welf}$ / hours$_{nonwelf}$)' (for people in households with heads of prime working age, 25–59).

	Germany	Netherlands	USA
Median 1985–94 (83–92)	0.11	0.15	0.17
Mean 1985–94 (83–92)	0.25	0.32	0.28

V   Target inefficiency

Eff 5A (frequency of overpayments): 'the proportion of persons receiving public transfers who are not poor (i.e. live in households with a total equivalent pre-government income of more than 50 per cent of median equivalent pre-government income across the nation as a whole); for multiple years, the proportion of persons receiving public transfers in each of N years who were poor in none of those N years' (for prime-working-aged population, aged 25–59).

Year	Germany (%)			Netherlands (%)			USA (%)		
	Means-tested	Non-means-tested	All	Means-tested	Non-means-tested	All	Means-tested	Non-means-tested	All
1987 (85)	6	64	65	22	63	69	3	17	18
1992 (90)	7	61	62	11	60	64	2	16	17
1985–89 (83–87)	0	52	52	4	44	48	1	4	4
1990–94 (88–92)	1	47	48	1	38	41	1	4	5
1985–94 (83–92)	0	40	40	0	31	34	0	2	2

Eff 5B (frequency of serious overpayments): 'the proportion of persons receiving public transfers who are nowhere near poor (i.e. live in households with a total equivalent pre-government income of more than 60 per cent of median equivalent pre-government income across the nation as a whole) for multiple years, the proportion of persons receiving public transfers in each of *N* years who were nowhere near poor in any of those *N* years' (for prime-working-aged population, aged 25–59).

Year	Germany (%)			Netherlands (%)			USA (%)		
	Means-tested	Non-means-tested	All	Means-tested	Non-means-tested	All	Means-tested	Non-means-tested	All
1987 (85)	6	63	64	22	62	69	2	17	18
1992 (90)	6	61	62	10	59	64	2	15	16
1985–89 (83–87)	1	51	51	4	44	48	1	3	4
1990–94 (88–92)	1	47	47	1	38	41	1	4	4
1985–94 (83–92)	0	39	39	0	31	35	0	2	2

Eff 5C (frequency of underpayments): 'the proportion of the poor (i.e. persons living in households with a total equivalent pre-government income of less than 50 per cent of median equivalent pre-government income across the nation as a whole) not receiving public transfers; for multiple years, the proportion of people who are poor in each of *N* years who never receive public transfers in any of those *N* years' (for prime-working-aged population, aged 25–59).

Year	Germany (%)			Netherlands (%)			USA (%)		
	Means-tested	Non-means-tested	All	Means-tested	Non-means-tested	All	Means-tested	Non-means-tested	All
1987 (85)	68	19	12	49	14	5	55	52	33
1992 (90)	70	19	15	69	11	5	57	64	38
1985–89 (83–87)	82	14	9	63	22	4	67	71	42
1990–94 (88–92)	91	32	24	84	14	1	64	77	42
1985–94 (83–92)	too few cases	too few cases	too few cases	88	44	0	65	70	39

Eff 5D (frequency of serious underpayments): 'the proportion of the very poor (i.e. persons living in households with a total equivalent pre-government income of less than 40 per cent of median equivalent pre-government income across the nation as a whole) not receiving public transfers from means-tested programmes; for multiple years, the proportion of people who are poor in each of N years who never receive public transfers in any of those N years' (for prime-working-aged population, aged 25–59).

Year	Germany (%)			Netherlands (%)			USA (%)		
	Means-tested	Non-means-tested	All	Means-tested	Non-means-tested	All	Means-tested	Non-means-tested	All
1987 (85)	63	16	9	48	14	5	45	46	23
1992 (90)	67	17	12	68	11	5	50	59	30
1985–89 (83–87)	81	15	11	62	21	3	55	63	27
1990–94 (88–92)	87	41	29	82	14	0	53	68	24
1985–94 (83–92)	too few cases	too few cases	too few cases	86	45	0	60	62	28

VI   Programme efficiency

Eff 6A (proportion of monies going to the poor (Beckerman index)): '(the proportion of programme expenditures going to persons who are poor) × (1 minus the proportion of benefits in excess of what it would take to lift the poor out of poverty, i.e. the "spillover"). NB: spillover for each individual = public transfers − poverty gap for that individual.

Year	Germany (%)			Netherlands (%)			USA (%)		
	Means-tested	Non-means-tested	All	Means-tested	Non-means-tested	All	Means-tested	Non-means-tested	All
1987 (85)	50	32	33	19	25	29	86	19	51
1992 (90)	29	29	29	5	27	29	86	30	42
1985–89 (83–87)	24	26	27	5	14	17	78	14	32
1990–94 (88–92)	25	25	25	7	20	21	83	21	33
1985–94 (83–92)	15	20	20	3	12	13	63	11	25

Eff 6B (proportion of monies going to the seriously poor (Beckerman index)): '(the proportion of programme expenditures going to persons who are seriously poor, i.e. < 40 per cent median equivalent income) × (1 minus the proportion of benefits in excess of what it would take to lift the poor out of poverty, i.e. the "spillover")'. NB: spillover for each individual = public transfers − poverty gap for that individual.

Year	Germany (%)			Netherlands (%)			USA (%)		
	Means-tested	Non-means-tested	All	Means-tested	Non-means-tested	All	Means-tested	Non-means-tested	All
1987 (85)	36	24	25	13	18	21	100	21	47
1992 (90)	14	22	22	3	20	22	100	27	38
1985–89 (83–87)	11	19	19	3	9	12	54	9	23
1990–94 (88–92)	14	18	18	4	14	16	53	13	23
1985–94 (83–92)	7	14	14	3	8	9	30	6	16

Appendix table A2   Indicators of poverty

I   Extent of poverty

Pov 1A (extent of poverty among people overall): 'the proportion of the total population of the country living in households with a total equivalent income of less than 50 per cent of median equivalent income across the nation as a whole'.

(a) *Pre-government*

Year	Germany (%)	Netherlands (%)	USA (%)
1987 (85)	25.1	19.4	21.1
1992 (90)	25.1	19.0*	21.9
1985–89 (83–87)	22.6	16.2	18.7
1990–94 (88–92)	23.5	18.2	20.6
1985–94 (83–92)	21.2	15.4	16.9

* There seems to be some problem with the 1992 Dutch data, which show pre-government poverty that year to be too low, given the weak Dutch economic performance that year; the true poverty rate should, if anything, be a bit higher than the two adjacent years (20.7 per cent for 1991 and 20.8 per cent for 1993).

(b) *Post-government*

Year	Germany (%)	Netherlands (%)	USA (%)
1987 (85)	7.6	4.3	18.0
1992 (90)	8.9	6.8*	18.2
1985–89 (83–87)	6.2	1.1	14.7
1990–94 (88–92)	7.1	1.4	16.3
1985–94 (83–92)	5.8	0.5	13.0

* There seems to be some problem with the 1992 Dutch data, as noted above; the true rate of post-government poverty should, if anything, be rather higher than that in the two adjacent years (7.4 per cent for 1991 and 7.2 per cent for 1993).

276

Pov 1B (extent of poverty among people in working-aged households): 'the proportion of the population living in working-aged households with a total equivalent income of less than 50 per cent of median equivalent income across the nation as a whole' (for individuals living in households whose head is aged under 60).

(a) *Pre-government*

Year	Germany (%)	Netherlands (%)	USA (%)
1987 (85)	9.8	10.5	17.5
1992 (90)	9.8	9.2	17.0
1985–89 (83–87)	7.8	6.1	14.3
1990–94 (88–92)	7.9	6.0	15.5
1985–94 (83–92)	6.1	4.9	12.0

(b) *Post-government*

Year	Germany (%)	Netherlands (%)	USA (%)
1987 (85)	7.6	3.6	17.8
1992 (90)	7.6	6.2	17.7
1985–89 (83–87)	5.6	0.8	13.9
1990–94 (88–92)	6.3	2.3	15.4
1985–94 (83–92)	5.2	0.3	12.0

Pov 1C (extent of the working poor): 'the proportion of people living in a household where the head of household is under 60 years and in paid labour who have a total equivalent income less than 50 per cent of median equivalent income across the nation as a whole'.

(a) *Pre-government*

Year	Germany (%)	Netherlands (%)	USA (%)
1987 (85)	9.8	10.5	16.6
1992 (90)	9.8	8.6	17.0
1985–89 (83–87)	7.8	6.1	14.3
1990–94 (88–92)	7.9	5.8	15.5
1985–94 (83–92)	6.1	4.6	11.5

(b) *Post-government*

Year	Germany (%)	Netherlands (%)	USA (%)
1987 (85)	7.6	3.6	17.0
1992 (90)	7.6	5.7	17.7
1985–89 (83–87)	5.6	0.8	10.9
1990–94 (88–92)	6.3	2.3	15.4
1985–94 (83–92)	5.2	0.3	11.7

Pov 1D (extent of aged poverty): 'the median proportion, over ten years, of total population aged 65 or over living in households with a total equivalent income of less than 50 per cent of median equivalent income across the nation as a whole'.

(a) *Pre-government*

Year	Germany (%)	Netherlands (%)	USA (%)
1987 (85)	83.6	60.7	52.4
1992 (90)	80.5	67.8	52.6
1985–89 (83–87)	84.7	65.2	51.9
1990–94 (88–92)	86.2	69.3	56.4
1985–94 (83–92)	87.6	71.4	56.1

(b) *Post-government*

Year	Germany (%)	Netherlands (%)	USA (%)
1987 (85)	11.1	2.2	26.8
1992 (90)	12.9	6.3	26.5
1985–89 (83–87)	11.3	0.5	22.8
1990–94 (88–92)	11.3	1.3	27.2
1985–94 (83–92)	11.8	0.3	25.9

Pov 1E (extent of child poverty): 'the proportion of those aged 16 and under who live in households with a total equivalent income of less than 50 per cent of median equivalent income across the nation as a whole'.

(a) *Pre-government*

Year	Germany (%)	Netherlands (%)	USA (%)
1987 (85)	11.7	12.3	20.4
1992 (90)	11.1	9.8	22.5
1985–89 (83–87)	9.2	7.0	17.8
1990–94 (88–92)	8.7	5.9	20.0
1985–94 (83–92)	7.6	4.9	14.6

(b) *Post-government*

Year	Germany (%)	Netherlands (%)	USA (%)
1987 (85)	9.3	3.4	19.9
1992 (90)	9.7	7.4	22.0
1985–89 (83–87)	7.0	0.6	17.3
1990–94 (88–92)	7.1	2.1	19.5
1985–94 (83–92)	5.6	0.8	13.8

Pov 1F (extent of single-parent poverty): 'the proportion of all people (children plus parents) living in single-parent households who have a total equivalent income of less than 50 per cent of median equivalent income across the nation as a whole'.

(a) *Pre-government*

Year	Germany (%)	Netherlands (%)	USA (%)
1987 (85)	40.6	58.4	61.8
1992 (90)	40.5	55.1	58.5
1985–89 (83–87)	31.0 but few cases	too few cases	71.7
1990–94 (88–92)	57.0 but few cases	too few cases	65.7
1985–94 (83–92)	23.6 but few cases	too few cases	68.0

(b) *Post-government*

Year	Germany (%)	Netherlands (%)	USA (%)
1987 (85)	22.9	4.0	60.5
1992 (90)	29.1	15.5	58.5
1985–89 (83–87)	19.2 but few cases	too few cases	73.9
1990–94 (88–92)	10.0 but few cases	too few cases	65.8
1985–94 (83–92)	15.3 but few cases	too few cases	71.7

II   Depth of poverty

Pov 2A (deep poverty): 'the proportion of the population which lives in households with a total equivalent income of less than 40 per cent of median equivalent income across the nation as a whole'.

(a) *Pre-government*

Year	Germany (%)	Netherlands (%)	USA (%)
1987 (85)	22.6	17.4	16.9
1992 (90)	22.9	15.5	17.8
1985–89 (83–87)	19.7	14.4	14.1
1990–94 (88–92)	20.2	14.7	16.0
1985–94 (83–92)	17.7	13.5	13.3

(b) *Post-government*

Year	Germany (%)	Netherlands (%)	USA (%)
1987 (85)	4.2	2.9	11.6
1992 (90)	5.2	4.3	12.3
1985–89 (83–87)	2.1	0.5	8.8
1990–94 (88–92)	3.2	1.1	10.6
1985–94 (83–92)	1.7	0.0	7.8

Poverty 2B (poor or nearly poor): 'the proportion of the population with a total equivalent income of less than 60 per cent of median equivalent income'.

(a) *Pre-government*

Year	Germany (%)	Netherlands (%)	USA (%)
1987 (85)	22.8	21.4	25.6
1992 (90)	28.0	20.5	26.1
1985–89 (83–87)	25.1	18.1	22.4
1990–94 (88–92)	25.7	18.5	25.7
1985–94 (83–92)	23.4	17.3	21.6

(b) *Post-government*

Year	Germany (%)	Netherlands (%)	USA (%)
1987 (85)	14.2	7.3	24.1
1992 (90)	15.3	11.1	24.4
1985–89 (83–87)	11.6	0.8	20.2
1990–94 (88–92)	13.1	6.5	23.6
1985–94 (83–92)	10.9	2.8	19.3

Pov 2C (average post-government poverty gap): 'the proportion by which the mean/median post-government income of those individuals who were post-government poor (i.e. with a post-government income of less than 50 per cent of median post-government equivalent income across the nation as a whole) fell short of the 50 per cent median level' (for household heads under age 60). (NB: pre-government poverty gaps are meaningless, given how many people have zero pre-government incomes.)

(a) *Percentage gap by which the* mean *post fisc incomes of the post-government poor fell below the 50 per cent median post-government poverty line.*

Year	Germany (%)	Netherlands (%)	USA (%)
1987 (85)	26.3	36.2	36.2
1992 (90)	34.4	39.4	37.4
1985–89 (83–87)	14.9	21.7	29.6
1990–94 (88–92)	14.8	28.4	34.5
1985–94 (83–92)	4.7	7.7	32.0

(b) *Percentage gap by which the* median *post-fisc incomes of the post-govern-ment poor fell below the 50 per cent median post-government poverty line.*

Year	Germany (%)	Netherlands (%)	USA (%)
1987 (85)	23.0	36.9	33.6
1992 (90)	29.5	33.6	34.9
1985–89 (83–87)	7.4	10.4	25.3
1990–94 (88–92)	3.1	21.8	33.2
1985–94 (83–92)	2.5	12.0	28.2

III   Duration of poverty

Pov 3A (duration of poverty): 'the period of unbroken time an individual's total equivalent income remains below 50 per cent of median equivalent income across the nation as a whole' (survival rates, spell analysis).

(a) *Pre-government*

Survival after	Germany (%)		Netherlands (%)		USA (%)	
		Unweighted error		Unweighted error		Unweighted error
1 year	66.7	0.009	66.7	0.015	61.6	0.006
2 years	55.0	0.010	58.3	0.016	46.3	0.007
3 years	49.8	0.010	50.4	0.017	38.1	0.007
4 years	46.6	0.011	46.4	0.018	33.0	0.007
5 years	40.2	0.012	42.3	0.019	29.4	0.007
6 years	37.8	0.012	40.2	0.019	26.8	0.007
7 years	36.3	0.013	39.5	0.019	26.0	0.008
8 years	33.8	0.014	Too few cases	–	25.6	0.008
9 years	Too few cases	–	Too few cases	–	Too few cases	–
10 years	Too few cases	–	Too few cases	–	Too few cases	–
% of cases censored	47.3 weighted	45.1 unweighted	48.0 weighted	47.6 unweighted	38.5 weighted	39.4 unweighted
Unweighted no. of spells	2,564		970		5,141	

(b) *Post-government*

Survival after	Germany (%)		Netherlands (%)		USA (%)	
		Unweighted error		Unweighted error		Unweighted error
1 year	48.6	0.012	34.4	0.017	59.6	0.006
2 years	34.4	0.012	19.4	0.016	42.5	0.007
3 years	25.8	0.012	14.9	0.015	33.5	0.007
4 years	20.9	0.012	10.6	0.014	28.6	0.007
5 years	16.7	0.012	Too few cases	–	24.6	0.007
6 years	14.3	0.012	Too few cases	–	22.3	0.007
7 years	11.5	0.013	Too few cases	–	20.8	0.007
8 years	11.1	0.013	Too few cases	–	19.8	0.008
9 years	Too few cases	–	Too few cases	–	Too few cases	–
10 years	Too few cases	–	Too few cases	–	Too few cases	–
% of cases censored	24.4 weighted	27.0 unweighted	20.1 weighted	18.2 unweighted	35.5 weighted	37.5 unweighted
Unweighted no. of spells	1,815		730		5,473	

IV   Recurrence of poverty

Pov 4A (recurrence of poverty): 'proportion of people whose equivalent income has been below 50 per cent of median equivalent income across the nation as a whole for N years out of 10' (hit rates).

(a) *Pre-government*

No. of times poor	Germany (%)	Netherlands (%)	USA (%)
Never poor	57.8	61.9	59.1
≥ 1 times	42.2	38.1	40.9
≥ 2 times	34.2	30.2	31.9
≥ 3 times	29.5	26.1	26.4
≥ 4 times	25.8	22.7	22.8
≥ 5 times	22.9	20.1	19.2
≥ 6 times	20.7	18.2	16.7
≥ 7 times	18.6	16.1	14.5
≥ 8 times	15.9	14.4	12.0
≥ 9 times	13.9	11.9	9.5
10 times	11.9	9.0	7.3

(b) *Post-government*

No. of times poor	Germany (%)	Netherlands (%)	USA (%)
Never poor	76.3	81.0	63.3
≥ 1 times	25.7	19.0	36.7
≥ 2 times	14.1	7.7	26.9
≥ 3 times	10.1	3.5	22.1
≥ 4 times	7.1	1.7	18.2
≥ 5 times	5.1	0.9	15.1
≥ 6 times	3.5	0.6	12.8
≥ 7 times	2.8	0.1	10.6
≥ 8 times	2.0	0.0	8.4
≥ 9 times	1.4	0.0	6.3
10 times	0.9	0.0	4.0

Pov 4B (seriously recurrent poverty): 'the proportion of individuals with total household equivalent incomes below 50 per cent of median equivalent income across the nation as a whole for five years or more out of ten' (1985–94 for Germany and Netherlands; 1983–92 for US)'.

	Germany (%)	Netherlands (%)	USA (%)
Pre-government	22.9	20.1	19.2
Post-government	5.1	0.9	15.1

V   Risk of poverty

Pov 5A (risk of poverty, in the top half of income distribution): 'the proportion of individuals with pre-government incomes in the top half of the pre-government income distribution in 1985 (1983 in US) who were in pre-government poverty for one or more of the subsequent years 1986–94 (1984–92 in US) for (a) all persons and (b) white (US) or non-guestworker (Germany) males of prime working age (25–59)'.

(a) *Pre-government*

	Germany		Netherlands		USA	
	All persons (%)	Prime-working-aged males (non-guest workers) (%)	All persons (%)	Prime-working-aged males (%)	All persons (%)	Prime working aged males (white) (%)
1986–94 (84–92)	24.3	5.9	18.5	7.4	21.5	7.8

(b) *Post-government*

	Germany		Netherlands		USA	
	All persons (%)	Prime-working-aged males (non-guest workers) (%)	All persons (%)	Prime-working-aged males (%)	All persons (%)	Prime working aged males (white) (%)
1986–94 (84–92)	12.8	4.9	13.9	6.1	17.6	10.3

VI   Government reduction of poverty

Pov 6A (government reduction of overall poverty): 'the difference, post-government less pre-government, in the proportion of the total population with a total equivalent income of less than 50 per cent of median equivalent income across the nation as a whole' (= (pre-government Pov1A minus post-government Pov1A) / pre-government Pov1A).

Year	Germany (%)			Netherlands (%)			USA (%)		
	Pre	Post	%+/−	Pre	Post	%+/−	Pre	Post	%+/−
1987 (85)	25.1	7.6	69.7	19.4	4.3	77.8	21.1	18.0	14.7
1992 (90)	25.1	8.9	64.5	19.0*	6.8*	64.9	21.9	18.2	16.9
1985–89 (83–87)	22.6	6.2	72.6	16.2	1.1	93.2	18.7	14.7	21.4
1990–94 (88–92)	23.5	7.1	69.8	18.2	1.4	92.3	20.6	16.3	20.9
1985–94 (83–92)	21.2	5.8	72.6	15.4	0.8	94.8	16.9	13.0	23.1

Note: The 1992 Netherlands pre- and post-government poverty statistics are problematic, as noted in the Pov 1A table; but the percentage by which government reduces poverty is largely unaffected (it would be 64.2 per cent, taking for 1992 the average of the 1991 and 1993 pre- and post-government poverty rates).

Pov 6B (government reduction in poverty in working-aged households): 'the difference, post-government less pre-government, in the proportion of those living in working-aged households (head aged under 60) with a total equivalent income of less than 50 per cent of median equivalent income across the nation as a whole' (= (pre-government Pov1B minus post-government Pov 1B) /pre-government Pov 1B).

Year	Germany (%)			Netherlands (%)			USA (%)		
	Pre	Post	%+/-	Pre	Post	%+/-	Pre	Post	%+/-
1987 (85)	9.8	7.6	22.4	10.5	3.6	65.7	17.5	17.8	-1.7
1992 (90)	9.8	7.6	22.4	8.6	6.2	27.9	17.0	17.7	-0.4
1985–89 (83–87)	7.8	5.6	28.2	6.1	0.8	86.9	14.3	13.9	2.8
1990–94 (88–92)	7.9	6.3	20.3	6.0	2.3	61.7	15.5	15.4	0.6
1985–94 (83–92)	6.1	5.2	14.8	4.9	0.3	93.9	12.0	12.0	0.0

Pov 6C (government reduction of the working poor): 'the difference, post-government less pre-government, in the proportion of those living in households with a head aged under 60 and in paid employment with a total equivalent income of less than 50 per cent of median equivalent income across the nation as a whole' (= (pre-government Pov1C minus post-government Pov 1C) /pre-government Pov 1C).

Year	Germany (%)			Netherlands (%)			USA (%)		
	Pre	Post	%+/-	Pre	Post	%+/-	Pre	Post	%+/-
1987 (85)	9.8	7.6	22.4	10.5	3.6	65.7	16.6	17.0	-2.4
1992 (90)	9.8	7.6	22.4	8.6	5.7	33.7	17.0	17.7	-0.4
1985–89 (83–87)	7.8	5.6	28.2	6.1	0.8	86.9	14.3	10.9	23.8
1990–94 (88–92)	7.9	6.3	20.3	5.8	2.3	60.3	15.5	15.4	0.6
1985–94 (83–92)	6.1	5.2	14.8	4.6	0.3	93.5	11.5	11.7	-0.2

Pov 6D (*government reduction/increase of aged poverty*): 'the difference, post-government less pre-government, in the proportion of the population aged 65 and over with a total equivalent income of less than 50 per cent of median equivalent income across the nation as a whole' (= (pre-government Pov1D minus post-government Pov 1D) / pre-government Pov 1D)'.

Year	Germany (%)			Netherlands (%)			USA		
	Pre	Post	%+/−	Pre	Post	%+/−	Pre	Post	%+/−
1987 (85)	83.6	11.1	86.7	60.7	2.2	96.4	52.4	26.8	48.9
1992 (90)	80.5	12.9	84.0	67.8	6.3	90.7	52.6	26.5	49.6
1985–89 (83–87)	84.7	11.3	86.7	65.2	0.5	99.2	51.9	22.8	56.1
1990–94 (88–92)	86.2	11.3	86.9	69.3	1.3	98.1	56.4	27.2	51.8
1985–94 (83–92)	87.6	11.8	86.5	71.4	0.3	99.6	56.1	25.9	53.8

Pov 6E (*government reduction of child poverty*): 'the difference, post-government less pre-government, in the proportion of total population aged 16 and under with a total equivalent income of less than 50 per cent of median equivalent income across the nation as a whole' (= (pre-government Pov1E minus post-government Pov 1E) /pre-government Pov 1E).

Year	Germany (%)			Netherlands (%)			USA (%)		
	Pre	Post	%+/−	Pre	Post	%+/−	Pre	Post	%+/−
1987 (85)	11.7	9.3	20.5	12.3	3.4	72.4	20.4	19.9	2.5
1992 (90)	11.1	9.7	12.6	9.8	7.4	24.5	22.5	22.0	2.2
1985–89 (83–87)	9.2	7.0	23.9	7.0	0.6	91.4	17.8	17.3	2.8
1990–94 (88–92)	8.7	7.1	18.4	5.9	2.1	64.4	20.0	19.5	2.5
1985–94 (83–92)	7.6	5.6	26.3	4.9	0.8	83.7	14.6	13.8	5.5

Pov 6F (*government reduction of single-parent poverty*): 'the difference, post-government less pre-government, in the proportion of households headed by single parents with a total post-government equivalent income of less than 50 per cent of median equivalent income across the nation as a whole' (= (pre- minus post-government Pov 1F) /pre-government Pov 1F).

Year	Germany (%)			Netherlands (%)			USA (%)		
	Pre	Post	%+/-	Pre	Post	%+/-	Pre	Post	%+/-
1987 (85)	40.6	22.9	43.6	58.4	4.0	93.2	61.8	60.5	2.1
1992 (90)	40.5	29.1	28.1	55.1	15.5	71.0	58.5	58.5	0.0
1985–89 (83–87)	31.0 but few cases	19.2 but few cases	38.1	too few cases	too few cases	–	71.7	73.9	–3.1
1990–94 (88–92)	57.0 but few cases	10.0 but few cases	82.5	too few cases	too few cases	–	65.7	65.8	–0.2
1985–94 (83–92)	23.6 but few cases	15.3 but few cases	35.2	too few cases	too few cases	–	68.0	71.7	–5.4

Pov 6G (step-wise effectiveness of government interventions in alleviating poverty under age 60): 'proportion of the population poor: (1) pre-government; (2) after being adjusted for social insurance (non-means-tested) payments; (3) after all that adjusted for public transfers (means-tested programmes); (4) after all that adjusted for tax (i.e. post-government poor)' (for heads of household under age 60).

(a) *Germany (%)*

Year	(1)	(2)	(3)	(4)
1987 (85)	9.8	8.1	5.6	7.6
1992 (90)	9.8	8.4	6.4	7.6
1985–89 (83–87)	7.8	5.9	3.6	5.6
1990–94 (88–92)	7.9	6.6	3.8	6.3
1985–94 (83–92)	6.1	4.9	2.5	5.2

(b) *Netherlands (%)*

Year	(1)	(2)	(3)	(4)
1987 (85)	10.5	9.9	1.9	3.6
1992 (90)	9.2	8.7	2.0	6.2
1985–89 (83–87)	6.1	5.3	0.2	0.8
1990–94 (88–92)	6.0	5.6	0.4	2.3
1985–94 (83–92)	4.9	4.4	0.0	0.3

(c) *USA (%)*

Year	(1)	(2)	(3)	(4)
1987 (85)	17.5	16.4	15.0	17.8
1992 (90)	17.0	16.1	15.1	17.7
1985–89 (83–87)	14.3	13.4	11.4	13.9
1990–94 (88–92)	15.5	14.4	13.5	15.4
1985–94 (83–92)	12.0	11.3	10.1	12.0

Pov 6H (step-wise effectiveness of government interventions in alleviating poverty among the aged): 'proportion of the population poor: (1) pre-government; (2) after being adjusted for social insurance (non-means-tested) payments; (3) after all that adjusted for public transfers (means-tested programmes); (4) after all that adjusted for tax (i.e. post-government poor)' (for heads of household ≥ age 65).

(a) *Germany (%)*

Year	(1)	(2)	(3)	(4)
1987 (85)	82.8	12.6	9.9	10.5
1992 (90)	77.2	13.1	11.8	11.4
1985–89 (83–87)	82.2	10.0	8.7	9.8
1990–94 (88–92)	84.0	7.6	6.0	10.2
1985–94 (83–92)	84.0	9.0	7.6	8.9

(b) *Netherlands (%)*

Year	(1)	(2)	(3)	(4)
1987 (85)	52.9	2.7	2.7	3.5
1992 (90)	59.6	5.0	4.5	6.1
1985–89 (83–87)	61.0	1.6	1.6	1.6
1990–94 (88–92)	62.8	0.3	0.3	1.1
1985–94 (83–92)	61.8	0.8	0.8	0.8

(c) *USA (%)*

Year	(1)	(2)	(3)	(4)
1987 (85)	51.8	27.5	25.2	25.4
1992 (90)	50.5	25.7	24.9	24.9
1985–89 (83–87)	53.2	24.7	23.9	23.9
1990–94 (88–92)	55.5	28.1	27.0	27.2
1985–94 (83–92)	55.5	26.0	25.6	25.5

Pov 6I (*effectiveness of public transfers in alleviating poverty overall*): 'the proportion of persons of prime working age lifted out of poverty (above 50 per cent of median household equivalent income) by all public transfers', i.e. (proportion post-government poor minus proportion pre-government poor) divided by pre-government poor (for individuals aged 25–59).

Year	Germany			Netherlands			USA		
	Means-tested prog. (%)	Non-means-tested prog. (%)	All public trans. prog. (%)	Means-tested prog. (%)	Non-means-tested prog. (%)	All public trans. prog. (%)	Means-tested prog. (%)	Non-means-tested prog. (%)	All public trans. prog. (%)
1987 (85)	12	42	53	43	74	78	5	14	15
1992 (90)	14	36	41	25	65	68	6	12	16
1985–89 (83–87)	32	66	74	69	89	93	19	40	40
1990–94 (88–92)	26	58	65	47	85	88	15	23	31
1985–94 (83–92)	29	69	76	100	100	100	31	48	49

Appendix table A3   Measures of inequality

I   Income inequality across individuals

Eq 1A (income inequality): 'the index of inequality in individuals' equivalent income' (for individuals with heads of household aged < 60).

(a) *Pre-government*

Year	Germany		Netherlands		USA	
	Theil-0	Gini	Theil-0	Gini	Theil-0	Gini
1987 (85)	0.305	0.430	0.294	0.396	0.439	0.435
1992 (90)	0.413	0.428	0.356	0.399	0.470	0.445
1985–89 (83–87)	0.152	0.390	0.184	0.349	0.256	0.396
1990–94 (88–92)	0.153	0.395	0.233	0.360	0.262	0.415
1985–94 (83–92)	0.115	0.363	0.173	0.334	0.212	0.389

(b) *Post-government*

Year	Germany			Netherlands			USA		
	Theil-0	Gini	90/10 ratio	Theil-0	Gini	90/10 ratio	Theil-0	Gini	90/10 ratio
1987 (85)	0.094	0.268	3.3	0.085	0.257	2.81	0.166	0.365	5.5
1992 (90)	0.124	0.276	3.5	0.102	0.279	3.13	0.222	0.376	6.0
1985–89 (83–87)	0.068	0.235	2.9	0.049	0.204	2.35	0.144	0.328	4.8
1990–94 (88–92)	0.081	0.250	3.1	0.063	0.231	2.73	0.164	0.354	5.2
1985–94 (83–92)	0.063	0.222	2.8	0.046	0.196	2.35	0.137	0.327	4.6

Eq 1B (inequality in earned income): 'the inequality in individuals' labour income per hour, for all people of prime working age' (aged 25–59).

Year	Germany		Netherlands		USA	
	90/10 ratio	75/25 ratio	90/10 ratio	75/25 ratio	90/10 ratio	75/25 ratio
1994 (92)	3.16	1.66	2.72	1.57	5.59	2.46

II   Social equality

Eq 2A (inequality in hours worked across individuals): 'the 75/25 ratio of annual number of hours of paid labour by members of households with heads of prime working age,' (aged 25–59).

Year	Germany		Netherlands		USA	
	Whole household	Men only	Whole household	Men only	Whole household	Men only
1987 (85)	2.00	1.18	1.71	1.08	1.95	1.32
1992 (90)	2.19	–	1.68	1.11	1.96	1.32
1985–89 (83–87)	1.80	1.30	1.58	1.12	1.78	1.26
1990–94 (88–92)	1.90	1.89	1.55	1.16	1.76	1.31
1985–94 (83–92)	1.65	1.24	1.50	1.13	1.65	1.30

Eq 2B (equality in education across individuals): 'the percentage of the population with no more than secondary-school education'.

Year	Germany (%)	Netherlands (%)	USA (%)
1994 (92)	86.1	87.7	59.6

III   Equal citizenship

Eq 3A (benefit universalism): 'the proportion of individuals receiving some public transfer payments in one or more years'.

(a) *Where head of household is aged < 60 (%)*

Year	Germany	Netherlands	USA
1987 (85)	73.4	82.1	25.7
1992 (90)	70.1	79.5	23.6
1985–89 (83–87)	77.6	95.0	47.7
1990–94 (88–92)	74.2	92.9	43.4
1985–94 (83–92)	92.9	100.0	59.6

(b) *Where head of household is aged ≥ 60 (%)*

Year	Germany	Netherlands	USA
1987 (85)	78.6	86.2	81.9
1992 (90)	71.1	80.3	81.4
1985–89 (83–87)	98.8	98.6	96.8
1990–94 (88–92)	97.3	97.1	94.6
1985–94 (83–92)	98.9	100.0	98.8

Eq 3B (universalism of old age pensions): 'the median, over ten years, of the proportion of households with heads aged 65 + receiving basic old-age pensions'.

Year	Germany (%)	Netherlands (%)	USA (%)
1985–94 (83–92)	96.90	100.0	95.15

Eq 3C (universalism of child benefits): 'the median, over ten years, of the proportions of households with children under 16 receiving child benefits (AFDC in the US)'.

Year	Germany (%)	Netherlands (%)	USA (%)
1985–94 (83–92)	100.0	100.0	7.4

Eq 3D (universalism of public transfers, excluding old age pensions and child benefits): 'the proportion of households receiving some public transfers in one or more years other than child benefits (AFDC in the US)' (where head of household is age < 60).

Year	Germany (%)	Netherlands (%)	USA (%)
1987 (85)	28.1	39.4	25.0
1992 (90)	29.1	32.5	23.3
1985–89 (83–87)	48.0	61.9	47.7
1990–94 (88–92)	48.5	58.1	43.1
1985–94 (83–92)	62.7	100.0	59.8

Eq 3E (inequality in the distribution of public transfer payments): 'the 90/10 index of inequality in the distribution of public transfer payments received by prime-aged individuals, among those receiving any public transfer payments at all' (persons aged 16–64).

Year	Germany	Netherlands	USA
1987 (85)	31.0	19.5	20.2
1992 (90)	39.2	14.1	6.1
1985–89 (83–87)	33.9	18.8	49.3
1990–94 (88–92)	34.5	18.9	58.9
1985–94 (83–92)	29.9	15.3	64.0

IV   Government reduction of inequality

Eq 4A (government reduction of inequality): 'proportional change in post-government to pre-government income inequality' (= (post-government equality – pre-government equality)/pre-government equality)'.

Year	Germany (%)		Netherlands (%)		USA (%)	
	Theil-0	Gini	Theil-0	Gini	Theil-0	Gini
1987 (85)	73.1	37.6	71.1	35.1	62.2	16.0
1992 (90)	70.0	35.4	71.3	30.1	52.8	15.5
1985–89 (83–87)	55.3	39.7	73.4	41.5	43.8	17.2
1990–94 (88–92)	47.1	36.7	73.0	35.8	37.4	14.5
1985–94 (83–92)	45.2	38.7	73.4	41.3	35.4	15.8

Appendix table A4   Indicators of integration

I   Integration into households

Integ 1A (proportion in shared households): 'the median proportion, over ten years, of adults (aged ≥ 16) who live in shared households (i.e. containing ≥ 2 adults)'.

Year	Germany (%)	Netherlands (%)	USA (%)
1985–94 (83–92)	76.2	85.0	78.4

II   Integration into the labour force

Integ 2A (labour force participation levels): 'the proportion of the working-aged population in full-time employment (i.e. who work > 30 hours for > 46 weeks) in the country in $\geq N$ years out of 10' (hit rates) (for three population groups: (1) all heads of household under age 60; (2) all persons aged 25–59; (3) males aged 25–59).

Years	Germany			Netherlands			USA		
	(1) (%)	(2) (%)	(3) (%)	(1) (%)	(2) (%)	(3) (%)	(1) (%)	(2) (%)	(3) (%)
≥ 1	94.8	75.5	97.2	91.5	65.4	91.3	96.6	88.5	97.6
> 2	92.8	72.0	96.2	89.4	59.5	88.7	94.2	84.6	96.7
≥ 3	90.8	68.6	94.6	88.2	56.5	87.2	92.7	80.9	95.3
≥ 4	88.2	64.7	92.2	87.2	54.1	85.0	91.1	77.8	94.0
≥ 5	84.9	61.6	89.6	85.5	51.8	83.5	89.7	74.6	92.5
≥ 6	80.0	56.1	84.9	83.5	49.8	82.1	87.1	70.5	90.6
≥ 7	71.3	49.2	76.1	81.4	47.5	79.7	83.8	66.2	87.5
≥ 8	65.6	45.0	71.0	78.1	44.2	75.7	79.0	60.7	83.0
≥ 9	58.2	39.4	62.4	74.1	41.1	70.7	72.5	54.0	76.6
≥ 10	41.6	28.1	45.9	64.0	34.3	59.8	57.6	41.7	61.9

III   Economic integration

Integ 3A (lack of shared financial fate): 'the proportion of individuals in the country changing, over ten years (1985–94 for Germany and Netherlands, 1983–92 for US), more than one quintile in the national income distribution' (for people aged 25–59).

	Germany (%)			Netherlands (%)			USA (%)		
	Up	Down	Total	Up	Down	Total	Up	Down	Total
Pre-government	12.3	16.0	28.3	13.3	13.9	27.2	8.8	12.2	21.0
Post-government	11.9	14.4	26.3	15.2	16.0	31.2	8.6	12.5	21.1

IV Social exclusion

Integ 4A (cumulative inequality across sectors): 'the proportion of households headed by people of prime working age in the country who are in the bottom quintile of post-government income and working hours and education' (income and hours aggregated over ten years and across all members of the household; for households with heads aged 25–59; 'male-headed' = male head for all ten years, 'female-headed' = female head for all ten years)

	Germany (%)			Netherlands (%)			USA (%)		
	All	Male-headed household	Female-headed household	All	Male-headed household	Female-headed household	All	Male-headed house-hold	Female-headed household
1985–94 (83–92)	2.7	1.9	13.8	4.4	3.7	28.7 (but few cases)	3.8	1.5	13.8

Appendix table A5   Indicators of social stability

I   Social stability

Stab 1A (instability of households): 'the number of times the head of a person's household changed over ten years' (operationalized by the age of the household changing by > 2 years from one year to the next).

No. of times head changed	Germany (%)	Netherlands (%)	USA (%)
≥ 1	17.8	9.9	24.5
≥ 2	1.8	3.6	7.1
≥ 3	0.6	0.5	1.6
≥ 4	0.2	0.1	0.4
≥ 5	0.0	0.0	0.1

II   Employment stability

Stab 2A (stability of full-time employment): 'the proportion of the prime-working-aged population in full-time employment (i.e. who work > 30 hours for > 46 weeks) in the country in ≥ N years out of 10' (hit rates) (for people of prime working age, 25–59).

Years	Germany (%)		Netherlands (%)		USA (%)	
	All aged 25–59	Males aged 25–59	All aged 25–59	Males aged 25–59	All aged 25–59	Males aged 25–59
≥ 1	75.5	97.2	65.4	91.3	88.5	97.6
> 2	72.0	96.2	59.5	88.7	84.6	96.7
≥ 3	68.6	94.6	56.5	87.2	80.9	95.3
≥ 4	64.7	92.2	54.1	85.0	77.8	94.0
≥ 5	61.6	89.6	51.8	83.5	74.6	92.5
≥ 6	56.1	84.9	49.8	82.1	70.5	90.6
≥ 7	49.2	76.1	47.5	79.7	66.2	87.5
≥ 8	45.0	71.0	44.2	75.7	60.7	83.0
≥ 9	39.4	62.4	41.1	70.7	54.0	76.6
≥ 10	28.1	45.9	34.3	59.8	41.7	61.9

III   Income stability

Stab 3A (instability of people's income across time): 'the median, across individuals, of the coefficient of variation (standard deviation divided by mean) in each individual's income across time' (people in households with head aged under 60) (includes only individuals with some income in two or more years).

(a) *Pre-government*

Year	Germany	Netherlands	USA
1985–94 (83–92) min-max (%)	42.0	41.3	39.3
1985–94 (83–92) coefficient of variant	0.33	0.28	0.37

(b) *Post-government: all individuals*

Year	Germany	Netherlands	USA
1985–94 (83–92) min-max (%)	53.5	53.3	44.0
1985–94 (83–92) coefficient of variation	0.20	0.20	0.26

(c) *Post-government: people in bottom half of post-government income distribution*

Year	Germany	Netherlands	USA
1985–94 (83–92) min-max (%)	51.5	56.9	39.4
1985–94 (83–92) coefficient of variation	0.21	0.18	0.29

Stab 3B (instability of prime-working-aged people's pre-government labour income across time): 'the median, across individuals, of the coefficient of variation (standard deviation divided by mean) in prime-working-aged people's labour income across time' (age 25–59; includes only individuals with non-zero individual labour income two or more years).

(a) *All prime-working-aged persons*

Year	Germany	Netherlands	USA
1985–94 (83–92) coefficient of variation	0.26	0.22	0.33
1985–94 (83–92) min-max (%)	44.53	49.82	34.21

(b) *All prime-working-aged persons in bottom half of income distribution*

Year	Germany	Netherlands	USA
1985–94 (83–92) coefficient of variation	0.28	0.21	0.36
1985–94 (83–92) min-max (%)	41.30	52.04	31.73

Stab 3C (instability of prime-working-aged males' pre-government labour income across time): 'the median, across individuals, of the coefficient of variation (standard deviation divided by mean) in prime-working-aged males' labour income across time' (males age 25–59; includes only individuals with non-zero individual labour income two or more years).

(a) *All prime-working-aged males*

Year	Germany	Netherlands	USA
1985–94 (83–92) coefficient of variation	0.32	0.26	0.36
1985–94 (83–92) min-max (%)	35.58	42.34	32.42

(b) *Prime-working-aged males in bottom half of income distribution*

Year	Germany	Netherlands	USA
1985–94 (83–92) coefficient of variation	0.38	0.26	0.38
1985–94 (83–92) min-max (%)	30.92	43.22	25.37

IV   Lifecourse-related income instability

Stab 4A (income instability due to separation or divorce): 'the median, across individuals, of the coefficient of variation (or min-max) in each individual's income across ten years for those individuals experiencing separation or divorce during the period'.

(a) *Pre-government*

Year	Germany		Netherlands		USA	
	Coefficient of variation	Min-max (%)	Coefficient of variation	Min-max (%)	Coefficient of variation	Min-max (%)
1985–94 (83–92) not experiencing	0.27	42.1	0.28	41.9	0.29	38.6
1985–94 (83–92) Experiencing	0.34	34.6	0.39	29.0	0.39	26.7

(b) *Post-government*

Year	Germany		Netherlands		USA	
	Coefficient of variation	Min-max (%)	Coefficient of variation	Min-max (%)	Coefficient of variation	Min-max (%)
1985–94 (83–92) not experiencing	0.19	55.2	0.20	53.6	0.25	45.8
1985–94 (83–92) Experiencing	0.29	40.0	0.27	42.5	0.35	31.7

Stab 4B (total income instability related to household breakdown): 'instability of post-government income due to – changes in the person's head of household' (operationalized as head of household aging > 2 years from one year to the next).

No. of changes of household	Germany		Netherlands		USA	
	Coefficient of variation	Min-max (%)	Coefficient of variation	Min-max (%)	Coefficient of variation	Min-max (%)
0	0.19	55.5	0.19	55.5	0.23	47.9
1	0.27	40.8	0.29	40.4	0.35	33.4
2	0.35	34.0	0.28	42.3	0.38	27.7
3	0.49	20.2	0.33	32.2	0.42	25.1
4	0.63	9.1	–	–	0.41	26.9
5	–	–	0.38	35.03	0.51	15.0
6					0.82	13.5

V   Transfer-based income stability

Stab 5A (replacement rate of public transfer payments, other than old age pensions): 'For individuals whose principal source of income was public transfers in year x and whose principal source of income was not public transfers in year $x - 1$ (the transfer income of that individual in year x divided by that individual's income in year $x - 1$ (median individual, median year) (for households with heads of prime working age, 25–59; for public transfer programmes other than old age pensions).

	Germany	Netherlands	USA
Wage + transfer income replaced (%)	74	76	67
Total household equivalent income replaced (%)	75	83	71

Stab 5B (replacement rate, old age pensions): 'For individuals whose principal source of income was the old age pension in year x and whose
principal source of income was not public transfers in year $x-1$, (the
transfer income of that individual in year x) divided by that individual's
income in year $x-1$ (median individual, median year) (for households
with heads age > 56).

	Germany	Netherlands	USA
Wage + transfer income replaced (%)	93	98	96
Total household equivalent income replaced (%)	89	74	75

Stab 5C (government reduction of income instability across time): 'the proportional reduction in the coefficient of variation in people's pre-government
to post-government income' (includes only individuals with some income
in at least two years) (= (post-government Stab 3A minus pre-government Stab3A) / pre-government Stab 3A).

Year	Germany (%)	Netherlands (%)	USA (%)
1985–94 (83–92) coefficient of variation	39.4	28.6	29.7
1985–94 (83–92) min-max (%)	27.4	29.1	1.8

Appendix table A6   Measures of autonomy

I   Social autonomy

Aut 1A (instability of households): 'the proportion of people living in households whose heads have chnged N times over ten years'.

No. of times head changed	Germany (%)			Netherlands (%)			USA (%)		
	All	>half median equivalent post-government income	<half median equivalent post-government income	All	>half median equivalent post-government income	<half median equivalent post-government income	All	>half median equivalent post-government income	<half median equivalent post-government income
>0	17.8	17.8	19.7	9.9	12.0	7.7	24.5	19.0	30.6
>1	1.8	1.6	1.8	3.6	4.8	2.4	7.1	5.1	9.4
>2	0.6	0.6	0.5	0.5	0.7	0.4	1.6	0.6	2.7
>3	0.2	0.1	0.2	0.1	0.2	0.0	0.4	0.1	0.8
>4	0.0	0.0	0.0	0.0	0.2		0.1	0.0	0.2
>5				0.0	0.0		0.1		0.0

II   Labour market autonomy

Aut 2A (autonomy in labour markets, by income group): 'the proportion of people working zero hours of paid labour' (for people of prime working age, 25–59).

Year	Germany (%)			Netherlands (%)			USA (%)		
	All	>half median equivalent post-government income	<half median equivalent post-government income	All	>half median equivalent post-government income	<half median equivalent post-government income	All	>half median equivalent post-government income	<half median equivalent post-government income
1987 (85)	33.7	26.1	44.1	33.8	22.6	48.7	14.7	10.0	19.6
1992 (90)	39.6	34.7	46.5	25.5	16.1	43.7	12.8	8.1	19.0

NB: Nows do not sum because medians used in each case.

III   Economic autonomy

Aut 3A (sources of economic autonomy): 'the percentage of prime-working-aged people with income above the poverty line on the basis of: asset income alone; that plus labour income; that plus private transfers; and that plus public transfers' (for people aged 25–59).

(a) *Germany*

Year	Asset income alone	Plus labour income	Plus private transfers	Plus public transfers
1987 (85)	1.4	91.4	91.8	96.7
1992 (90)	2.5	90.3	90.6	95.2
1985–89 (83–87)	1.4	93.8	94.3	98.2
1990–94 (88–92)	2.5	94.6	94.9	98.3
1985–94 (83–92)	1.6	95.9	96.0	98.8

(b) *Netherlands*

Year	Asset income alone	Plus labour income	Plus private transfers	Plus public transfers
1987 (85)	5.8	84.2	85.8	96.9
1992 (90)	3.5	86.1	88.2	96.6
1985–89 (83–87)	6.0	89.6	90.6	98.9
1990–94 (88–92)	2.0	91.1	92.1	94.3
1985–94 (83–92)	2.1	92.4	92.4	99.9

(c) *USA*

Year	Asset income alone	Plus labour income	Plus private transfers	Plus public transfers
1987 (85)	3.2	83.6	85.5	87.9
1992 (90)	2.9	82.6	84.5	87.0
1985–89 (83–87)	8.1	78.9	82.3	90.5
1990–94 (88–92)	4.2	90.6	91.8	94.6
1985–94 (83–92)	4.2	92.2	93.0	96.2

Aut 3B (independent income): 'the ratio of median non-heads' labour income to the labour income of the head of their household' (for people of prime working age, 25–59).

Year	Germany (%)	Netherlands (%)	USA (%)
1985 (83)	9.0	0	30.7
1990 (88)	21.5	0	41.1
1994 (92)	35.4	too few cases	52.4

IV Temporal autonomy

Aut 4A (leisure time): 'the median, across ten years, of the median number of hours per week spent in paid work, unpaid work and leisure'.

	Germany			Netherlands			USA		
	Paid work	Unpaid work	Leisure	Paid work	Unpaid work	Leisure	Paid work	Unpaid work	Leisure
All persons 25–59	33.5	20.0	42.0	29.2	20.0	48.9	37.1	20.0	36.0
Males 25–59	39.0	13.5	42.0	34.9	13.5	44.6	40.0	13.5	39.5
Females 25–59	4.8	33.5	41.5	4.5	33.5	60.0	30.4	33.5	31.6
All 25–59 with children at home	29.0	31.0	33.5	21.5	31.0	45.5	36.3	31.0	25.7
Single mothers, 25–59 with children at home	9.2	45.5	30.5	8.6	45.5	49.0	32.7	45.5	28.1
All 65 +	0.0	23.0	75.0	0.0	23.0	75.0	0.0	23.0	75.0

NB: Rows do not sum because medians used in each case.

Aut 4B (leisure time related to income): 'the median, across ten years, of the median number of leisure hours per week and leisure, pre-, post-government income as fraction of the poverty line'.

	Germany				Netherlands				USA			
	Leisure time	Indiv labour inc / pov line	Pre-gov equiv inc / pov line	Post-gov equiv inc / pov line	Leisure time	Indiv labour inc / pov line	Pre-gov equiv inc / pov line	Post-gov equiv inc / pov line	Leisure time	Indiv labour inc / pov line	Pre-gov equiv inc / pov line	Post-gov equiv inc / pov line
All persons 25–59	42.0	2.5	2.9	2.2	48.9	2.8	3.5	2.2	36.0	2.0	2.6	2.4
Males 25–59	42.0	3.2	2.9	2.3	44.6	4.0	3.6	2.3	39.5	3.0	2.8	2.6
Females 25–59	41.5	0.8	2.8	2.2	60.0	0.3	3.4	2.2	31.6	1.2	2.5	2.3
All 25–59 with children at home	33.5	2.4	2.5	2.0	45.5	2.3	3.1	1.9	25.7	1.8	2.3	2.2
Single mothers 25–59 with children at home	30.5	0.8	0.9	1.0	49.0	0.1	0.6	1.5	28.1	1.0	0.9	0.9
All 65 +	75.0	0.0	0.0	1.7	75.0	0.0	0.5	1.7	75.0	0.0	1.0	1.7

V   Combined resource autonomy

Aut 5A (frequency of combined resource autonomy, various groups): 'the proportion of the population that works less than 40 hours a week and has an income above the poverty line' (for various age groups, as specified in the table; and for three sources of income: (1) individual labour income; (2) pre-government household equivalent income; (3) post-government household equivalent income).

	Germany (%)			Netherlands (%)			USA (%)		
	(1)	(2)	(3)	(1)	(2)	(3)	(1)	(2)	(3)
Males 25–59									
1987 (85)	46.5	50.2	52.5	68.5	72.6	79.9	40.0	43.7	43.9
1992 (90)	81.9	87.9	90.9	80.3	85.5	91.4	37.0	39.5	39.7
Females 25–59									
1987 (85)	32.3	76.5	81.6	29.3	86.3	96.8	39.5	70.9	71.6
1992 (90)	45.1	86.5	90.6	37.4	86.5	95.8	39.7	68.1	68.9
All 25–59 with children < 13									
1987 (85)	34.1	64.8	66.3	45.9	80.7	86.5	36.7	55.8	56.3
1992 (90)	58.2	88.5	90.6	60.4	89.6	94.3	35.4	53.4	54.0
All 65 +									
1987 (85)	(too few	(too few	(too few	(too few	(too few	(too few	4.7	46.3	71.7
1992 (90)	cases)	cases)	cases)	cases)	cases)	cases)	4.2	46.1	72.3

Aut 5B (frequency of combined resource autonomy, all individuals): 'the proportion of the population that works less than 40 hours a week and has an income above the poverty line' (for various measures of income, as specified in table).

(a) *(1) Individual labour income and (2) household equivalent income pre-government (%)*

Year	Netherlands		Germany		USA	
	(1)	(2)	(1)	(2)	(1)	(2)
1987 (85)	23.2	59.8	29.4	75.9	25.3	63.2
1992 (90)	35.8	73.5	35.6	79.0	22.8	60.8
1985–89 (83–87)	24.6	61.2	37.7	81.3	40.0	65.9
1990–94 (88–92)	35.1	72.5	36.5	81.8	34.1	63.0
1985–94 (83–92)	34.5	71.2	43.6	84.8	40.2	66.9

(b) *Household equivalent income post-government (%)*

Year	Germany	Netherlands	USA
1987 (85)	76.9	91.2	66.6
1992 (90)	89.7	91.6	64.7
1985–89 (83–87)	77.0	93.8	69.9
1990–94 (88–92)	88.9	97.0	67.5
1985–94 (83–92)	86.6	97.0	70.9

NB: Government taxes and transfers are calculated on the basis of individuals' (and often households') income from all sources; it therefore makes little sense to try to calculate individual labour income on a post-government basis.

Aut 5C (recurrence of combined resource autonomy, all individuals): 'the proportion of the population that works less than 40 hours a week and has an income above the poverty line in N years out of 10' (hit rates) (for three measures of income: (1) individual labour income; (2) pre-government household equivalent income; (3) post-government household equivalent income (%)).

Years	Germany			Netherlands			USA		
	(1)	(2)	(3)	(1)	(2)	(3)	(1)	(2)	(3)
≥ 1	55.7	87.6	98.6	47.7	90.3	99.8	56.4	88.1	91.4
> 2	50.6	84.9	97.7	43.6	87.1	99.5	47.2	82.0	85.6
≥ 3	45.7	82.0	96.8	40.9	84.3	99.1	39.7	76.6	80.2
≥ 4	41.0	78.4	95.2	37.7	82.2	98.5	33.3	71.0	75.0
≥ 5	33.7	72.4	90.6	34.1	79.6	97.7	27.5	65.7	69.9
≥ 6	26.1	64.7	83.4	31.6	76.6	96.7	22.0	60.2	64.5
≥ 7	20.3	58.5	77.7	28.0	72.6	94.3	17.0	54.1	58.7
≥ 8	15.4	51.3	70.3	24.1	67.7	89.6	13.1	47.7	52.0
≥ 9	11.1	43.4	61.5	20.0	60.0	80.5	8.8	40.3	44.9
≥ 10	6.1	32.6	48.0	14.5	44.1	57.9	5.0	29.4	33.6

Aut 5D (frequency of combined resource autonomy, all individuals of prime working age): 'the proportion of the population that works less than 40 hours a week and has an income above the poverty line' (for people aged 25–59; and for two measures of income, specified in table).
(a) (1) *Individual labour income and (2) household equivalent income (%).*

Year	Germany		Netherlands		USA	
	(1)	(2)	(1)	(2)	(1)	(2)
1987 (85)	39.5	63.3	48.9	76.9	42.6	58.1
1992 (90)	63.5	64.0	61.4	86.3	39.0	54.7
1985–89 (83–87)	37.4	61.9	57.8	83.0	45.4	60.5
1990–94 (88–92)	59.1	85.0	63.2	88.5	40.4	55.6
1985–94 (83–92)	50.5	76.6	66.7	90.4	44.8	59.6

(b) *Household equivalent income post-government (%)*

Year	Germany	Netherlands	USA
1987 (85)	67.0	86.3	58.6
1992 (90)	90.8	91.6	55.2
1985–89 (83–87)	65.2	88.7	61.4
1990–94 (88–92)	87.7	96.2	56.8
1985–94 (83–92)	78.9	94.6	60.5

NB: Government taxes and transfers are calculated on the basis of individuals' (and often households') income from all sources; it therefore makes little sense to try to calculate individual labour income on a post-government basis.

Aut 5E (recurrence of combined resource autonomy, all people of prime working age): 'the proportion of the prime-working-aged population that works less than 40 hours a week and has an income above the poverty line in *N* years out of 10' (hit rates) (ages 25–59) (for three measures of income: (1) individual labour income; (2) pre-government household equivalent income; (3) post-government household equivalent income).

Years	Germany (%)			Netherlands (%)			USA (%)		
	(1)	(2)	(3)	(1)	(2)	(3)	(1)	(2)	(3)
≥ 1	79.0	97.8	99.2	74.3	95.4	99.5	77.9	87.5	88.8
> 2	75.3	96.7	98.0	70.3	94.0	99.0	67.3	79.6	80.0
≥ 3	71.1	95.2	97.2	66.9	92.6	98.5	58.7	73.1	73.5
≥ 4	66.7	92.3	95.2	63.5	90.2	97.5	51.3	66.8	66.8
≥ 5	56.5	84.0	87.2	59.8	86.8	95.8	43.5	60.5	60.8
≥ 6	45.2	73.1	76.4	56.9	84.5	94.5	36.3	54.5	54.5
≥ 7	37.4	65.5	68.9	52.7	81.4	92.1	29.7	48.0	48.2
≥ 8	30.1	56.9	61.2	48.2	76.8	88.0	24.0	41.9	41.6
≥ 9	23.2	48.3	52.0	41.5	69.7	79.6	16.9	33.7	33.7
≥ 10	13.8	36.6	39.0	30.7	53.7	61.5	9.7	22.9	23.2

VI   Government/family/market contribution to combined resource autonomy

Aut 6A (government increase in combined resource autonomy, all individuals): 'the increase in the proportion of the population with combined resource autonomy (works less than 40 hours a week, and has a household equivalent income above the poverty line) as a result of public taxes and transfers' (= (Aut 5B post-government minus Aut 5B pre-government) / Aut 5B pre-government).

Year	Germany (%)	Netherlands (%)	USA (%)
1987 (85)	28.6	20.2	5.4
1992 (90)	22.0	15.9	6.4
1985–89 (83–87)	25.8	15.4	6.1
1990–94 (88–92)	22.6	18.6	7.1
1985–94 (83–92)	21.9	15.1	6.0

Aut 6B (government increase in combined resource autonomy, people of prime working age): 'the increase in the proportion of the prime-working-aged population (age 25–59) with combined resource autonomy (works less than 40 hours a week, and has a household equivalent income above the poverty line) as a result of public taxes and transfers' (= (Aut 5D post-government minus Aut 5D pre-government) / Aut 5D pre-government).

Year	Germany (%)	Netherlands (%)	USA (%)
1987 (85)	5.8	12.2	0.9
1992 (90)	41.9	6.1	0.9
1985–89 (83–87)	5.3	6.9	1.5
1990–94 (88–92)	3.2	8.7	1.4
1985–94 (83–92)	3.0	4.6	1.5

Aut 6C (market/family/government contribution to combined resource autonomy): 'the proportion of the population with combined resource autonomy (works less than 40 hours a week, and has an income above the poverty line) as a result of (1) individual labour income, (2) sharing of household pre-government equivalent income and (3) post-government taxes and transfers'.

(a) *All individuals*

Year	Germany (%)			Netherlands (%)			USA (%)		
	(1)	(2)	(3)	(1)	(2)	(3)	(1)	(2)	(3)
1987 (85)	23.2	59.8	76.9	29.4	75.9	91.2	25.3	63.2	66.6
1992 (90)	35.8	73.5	89.7	35.6	79.0	91.6	22.8	60.8	64.7
1985–89 (83–87)	24.6	61.2	77.0	37.7	81.3	93.8	40.0	65.9	69.9
1990–94 (88–92)	35.1	72.5	88.9	36.5	81.8	97.0	34.1	63.0	67.5
1985–94 (83–92)	34.5	71.2	86.6	43.6	84.8	97.0	40.2	66.9	70.9

(b) *Individuals of prime working age (25–59)*

Year	Germany (%)			Netherlands (%)			USA (%)		
	(1)	(2)	(3)	(1)	(2)	(3)	(1)	(2)	(3)
1987 (85)	39.5	63.3	67.0	48.9	76.9	86.3	42.6	58.1	58.6
1992 (90)	63.5	64.0	90.8	61.4	86.3	91.6	39.0	54.7	55.2
1985–89 (83–87)	37.4	61.9	65.2	57.8	83.0	88.7	45.4	60.5	61.4
1990–94 (88–92)	59.1	85.0	87.7	63.2	88.5	96.2	40.4	55.6	56.8
1985–94 (83–92)	50.5	76.6	78.9	66.7	90.4	94.6	44.8	59.6	60.5

References

Aaberge, Rolf; Anders Björklund; Markus Jäntti; Mårten Palme; Peder J. Pedersen; Nina Smith; and Tom Wennemo. 1996. Income inequality and mobility in the Scandinavian countries compared to the United States. Discussion Papers no. 168, Research Department, Statistics Norway. Oslo: Statistics Norway.

Aaron, Henry J. 1978. *Politics and the Professors: The Great Society in Perspective*. Washington, D.C.: Brookings Institution.

Aaron, Henry J. and Barry P. Bosworth. 1997. Preparing for the baby boomers' retirement. In Reischauer 1997, pp. 263–301.

Abbot, Edith. 1940. *Public Assistance*. Chicago: University of Chicago Press.

Åberg, Rune. 1989. Distributive mechanisms of the welfare state – a formal analysis and an empirical application. *European Sociological Review* 5: 167–82.

Addams, Jane. 1919. *Twenty Years at Hull House*. New York: Macmillan.

Alber, Jens. 1986. Germany. In Flora 1986, vol. II, pp. 1–154 and vol. IV, pp. 247–96.

1996. Selectivity, universalism and the politics of welfare retrenchment in Germany and the United States. Presented to the Annual Meetings of the American Political Science Association, San Francisco, 31 Aug. 1996.

Aldrich, Jonathan. 1982. Earnings replacement rates of old-age benefits in 12 countries, 1969–80. *Social Security Bulletin* 45 (Nov): 3–11.

Alesina, Alberto and Daniel Rodrik. 1991. *Distributive Politics and Economic Growth*. NBER Working Paper no. 3668. New York: National Bureau of Economic Research.

Andersen, Jørgen Goul. 1997. The Scandinavian welfare model in crisis? Achievements and problems of the Danish welfare state in an age of unemployment and low growth. *Scandinavian Political Studies* 20: 1–31.

Arneson, Richard J. 1990. Is work special? Justice and the distribution of employment. *American Political Science Review* 84: 1127–47.

Arrow, Kenneth J. and Frank Hahn. 1971. *General Competitive Analysis*. San Francisco: Holden-Day.

Atkinson, A. B. 1975. *The Economics of Inequality*. Oxford: Clarendon Press.

1985. Income maintenance and social insurance. Welfare State Programme Discussion Paper no. 5. London: STICERD, LSE. Printed in *Handbook of Public Economics*, ed. Alan J. Auerbach and Martin Feldstein. Amsterdam: North-Holland, 1985–1987 (2 vols.).

1989a. *Poverty and Social Security*. London: Harvester Wheatsheaf.

1989b. The take-up of social security benefits. In Atkinson 1989a, pp. 190–297.

1995a. *Incomes and the Welfare State*. Cambridge: Cambridge University Press.

1995b. *Public Economics in Action: The Basic Income/Flat Tax Proposal*. Oxford: Oxford University Press.

1995c. The welfare state and economic performance. Discussion Paper WSP/109, Welfare State Programme. London: STICERD, LSE.

1998a. Bringing income distribution in from the cold. *Economic Journal* 107: 297–321.

1998b. *Poverty in Europe*. Oxford: Blackwell.

1998c. Social exclusion, poverty and unemployment. In Atkinson and Hills 1998, pp. 1–20.

1999. *The Economic Consequences of Rolling Back the Welfare State*. Cambridge, Mass.: MIT Press.

Atkinson, A. B.; F. Bourguignon; and C. Morrisson. 1992. *Empirical Studies of Earnings Mobility*. Chur, Switzerland: Harwood Academic Publishers.

Atkinson, A. B. and John Hills. 1998 eds. *Exclusion, Employment and Opportunity*. CASE paper 4, Centre for Analysis of Social Exclusion. London: STICERD, LSE.

Atkinson, A. B. and John Micklewright. 1992. *Economic Transformation in Eastern Europe*. Cambridge: Cambridge University Press.

Atkinson, A. B.; Lee Rainwater; and Timothy M. Smeeding. 1995. *Income Distribution in OECD Countries: The Evidence from the Luxembourg Income Study (LIS)*. Social Policy Studies no. 18. Paris: OECD. Reprinted in part in Atkinson 1995a, ch. 2.

Atkinson, A. B. and Holly Sutherland. 1989. Inter-generational continuities in deprivation. In Atkinson 1989a, pp. 87–96.

Australian Bureau of Statistics (ABS). 1994. *How Australians Use their Time*. Catalogue No. 4153.0. Canberra: ABS.

Baldwin, Peter. 1988. How socialist is solidaristic social policy? *International Review of Social History* 33: 121–47.

1990. *The Politics of Social Solidarity: Class Bases of the European Welfare State 1875–1975*. Cambridge: Cambridge University Press.

Bane, Mary Jo and David T. Ellwood. 1986. Slipping into and out of poverty: the dynamics of spells. *Journal of Human Resources* 21: 1–23.

1994. *Welfare Realities: From Rhetoric to Reform*. Cambridge, Mass.: Harvard University Press.

Barr, Nicholas. 1985. Economic welfare and social justice. *Journal of Social Policy* 14: 175–87.

1987. *The Economics of the Welfare State*. London: Weidenfeld and Nicolson.

1989. Social insurance as an efficiency device. *Journal of Public Policy* 9: 59–82.

1992. Economic theory and the welfare state: a survey and an interpretation. *Journal of Economic Literature* 30: 741–803.

Barrett, Michèle and Mary McIntosh. 1982. *The Anti-Social Family*. London: Verso.

Barry, Brian. 1973. *The Liberal Theory of Justice*. Oxford: Clarendon Press.

1990. *Political Argument.* Reissue, with new introduction. New York: Harvester-Wheatsheaf; originally published 1965.

Baxter, Janeen and Diane Gibson with Mark Lynch-Blosse. 1990. *Double Take: The Links Between Paid and Unpaid Work.* Canberra: Australian Government Publishing Service.

Becker, Gary S. 1965. A theory of the allocation of time. *Economic Journal* 75: 493–517.

Beckerman, Wilfred. 1979a. The impact of income maintenance payments on poverty in Britain, 1975. *Economic Journal* 89: 261–79.

1979b. *Poverty and the Impact of Income Maintenance Programmes in Four Developed Countries.* Geneva: International Labour Organisation.

Becketti, Sean; William Gould; Lee Lilliard; and Finis Welch. 1988. The Panel Study of Income Dynamics after fourteen years: an evaluation. *Journal of Labour Economics* 6: 472–92.

Benhabib, Seyla. 1992. *Situating the Self.* Oxford: Polity.

Berben, Theo and Joop Roebroek. 1986. The Netherlands. In Flora 1986, vol. IV, pp. 671–750.

Berger, Peter L. and Richard John Neuhaus. 1977. *To Empower People: The Role of Mediating Structures in Public Policy.* Washington, D.C.: American Enterprise Institute.

Berlin, Isaiah. 1958. Two concepts of liberty. Pp. 118–72 in *Four Essays on Liberty.* Oxford: Oxford University Press, 1969.

Bermann, George A. 1994. Taking subsidiarity seriously: federalism in the European Community and the United States. *Columbia Law Review* 94: 331–456.

Beveridge, William H. 1907. Labour exchanges and the unemployed. *Economic Journal,* 17: 66–81.

1942. *Social Insurance and Allied Services.* Cmnd. 6404. London: HMSO.

1945. *Full Employment in a Free Society.* London: Allen and Unwin.

1948. *Voluntary Action.* London: Allen and Unwin.

Bittman, Michael. 1992. *Juggling Time: How Australian Families Use Time,* 2nd edn. Canberra: Australian Government Publishing Service.

Bittman, Michael and Robert E. Goodin. 1998. An equivalence scale for time. SPRC Discussion Paper no. 85. Kensington, NSW: Social Policy Research Centre, University of New South Wales.

Björklund, Anders. 1993. A comparison between actual distributions of annual and lifetime income: Sweden 1951–89. *Review of Income and Wealth* 39: 377–86.

Blaug, Marc. 1963. The myth of the old poor law and the making of the new. *Journal of Economic History* 23: 151–84.

Block, Fred. 1990. *Postindustrial Possibilities.* Berkeley: University of California Press.

Blom, Hans W. 1995. Citizens and the ideology of citizenship in the Dutch Republic: Machiavellianism, wealth and nation in the mid-seventeenth century. *Yearbook of European Studies,* 8: 131–52.

Bolderson, Helen and Deborah Mabbett. 1995. Mongrels or thoroughbreds: a cross-national look at social security systems. *European Journal of Political Research* 28: 119–39.

Booth, Charles. 1892–1903. *Life and Labour of the People in London*, 16 vols. London: Macmillan.

Bowles, Samuel and Herbert A. Gintis. 1990. Contested exchange: new microfoundations for the political economy of capitalism. *Politics and Society* 18: 165–222.

Bradley, F. H. 1876. My station and its duties. Pp. 98–147 in *Ethical Studies*, ed. Ralph G. Ross. Indianapolis, Ind.: Bobbs-Merrill, 1951.

Braybrooke, David. 1987. *Meeting Needs*. Princeton, N.J.: Princeton University Press.

Brittan, Samuel. 1988. *A Restatement of Economic Liberalism*, 2nd edn. London: Macmillan; first edition published 1973 under the title *Capitalism and the Permissive Society*.

Brown, J. Douglas. 1956. The American philosophy of social insurance. *Social Service Review* 39: 1–8.

Browning, Edgar K. 1993. The marginal cost of redistribution. *Public Finance Quarterly* 21: 3–23.

Buchanan, James M. and Gordon Tullock. 1962. *The Calculus of Consent*. Ann Arbor, Mich.: University of Michigan Press.

Budge, Ian; David Robertson; and Derek Hearl. 1987. eds. *Ideology, Strategy and Party Change*. Cambridge: Cambridge University Press.

Buhmann, B.; L. Rainwater; G. Schmaus; and T. M. Smeeding. 1988. Equivalence scales, well-being, inequality and poverty: sensitivity estimates across ten countries using the Luxembourg Income Study (LIS) database. *Review of Income and Wealth* 34: 115–42.

Bundesarbeitsgemeinschaft Wohnungslosen e.V. 1994. Antworten auf den Fragenkatalog zur öffentlichen Anhörung am 15 Juni 1994. Wohnungslosigkeit – Obdachosigkeit und Wohnungsnotfälle in der Bundesrepublik Deutschland und Maßnahmen zu ihrer Bekämpfun. Drucksache 12/5250. Bielefeld: Bundesarbeitsgemeinschaft Wohnungslosen e.V.

Burkhauser, Richard V. and John G. Poupore. 1997. A cross-national comparison of permanent inequality in the US and Germany. *Review of Economics and Statistics* 79: 10–17.

Burtles, Gary; R. Kent Weaver; and Joshua M. Wiener. 1997. The future of the social safety net. In Reischauer 1997, pp. 75–122.

Bussemaker, Jet and Kees van Kersbergen. 1994. Gender and welfare states: some theoretical reflections. In Sainsbury 1994, pp. 8–25.

Calmfors, Lars and Per Skedinger. 1995. Does active labour-market policy increase employment? Theoretical considerations and some empirical evidence from Sweden. *Oxford Review of Economic Policy* 11 (no. 1, spring): 91–109.

Cameron, David R. 1978. The expansion of the public economy: a comparative analysis. *American Politial Science Review* 72: 1243–61.

Case, Anne and Angus Deaton. 1998. Large cash transfers to the elderly in South Africa. *Economic Journal* 108: 1330–61.

Cass, Bettina. 1995. Overturning the male breadwinner model in the Australian social protection system. In *Social Policy and the Challenges of Social Change*, ed. Peter Saunders and Sheila Shaver. Social Policy Research Centre Reports and Proceedings no. 112. Sydney: SPRC, University of New South Wales.

Castles, Francis G. 1978. *The Social Democratic Image of Society*. London: Routledge and Kegan Paul, 1978.

1985. *The Working Class and the Welfare State: Reflections on the Political Development of the Welfare State in Australia and New Zealand, 1890–1980*. Sydney: Allen and Unwin.

1993 ed. *Families of Nations: Patterns of Public Policy in Western Democracies*. Aldershot: Dartmouth.

1996a. The institutional design of the Australian welfare state. Presented to the Reshaping Australian Institutions Workshop. Research Committee 19 (Poverty, Social Welfare and Social Policy) Annual Meeting, Canberra, 19–23 August.

1996b. Needs-based strategies of social protection in Australia and New Zealand. Ch. 4 in Esping-Andersen 1996b.

1997. The institutional design of the Australian welfare state. *International Social Security Review* 50: 25–42.

1998. *Comparative Public Policy: Patterns of Post-war Transformation*. Cheltenham: Elgar.

Castles, Francis G. and Stephen Dowrick. 1990. The impact of government spending levels on medium-term economic growth in the OECD. *Journal of Theoretical Politics* 2: 173–204.

Castles, Francis G. and Deborah Mitchell. 1990. Three worlds of welfare capitalism or four? Mimeo, Graduate Programme in Public Policy, Australian National University. Reprinted as Castles and Mitchell 1992.

1992. Identifying welfare state regimes: the links between politics, instruments and outcomes. *Governance* 5: 1–26. Reprinted in Castles 1993, ch. 3.

1997. Between a rock and a hard place: instituional designs of the welfare state and their limitations. Paper presented to the XVIIth World Congress of the International Political Science Association, Seoul, August 1997.

Childs, Marquis. 1936. *Sweden: The Middle Way*. New Haven, Conn.: Yale University Press.

1980. *Sweden: The Middle Way on Trial*. New Haven, Conn.: Yale University Press.

Citro, Constance F. and Robert T. Michael. 1995. *Measuring Poverty: A New Approach*. Washington D.C.: National Academic Press.

Clasen, Jochen and Arthur Gould. 1995. Stability and change in welfare states: Germany and Sweden in the 1990s. *Policy and Politics* 23: 189–202.

Cohen, G. A. 1983. The structure of proletarian unfreedom. *Philosophy and Public Affairs* 12: 3–33.

1989. On the currency of egalitarian justice. *Ethics* 99: 906–44.

Collier, David and Richard Messick. 1975. Prerequisites versus diffusion: testing alternative explanations of social security adoption. *American Political Science Review* 69: 1296–315.

Commission on Social Justice, UK Labour Party. 1993. *The Justice Gap*. London: Vintage/Random House.

1994. *Social Justice: Strategies for National Renewal*. London: Vintage/Random House.

Cornford, James. 1972. The political theory of scarcity. Pp. 27–44 in P. Laslett, W. G. Runciman and Q. Skinner, eds., *Philosophy, Politics and Society*, 4th series. Oxford: Blackwell.

Cornuelle, Richard C. 1965. *Reclaiming the American Dream*. New York: Random House.

Coulter, F. A. E.; Frank A. Cowell; and S. P. Jenkins. 1992. Equivalence scale relativities and the extent of the inequality and poverty. *Economic Journal* 102: 1067–82.

Cox, Robert H. 1993. *The Development of the Dutch Welfare State: From Workers' Insurance to Universal Entitlement*. Pittsburgh: University of Pittsburgh Press.

Cutright, Phillips. 1965. Political structure, economic development and national social security programs. *American Journal of Sociology* 70: 537–50.

Daalder, Hans. 1966. The Netherlands: opposition in a segmented society. Pp. 188–236 in *Political Oppositions in Western Democracies*, ed. Robert A. Dahl. New Haven: Yale University Press.

Dahrendorf, Ralf. 1990. *Reflections on the Revolution in Europe*. London: Chatto and Windus.

Daly, Herman E. and John B. Cobb, Jr. 1989. *For the Common Good: Redirecting the Economy Toward Community, the Environment and a Sustainable Future*. Boston: Beacon Press.

Daniels, Norman. 1981. Conflicting objectives and the priorities problem. Pp. 147–64 in *Income Support: Conceptual and Policy Issues*, ed. Peter G. Brown, Conrad Johnson and Paul Vernier. Totowa, N.J.: Rowman and Littlefield.

Danziger, Sheldon and Robert Haveman. 1978. An economic concept of solidarity: its application to poverty and income distribution in the United States. *Labour and Society* 3: 377–86.

Danziger, Sheldon; Robert Haveman; and Robert Plotnick. 1981. How income transfer programs affect work, savings and income distribution. *Journal of Economic Literature* 19: 975–1028.

Dasgupta, Partha. 1993. *An Inquiry into Well-being and Destitution*. Oxford: Clarendon Press.

Davidoff, Leonore. 1995. *Worlds Between: Historical Perspectives on Gender and Class*. Oxford: Polity Press.

Deacon, Bob. 1983. *Social Policy and Socialism: The Struggle for Socialist Relations of Welfare*. London: Pluto Press.

Deaton, Angus. 1997. *The Analysis of Household Surveys*. Baltimore, Md.: Johns Hopkins University Press for the World Bank.

Delors, Jacques. 1991. *Subsidiarity: The Challenge of Change*. Maastricht: European Institute of Public Administration.

Dickens, Charles. 1854. *Hard Times*. Harmondsworth, Mddx.: Penguin, 1969.

Dierickx, Guido. 1994. Christian democracy and its ideological rivals. Pp. 15–30 in *Christian Democracy in Europe: A Comparative Perspective*, ed. David L. Hanley. London: Pinter.

Dirven, Henk-Jan. 1995. Income dynamics and social protection: a comparison of Germany and the Netherlands. Paper presented at the conference on the Economics of Poverty and Social Exclusion, Leuven, Belgium, 15–16 Dec.

1995.

Dirven, Henk-Jan and Jos Berghman. 1995. The evolution of income poverty in the Netherlands: results from the Dutch Socio-economic Panel Survey. *Innovation* 8: 75–94.

Dirven, Henk-Jan and Didier Fouarge. 1995. Impoverishment and social exclusion: a dynamic perspective on income poverty and relative deprivation in Belgium and the Netherlands. Paper presented at the International Conference on Empirical Poverty Research, Bielefeld, Germany, 17–18 Nov. 1995.

Dirven, Henk-Jan; Didier Fouarge; and Ruud Muffels. 1998. Netherlands. Pp. 136–70 in *Poverty: A Persistent Global Reality*, ed. J. Dixon and D. Macarovi. London: Routledge.

Disraeli, Benjamin. 1875. *Sybil; or, The Two Nations*. London: Longmans, Green.

Döring, Diether. 1997. Is the German welfare state sustainable? In Koslowski and Føllesdal 1997 pp. 38–61.

Doyal, Len and Ian Gough. 1991. *A Theory of Human Need*. London: Macmillan.

Drèze, Jacques H. and Edmond Malinvaud. 1994. Growth and employment: the scope for a European initiative. *European Economy (Reports and Studies)* 1: 77–106.

Drèze, Jean and Amartya Sen. 1989. *Hunger and Public Action*. Oxford: Clarendon Press.

Dryzek, John S. 1996. Political inclusion and the dynamics of democratization. *American Political Science Review* 90: 475–87.

Duncan, Greg J. 1994. Using panel studies to understand household behaviour and well-being. Paper presented to the Aldi Hagenaars Memorial Conference, 28–29 August.

Duncan, Greg J.; with Richard D. Coe; Mary E. Corcoran; Martha S. Hill; Saul D. Hoffman; and James N. Morgan. 1984. *Years of Poverty, Years of Plenty: The Changing Economic Fortunes of American Workers and Families*. Ann Arbor, Mich.: Survey Research Center, Institute for Social Research, University of Michigan.

Duncan, Greg J.; Björn Gustafsson; Richard Hauser; Günther Schmaus; Stephen Jenkins; Hans Messinger; Ruud Muffels; Brian Nolan; Jean-Claude Ray; and Wolfgang Voges. 1995. Poverty and social-assistance dynamics in the United States, Canada and Europe. Pp. 67–108 in *Poverty, Inequality and the Future of Social Policy*, ed. Katherine McFate, Roger Lawson and William Julius Wilson. New York: Russell Sage Foundation.

Duncan, Greg J.; Björn Gustafsson; Richard Hauser; Günther Schmaus; Hans Messinger; Ruud Muffels; Brian Nolan; and Jean-Claude Ray. 1993. Poverty dynamics in eight countries. *Journal of Population Economics* 6: 215–34.

Duncan, Greg J. and Daniel H. Hill. 1985. An investigation of the extent and consequences of measurement error in labor-economic survey data. *Journal of Labor Economics* 3: 508–32.

Duncan, Greg J.; Martha S. Hill; and Saul D. Hoffman. 1988. Welfare dependence within and across generations. *Science* 239: 467–71.

Duncan, Greg J. and James N. Morgan. 1973 *et seq.* eds. *Five Thousand American Families – Patterns of Economic Progress*, vols. I *et seq.* Ann Arbor, Mich.:

Survey Research Center, Institute for Social Research, University of Michigan.

Duncan, Greg J. and Wolfgang Voges. 1993. Do generous social-system programs lead to dependence? A comparative study of lone-parent families in Germany and the United States. Working Paper 11/1993. Bremen: Centre for Social Policy Research, University of Bremen.

Dworkin, Ronald M. 1978. Liberalism. Pp. 113–43 in *Public and Private Morality*, ed. Stuart Hampshire. Cambridge: Cambridge University Press.

1981. What is equality? *Philosophy and Public Affairs* 10: 185–246, 283–345.

Eardley, Tony; Jonathan Bradshaw; J. Ditch; Ian Gough; and Peter Whiteford. 1996. *Social Assistance in OECD Countries*. Department of Social Security Research Report No. 47. London: HMSO.

Edin, Kathryn. 1991. Surviving the welfare system: how AFDC recipients make ends meet in Chicago. *Social Problems* 38: 462–74.

Ellwood, David T. 1988. *Poor Support: Poverty in the American Family*. New York: Basic.

Elster, Jon. 1978. Exploring exploitation. *Journal of Peace Research* 15: 3–17.

1988. Is there (or should there be) a right to work? Pp. 52–78 in *Democracy and the Welfare State*, ed. Amy Gutmann. Princeton, N.J.: Princeton University Press.

1990. Local justice. *Archives Européennes de Sociologie* 31: 117–40.

1992. *Local justice*. New York: Russell Sage Foundation.

1995 ed. *Local Justice in America*. New York: Russell Sage Foundation.

Elsthain, Jean Bethke. 1981. *Public Man, Private Woman*. Princeton, N.J.: Princeton University Press.

England, Paula and B. S. Kilbourne. 1990. Markets, marriages and other mates. In *Beyond the Marketplace: Rethinking Economy and Society*, ed. Roger Friedland and A. F. Robertson. New York: de Gruyter.

Erikson, Robert and Rune Åberg. 1987. *Welfare in Transition: A Survey of Living Conditions in Sweden 1968–1981*. Oxford: Oxford University Press.

Esping-Andersen, Gøsta. 1985a. *Politics Against Markets: The Social Democratic Road to Power*. Princeton, N.J.: Princeton University Press.

1985b. Power and distributional regimes. *Politics and Society* 14: 223–56.

1987a. Citizenship and socialism: de-commodification and solidarity in the welfare state. In Rein, Esping-Andersen and Rainwater 1987, pp. 78–101.

1987b. The comparison of policy regimes: an introduction. In Rein, Esping-Andersen and Rainwater 1987, pp. 3–12.

1990. *The Three Worlds of Welfare Capitalism*. Oxford: Polity.

1994. Welfare states and the economy. Pp. 711–32 in *The Handbook of Economic Sociology*, ed. Neil J. Smelser and Richard Swedberg. Princeton, N.J.: Princeton University Press.

1996a. After the golden age? Welfare state dilemmas in a global economy. In Esping-Andersen 1996b, pp. 1–30.

1996b. *Welfare States in Transition: National Adaptations in Global Economies*. London: Sage for the United Nations Research Institute for Social Development.

1996c. Welfare states without work: the impasse of labour shedding and familialism in continental European social policy. In Esping-Andersen 1996b, pp. 66–87.

1999. *Social Foundations of Post-industrial Economics.* Oxford: Oxford University Press.

Esping-Andersen, Gøsta and Walter Korpi. 1984. Social policy as class politics in post-war capitalism: Scandinavia, Austria and Germany. In Goldthorpe 1984, pp. 179–208.

Esping-Andersen, Gøsta and Kees van Kersbergen. 1992. Contemporary research on social democracy. *Annual Review of Sociology* 18: 187–208.

Etzioni, Amitai. 1993. *The Spirit of Community.* New York: Crown Books.

Etzioni, Amitai *et al.* 1991/2. The responsive communitarian platform: rights *and* responsibilities. *The Responsive Community* 2: 4–20. Reprinted in Etzioni 1993, pp. 251–67.

Evans, Martin; Serge Paugam; and Joseph A. Prélis. 1995. Chunnel vision: poverty, social exclusion and the debate on social welfare in France and Britain. Discussion Paper WSP/115, Welfare State Programme, STICERD, London School of Economics.

Falkingham, Jane and John Hills. 1995 eds. *The Dymanic of Welfare: The Welfare State and the Life Cycle.* New York: Prentice Hall/Harvester Wheatsheaf.

Falkingham, Jane; John Hills; and C. Lessof. 1993. William Beveridge versus Robin Hood: social security and redistribution over the life cycle. Discussion Paper WSP/88. London: Suntory-Toyota International Centre for Economics and Related Disciplines, London School of Economics.

Favell, Adrian. 1998. *Philosophies of Integration.* London: Macmillan.

Feldstein, Martin. 1980. International differences in social security and savings. *Journal of Public Economics* 14: 225–44.

1996. The missing piece in policy analysis: social security reform. *American Economic Review (Papers and Proceedings)* 86 (2): 1–14.

Feldstein, Martin and Anthony Pellechio. 1979. Social security and household wealth accumulation: new micro econometric evidence. *Review of Economics and Statistics* 61: 361–8.

Flora, Peter. 1986 ed. *Growth to Limits: The West European Welfare State Since World War II.* 4 vols. Berlin: Walter de Gruyter.

Flora, Peter and Arnold J. Heidenheimer. 1981 eds. *The Development of Welfare States in Europe and America.* New Brunswick, N.J.: Transaction.

Folbre, Nancy. 1982. Exploitation comes home: a critique of the Marxian theory of family labour. *Cambridge Journal of Economics*, 6: 317–29.

1991. The unproductive housewife: her evolution in nineteenth century economic thought. *Signs* 16: 463–84.

1996. Engendering economics: new perspectives on women, work, and demographic change. Pp. 127–53 in *Annual World Bank Conference on Development Economics*, ed. Michael Bruno and Boris Pleskovic. Washington, D.C.: World Bank.

Føllesdal, Andreas. 1998. Survey article: subsidiarity. *Journal of Political Philosophy*, 6: 190–218.

Foster, J.; J. Greer; and E. Thorbecke. 1984. A class of decomoposable poverty measures. *Econometrica* 52: 761–6.

Fouarge, Didier and Henk-Jan Dirven. 1995. Income dynamics among the elderly: results of an international comparative study. Pp. 409–30 in *Actes des XVe Journées de l'Association d'Economie Sociale*. Nancy: Berger-Levrault GTI.

Fraser, Nancy. 1994. After the family wage: gender equity and the welfare state. *Political Theory* 22: 591–618.

Fraser, Nancy and Linda Gordon. 1994. 'Dependency' demystified: inscriptions of power in a keyword of the welfare state. *Social Politics* 1 (spring): 4–31; revised version of paper originally published in *Signs* 19 (1994): 1–29. Reprinted in Robert E. Goodin and Philip Pettit, eds., *Contemporary Political Philosophy: An Anthology* (Oxford: Blackwell, 1997), pp. 618–33.

Freeden, Michael. 1978. *The New Liberalism*. Oxford: Clarendon Press.

Friedlander, Danile and Gary Burtless. 1995. *Five Years After: The Long-Term Effects of Welfare-to-Work Programs*. New York: Russell Sage Foundation.

Friedman, Milton. 1962. *Capitalism and Freedom*. Chicago: University of Chicago Press.

Friedman, Milton and Rose Friedman. 1979. *Free to Choose*. New York: Harcourt, Brace, Jovanovich.

Furniss, Norman and Timothy Tilton. 1977. *The Case for the Welfare State: From Social Security to Social Equality*. Bloomington: Indiana University Press.

Gal, John. 1997. Categorical benefits in welfare states: findings from Britain and Israel. Discussion Paper WSP/132, Welfare State Programme. London: STICERD, LSE.

Galler, H. P. and Gert Wagner. 1986. The microsimulation model of the Sfb3 for the analysis of economic and social policies. Pp. 227–47 in *Microanalytic Simulation Models to Support Social and Financial Policy*, ed. Guy H. Orcutt, Joachim Merz and Hermann Quinke. Amsterdam: North-Holland.

Ganßmann, Heiner. 1983. After unification: problems facing the German welfare state. *Journal of European Social Policy* 3: 79–90.

Garfinkel, Irving and Robert Haveman. 1977. *Earnings Capacity, Poverty and Inequality*. New York: Academic Press.

Gibson, Diane. 1998. *Aged Care: Old Policies, New Problems*. Cambridge: Cambridge University Press.

Gilbert, Neil. 1995. *Welfare Justice: Restoring Social Equity*. New Haven, Conn.: Yale University Press.

Gilbert, Neil and A. Moon. 1988. Analyzing welfare effort: an appraisal of comparative methods. *Journal of Policy Analysis and Management* 7: 328–32.

Gilder, George. 1981. *Wealth and Poverty*. New York: Basic Books.

Ginneken, W. van and J. Park. 1984. *Generating Internationally Comparable Income Distribution Estimates*. Geneva: International Labour Office.

Glennerster, Howard. 1995. *British Social Policy Since 1945*. Oxford: Blackwell.

Goldschmidt-Clermont, L. and E. Pagnossin-Aligisakis. 1995. *Measures of Unrecorded Economic Activities in Fourteen Countries*. Occasional Paper no. 20, Human Development Report Office. New York: United Nations Development Program.

Goldthorpe, John H. 1994 ed. *Order and Conflict in Contemporary Capitalism: Studies in the Political Economy of Western European Nations*. Oxford: Clarendon Press.

Goodin, Robert E. 1982. *Political Theory and Public Policy*. Chicago: University of Chicago Press.

— 1985. Erring on the side of kindness in social welfare policy. *Policy Sciences* 18: 141–56.

— 1988. *Reasons for Welfare*. Princeton, N.J.: Princeton University Press.

— 1990a. Relative needs. In Ware and Goodin 1990, pp. 12–33.

— 1990b. Stabilizing expectations: the role of earnings-related benefits in social welfare policy. *Ethics* 100: 530–53.

— 1991. Compensation and redistribution. Pp. 143–77 in John W. Chapman, ed., *Nomos XXXIII: Compensatory Justice*. New York: New York University Press.

— 1993. *Motivating Political Morality*. Oxford: Blackwell.

— 1996. Inclusion and exclusion. *Archives Européennes de Sociologie*, 37: 343–71.

— 1996 ed. *The Theory of Institutional Design*. Cambridge: Cambridge University Press.

— 1998a. Communities of enlightenment. *British Journal of Political Science*, 28: 531–58.

— 1998b. Social welfare as a collective social responsibility. In Schmidtz and Goodin 1998, pp. 97–194.

Goodin, Robert E. and John Dryzek. 1986. Risk-sharing and social justice: the motivational foundations of the post-war welfare state. *British Journal of Political Science*, 16: 1–34. Reprinted in Goodin, Le Grand *et al.* 1987, pp. 37–75.

Goodin, Robert E.; Julian Le Grand; *et al.* 1987. *Not Only the Poor*. London: Allen and Unwin.

Goodman, Roger and Ito Peng. 1977. The East Asian welfare states: peripatetic learning, adaptive change, and nation-building. In Esping-Andersen 1997b, pp. 192–224.

Gorz, André. 1989. *Critique of Economic Reason*, trans. Gillian Handyside and Chris Turner. London: Verso; originally published 1988.

— 1997. *Misères du Présent, Richesse du Possible*. Paris: Galilée.

Gottshalk, Peter and Robert Moffitt. 1994. Welfare dependence: concepts, measures and trends. *American Economic Review* 84: 38–42.

Gottshalk, Peter and Timothy M. Smeeding. 1997. Cross-national comparisons of earnings and income inequality. *Journal of Economic Literature* 35: 633–87.

Gough, Ian. 1979. *The Political Economy of the Welfare State*. London: Macmillan.

Green, David. 1985. *Working Class Patients and the Medical Establishment: Self-help in Britain from the Mid-Nineteenth Century to 1948*. Aldershot: Gower.

— 1993. *Reinventing Civil Society: The Rediscovery of Welfare without Politics*. London: Institute of Economic Affairs, Health and Welfare Unit.

Gregory, Robert. 1996. Wage regulation, low paid workers and full employment. Pp. 81–101 in *Dialogues on Australia's Future*, ed. P. Sheehan, B. Grewel and M. Kumnick. Melbourne: Victoria University Centre for Strategic Economic Studies.

Guibert-Lantoine, Catherine de and Alain Monnier. 1997. La conjoncture démographique: L'Europe et les pays développés d'outre-mer. *Population* 5:

1187–216.

Guillemard, Anne-Marie and Herman van Gunsteren. 1991. Pathways and their prospects: a comparative interpretation of the meaning of early exit. In Kohli *et al.* 1991, pp. 362–88.

Gunsteren, Herman van and Martin Rein. 1985. The dialectic of public and private pensions. *Journal of Social Policy* 14: 129–49.

Gutmann, Amy. 1985. Communitarian critics of liberalism. *Philosophy and Public Affairs* 14: 308–22.

Habermas, Jürgen. 1962/1989. *The Structural Transformation of the Public Sphere*, trans. Thomas Burger and Frederick Lawrence. Oxford: Polity; originally published 1962.

    1975. *Legitimation Crisis*, trans. T. McCarthy. Boston: Beacon Press.

Hagenaars, A. J. M. 1986. *The Perception of Poverty*. Amsterdam: North-Holland.

    1991. The definition and measurement of poverty. Pp. 134–56 in *Economic Inequality and Poverty: International Perspectives*, ed. L. Osberg. New York: M. E. Sharpe.

Haminga, Bert. 1995. Demoralizing the labor market. *Journal of Political Philosophy* 3: 23–35.

Hancock, Keith. 1979. The first half-century of Australian wage policy. *Journal of Industrial Relations* 21: 129–60.

Handler, Joel F. 1979. *Protecting the Social Service Client.* New York: Academic Press.

Harding, Ann. 1993a. *Lifetime Income Distribution and Redistribution in Australia: Applications of a Microsimulation Model*. Amsterdam: North-Holland.

    1993b. Lifetime vs annual tax-transfer incidence: how much less progressive? *Economic Record* 69: 179–91.

    1995. The impact of health, education and housing outlays on income distribution in Australia in the 1990s. Discussion Paper no. 7. Canberra: NATSEM.

Harrington, Michael. 1962. *The Other America: Poverty in the United States.* New York: Macmillan.

Hartz, Louis. 1955. *The Liberal Tradition in America.* New York: Harcourt, Brace.

Hauser, Richard. 1995. Problems of the German welfare state after unification. *Oxford Review of Economic Policy* 11 (no. 3, Autumn): 44–58.

Haveman, Robert and Andrew Berkshadker. 1998. Self-reliance as a poverty criterion: trends in earning-capacity poverty, 1975–92. *American Economic Review (Papers and Proceedings)* 88 (2): 342–7.

Haveman, Robert and L. F. Buron. 1993. Escaping poverty through work – the problem of low earnings capacity in the United States, 1973–88. *Review of Income and Wealth* 38: 1–15.

Hayek, Friedrich A. 1960. *The Constitution of Liberty.* London: Routledge and Kegan Paul.

    1973–79. *Law, Legislation and Liberty*, 3 vols. Chicago: University of Chicago Press.

Headey, Bruce; Robert E. Goodin; Ruud Muffels; and Henk-Jan Dirven. 1997. Welfare over time: three worlds of welfare capitalism in panel perspective. *Journal of Public Policy* 17: 329–59.

Headey, Bruce and Peter Krause. 1994. Inequalities of income, health and happiness: the stratification paradigm and alternatives. Pp. 133–76 in *Contemporary Issues in Income Distribution Research*, ed. Bruce Bradbury. SPRC Reports and Proceedings no. 115. Sydney: Social Policy Research Centre, University of New South Wales.

Headey, Bruce W.; Peter Krause; and Roland Habich. 1994. Long and short term poverty: is Germany a two-thirds society? *Social Indicators Research* 31: 1–25.

Heidenheimer, Arnold J.; Hugh Heclo; and Carolyn Teich Adams. 1975. *Comparative Public Policy: The Politics of Social Choice in Europe and America*. London: Macmillan.

1990. *Comparative Public Policy: The Politics of Social Choice in America, Europe and Japan*, 3rd edn. London: Macmillan.

Heisler, Barbara Schmitter. 1996. Institutional dimensions of social exclusion in the welfare state: an assessment of trends in the Netherlands and Germany 1985–1992. *Journal of European Public Policy* 3: 168–91.

Hemerijck, Anton and Kees van Kersbergen. 1997. A miraculous model? Explaining the new politics of the welfare state in the Netherlands. *Acta Politica* 23: 258–80.

Hernes, Helga. 1987. *Welfare State and Woman Power*. Oslo: Universiteitsforlaget.

Hicks, A. and D. Swank. 1992. Politics, institutions and welfare spending in industrialized democracies. *American Political Science Review* 86: 658–74.

Hills, John. 1998. Does income mobility mean that we do not need to worry about poverty? In Atkinson and Hills 1998, pp. 31–54.

Hills, John; John Ditch; and Howard Glennerster. 1994 eds. *Beveridge and Social Security: An International Retrospective*. Oxford: Oxford University Press.

Himmelfarb, Gertrude. 1984. *The Idea of Poverty*. London: Faber and Faber.

1994. A demoralized society: the British/American experience. *Public Interest* 117: 57–80.

Hinrichs, Karl. 1998. Reforming the public pension scheme in Germany: the end of the traditional consensus? Paper presented to Research Committee 19, XVIth World Congress of the International Sociological Association, Montreal, July 1998.

Hirsch, Fred. 1976. *Social Limits to Growth*. Cambridge, Mass.: Harvard University Press.

Hirshleifer, Jack. 1987. Disaster behavior: altruism or alliance? Pp. 134–41 in Hirshleifer, *Economic Behavior in Adversity*. Brighton: Wheatsheaf.

Hitch, Charles J. and Roland N. McKean. 1960. *The Economics of Defense in the Nuclear Age*. Cambridge, Mass.: Harvard University Press.

Hobsbawm, E. H. 1975. Fratrernity. *New Society* 34 (no. 686, 27 Nov.): 471–3.

Hochschild, Arlie Russell. 1989. *The Second Shift: Working Parents and the Revolution at Home*. New York: Viking.

1997. *The Time Bind*. New York: Metropolitan Books.

Hofferbert, Richard I. and David Louis Cingrinelli. 1996. Comparative policy studies. Pp. 593–609 in *A New Handbook of Political Science*, ed. Robert E. Goodin and Hans-Dieter Klingemann. Oxford: Oxford University Press.

Horst, Han van der. 1996. *The Low Sky: Understanding the Dutch*, trans. Andy Brown. The Hague: Scriptum Books.

Inglehart, Ronald. 1977. *The Silent Revolution*. Princeton, N.J.: Princeton University Press.

International Labour Office (ILO). Various years, 1984–96. *Yearbook of Labour Statistics*. Geneva: ILO.

1996. *International Labour Conventions and Recommendations*, 3 vols. Geneva: ILO.

Jackman, Robert. 1972. *Politics and Social Equality*. New York: Wiley.

Jacobs, Eva E. 1997 ed. *Handbook of US Labor Statistics: Employment, Earnings, Prices, Productivity and Other Labor Data*, 1st edn. Lanham, Md.: Bernan Press.

Jahoda, M. 1982. *Employment and Unemployment*. Cambridge: Cambridge University Press.

Jahoda, M.; Paul F. Lazarsfeld; and Hans Zeisel. 1933/1972. *Marienthal*. London: Tavistock; originally published 1933.

James, Susan. 1992. The good-enough citizen: female citizenship and independence. Pp. 48–65 in *Beyond Equality and Difference*, ed. Gissela Bock and Susan James. London: Routledge.

Janoski, Thomas. 1994. Direct state intervention in the labor market: the explanation of active labor market policy from 1950 to 1988 in social democratic, conservative and liberal regimes. Pp. 54–92 in *The Comparative Political Economy of the Welfare State*, ed. Thomas Janoski and Alexander M. Hicks. New York: Cambridge University Press.

Jencks, Christopher. 1994. *The Homeless*. Cambridge, Mass.: Harvard University Press.

Jenson, Jane and Rianne Mahon. 1993. Representing solidarity: class, gender and the crisis in social-democratic Sweden. *New Left Review* 201: 76–100.

Jones, Catherine. 1990. Hong Kong, Singapore and Taiwan: oikonomic welfare states. *Government and Opposition* 25: 447–62.

1993. The Pacific challenge. Pp. 198–220 in *New Perspectives on the Welfare State in Europe*, ed. Catherine Jones. London: Routledge.

Jones, Peter. 1982. Freedom and the redistribution of resources. *Journal of Social Policy* 11: 217–38.

Jong, Philip de; Michiel Herweijer; and Jaap de Wildt. 1990. *Form and Reform of the Dutch Social Security System*. Deventer: Kluwer Law and Taxation Publishers, for the Ministry of Social Affairs and Employment.

Jordan, Bill. 1996. *A Theory of Poverty and Social Exclusion*. Oxford: Polity.

Josephson, Matthew. 1934. *The Robber Barons: The Great American Capitalists, 1861–1901*. New York: Harcourt, Brace.

Kakwani, Nanak. 1986. *Analysing Redistribution Policies*. Cambridge: Cambridge University Press.

Kangas, Olli and Joakim Palme. 1998. Does social policy matter? Poverty cycles in OECD Countries. Paper presented to XVIth World Congress of International Sociological Association, Montreal.

Kapteyn, A.; P. Kooreman; and R. Willemse. 1988. Some methodological issues in the implementation of subjective poverty definitions. *Journal of Human Resources* 23 (no. 2): 222–42.

Katz, Michael B. 1986. *In the Shadow of the Poorhouse: A Social History of Welfare in America*. New York: Basic Books.

Kersbergen, Kees van. 1995. *Social Capitalism: A Study of Christian Democracy and the Welfare State*. London: Routledge.

Kersbergen, Kees van and Uwe Becker. 1988. The Netherlands: a passive social democratic welfare state in a Christian democratic ruled society. *Journal of Social Policy* 17: 477–99.

King, Desmond S. 1995. *Actively Seeking Work? The Politics of Unemployment and Welfare Policy in the United States and Great Britain*. Chicago: University of Chicago Press.

King, Desmond S. and Jeremy Waldron. 1988. Citizenship, social citizenship and the defence of welfare provision. *British Journal of Political Science* 18: 415–43. Reprinted in Waldron 1993, pp. 271–308.

King, Gary; Robert O. Keohane; and Sidney Verba. 1994. *Designing Social Inquiry: Scientific Inference in Qualitative Research*. Princeton, N.J.: Princeton University Press.

Kirchheimer, Otto. 1966. Germany: the vanishing opposition. Pp. 237–59 in *Political Oppositions in Western Democracies*, ed. Robert A. Dahl. New Haven, Conn.: Yale University Press.

Klein, Rudolf. 1993. Ogoffe's tale. Pp. 7–17 in *New Perspectives on the Welfare State in Europe*, ed. Catherine Jones. London: Routledge.

Kloosterman, Robert C. 1994. Three worlds of welfare capitalism? The welfare state and the post-industrial trajectory in the Netherlands after 1980. *West European Politics* 17 (no. 4, Oct.): 166–89.

Knijn, Trudie. 1994. Fish without bikes: revision of the Dutch welfare state and its consequences for the (in)dependence of single mothers. *Social Politics* 1 (no. 1): 83–105.

Kohli, Martin; Martin Rein; Anne Marie Guillemard; and Herman van Gunsteren. 1991 eds. *Time for Retirement: Comparative Studies of Early Exit from the Labor Force*. Cambridge: Cambridge University Press.

Korpi, Walter. 1983. *The Democratic Class Struggle*. London: Routledge and Kegan Paul.

1985. Economic growth and the welfare state: leaky bucket or irrigation system? *European Sociological Review* 1: 97–118.

1989. Power, politics and state autonomy in the growth of social citizenship: social rights during sickness in eighteen OECD countries since 1930. *American Sociological Review* 54: 309–28.

1990. The development of the Swedish welfare state in comparative perspective. Stockholm: Swedish Institute. Reprint no. 309, Swedish Institute for Social Research, Stockholm University.

1995. The position of the elderly in the welfare state: comparative perspectives on old-age care in Sweden. *Social Service Review* 69: 242–73.

1997. Bringing conflict and power into rational choice analysis of institutions: a comparative study of the emergence and change of welfare state institutions. Mimeo, Swedish Institute for Social Research, Stockholm University.

Korpi, Walter and Joakim Palme. 1998. The paradox of redistribution and strategies of equality: welfare state institutions, inequality and poverty in the Western countries. *American Sociological Review* 63: 661–87.

Koslowski, Peter and Andreas Føllesdal. 1997 eds. *Restructuring the Welfare State: Theory and Reform of Social Policy*. Berlin: Springer-Verlag.

Koslowski, Stefan. 1997. Origins of the 'social state' in German philosophy and 'staatswissenschaft'. In Koslowski and Føllesdal 1997, pp. 119–42.

Lampman, Robert J. 1974. What does it do for the poor? – a new test for national policy. *Public Interest* 34: 66–82; reprinted pp. 66–82 in *The Great Society: Lessons for the Future*, ed. Eli Ginzberg and Robert M. Solow. New York: Basic Books, 1974.

Land, Hilary. 1975. The introduction of family allowances: an act of historic justice? Pp. 157–230 in *Change, Choice and Conflict in Social Policy*, ed. Pheobe Hall, Hilary Land, Roy Parker and Adrian Webb. London: Heinemann.

    1978. Who cares for the family? *Journal of Social Policy* 7: 257–84.

    1980. The family wage. *Feminist Review* 6: 55–77.

    1994. The demise of the male breadwinner – in practice but not in theory: a challenge for social security systems. Pp. 100–15 in *Social Security in Transition*, ed. Sally Baldwin and Jane Falkingham. New York: Harvester-Wheatsheaf.

Landis, Michele L. 1998. 'Let me next time be "tried by fire"': disaster relief and the origins of the American welfare state 1789–1874. *Northwestern University Law Review* 92: 969–1036.

Layard, Richard. 1977. The lifetime redistribution of income. Pp. 45–72 in *The Economics of Public Services*, ed. Martin S. Feldstein and Robert P. Inman. London: Macmillan for International Economic Association.

Le Grand, Julian. 1982. *The Strategy of Equality*. London: Allen and Unwin.

    1990. Equity versus efficiency: the elusive trade-off. *Ethics* 100: 554–68.

Lehmbruch, Gerhard. 1984. Concertation and the structure of corporatist networks. Pp. 60–80 in *Order and Conflict in Contemporary Capitalism*, ed. John H. Goldthorpe. Oxford: Clarendon Press.

Leibenstein, Harvey. 1966. Allocative efficiency vs. x-efficiency. *American Economic Review* 56: 392–415.

Leibfried, Stephan. 1992. Nutritional minima and the state: on the institutionalization of professional knowledge in national social policy in the US and Germany. ZeS Abeitspapier Nr. 10/92. Bremen, Zentrum für Sozialpolitik, Universität Bremen.

    1993. Towards a European welfare state. Pp. 133–56 in *New Perspectives on the Welfare State in Europe*, ed. Catherine Jones. London: Routledge.

Leisering, Lutz and Stephan Leibfried. 1998. *Time, Life and Poverty: Social Assistance Dynamics in the German Welfare State*, trans. J. Veit-Wilson and Lutz Leisering. Cambridge: Cambridge University Press.

Levitan, Sar A. and Richard S. Belous. 1977. *Shorter Hours, Shorter Weeks: Spreading the Work to Reduce Unemployment*. Baltimore, Md.: Johns Hopkins University Press.

Levy, Frank. 1977. How big is the American underclass? Working Paper 0090–1. Washington, D.C.: Urban Institute.

Levy, Frank and Richard J. Murname. 1992. US earnings level and earnings inequality: a review of recent trends and proposed explanations. *Journal of*

Economic Literature 30: 1333–81.

Lewis, Jane. 1992. Gender and welfare regimes. *Journal of European Social Policy*, 2: 159–71.

Lewis, Jane and Gertrud Astrom. 1992. Equality, difference and state welfare: labor markets and family policies in Sweden. *Feminist Studies* 18: 59–87.

Liebow, Elliot. 1967. *Tally's Corner: A Study of Negro Streetcorner Men*. Boston: Little, Brown.

Lilliard, Lee A. 1977. Inequality: earnings versus human wealth. *American Economic Review*, 67: 42–53.

Lindbeck, Assar. 1995. Hazardous welfare-state dynamics. *American Economic Review (Papers and Proceedings)* 85 (May): 9–15.

——— 1997. The Swedish experiment. *Journal of Economic Literature* 85: 1273–1319.

Lindbeck, Assar; Per Molander; Torsten Persson; Olof Petersson; Agnar Sandmo; Birgitta Swedenborg; and Niels Thygesen. 1994. *Turning Sweden Around*. Cambridge, Mass.: MIT Press.

Linder, Staffan B. 1970. *The Harried Leisure Class*. New York: Columbia University Press.

Lipset, Seymour Martin. 1996. *American Exceptionalism*. New York: Norton.

Lipsey, Richard G. and Kelvin J. Lancaster. 1956. The general theory of second best. *Review of Economic Studies* 24: 11–33.

Lipsky, Michael. 1984. Bureaucratic disentitlement in social welfare programs. *Social Service Review* 58: 3–27.

Lijphart, Arend. 1975. *The Politics of Accommodation: Pluralism and Democracy in the Netherlands*, 2nd edn. Berkeley, Calif.: University of California Press; originally published 1968.

Lundberg, S. and R. A. Pollack. 1993. Separate spheres bargaining and the marriage market. *Journal of Political Economy* 101: 988–1010.

Lydall, Harold. 1955. The life-cycle in income, saving and asset ownership. *Econometrica* 23: 131–50.

MacCallum, Gerald C. 1966. Legislative intent. *Yale Law Journal* 75: 754–87.

MacDonald, Martha. 1998. Gender and social security policy: pitfalls and possibilities. *Feminist Economics* 4: 1–25.

MacIntyre, Alasdair C. 1988. *Whose Justice? Which Rationality?* Notre Dame, Ind.: University of Notre Dame Press.

Mahon, Rianne. 1991. From solidaristic wages to solidaristic work: a post-Fordist historic compromise for Sweden? *Economic and Industrial Democracy* 12: 295–325.

Malcolm X. 1965. *The Autobiography of Malcolm X*. New York: Grove.

Marmor, Theodore R.; Jerry L. Mashaw; and Philip L. Harvey. 1990. *America's Misunderstood Welfare State: Persistent Myths, Enduring Realities*. New York: Basic Books.

Marshall, T. H. 1949. Citizenship and social class. Reprinted pp. 70–134 in Marshall, *Class, Citizenship and Social Development*. Chicago: University of Chicago Press, 1963.

——— 1977. *Social Policy in the Twentieth Century*. London: Hutchinson.

Mathies, H.; U. Mückenberger; C. Offe; E. Peter; and S. Raasch. 1994. *Arbeit 2000*. Reinbek: Rowohlt.

McQustra, C. 1990. *Love in the Economy: Catholic Social Doctrine for the Individual.* Slough: St Paul.

Mead, Lawrence M. 1986. *Beyond Entitlement: The Social Obligations of Citizenship.* New York: Free Press.

1992. *The New Politics of Poverty: The Nonworking Poor in America.* New York: Basic Books.

Meade, James E. 1984. Full employment, new technology and the distribution of income. *Journal of Social Policy* 13: 129–46.

Mill, John Stuart. 1843. *A System of Logic.* London: Parker.

1859. *On Liberty.* Harmondsworth, Mddx.: Penguin, 1974.

Mills, C. Wright. 1959. *The Sociological Imagination.* New York: Oxford University Press.

Mishra, Ramesh. 1984. *The Welfare State in Crisis.* Hemel Hempstead: Wheatsheaf.

Mitchell, Deborah. 1991. *Income Transfers in Ten Welfare States.* Aldershot: Avebury.

Moene, Karl Ove and Michael Wallerstein. 1993. What's wrong with social democracy? In *Market Socialism: The Current Debate,* ed. Pranab Bardhan and John Roemer. New York: Oxford University Press.

1995. How social democracy worked: labor-market institutions. *Politics and Society* 23: 185–212.

Moffitt, Robert. 1992. Incentive effects of the US welfare system: a review. *Journal of Economic Literature* 30: 1–61.

Mommsen, Wolfgang J. 1981 ed. *The Emergence of the Welfare State in Britain and Germany, 1850–1950.* London: Croom Helm.

Moore, Barrington Jr. 1967. *Social Origins of Dictatorship and Democracy.* London: Allen Lane.

Morgan, James N. 1965. Measuring the economic status of the aged. *International Economic Review* 6: 1–17.

Morris, Jenny. 1993. *Independent Lives: Community Care and Disabled People.* London: Macmillan.

Moynihan, Daniel Patrick. 1973. *The Politics of a Guaranteed Income: The Nixon Administration and the Family Assistance Plan.* New York: Random House.

1995. It will shame the Congress. Speech in the US Senate, 16 September 1995. Reprinted in *New York Review of Books* 42 (no. 16, 19 Oct.): 71–2.

Muffels, R. J. A. 1993. *Welfare Economic Effects of Social Security: Essays on Poverty, Social Security and Labour Market – Evidence from Panel Data.* Series on Social Security Studies, Reports, no. 21. Tilburg: KUB.

Muffels, Ruud and Henk-Jan Dirven. 1993. Income mobility and poverty persistence: persistent poverty measures and comparative analyses of Dutch and American panel data. Working Papers of the European Scientific Network on Household Panel Studies, Paper no. 75. Colchester: University of Essex.

1995. Long-term income and deprivation-based poverty: a comparative study on the Dutch and German panel data. WORC Paper 95.12.029/2. Presented at the International Conference on Empirical Poverty, Bielefeld, Germany, 17–18 Nov. 1995.

Murray, Charles. 1982. The two wars against poverty: economic growth and the

Great Society. *Public Interest* 69: 3–16.

1984. *Losing Ground: American Social Policy, 1950–80.* New York: Basic Books.

Myles, John. 1988. Postwar capitalism and the extension of Social Security into a retirement wage. In Weir, Orloff and Skocpol 1988, pp. 265–84.

1989. *Old Age in the Welfare State: The Political Economy of Public Pensions,* revised edn. Lawrence: University of Kansas Press; originally published by Little, Brown, 1984.

1996. When markets fail: social welfare in Canada and the United States. In Esping-Andersen 1996b, pp. 116–40.

Myrdal, Alva. 1944. *Nation and Family: The Swedish Experiment in Democratic Family and Population Policy.* London: Kegan Paul, Trench, Trubner.

Nell [O'Neill], Onora. 1980. How do we know when opportunities are equal? *Philosophical Forum,* 5 (nos. 1–2): 334–46. Reprinted in *Women and Philosophy,* ed. Carol C. Gould and Marx. W. Wartofsky (New York: Putnam, 1980), pp. 334–46.

Netherlands Ministry of Social Affairs and Employment. 1990. *Social Security in the Netherlands.* Deventer: Kluwer Law and Taxation Publishers.

1996a. *The Dutch Welfare State from an International and Economic Perspective.* The Hague: Ministry of Social Affairs and Employment.

1996b. *Social and Economic Aspects of the Netherlands,* volume I: *Policies.* The Hague: Ministry of Social Affairs and Employment.

Nozick, Robert. 1974. *Anarchy, State and Utopia.* Oxford: Blackwell.

Oakeshott, Michael. 1962. *Rationalism in Politics.* London: Methuen. New edition, Indianapolis, Ind.: Liberty Press, 1991.

O'Connor, James R. 1973. *The Fiscal Crisis of the State.* New York: St Martin's Press.

Offe, Claus. 1984. *Contradictions of the Welfare State.* Cambridge, Mass.: MIT Press.

1992. A non-productivist design for social policies. Pp. 61–80 in Philippe Van Parijs, ed., *Arguing for Basic Income.* London: Verso.

1995. Full employment: asking the wrong question? *Dissent* (winter): 77–81.

1996. *Modernity and the State : East, West.* Cambridge, Mass.: MIT Press.

1997. Towards a new equilibrium of citizens' rights and economic resources. Pp. 81–108 in *Social Cohesion and the Globalizing Economy: What Does the Future Hold?* Paris: OECD.

1998. The German welfare state: principles, performance, prospects. Paper presented to conference on 'The welfare state at century's end: current dilemmas and possible futures', Tel Aviv, 5–7 January 1998.

Offe, Claus; Rolf G. Heinze, *et al.* 1992. *Beyond Employment: Time, Work, and the Informal Economy,* trans. Alan Braley. Oxford: Polity.

O'Higgins, Michael and S. Jenkins. 1990. Poverty in the EC: 1975, 1980, 1985. In *Analysing Poverty in the European Community,* ed. Rudolf Teekens and Bernard Van Praag. Eurostat News, special edition, no. 1. Luxembourg: EUROSTAT.

Okun, Arthur. 1975. *Equality and Efficiency: The Big Tradeoff.* Washington, D.C.: Brookings Institution.

Olson, Mancur Jr. 1982. *The Rise and Decline of Nations.* New Haven, Conn.: Yale

University Press.

Oorschot, Wim van. 1991. Non-take-up of social security benefits in Europe. *Journal of European Social Policy* 1: 15–30.

——— 1997. The common good, nearness and dependence: on solidarity and its motives. Working Paper 97/12. Utrecht: Onderzoekschool AWSB.

Organisation for Economic Co-operation and Development (OECD). 1981. *The Welfare State in Crisis*. Paris: OECD.

——— 1983. *Historical Statistics, 1960–81*. Paris: OECD.

——— 1988a. *The Future of Social Protection*. OECD Social Policy Studies no. 6. Paris: OECD.

——— 1988b. *Reforming Public Pensions*. OECD Social Policy Studies no. 5. Paris: OECD.

——— 1990a. *Labour Market Policies for the 1990s*. Paris: OECD.

——— 1990b. *Main Economic Indicators*. Paris: OECD.

——— 1991. *Revenue Statistics of OECD Member Countries 1965–90*. Paris: OECD.

——— 1994. *New Orientations for Social Policy*. OECD Social Policy Studies no. 12. Paris: OECD.

——— 1996a. *Historical Statistics, 1960–94*. Paris: OECD.

——— 1996b. *National Accounts, 1982–1994*, vol. II: *Detailed Tables*. Paris: OECD.

——— 1996c. *Social Expenditure Statistics of OECD Member Countries (Provisional Version)*. OECD Labour Market and Social Policy, Occasional Papers no. 17, OCDE/GD(96)49. Paris: OECD.

——— 1996d. *Labour Force Statistics*. Paris: OECD.

——— 1996e. Making work pay. Pp. 25–56 in *Employment Outlook*. Paris: OECD. Subsequently published in expanded form as: *Making Work Pay: Taxation, Benefits, Employment and Unemployment*. Paris: OECD, 1997.

——— 1996f. *Economic Outlook*, no. 60. Paris: OECD.

——— 1996g. *National Accounts, 1960–94*, vol I: *Main Aggregates*. Paris: OECD.

——— 1997. *Ageing in OECD Countries: A Critical Policy Challenge*. OECD Social Policy Studies no. 20. Paris: OECD.

——— 1998. *National Accounts, 1960–96*, vol. I: *Main Aggregates*. Paris: OECD.

——— Various years, 1984–1995. *Employment Outlook*. Paris: OECD.

Orloff, Ann Shola. 1988. The political origins of America's belated welfare state. In Weir, Orloff and Skocpol 1988, pp. 37–80.

——— 1993. Gender and the social rights of citizenship: the comparative analysis of gender relations and welfare states. *American Sociological Review* 58: 303–28.

——— 1996. Gender in the welfare state. *Annual Review of Sociology* 22: 51–78.

Orloff, Ann Shola and Theda Skocpol. 1984. Why not equal protection? Explaining the politics of public social spending in Britain, 1900–1911, and the United States, 1880s–1920. *American Sociological Review* 49: 726–50.

Orshansky, M. 1965. Counting the poor: another look at the poverty profile. *Social Security Bulletin* 28 (1): 3–29; reprinted *Social Security Bulletin* 51 (10) (1988): 25–51.

Orwell, George. 1933. *Down and Out in Paris and London*. New York: Harcourt Brace Jovanovich, 1961; originally published 1933.

Pahl, Jan. 1983. The allocation of money and the structuring of inequality within marriage. *Sociological Review* 31: 237–62.

1989. *Money and Marriage.* London: Macmillan.

Palda, Filip. 1997. Fiscal churning and political efficiency. *Kyklos* 50: 189–206.

Palme, Joakim. 1990a. Models of old-age pensions. In Ware and Goodin 1990, pp. 104–25. Reprinted (expanded) in Palme 1990b, ch. 4.

1990b. *Pension Rights in Welfare Capitalism: The Development of Old-Age Pensions in 18 OECD Countries 1930 to 1985.* Stockholm: Swedish Institute for Social Research, University of Stockholm.

Palmer, John L.; Timothy Smeeding; and Barbara Boyle Torrey. 1988 eds. *The Vulnerable.* Washington, D.C.: Urban Institute Press.

Pateman, Carole. 1988a. The patriarchal welfare state. Pp. 231–60 in *Democracy and the Welfare State,* ed. Amy Gutmann. Princeton, N.J.: Princeton University Press.

1988b. *The Sexual Contract.* Oxford: Polity Press.

Pechman, Joseph A. and M. S. Mazur. 1984. The rich, the poor and the taxes they pay: an update. *Public Interest* 77: 28–36.

Pettit, Philip. 1997. *Republicanism.* Oxford: Clarendon Press.

Piachaud, David. 1981. Peter Townsend and the Holy Grail. *New Society* 54 (no. 982): 419–21.

1982. Patterns of income and expenditure within families. *Journal of Social Policy* 11: 469–82.

Pierson, Paul. 1994. *Dismantling the Welfare State? Reagan, Thatcher and the Politics of Retrenchment.* Cambridge: Cambridge University Press.

Ploug, N. and J. Qvist. 1994 eds. *Recent Trends in Cash Benefits in Europe.* Copenhagen: Danish National Institute of Social Research.

Polanyi, Karl. 1944. *The Great Transformation.* New York: Rinehart Press.

Pollack, R. A. and M. L. Watcher. 1975. The relevance of the household production function and its implicatons for the allocation of time. *Journal of Political Economy* 83: 255–77.

Pryor, Frederic L. 1968. *Public Expenditure in Communist and Capitalist Nations.* London: Allen and Unwin.

Przeworski, Adam and John Sprague. 1986. *Paper Stones: A History of Electoral Socialism.* Chicago: University of Chicago Press.

Przeworski, Adam and Henry Teune. 1970. *The Logic of Comparative Social Inquiry.* New York: Wiley.

Purdy, D. 1994. Citizenship, basic income and the state. *New Left Review* 208: 30–48.

Putnam, Robert D. 1993. *Making Democracy Work: Civic Traditions in Modern Italy.* Princeton, N.J.: Princeton University Press.

Quandango, Jill S. 1988a. From old-age assistance to supplemental security income: the political economy of relief in the South, 1935–72. In Weir, Orloff and Skocpol 1988, pp. 235–64.

1988b. *The Transformation of Old Age Security: Class and Politics in the American Welfare State.* Chicago: University of Chicago Press.

Rae, Douglas W. 1981. *Equalities.* Cambridge, Mass.: Harvard University Press.

Rainwater, Lee. 1974. *What Money Buys: Inequality and the Social Meaning of Income.* New York: Basic.

Rainwater, Lee; Martin Rein; and Joseph Schwartz. 1986. *Income Packaging in the*

Welfare State. Oxford: Clarendon Press.

Rawls, John. 1971. *A Theory of Justice.* Cambridge, Mass.: Harvard University Press.

Raz, Joseph. 1990. Facing diversity: the case of epistemic abstinence. *Philosophy and Public Affairs* 19: 3–46. Reprinted in Raz, *Ethics in the Public Domain* (Oxford: Clarendon Press, 1994), pp 60–96.

Reich, Charles A. 1964. The new property. *Yale Law Journal* 73: 733–87.

Rein, Martin; Gøsta Esping-Andersen; and Lee Rainwater. 1987 eds. *Stagnation and Renewal in Social Policy: The Rise and Fall of Policy Regimes.* Armonk, N.Y.: M. E. Sharpe.

Rein, Martin and John Turner. 1997. Work, family, state and market: income at the last stages of the working career. *Lien Social et Politique* 38: 101–12.

Reischauer, Robert D. 1997 ed. *Setting National Priorities: Budget Choices for the Next Century.* Washington, D.C.: Brookings Institution.

Rimlinger, Gaston V. 1971. *Welfare Policy and Industrialization in Europe, America and Russia.* New York: Wiley.

1987. Social policy under German fascism. In Rein, Esping-Andersen and Rainwater 1987, pp. 59–77.

Ringen, Stein. 1987. *The Possibility of Politics: A Study in the Political Economy of the Welfare State.* Oxford: Clarendon Press.

1988. Direct and indirect measures of poverty. *Journal of Social Policy* 17: 351–65.

1991. Households, standard of living and inequality. *Review of Income and Wealth* 37: 1–13.

1996a. Can inequality be reformed? *Czech Sociological Review* 4: 19–28.

1996b. Households, goods and well-being. *Review of Income and Wealth* 42: 421–31.

Rivlin, Alice M. 1971. *Systematic Thinking for Social Action.* Washington, D.C.: Brookings Institution.

Robinson, Joan. 1933. *The Economics of Imperfect Competition.* London: Macmillan.

Roemer, John. 1982. *A General Theory of Exploitation and Class.* Cambridge, Mass.: Harvard University Press.

1985. Equality of resources implies equality of welfare. *Quarterly Journal of Economics* 101: 751–84.

Rogers, Gerry. 1995. What is special about a social exclusion approach? In Rogers, Gore and Figueiredo 1995, pp. 43–56.

Rogers, Gerry; Charles Gore; and José B. Figueiredo. 1995 eds. *Social Exclusion: Rhetoric, Reality, Responses.* Geneva: International Institute for Labour Studies, International Labour Organisation and United Nations Development Programme.

Room, Graham. 1995. Poverty in Europe: competing paradigms and analysis. *Policy and Politics* 23: 103–13.

Rosanvallon, Pierre. 1995. *La nouvelle question sociale. Repenser de l'Etat- Providence.* Paris: Seuil.

Rose, Richard. 1976. On the priorities of citizenship in the deep South and Northern Ireland. *Journal of Politics* 38: 247–91.

1984. *Understanding Big Government*. London: Sage.

Rosenthal, Albert H. 1967. *The Social Programs of Sweden*. Minneapolis: University of Minnesota Press.

Rothstein, Bo. 1996. *The Social Democratic State: The Swedish Model and the Bureaucratic Problem of Social Reforms*. Pittsburgh: University of Pittsburgh Press.

Rowntree, Seebohm. 1901. *Poverty: A Study of Town Life*, 2nd edn. London: Macmillan.

1941. *Poverty and Progress: A Second Social Survey of York*. London: Longmans, Green.

Ruggles, Patricia. 1990. *Drawing the Line: Alternative Poverty Measures and their Implications for Public Policy*. Washington, D.C.: Urban Institute.

Runciman, W. G. 1966. *Relative Deprivation and Social Justice*. Harmondsworth, Mddx.: Penguin.

Sainsbury, Diane. 1994 ed. *Gendering Welfare States*. London: Sage.

Sainsbury, Diane. 1996. *Gender, Equality and Welfare States*. Cambridge: Cambridge University Press.

Sandel, Michael J. 1982. *Liberalism and the Limits of Justice*. Cambridge: Cambridge University Press

Sandel, Michael J. 1984 ed. *Liberalism and its Critics*. Oxford: Blackwell.

Saunders, Peter. 1985. Public expenditures and economic performance in OECD countries. *Journal of Public Policy* 5: 1–21.

1991. Selectivity and targeting income support: the Australian experience. *Journal of Social Policy* 20: 299–326.

1994. *Welfare and Inequality: National and International Perspectives in the Australian Welfare State*. Cambridge: Cambridge University Press.

Saunders, Peter; Inge O'Connor; and Timothy Smeeding. 1994. The distribution of welfare: inequality, earnings capacity and household production in comparative perspective. SPRC Discussion Papers 51. Social Policy Research Centre, University of New South Wales.

Sawyer, Michael. 1976. Income distribution in OECD countries. In *OECD Economic Outlook – Occasional Studies*. Paris: OECD.

Schmidtz, David and Robert E. Goodin. 1998. *Social Welfare and Individual Responsibility*. Cambridge: Cambridge University Press.

Schmitter, Philippe. 1981. Interest intermediation and regime governability in contemporary Western Europe and North America. Pp. 287–330 in *Organizing Interests in Western Europe*, ed. Suzanne Berger. Cambridge: Cambridge University Press.

Schmitter, Philippe and Gerhard Lehmburch. 1975 eds. *Trends Toward Corporatist Intermediation*. London: Sage.

Schor, Juliet B. 1991. *The Overworked American: The Unexpected Decline of Leisure*. New York: Basic Books.

Schluter, Christian. 1996a. Income distribution and inequality in Germany: evidence from panel data. Discussion paper no. DAPR 16, Distributional Analysis Research Programme. London: STICERD, LSE.

1996b. Income mobility in Germany: evidence from panel data. Discussion paper no. DAPR 17, Distributional Analysis Research Programme. London:

STICERD, LSE.
1998. Income dynamics in Germany, the USA and the UK: evidence from panel data. CASE paper Case/8, Centre for Analysis of Social Exclusion. London: STICERD, LSE.

Schumpeter, Joseph A. 1954. *History of Economic Analysis*, ed. E. B. Schumpeter. London: Routledge, 1994.

Schuyt, Kees. 1997. Is the welfare system of the Netherlands sustainable? In Koslowski and Føllesdal 1997, pp. 21–37.

Scott, James C. 1997. *Seeing Like a State*. New Haven, Conn.: Yale University Press.

Sen, Amartya. 1973. *On Economic Inequality*. Oxford: Clarendon Press.

1976. Poverty: an ordinal approach to measurement. *Econometrica* 44: 219–31.

1977. Rational fools: a critique of the behavioral foundations of economic theory. *Philosophy and Public Affairs* 6: 317–44.

1979. Issues in the measurement of poverty. *Scandanavian Journal of Economics* 81: 285–307.

1980. Equality of what? Pp. 195–220 in *Tanner Lectures on Human Values*, vol. I, ed. Sterling M. McMurrin. Salt Lake City: University of Utah Press.

1981. *Poverty and Famines*. Oxford: Clarendon Press.

1983. Poor, relatively speaking. *Oxford Economic Papers* 35: 153–69.

Shorrocks, Anthony. 1978. Income inequality and income mobility. *Journal of Economic Theory* 19: 376–93.

1980. The class of additively decomposable inequality measures. *Econometrica* 48: 613–25.

Shue, Henry, 1974. The current fashions: trickle-down by Arrow and close-knit by Rawls. *Journal of Philosophy* 71: 319–27.

Silver, Hilary. 1994. Social exclusion and social solidarity: three paradigms. Discussion Paper DP/69/1994, Labour Institutions and Development Programme. Geneva: International Institute for Labour Studies, International Labour Organisation.

1995. Reconceptualizing social disadvantage: three paradigms of social exclusion. In Rogers, Gore and Figueiredo 1995, pp. 57–81.

Skocpol, Theda. 1992. *Protecting Soldiers and Mothers: The Political Origins of Social Policy in the United States*. Cambridge, Mass.: Harvard University Press.

1995. *Social Policy in the United States: Future Possibilities in Historical Perspective*. Princeton, N.J.: Princeton University Press.

Skocpol, Theda and Ann Shola Orloff. 1986. Explaining the origins of welfare states: a comparison of Britain and the United States, 1880s–1920s. Pp. 229–54 in *Approaches to Social Theory*, ed. S. Lindenberg, J. Coleman and S. Nowak. New York: Russell Sage Foundation.

Smeeding, Timothy M. *et al.* 1985. Poverty in major industrialised countries. Luxembourg Income Study Working Paper no. 2. Luxembourg: LIS-CEPS Institute.

Smeeding, Timothy M.; Michael O'Higgins; and Lee Rainwater. 1990 eds. *Poverty, Inequality and Income Distribution in Comparative Perspective: The Luxembourg Income Study*. London: Harvester-Wheatsheaf.

Smeeding, Timothy M.; Peter Saunders; J. Coder; S. Jenkins; J. Fritzell; A. J. M. Hagenaars; and M. Wolfson. 1993. Poverty, inequality and family living standards across seven nations: the effect of non-cash subsidies for health, education and housing. *Review of Income and Wealth* 39: 229–56.

Soskice, David. 1991. The institutional infrastructure of international competitiveness: a comparative analysis of the UK and Germany. Pp. 45–66 in *Economics for the New Europe*, ed. A. B. Atkinson and Renato Brunetta. New York: New York University Press.

Sraffa, Piero. 1926. The laws of return under competitive conditions. *Economic Journal* 36: 535–50.

Standing, Guy. 1996. Social protection in Central and Eastern Europe: a tale of slipping anchors and torn safety nets. In Esping-Andersen 1996b, pp. 225–55.

1997. The folly of social safety nets: why basic income is needed in Eastern Europe. *Social Research* 64: 1339–79.

Steinbeck, John. 1963. *The Grapes of Wrath*. London: Heinemann.

Steinmetz, George. 1991. Workers and the welfare state in Imperial Germany. *International Labor and Working Class History* 40: 18–46.

Steinmo, Sven; Kathleen Thelen and Frank Longstreth. 1992 eds. *Structuring Politics: Historical Institutionalism in Comparative Analysis*. New York: Cambridge University Press.

Stephens, John D. 1996. The Scandinavian welfare states: achievements, crises and prospects. In Esping-Andersen 1996b, pp. 32–65.

Stevens, A. H. 1994. The dynamics of poverty spells: updating Bane and Ellwood. *American Economic Review (Papers and Proceedings)* 84 (no. 5, May): 34–7.

Stewart, Mark B. and Joanna K. Swaffield. 1997. Constraints on the desired hours of work of British men. *Economic Journal* 107: 520–35.

Stouffer, Samuel. 1949. *The American Soldier*. Princeton, N.J.: Princeton University Press.

Streeck, Wolfgang. 1984. Neo-corporatist industrial relations and the economic crisis in West Germany. In Goldthorpe 1994, pp. 291–314.

1997. German capitalism: does it exist? can it survive? *New Political Economy* 2: 237–56.

Sutherland, Holly. 1995. Static microsimulation models in Europe: a survey. DAE Working Paper MU9503. Microsimulation Unit, Department of Applied Economics, University of Cambridge.

Sweden. Ministry of Finance. 1996. *Report on Income Distribution*. Stockholm: Printing Works of the Cabinet Office and Ministries.

Syracuse University Center for Aging and Demography and German Institute for Economic Research. 1997. PSID-GSOEP Equivalent File, 1980–1995. Syracuse: Syracuse University.

Tamir, Yael. 1993. *Liberal Nationalism*. Princeton, N.J.: Princeton University Press.

Tanzi, Vito and Ludger Schuknecht. 1995. *The Growth of Government and the Reform of the State in Industrial Countries*. International Monetary Fund working paper. Washington, D.C.: IMF.

Tawney, R. H. 1921. *The Acquisitive Society*. New York: Harcourt, Brace.
1931. *Equality*. London: Unwin.

Taylor, Charles. 1989. *Sources of the Self*. Cambridge: Cambridge University Press.

Theil, Henri. 1967. *Economics and Information Theory*. Amsterdam: North-Holland.

Therborn, Göran. 1986. *Why Some Peoples Are More Unemployed Than Others*. London: Verso.
1989. 'Pillarization' and 'popular movements' – two variants of welfare state capitalism: the Netherlands and Sweden. Pp. 192–241 in *The Comparative History of Public Policy*, ed. Francis G. Castles. Oxford: Polity.
1992. Swedish social democracy and the transition from industrial to post-industrial politics. Pp. 101–23 in Frances Fox Piven, ed., *Labour Parties in Post-industrial Societies*. New York: Oxford University Press.

Thurow, Lester C. 1996. *The Future of Capitalism*. Sydney: Allen and Unwin.

Tilton, Timothy A. 1990. *The Political Theory of Swedish Social Democracy*. Oxford: Clarendon Press.

Timpane, P. Michael and Joseph A. Pechman. 1975 eds. *Work Incentives and Income Guarantees: The New Jersey Negative Income Tax Experiment*. Washington, D.C.: Brookings Institution.

Titmuss, Richard M. 1958. The social division of welfare: some reflections on the search for equity. Pp. 34–55 in *Essays on 'the Welfare State'*. London: Allen and Unwin. Reprinted in Titmuss 1987, pp. 39–59.
1967. Universal and selective social services. Pp. 113–23 in Titmuss, *Commitment to Welfare*. London: Allen and Unwin. Reprinted in Titmuss 1987, pp. 128–40.
1971. Welfare 'rights', law and discretion. *Political Quarterly* 42: 113–32.
1974. *Social Policy*. London: Allen and Unwin.
1987. *The Philosophy of Welfare: Selected Writings of Richard M. Titmuss*, ed. Brian Abel-Smith and Kay Titmuss. London: Allen and Unwin.

Tobin, James. 1970. On limiting the domain of inequality. *Journal of Law and Economics* 13: 363–78.

Tocqueville. Alexis de. 1835. Address to the Royal Academy of Cherbourg. Pp. 1–27 in *Tocqueville and Beaumont on Social Reform*, ed. and trans. Seymour Drescher. New York: Harper and Row, 1968. Reprinted as: Memoir on pauperism. *The Public Interest* 70 (1983): 102–20.

Townsend, Peter. 1954. Measuring poverty. *British Journal of Sociology* 5: 130–7.
1962. The meaning of poverty. *British Journal of Sociology* 13: 210–27.
1975. *Sociology and Social Policy*. Harmondsworth, Mddx.: Penguin.
1979. *Poverty in the United Kingdom*. Harmondsworth, Mddx.: Penguin.

Travers, Peter and Sue Richardson. 1993. *Living Decently: Material Well-being in Australia*. Melbourne: Oxford University Press.

Unger, Roberto Mangabeira. 1975. *Knowledge and Politics*. New York: Free Press.

Ungerson, Clare. 1987. *Policy is Personal: Sex, Gender and Informal Care*. London: Tavistock.

United Nations (UN) Department of Economic and Social Information and Policy Analysis. Various years. *Demographic Yearbook*. New York: UN.

United States Department of Health, Education and Welfare (US DHEW). 1969. *Toward a Social Report*. Washington, D.C.: Government Printing Office.

United States Department of Labor. 1997. *Handbook of U.S. Labor Statistics*. Washington, D.C.: Government Printing Office.

United States Social Security Administration (US SSA). 1983. *Social Security Programs Throughout the World*. Research Report 59. Washington, D.C.: Government Printing Office.

1993. *Social Security Programs Throughout the World*. Research Report 63. Washington, D.C.: Government Printing Office.

Van Berkel, Michel and Nan Dirk De Graaf. 1998. Married women's economic dependency in the Netherlands, 1979–1991. *British Journal of Sociology* 49: 97–117.

Van Parijs, Philippe. 1990. The second marriage of justice and efficiency. *Journal of Social Policy* 19: 1–25. Reprinted pp. 215–43 in Van Parijs, ed., *Arguing for Basic Income*. London: Verso.

1991. Why surfers should be fed: the liberal case for an unconditional basic income. *Philosophy and Public Affairs* 20: 101–31.

1992 ed. *Arguing for Basic Income*. London: Verso.

1995. *Real Freedom for All*. Oxford: Clarendon Press.

Van Praag, B. M. S. 1993. The relativity of the welfare concept. Pp. 362–85 in *The Quality of Life*, ed. Martha C. Nussbaum and Amartya Sen. Oxford: Clarendon Press.

Van Praag, B. M. S.; A. J. M. Hagenaars; and J. van Weeren. 1982. Poverty in Europe. *Review of Income and Wealth* 28: 345–59.

Veblen, Thorsten. 1925. *The Theory of the Leisure Class*. London: Unwin.

Veen, Robert van der. 1998a. Real freedom versus reciprocity: competing views on the justice of unconditional basic income. *Political Studies* 46: 140–63.

1998b. Participate or sink: threshold equality behind the dykes. Paper presented to the 'Uncertain future of the welfare state' Workshop, European Consortium for Political Research, Warwick.

Veen, Robert van der and Philippe Van Parijs. 1987. A capitalist road to communism. *Theory and Society* 15: 635–55.

Vickery, Clair. 1977. The time-poor: a new look at poverty. *Journal of Human Resources* 12: 27–48.

Visser, Jelle and Anthon Hemerijck. 1997. *A Dutch Miracle: Job Growth, Welfare Reform and Corporatism in the Netherlands*. Amsterdam: Amsterdam University Press.

Vroom, Bert de and Martin Blomsma. 1991. The Netherlands: an extreme case. In Kohli *et al.* 1991, pp. 97–126.

Wagner, Gert; Richard V. Burkhauser; and Friederike Behringer. 1993. The English language public use file of the German Socio-Economic Panel. *Journal of Human Resources* 28: 429–33.

Waldron, Jeremy. 1986. Welfare and images of charity. *Philosophical Quarterly* 36: 463–82. Reprinted in Waldron 1993, pp. 225–49.

1987. Theoretical foundations of liberalism. *Philosophical Quarterly* 37: 127–50. Reprinted in Waldron 1993, pp. 35–62.

1991. Homelessness and the issue of freedom. *UCLA Law Review* 39: 295–324. Reprinted in Waldron 1993, pp. 309–38.

1993. *Liberal Rights.* Cambridge: Cambridge University Press.

Walzer, Michael. 1983. *Spheres of Justice.* Oxford: Martin Robertson.

Ware, Alan and Robert E. Goodin. 1990 eds. *Needs and Welfare.* London: Sage.

Waring, Marilyn. 1988. *Counting for Nothing: What Men Value and What Women Are Worth.* Wellington, New Zealand: Allen and Unwin. Published in the US under the title: *If Women Counted: A New Feminist Economics.* New York: Harper and Row.

Weir, Margaret; Ann Shola Orloff; and Theda Skocpol. 1988 eds. *The Politics of Social Policy in the United States.* Princeton, N.J.: Princeton University Press.

Weisbrod, B. A. 1970. Collective action and the distribution of income: a conceptual approach. Pp. 117–41 in *Public Expenditure and Policy Analysis*, ed. R. H. Haveman and J. Margolis. Chicago: Markham.

Weitzman, Lenore J. 1985. *The Divorce Revolution.* New York: Free Press.

Whiteford, Peter. 1995. The use of replacement rates in international comparisons of benefit systems. *International Social Security Review* 48: 3–30.

Wildavsky, Aaron. 1973. If planning is everything, maybe it's nothing. *Policy Sciences* 4: 127–53.

Wilensky, Harold L. 1975. *The Welfare State and Equality.* Berkeley: University of California Press.

Wilensky, Harold L. and C. N. Lebeaux. 1958. *Industrial Society and Social Welfare.* New York: Russell Sage Foundation.

Williams, Bernard. 1973. A critique of utilitarianism. Pp. 75–150 in J. J. C. Smart and Bernard Williams, *Utilitarianism, For and Against.* Cambridge: Cambridge University Press.

Williamson, John B. and Fred C. Pampel. 1993. *Old-Age Security in Comparative Perspective.* New York: Oxford University Press.

Wilson, William Julius. 1987. *The Truly Disadvantaged: The Inner City, the Underclass, and Public Policy.* Chicago: University of Chicago Press.

Wolfe, Barbara L.; Philip R. de Jong; Robert H. Haveman; Victor Halberstadt; and Kees P. Goudswaard. 1984. Income transfers and work effort: the Netherlands and the United States in the 1970s. *Kyklos* 37: 609–37.

World Bank. 1994. *Averting the Old Age Crisis.* Oxford: Oxford University Press for the World Bank.

1996. *World Bank Atlas 1996.* Washington, D.C.: World Bank.

Young, I. M. 1995. Mothers, citizenship, and independence: a critique of pure family values. *Ethics* 105: 535–56.

Young, Michael. 1952. Distribution of income within the family. *British Journal of Sociology* 3: 305–21.

Young, Michael and A. H. Halsey. 1995. Family and community socialism. IPPR Monograph. London: Institute for Public Policy Research.

Zeckhauser, Richard J. 1973. Time as the ultimate source of utility. *Quarterly Journal of Economics* 87: 668–75.

1974. Risk spreading and distribution. Pp. 206–28 in *Redistribution Through Public Choice*, ed. Harold M. Hochman and George E. Peterson. New York: Columbia University Press.

Index